Creation and Chaos Talk

Princeton Theological Monograph Series

K. C. Hanson, Charles M. Collier, D. Christopher Spinks,
and Robin Parry, Series Editors

Recent volumes in the series:

Paul W. Chilcote
*Making Disciples in a World Parish:
Global Perspectives on Mission and Evangelism*

Jennifer R. Ayres
*Waiting for a Glacier to Move:
Practicing Social Witness*

Susan Marie Smith
*Christian Ritualizing and the Baptismal Process:
Liturgical Explorations toward a Realized Baptismal Ecclesiology*

Jon Paul Sydnor
*Ramanuja and Schleiermacher:
Toward a Constructive Comparitive Theology*

Eric G. Flett
*Persons, Powers, and Pluralities:
Toward a Trinitarian Theology of Culture*

Vladimir Kharlamov
Theosis: Deification in Christian Theology, Volume Two

Gale Heide
*Timeless Truth in the Hands of History:
A Short History of System in Theology*

Creation and Chaos Talk

Charting a Way Forward

ERIC M. VAIL

☙PICKWICK *Publications* · Eugene, Oregon

CREATION AND CHAOS TALK
Charting a Way Forward

Princeton Theological Monograph Series 185

Copyright © 2012 Eric M. Vail. All rights reserved. Except for brief quotations in critical publications or reviews, no part of this book may be reproduced in any manner without prior written permission from the publisher. Write: Permissions, Wipf and Stock Publishers, 199 W. 8th Ave., Suite 3, Eugene, OR 97401.

Pickwick Publications
An Imprint of Wipf and Stock Publishers
199 W. 8th Ave., Suite 3
Eugene, OR 97401

www.wipfandstock.com

ISBN 13: 978-1-60899-791-6

Cataloging-in-Publication data:

Vail, Eric M.

    Creation and chaos talk : charting a way forward / Eric M. Vail.

    Princeton Theological Monograph Series 185

    x + 276 p.; 23 cm—Includes bibliographical references.

    ISBN 13: 978-1-60899-791-6

    1. Creation. 2. Chaos (Christian theology). I. Title. II. Series.

BT695 V20 2012

Scriptures marked (NRSV) come from the New Revised Standard Version Bible, copyright 1989, Division of Christian Education of the National Council of the Churches of Christ in the United States of America. Used by permission. All rights reserved.

Manufactured in the USA

To Carrie, Dalan, and Rowan

Contents

Preface / ix

Introduction / 1

1. Immersion into "Chaos" Talk / 10

2. Shifting Contexts: Theology, Scripture, and Science / 26

3. The Growing Debate around "Chaos" Language in Biblical Studies: Jon D. Levenson's Position / 77

4. The Growing Debate around "Chaos" Language in Biblical Studies: David T. Tsumura's Position / 121

5. Catherine Keller's Tehomic Theology: A Theology of Becoming / 155

6. A New *Creatio ex Nihilo* Framework / 182

7. The Place for "Chaos" in Theological Discourse / 210

8. Conclusion / 246

Bibliography / 263

Preface

IN PREPARING THIS BOOK, IT HAS BEEN ENJOYABLE FOR ME TO LISTEN AT the intersections of scholarship in theology, science, Bible, and ancient Near Eastern studies—particularly in the ways "chaos" is understood. There has been a great deal of cross-pollination between these fields on the topic of chaos that deserves close reflection. It is my goal that readers will find much to consider about the ongoing discussions of chaos, especially in relation to how Christians understand and speak about God's creative activity in our present context.

This book is a reworking of my PhD dissertation at Marquette University, "Using 'Chaos' in Articulating the Relationship of God and Creation in God's Creative Activity." In addition to those I thanked at the time of that project's completion, I want to thank both the team at Pickwick Publications for helping to bring this book to publication and First Church of the Nazarene in St. Joseph, Missouri, for being supportive of me as their pastor during the revision process.

Introduction

THERE HAS BEEN NO SHORTAGE OF CONVERSATIONS CONCERNING either creation or chaos in recent years. At times the two topics are linked. The number of voices and perspectives in these conversations is daunting. Yet it is into this milieu this project travels. The question this book seeks to answer is what is the place of chaos-language in articulating the relationship of God and creation when speaking of God's creative activity.

In answering this question, first of all, a way will be suggested of speaking about a theology of creation. During this time in church history, where the broader intellectual context has shifted, there is not yet consensus on how to talk about God's creative activity and relationship to creation. Some theologians are venturing suggestions of varying merit, but the conversation is still far from equilibrium. It is hoped that the framework proposed in this book, with others of related thought, can provide a viable and attractive point around which conversation can amass.

Second, in the proposals offered thus far, the language of chaos—governing many different notions—has commonly made appearances. The language of chaos is powerful; it is quite gripping for the imagination; it elicits feelings of being overwhelmed, in danger, disoriented, and helpless. Yet to this point, many of the proposals employing "chaos" have dabbled in notions akin to some from which the Christian tradition has long shied away. Even in a new context, differently rendered manifestations of old dismissed ideas may not be a viable option.

In seeking to find a viable and attractive theology of creation for moving forward, this book seeks to follow in the wisdom of the tradition. Thus, "chaos" will be employed in a manner that utilizes the forcefulness of its connotation while being careful to avoid suggestions that would be conversation ending for tradition-loyal people who are in search of context-appropriate grammar about creation. The timeliness of this project could not be more fitting both for the unsettled condition of creation theology and the relative youth of the reemergence of chaos language within recent theological discourse.

This book does not stand alone in asserting that we have moved into a new, different context, which demands that theologians find fresh ways to articulate creation theology. There is a variety of available resources for that task. From biblical scholars have come suggestions for interpreting Genesis 1 that are viable and rich for building a theology of creation. Likewise, scientists are making suggestions that seem to be ready-made for entry into this theological discussion.

Some theologians have already begun using these fertile possibilities from both sides for dialogue. Their frameworks may not all be palatable for those looking for more traditional-sounding proposals, but this does not mean that their work should not be given a careful audience in order to glean their useful insights. It is the goal of this project to listen to the various voices of biblical studies, science-theology dialogue, and theology to freshly articulate a way to use the language of chaos in a tradition-honoring creation theology.

In answering the question about the place of "chaos" in describing God's relation to creation, the following thesis will be developed. "Chaos" should not be used to refer to conditions before or at the start of God's creative activity; rather, chaos is introduced within creation as discordant expressions of any part of creation in relation to God and others. In the framework that will be constructed chaos will be understood as instances when any part of creation (organic or inorganic) holds its breath and/or is out of tune with the inseparably operating Spirit and Word, who would have something more beautiful, abundantly life affirming, and rightly related for the whole community.

The ambitions of this project take the role of theology one step beyond making sense of our faith in a *given* context. It is assumed herein that theology should take a seat at the table in wrestling with how to speak about and frame the data of the various disciplines. For example, during the seventeenth-century, thinkers were sensitive to the fact that their accounts of reality through the exposition of physics had theological implications.[1] Data is neither self-collecting nor self-interpreting. It is

---

1. E.g., Spinoza (1632–1677) was one who used that to his advantage in his work to undermine the place of religion in all fields and facets of thinking. As a counterpoint, Sir

sought, named, and given meaning through being placed in a linguistic framework. Whether acknowledged or not, theological considerations are at stake when deciding what to name and how to frame the findings of any discipline—biblical studies as well as science. Even if the other disciplines do not attend to the theological implications of their linguistic construals, theologians need to keep assessing these frameworks and challenging the theology that is implicitly being stated. The methodology employed in this study engages in some of that work. It is hoped that the proposals being made can help provide a framework on which our experiences of the world can be hung.

The Relation of These Positions to Others Previous

Few positions concerning the activity of creation do not speak of it as solely an activity of God. For most theologians creation is by divine fiat—period. There has been sound reason for this. Defining "creation" in terms of *being* has been common for quite some time. In that paradigm, it is inconceivable to speak about *being* ultimately having any other source than God; God was defined in terms of primary causation, as Being. In the paradigm being proposed, God's activity of creation is not defined in the framework of primary causation in the classical sense. As will be described later, God's creative activity includes within it the response of the non-preexistent other. God's creative activity is intrinsically synergistic with the very other being created. This changes the way *creatio ex nihilo* is articulated while avoiding the lean toward dualism some theologians have opted for in their incorporation of chaos language.

Some thinkers have suggested that in creating God overcomes chaos, transforms chaos, makes a chaos (a raw material), or that chaos is intrinsic to the design of the creation God has made. Instead of these types of suggestions, "chaos" will be defined as something that comes into being in the event of creation; but, since creation is not something God does by fiat or monergistically, chaos does not have to be, nor should it be, attributed to God. Unlike nearly every instance of the use of "chaos" by other scholars, "chaos" is improper response embodied in the coming to be of the other, which is being created. The other being created can be anything from the smallest of particles to living organisms to

---

Isaac Newton (1634–1727) consciously tried to keep God in the universe in his physical account of reality.

the largest systems. More will be said in the coming chapters both about the proposals being made and their merits relative to other positions; but for now, it will simply be noted that the positions being put forth concerning creation and chaos have advantages over others both in issues of theodicy but more importantly in the claims about God's relationship to creation in and through God's creative activity.

One important benefit, which will become apparent as "chaos" is defined in greater detail, is that the *problem* creation faces can be defined uniformly for inorganic creation and for living beings. Additionally, the definition of "chaos" functions for both individuals and communities, or systems. Much of this is due to the way in which the chaos of improper response is defined relationally, in a dynamic and historical way. Improper responses establish and/or change relationships, which are ever in dynamic flux. This way of speaking in this context affirms Christianity's concern about the deep seated affects of original sin. It simply speaks differently than in past contexts where the fall was talked about as a one time, once upon a time, deforming change in creation.

The problem of chaos is an issue arising in the response of becoming. Thus, the manner in which creation's predicament is defined takes embodiment and materiality seriously. Matter is not the problem, but rather the manner of response in coming to be is the problem. Lastly, the notion of chaos as improper response will circumvent debates about intentionality or willfulness. Regardless of why the coming-to-be-other responded improperly, the reality of chaos is a serious problem from which repentance and recapitulation is needed.

The benefits of this way of speaking about chaos also make God's response to rectify creation's problem uniform, whether it is for material creation or for living beings. It is significant to note that the theme of salvation for *all* creation—which progressively dwindled away in Christian writing[2]—is once again being recovered. Salvation is not narrowly for humanity alone. Salvation is also not about escape from materiality, but about its being made new and being fulfilled in the Glory of God.[3] The aim of this project is focused toward talking about the problem of chaos within the context of God's relationship to creation in God's creative activity. Nevertheless, it is hoped that, in brief, the soteriological trajectory

---

2. This will be explained further in chapter 2; cf. Otten, "Nature and Scripture," 282.

3. See Middleton, "A New Heaven and a New Earth," 73–97, for a good summary of Scripture's position on this.

of the proposed paradigm will be seen enough that the relational dynamic between God and creation in the activity of creation, full of dynamism and synergism, is the same dynamic at work in God's saving activity.

Outline of Chapters

The language of chaos is typically used both in biblical studies and theology in the arena of creation theology. As a starting point for this project, in the following chapter, an introduction to chaos-talk will be offered. In the second chapter, the history of creation theology in Christianity will be examined in order to show major themes and developments up to the present context. It has been suggested that there have been shifts in how Christians have conceptualized God's creative activity and God's relationship to creation through the centuries that have been in step with changes in the broader cultural-intellectual context. A sketch of this history will be offered. This will highlight some differences in this context versus those in which traditional articulation of creation theology were developed. It will also give some context of why some theologians have been venturing different ways of speaking about creation. This portion of the book will serve the purpose of providing background and context for the current theological milieu in which the posed question will need to be answered.

Several scholarly investigations have already been done on key parts of creation theology's journey in the tradition; their work will be utilized in presenting this important background. For example, Gerhard May has presented the early journey of *creatio ex nihilo* becoming the orthodox position in *Creatio ex Nihilo: The Doctrine of "Creation Out of Nothing" in Early Christian Thought*. Christopher Kaiser has tracked the shifts in creation theology through the various changes in thinking over the centuries in *Creational Theology and the History of Physical Science: The Creationist Tradition from Basil to Bohr*. Kaiser's framing of the history is especially helpful to this study because he tracks developments in thinking within natural science along with corresponding shifts in thinking about creation theology.

This provides excellent background for not only the current work being done in creation theology, but also the rise of certain notions of chaos in science. Since the language of chaos in science is a significant influence on the use of this language in theology these scientific notions will be examined as part of this historical background. By looking at the background of chaos language in science—and later in biblical studies—the strength or validity of their choice of terms (i.e., their construal of the world) given the data about which they are speaking will be examined. Another key component to the change in context in which creation theology is being done today is the way in which the function of the Bible for theology has changed. This will also be noted in chapter 2.

Chapters 3 and 4 will address the use of "chaos" in biblical studies. Since the nineteenth-century proposals of George Smith and Herman Gunkel, much has been written about chaos in biblical and ancient Near Eastern (ANE) comparative studies. Smith's and Gunkel's initial focus was on the relation of Genesis 1 to *Enuma elish*. Since their proposals, the number of alleged references to chaos within the Bible has multiplied. In an effort to be comprehensive, there have been several scholars who have sought to examine each supposed reference to chaos in Scripture with far differing outcomes.[4]

This study will focus almost exclusively on Genesis 1 within these broader comparative discussions. Among all the possible texts within Scripture that are undisputedly about creation, this cosmology stands apart. It is a complete literary unit, which is highly developed in its artistry, structure, and theology. Also, the Priestly cosmology was given primacy in its canonical position. Furthermore, this text provides an excellent case study for how differently the message of a text can be viewed based on what background is presumed for the text. For those who believe it fits within a tradition of chaos references in the Bible its message sounds very different than those who question this now common way of reading these references.

The goal is to show this contrast in interpretation of the Priestly message. The goal is not to prove that one side is conclusively correct, but to show that extreme caution is warranted in repeating long-accepted positions within ANE comparative studies in light of recent investigations into the available data upon which they were built. This will indirectly show that theologians who build their creation theology on many of those chaos notions are at best building on shaky ground. There are other available interpretations of the biblical text that offer a

---

4. Contrast, e.g., Watson, *Chaos Uncreated*, and Tsumura, *Creation and Destruction*, with Levenson, *Creation and the Persistence of Evil*, and Day, *God's Conflict with the Dragon and the Sea*.

more compelling account of the text. Moreover, these chaos-free interpretations offer a better foundation upon which to develop a theology of creation in our context.

In order to show the contrast in readings between those who affirm chaos notions and those who reject them, a representative position from each side will be examined. Jon D. Levenson's *Creation and the Persistence of Evil: The Jewish Drama of Divine Omnipotence* has been chosen as a representative work in which Genesis 1 and the Priestly tradition as a whole is read against a chaos background.[5] David T. Tsumura's *Creation and Destruction: A Reappraisal of the Chaoskampf Theory in the Old Testament* will be used as a representative of an anti-chaos reading of the text. Even though both works address other biblical passages, they both have extensive treatments of Genesis 1 in relation to the broader ANE milieu. This helps in having a balance between the extensiveness of the Genesis 1 treatments in the two texts. Also, both authors are trying to instruct their readers on how to read the terms and images of Scripture. This is helpful in placing them in dialogue.

Levenson's and Tsumura's approaches also demonstrate a difference in methodology that is, for the most part, representative of others from their sides of the debate. This difference will factor significantly in evaluating their claims. According to Richard S. Hess, there is a need for the union of literary approaches "with their concern for context and/or contextualization" with comparative approaches in examining specific terms, images, and texts.[6] Contextual and comparative studies done

---

5. Levenson's position reflects a commonly presupposed view on how to read the language of Scripture. Even those who work outside of biblical studies make reference to Levenson's position; see, e.g., Burrell, *Freedom and Creation in Three Traditions*, 16ff. Others are responding to it; see, e.g., Levering, "Jon D. Levenson on the God of Israel," 77–82; and Keller, *Face of the Deep*, 26ff.

6. Hess, "One Hundred Fifty Years," 24. K. A. Kitchen writes an excellent evaluation of the manner in which scholars in ANE studies and biblical studies have operated and he provides some good cautions about procedure for those in biblical studies (*The Ancient Orient and Old Testament*, 28ff.). He gives these cautions because there are principles and methods being imposed on Old Testament data that have been demonstrated to be "false when applied to firsthand Ancient Near Eastern data" (ibid., 28). For example, his first rule is that "priority must always be given to tangible, objective data, and to external evidence, over subjective theory or speculative opinions. Facts must control theory, not vice versa" (ibid.). He suggests instances in which this rule has not been stressed in biblical studies to the degree it has been in ANE studies.

together on both biblical and nonbiblical ANE texts are Hess's recommendation toward the fullest and soundest understanding of the texts.

In evaluating opposing arguments within biblical studies, weight will be given to conclusions supported with detailed examination of texts in their literary contexts and to comparisons that are made when the contextual evidence provides warrant. This method first presupposes the unique voice of each text; it seeks to find that voice and preserve the integrity of it while understanding it further through placing it beside other ANE voices. As Richard J. Clifford states, "If comparison with other cosmogonies does not prove dependence, it does reveal the emphases in Genesis."[7] In sum, the concern of chapters 3 and 4 is: 1) to evaluate chaos language in biblical studies, particularly as it relates to the interpretation of Genesis 1; 2) to outline representative positions from the two sides of the biblical studies debate over "chaos" and ANE comparative studies, especially where it concerns Genesis 1; and 3) to track a way of reading Genesis 1 that holds promise for doing creation theology.

The fifth chapter investigates a growing phenomenon in systematic theology in the use of chaos. Within the world of systematic theology, there is a growing wave of scholars who are dialoguing with science and biblical studies on their use of "chaos." Nevertheless, there are others who are making proposals about chaos in the realm of creation theology that move beyond simply dialogue with science and biblical studies. Among these theologians who are making notions of "chaos" more central in their creation theology, Catherine Keller's proposal in *Face of the Deep: A Theology of Becoming* stands out above others in its sophistication, coherence, comprehensibility, insightfulness, and sensitivity to the contemporary intellectual, philosophical context. She pays attention to philosophy's turn to language. She does not ask objectively what the Genesis text meant and then try to apply that for today; rather she listens to the way the text reverberates in her world. Her work is commendable in that she tries to give an account of the faith for today. Important as well to this project, she interacts extensively with Genesis 1 in her work. As one who works within the framework of process thought, her approach to chaos represents a distinct position from those who more simply interact with biblical studies' or science's discussions of chaos. By examining her position on "chaos," this third approach to the language

---

7. Clifford, *Creation Accounts in the Ancient Near East and in the Bible*, 143.

of chaos will be evaluated and critiqued.[8] Even though her framework and use of "chaos" will not be supported, Keller has great sensitivity to the present intellectual context and thus makes some useful suggestions.

The goal of examining the use of "chaos" in science-theology dialogue, biblical studies, and theologians such as Keller is to show the questionability of their starting points. By examining these positions and raising questions about them, it is hoped that a different theological account of God's creative activity and relationship to creation can be offered in which the term "chaos" can be employed differently than it has been. Chapter 6 offers a theology of creation that builds upon the work of Lyle Dabney on pneumatology. It is within that framework of God's relationship to creation in God's creative activity that "chaos" will be defined in chapter 7. The goal of this proposal is to remain faithful to the spirit of Scripture and the Christian tradition while finding a way to articulate this mystery of our faith in and for the present context.

There are some topics that have a close connection with the investigation being proposed. The focus of this research is the theological use of "chaos" in speaking of God's relation to creation in God's creative activity. Metaphysical concerns are key among the connected topics. These concerns are certainly relevant and worthy of investigation. However, the purpose of this project is to address an ongoing trend in using "chaos"; it suggests doing so from a different perspective than has been represented thus far. Examining and developing answers to the metaphysical issues surrounding this conversation would need to be taken up in subsequent works.

---

8. The only other type of use of chaos language that exists other than uses that focus on biblical, scientific, or philosophical notions is that used by authors such as Stuart Chandler or Timothy Beal. In their work they focus on the sociological/psychological role of monsters (manifestations of chaos). "Chaos" is either the name for that which makes us feel not-at-home in the world (e.g., Timothy Beal), or it is a category we have within *our world* for new experiences or information we have that may demand we adjust our understanding of *world* (e.g., Stuart Chandler). These uses have more to do with how we make sense of the world—categorize it—individually or as a group. It will not be addressed in this project because, while the concern of this project is on the appropriateness of the language we use to call things, its focus is not on the phenomena or usefulness of having categories of chaos or the monstrous in our thought-worlds. Although, coupled with some of Catherine Keller's comments, these voices serve as a caution against demonizing certain things in the world as chaos simply because they are unlike us or do not fit neatly in our idyllic visions of the world.

1

Immersion into "Chaos" Talk

"CHAOS" ELICITS FEELINGS OF UNCERTAINTY AND CONFUSION, BEING IN danger or out of control. Using the term is in vogue within many academic disciplines. Scanning through a listing of recent publications will yield multiple titles from nearly every discipline with "chaos" in them. Even so, there is a great deal of divergence in what is meant by the term, whether it is used in a technical way for discipline-specific notions or in a popular sense as a synonym for *confusion*.

Biblical and theological studies are no exception to this growing surge of "chaos" use. The stated impetus for theologians who incorporate "chaos" language with varying accompanying notions is typically from two fronts. One front is the field of biblical studies and the use of "chaos" therein. According to the testimony of James Hutchingson, who himself has developed a theology incorporating "chaos," "Chaos would likely not emerge as an important theological concept were it not for the prominent role it plays in the initial verses of the Bible."[1] The second front is the host of changes in Western intellectual thought in the past few centuries, particularly in the sciences, that has given rise to new cosmologies, especially ones including notions of chaos.

In the center between these fronts is the concern of theology to offer an account of the faith in the present milieu. Some theologians feel that incorporating notions of chaos, which are being proposed along these two fronts, has promise for articulating the Christian faith within the broader intellectual and cultural milieu. There have been several theologians to take up the challenge of listening to the "chaos" language

---

1. Huchingson, *Pandemonium Tremendum*, 99.

being used on these fronts and incorporating these various notions in their theology.[2]

In looking at the first front—from biblical studies—there has been much fodder for theological talk about chaos. Much of this development can be attributed to archeological discoveries made in the last 150 years, which have been extremely helpful in reconstructing the worldviews of people in the ancient world. Of particular usefulness have been the uncovering and translation of Egyptian, Babylonian, and Canaanite religious writings. With these discoveries it was natural to compare the writings of these people with the more familiar writings of the Israelites, especially the cosmogonies of these various peoples.[3] In addition, there was a desire in the nineteenth century to replace many of the ways in which the Old Testament and its theological views had been portrayed to that point. Comparative studies were embraced as a means for providing new ways of framing Israel's writings and theology.[4]

Several Babylonian texts have been popular reference points in reframing biblical texts. While working as a repairer of cuneiform tablets, George Smith was the person to locate both the *Epic of Gilgamesh* and *Enuma elish* in the British Museum's collections.[5] In 1876, when Smith published *Enuma elish* under the title *The Chaldean Account of Genesis*, he was the first to identify a literary form he called a "chaos myth" and to suggest that the Babylonian *Enuma elish* was the oldest source for this myth in the ancient Middle East. E. Schrader had already suggested in 1863 that there exists in the early chapters of Genesis the idea of a

---

2. E.g., Keller, *Face of the Deep*; Inch, *Chaos Paradigm*; McDonough, *Between Chaos and New Creation*; Huchingson, *Pandemonium Tremendum*; Bruteau, *God's Ecstasy*; Cupitt, *Creation out of Nothing*; Page, *God and the Web of Creation*; Neiman, "The Myth of Chaos."

3. Rebecca Watson in *Chaos Uncreated* offers a helpful distinction between *cosmology* and *cosmogony* that will be used throughout this book. *Cosmology* is a group's perception of nature and the structure of the universe. *Cosmogony* is the group's mythology of its formation (3n8). Rémi Brague also has helpful descriptions of these terms. *Cosmogony* concerns the emergence of things and *cosmology* is a reflection on the nature of them (*The Wisdom of the World*, 3). He also uses the term *cosmography* to cover some of what Watson includes under cosmology; he uses it to indicate "the drawing or description (*graphein*) of the world as it appears at a given moment, with regard to its structure, its possible division into levels, regions, and so on" (3). This term may at times be employed.

4. Kitchen, *The Ancient Orient and Old Testament*, 17ff.

5. See Dobson, *A Chaos of Delight*, 382n147.

preexistent chaos.[6] Smith made the additional suggestion that Israel's own creation account, with its preexistent chaos, is dependent on the older text of its neighbor.[7]

Nearly twenty years after Smith, Hermann Gunkel, out of his studies of *Enuma elish*, was the first to claim that just as there is in *Enuma elish* a connection between divine *combat* with the chaotic sea—the sea-monster Tiamat—and the establishment of order from Tiamat's corpse, so also in the Old Testament there are integrally related themes of "chaos–conflict–creation" (i.e., *Chaoskampf*).[8] These claims concerning: 1) the presence of chaos in Scripture; 2) the dependence of Israel's writings on its neighbors; and 3) the presence of *Chaoskampf* in both ancient Near East (ANE) and biblical texts have been often repeated since.

The field of biblical studies is not alone in presenting a chaos/creation paradigm. On the second front there have been centuries-long progressions in scientific thinking that have led to a more widespread embrace of talk about self-organizing complexities emerging out of chaos. It is important to note that most scientists mean something quite different by the term "chaos" than is typically used by biblical scholars.

In using "chaos" as a technical term, scientists largely mean unpredictability. Unpredictability comes from some admitted problems with making any accurate predictions on chaotic systems. The most famous feature of these systems is "sensitivity on initial conditions."[9] This basically means that "small causes can have enormous and unexpected consequences."[10] A small cause can *unpredictably* snowball into

---

6. Watson, *Chaos Uncreated*, 15n24.

7. Ibid., 15.

8. Ibid., 16. Gunkel claimed this in his 1895 work, *Schöpfung und Chaos in Urzeit und Endzeit*. This work is now available in an English translation—*Creation and Chaos in the Primeval Era and the Eschaton: A Religio-Historical Study of Genesis 1 and Revelation 12*, translated by K. William Whitney, Jr. Gunkel's construction of events in the transmission of the myth to Israel starts with the Marduk myth, which is transferred to Israel. There is then a "poetic recension of the YHWH myth" (*Creation and Chaos*, 82). In this recension there is a loss of many mythological and polytheistic facets. Eventually in this sequence is the writing of Genesis 1, in which the Marduk myth was, "as far as it was possible, completely Judaized" (82). Gunkel's hypothesis becomes quite foundational for comparative studies done by biblical scholars after Gunkel. It has not gone without criticism. E.g., Alexander Heidel critiqued it in his 1963 translation of *Enuma elish* (cf. Seo, "Creation and Conflict in the Beginning," 115)

9.. Smedes, *Chaos, Complexity, and God*, 242.

10. Ibid.

progressively bigger effects. The final result is vastly disproportionate to the smallest of influences. The smallest of influences causes problems for calculations as well. Because every computer has limitations of memory and the certain ways its software is programmed to make calculations, it will inevitably have to round off decimals at some point. This rounding off can make enormous differences in the final calculations, which could drastically differ from the *true* values.[11] Every calculation on these complex systems at best is an approximation.

Another issue with these chaotic systems is that in order to predict where the system will be in the future "one needs to have knowledge of the exact details of the initial conditions."[12] This knowledge of initial conditions eludes us. According to the Heisenberg Principle, you can measure the location of a particle, but not its motion at the same time. In measuring one you disturb the other and vice versa. Thus "in chaotic systems it is fairly easy to explain how unpredictability arises: it is due to our inability to know and, even with the help of computers, to calculate the exact values of the initial conditions (these are thus external factors), and since there is sensitivity on initial conditions (which is an internal factor of the system), the indeterminacy will result in longer-term unpredictability."[13] In the world of science, unpredictable systems are chaotic systems.

There is a second use of "chaos" in science that more closely mirrors popular use. Systems lacking clear order, ones with a great deal of entropy, are often labeled as chaos. Thus, structures or order are said to develop in and/or out of "chaos." This usage often provides an easy bridge to the way in which "chaos" is used in biblical studies. However, the differences in worldview between the ANE and contemporary science can be easily blurred in bringing into a single conversation the use of "chaos" by scholars in the fields of science, theology, or biblical studies.

At the same time that there has been an influx in the use of "chaos" within both biblical studies and science, within the arena of theology there have been unsettling undulations concerning the doctrine of creation. Suggestions of there being anything primordial to "creation"—which is included in some of the notions of chaos—were once taboo for Christians for several reasons. One reason was the potentially dualistic

11. Ibid., 241.
12. Ibid., 243.
13. Ibid, 251.

implications—having two eternal entities. Another reason was that *creation* for over a millennium was defined in terms of giving *being*. It would have been nonsensical to talk of the *existence* (being) of anything other than Being itself (God) prior to God's *creative* act.[14] The only options, other than the orthodox formulations of creation out of nothing, were believed to be emanationism/pantheism or dualism.

Multiple features have changed, however, on the landscape on which creation theology presently is being done. These changes will be examined in more detail in the following chapters; however, for now it should be noted that some of those changes include broader shifts in Western intellectual thinking, the role of Scripture in theological discourse, and claims about the theology of biblical texts.

On this new landscape, where familiar landmarks for Christianity's traditional way of speaking about creation are now eroded away, there is not yet consensus about how to speak intelligibly about God's creative activity and relationship to creation. Some theologians have built upon an array of chaos notions from biblical studies and/or science in developing a theology of creation. Because of the new landscape our closer attention to the work of recent theologians is warranted before dismissing them offhand as heterodox. In this present work it is assumed that there is wisdom in the tradition concerning certain things that Christians want to affirm about God and God's relationship to creation. There is also wisdom in some cautions offered in the tradition against certain positions that are best avoided because of their undesirable implications. Nevertheless, with different and altered landmarks on the landscape, not only will things we want to affirm have to be said differently, but new things may need to be said as well, which were not at issue in prior contexts.

The heart of the problem being investigated is thus the intersection of several discourses. First, to continue the geographical metaphor a moment longer, there is a lack of consensus on how to speak theologically about God's creative activity and relationship to creation in this altered environment; the features of the landscape are still being investigated along with how to communicate Christianity's convictions anew within this new environment. Some of the proposals being put forth

---

14. Defining *creation* in terms of being, although not uncommon today, as will be seen, is no longer used to the exclusion of other definitions by all scholars; it is not thought to be comprehensive enough.

lie outside the comfort levels of many who view traditional theological formulas of the church as binding. Their discomfort is not even as much because of the new ways of communicating issues of theology, but because these new suggestions sound like they affirm things about God, the world, and/or God's relationship to creation that have been shunned throughout the tradition. There remains the task of giving a palatable account of the church's faith for this age just as Aquinas did in his day when Aristotelianism replaced Platonism as the dominant philosophical framework.

Second, within the realm of biblical studies long-standing conclusions are coming under increasing fire. Since the suggestions of Schrader, Smith, and Gunkel in the nineteenth century there have been three trends. First, "chaos" has been used frequently as the controlling category or descriptor for many Old Testament images. A significant problem, which has arisen in this trend, is how "unclear and inconsistently applied"[15] the term "chaos" is. Second, the dependence of Israel's writings upon those of its neighbors has been frequently repeated. It is common practice to identify terms, images, myths, or specific texts from other ANE cultures that may have been sources for Israel's writings. Authors will claim in differing ways that Israel's writings show "dependence" upon them, "borrow" from them, or these other ANE texts "lie in the background."[16] Third, the presence of a narrative within *Enuma elish*, other ANE writings, and the Bible in which creation-as-ordering comes out of *Chaoskampf* is frequently cited.

These three suggestions have been cited as fact without ever having been incontrovertibly proven. These ideas were not incontrovertibly proved based on the data when they were first suggested and have not been since. If anything, evidence against them has increased at the same time these ideas have gained wider currency. Even though proponents have never proved their case, the truth of their framework is so taken for granted that the burden of proof is now on the side of the naysayers. These three ideas are simply presumed as a sound framework for interpreting Scripture and making additional comparisons between the Bible and other ANE texts. Even more troubling, the use of the term

---

15. Watson, *Chaos Uncreated*, 18.

16. Bernhard W. Anderson is one author who employs such phrases: see, e.g., *Creation versus Chaos*, 168, 172. It should be noted, however, that Anderson became more moderate in his comparative claims over the course of his career.

"chaos," Israel's adoption of the "chaos myth," and a narrative framework of "chaos–conflict–creation" (*Chaoskampf*) has moved into the theological arena.[17] A closer examination into the current level of the evidence needs to be made before basing theology on this wave.

Third, within the realm of science, the use of the adjective *chaotic* to describe systems that are unpredictable—do not exhibit linear determinacy—is misleading. There is not total confusion and randomness in these systems; rather, it is a matter of epistemic limitation and finitude of our calculation machines that is currently at issue. The systems may or may not *be* chaotic; we do not know. Things that we do know are that the "apparent randomness of chaotic behavior is complemented by an underlying orderliness of behavior."[18] There are patterns in these systems, "constants,"[19] areas called attractors, etc. Chaotic behavior in science is not erratic.[20] Thus, in both biblical studies and science "chaos" is commonly used, but it is used quite differently and there are questions being raised about doing so in both fields.

This leads to the main problem: the intersection of these issues. In attempting to find ways to express God's creative activity and God's relationship to creation for the present era, it is increasingly becoming popular to use "chaos" language borrowed from biblical studies and/or science, as questionable as that language may be in the respective fields. This contributes to the inclusion of ideas within theology that themselves are raising concerns. There is a need to not only evaluate what is happening in these discourses, but to find a way to move forward with the task of theology.

As chaos discourse intersects between the various fields, one of the greatest difficulties with the use of the term "chaos," especially in biblical and ANE studies, is its lack of clear definition and consistent application. A good analogy for what is going on in biblical studies is that there is an entire menu of ingredients from which authors select—even at times moving between ingredients in a single work—when arguing for various notions they label as "chaos." Ingredients from which authors typically pick include:

1) whether chaos is created or not

---

17. Watson, *Chaos Uncreated*, 18ff.
18. Smedes, *Chaos, Complexity, and God*, 251.
19. Ibid., 246.
20. Ibid., 251.

2) whether chaos should be properly conceived of as either concretely existing or not existing
3) chaos's relationship to God's initial creative act
4) chaos's value or morality
5) whether chaos is an active force (sometimes personified) or inert stuff, a condition
6) whether chaos is in motion or stationary
7) the nature of chaos's activity within creation and its fate
8) the arena(s) in which "chaos" will be discussed (matter/cosmos,[21] individual human activity,[22] history and politics,[23] etc.)
9) the nature of God's relationship toward chaos
10) what God's activity relative to chaos is.

The switches that some authors make in the ingredients they include in their recipe for "chaos" at times can be attributed to the particular text they are discussing at the time. However, instead of being a defense, this shows how amorphously this term functions in the field as a catchall for so many divergent ideas.

This listing of ingredients needs further explanation. 1) Whether God created chaos or not is at issue. Some scholars suggest that God began by creating chaos;[24] others suggest that chaos (or certain images

21. This is by far the most common arena for discussion, often the only arena in which authors will discuss "chaos."

22. See, e.g., Anderson, "The Persistence of Chaos in God's Creation," 44; Inch, *Chaos Paradigm*, 16; McDonagh, *Between Chaos and New Creation*, 51.

23. See, e.g., Anderson, "The Persistence of Chaos in God's Creation," 44; Angel, *Chaos and the Son of Man*, 11; Beal, *Religion and Its Monsters*, 30, 33, 36; McDonagh, *Between Chaos and New Creation*, 51. Some authors clearly emphasize notions of chaos within multiple realms; see, e.g., Hutchingson, *Pandemonium Tremendum*, 96; Levenson, *Creation and the Persistence of Evil*, 35ff.

24. See, e.g., Copan and Craig, *Creation out of Nothing*, 33–34; and Küng, *The Beginning of All Things*, 115. Brevard S. Childs (*Myth and Reality in the Old Testament*, 31) and Claus Westermann (*Genesis 1–11*, 109) speak against this position. Whether authors believe God started by creating chaos or that God used a primordial chaos, it is not uncommon for authors to assert that this chaos was viewed as the material for creation within the Bible (see, e.g., cf., Beal, *Religion and Its Monsters*, 14–15, Bouteneff, *Beginnings*, 3, 13; Hahn, "Tohu Va-Vohu," 51; Levenson, *Creation and the Persistence of Evil*, 122; McDonagh, *Between Chaos and New Creation*, 4; Sarna, *Genesis*, 6; Stadelmann, *The Hebrew Conception of the World*, 12). This same type of suggestion was made in the twelfth-century CE by those trying to link the biblical images with Plato's *Timaeus* (Otten, "Reading Creation," 240). Similar ideas of cosmos being made out of chaos have been suggested in science, although careful attention to what is meant by "chaos" is necessary; cf. Benz, *The Future of the Universe*, 35, 132. This notion in science

or manifestations of it) are uncreated[25] or primordial;[26] still others bypass altogether the conversation about the Bible's position by remaining ambiguous.[27] 2) Depending on the opinion of whether or not chaos is believed to be created, there are different options concerning whether it exists autonomously/independently from God,[28] is dependent on God,[29] or should not even be categorized as existing or not existing.[30]

3) These first two opinions affect how people see the relationship of chaos to God's initial creative act: whether chaos exists only before that chaos-ending act, whether chaos exists before and after God's initial

---

has grown since Immanuel Kant; following him, others theorized about gravity pulling a chaos into the various masses we now have (cf. Kaiser, *Creational Theology and the History of Physical Science*, 335).

25. There are plenty of scholars who believe this is part of the biblical tradition; see, e.g., Knight, "Cosmogony and Order," 136, 138–39; Batto, *Slaying the Dragon*, 76, 79, 85, 87; and Keller, *Face of the Deep*, 5, 10. Others suggest such a notion is contradictory to Scripture and Israelite thinking in general; see, e.g., Gunkel, *Creation and Chaos*, 81. Gunkel was surprised that he was seeing what he thought to be remnants of ideas foreign to Israel's monotheism in Scripture. Suggestions that the Bible teaches an unoriginate matter are not new; Justin Martyr suggested the similarity between Genesis 1 and the *khora* of Plato's *Timaeus* (May, *Creatio Ex Nihilo*, 122).

26. For examples of those who believe the Bible speaks of a primordial chaos see, e.g., Angel, *Chaos and the Son of Man*, 11; Batto, *Slaying the Dragon*, 3, 47, 76, 84, 85, 87; Beal, *Religion and Its Monsters*, 44; Benz, *The Future of the Universe*, 132; Chandler, "When the World Falls Apart," 467; Levenson, *Creation and the Persistence of Evil*, 47; Löning and Zenger, *To Begin with, God Created*, 20; Morales, *Creation Theology*, 16–17, 18, 110; Stadelmann, *The Hebrew Conception of the World.*, 12. Even Claus Westermann, who rejects a notion of primordial chaos in Genesis 1 (*Genesis 1–11*, 102, 109), believes the Psalms still have some texts supporting the idea (29). Rebecca Watson's investigation of possible chaos references in the Psalms, through which she rejects the claim of there being chaos or *Chaoskampf* therein, is a challenge to Westermann's concession; see, e.g., her direct rejection of his reading of Ps 93:3–4 (*Chaos Uncreated*, 134). In the work of James Hutchingson one can see the way a systematic theologian has integrated this allegedly biblical notion of primordial chaos into theology (cf., e.g., *Pandemonium Tremendum*, 101).

27. See, e.g., Anderson, "The Persistence of Chaos in God's Creation," 19; Benz, *The Future of the Universe*, 35; Bouteneff, *Beginnings*, 3, 13; Morales, *Creation Theology*, 18; Wilson, "The Nature of the Universe," 52.

28. See, e.g., Batto, *Slaying the Dragon*, 76, 84, 87, 98; Levenson, *Creation and the Persistence of Evil*, 5ff. For opposing views see Westermann, *Genesis 1–11*, 110; and Brown, *Structure, Role, and Ideology*, 72.

29. See, e.g., Inch, *Chaos Paradigm*, 3; Küng, *The Beginning of All Things*, 115.

30. This is primarily the categorization proposed by Keller, *Face of the Deep*, 12, 161, 169. However, Bruteau, *God's Ecstasy*, 9, and Hutchingson, *Pandemonium Tremendum*, 101, also have positions in which chaos itself plays a part in generation/creation.

act,[31] whether chaos is a primordial material that God formed/forms into cosmos, whether it is created and then formed into cosmos, whether it is a facet of creation (e.g., this is a chaosmos),[32] or there is a kind of chaos that is a later introduction within creation.[33]

4) Value judgments about chaos and assertions about its morality differ no matter how people view chaos in relation to God's first creative act; some view it as negative and/or evil[34] while others view it as positive and/or a created good.[35] There are other options in which chaos is viewed simply as a fact, as neutral.[36] Some also claim that there is in chaos the possibility for evil or good, or it is the source of both.[37]

5) There are so many notions of chaos that have been proposed implicitly and explicitly that its proposed activity or place within creation is quite diverse. It can be seen as an active anti-creation anarchical

---

31. See, e.g., Batto, *Slaying the Dragon*, 85, 98; Keller, *Face of the Deep*, 12, 161; Levenson, *Creation and the Persistence of Evil*, 47, 122.

32. See, e.g., Anderson, "The Persistence of Chaos in God's Creation," 19; Bruteau, *God's Ecstasy*, 9; Hutchingson, *Pandemonium Tremendum*, 98; Inch, *Chaos Paradigm*, 3, 71, 77; Keller, *Face of the Deep*, 168f, 194; McDonagh, *Between Chaos and New Creation*, 6.

33. See, e.g., Anderson, "The Persistence of Chaos in God's Creation," 19, 44; McDonagh, *Between Chaos and New Creation*, 4.

34. See, e.g., Batto, *Slaying the Dragon*, 3, 84, 87, 98; Levenson, *Creation and the Persistence of Evil*, 16, 47. Even Claus Westermann speaks negatively about the darkness in Genesis 1:2 (*Genesis 1–11*, 104). Catherine Keller believes that there has been a trend in Western culture to demonize chaos; she claims we are tehomophobic (*Face of the Deep*, 15, 26).

35. See, e.g., Bruteau, *God's Ecstasy*, 9; Keller, *Face of the Deep*, 166; Haught, "Chaos, Complexity, and Theology," 189. Claus Westermann points out that the waters of the deep can just as often bless as they can destroy (*Genesis 1–11*, 105); Rebecca Watson shows in the Psalms how much more often this positive function is the case; see, e.g., *Chaos Uncreated*, 52, 65, 136, 140, 271.

36. This type of position has been more common in those describing positions earlier in history, in Greek, early church, or Enlightenment contexts. See, e.g., May, *Creatio Ex Nihilo*, 22, 122; Brown, "Divine Act," 21; Kaiser, *Creational Theology and the History of Physical Science*, 335.

37. For those who see chaos as possibility for either, see Keller, *Face of the Deep*, 29, 80, 122ff; Inch, *Chaos Paradigm*, 4. James Hutchingson suggests that chaos can be both the possibility and source for either (*Pandemonium Tremendum*, 101, 105).

force,[38] something nonpersonified, which *threatens* order,[39] or simply an instance of disorder, which is seen as the opposite of creation.[40] On the other extreme it can be seen as being generative, something that capacitates beginning or self-organization.[41] Some even see its function as being a reservoir of all possibilities, potentiality, or novelty.[42] With many authors' positions, however, it is nonsensical to talk about the *activity* of "chaos." It is simply an inert stuff,[43] or the term is a description of a disordered or formless condition.[44] It is challenging to locate the posi-

38. For those who see this theme in the Bible see, e.g., Angel, *Chaos and the Son of Man*, 1, 18; Batto, *Slaying the Dragon*, 3, 48, 76, 79, 84–85 98, 213n19; Beal, *Religion and Its Monsters*, 5–6, 9, 14, 30, 44; Hahn, "*Tohu Va-Vohu*," 40–41; Levenson, *Creation and the Persistence of Evil*, 16, 47. Several authors explicitly reject this type of reading of the biblical text; see Tsumura, *Creation and Destruction*, 190; Westermann, *Genesis 1–11*, 104ff.

39. See, e.g., Benz, *The Future of the Universe*, 167n4; Stadelmann, *The Hebrew Conception of the World*, 18. Some authors who are developing their own ideas of chaos see it as acting in this way; see, e.g., Beal, *Religion and Its Monsters*, 14; Keller, *Face of the Deep*, 186.

40. This is a common interpretation of the biblical imagery; see, e.g., Anderson, "The Persistence of Chaos in God's Creation," 44; Bouteneff, *Beginnings*, 3; Hahn, "*Tohu Va-Vohu*," 29, 45; Löning and Zenger, *To Begin with, God Created*, 10; Sarna, *Genesis*, 6. Others speak in these polarities of chaos and order (creation) in nature; McDonagh, *Between Chaos and New Creation*, 5; Polkinghorne, *Quarks, Chaos, and Christianity*, 84. Theologians have either adopted this type of juxtaposition—see Hutchingson, *Pandemonium Tremendum*, 97ff; Küng, *The Beginning of All Things*, 1—or, as Stuart Chandler points out ("When the World Falls Apart," 471), taken a theological position against chaos—see Karl Rahner, *Foundations of Christian Faith*, 33–34; Tillich, *Systematic Theology*, 1:187–99; Barth, *Church Dogmatics*, III/3, 209–368.

41. See, e.g., Beal, *Religion and Its Monsters*, 14–15; Brown, "Divine Act," 32. Some theologians have taken up this suggestion; see Hutchingson, *Pandemonium Tremendum*, 101; Keller, *Face of the Deep*, 123, 166, 188, 190, 194, 213.

42. See, e.g., Bruteau, *God's Ecstasy*, 85; Chandler, "When the World Falls Apart," 468; Haught, "Chaos, Complexity, and Theology," 189; Hutchingson, *Pandemonium Tremendum*, 98, 101, 109; Inch, *Chaos Paradigm*, 4, 71, 90; Keller, *Face of the Deep*, 12, 80, 115, 122–23, 169, 191; Polkinghorne, *Quarks, Chaos, and Christianity*, 84.

43. See, e.g., Knight, "Cosmogony and Order," 139; Chandler, "When the World Falls Apart," 468; Copan and Craig, *Creation out of Nothing*, 33; Küng, *The Beginning of All Things*, 115; Levenson, *Creation and the Persistence of Evil*, 122; Sarna, *Genesis*, 6; Stadelmann, *The Hebrew Conception of the World*, 12, 14.

44. For views that believe this is part of the biblical worldview, see Keller, *Face of the Deep*, 5; McDonagh, *Between Chaos and New Creation*, 4; Morales, *Creation Theology*, 15; Sarna, *Genesis*, 6; Stadelmann, *The Hebrew Conception of the World*, 12. Arnold Benz believes this facet of the biblical worldview fits well with science (*The Future of the Universe*, 132). It is presumed by Stuart Chandler that this view is the Judeo-Christian view ("When the World Falls Apart," 467). Claus Westermann contends this, however,

tions of some authors because they use "chaos" as a noun or an adjective depending on the context. Even more drastic in the conversation—given the recent trends—are those who choose a more original Greek meaning for the term and speak of chaos in the biblical text as a void/nothingness or gap/abyss.[45]

Given the divergence of views about the place of chaos within creation, what happens with chaos at the eschaton also varies widely. Some think it is eliminated,[46] and others think it is forever part of reality.[47] Some authors feel it is fully and finally brought under God's control,[48] while others claim that everything returns to chaos in order for new creation to emerge.[49]

6) God's relationship toward chaos is quite varied among authors. Most commonly God is believed to have an adversarial relationship with chaos.[50] For others, however, God's relationship with chaos is positive,[51] or God is mixed up with chaos in varying ways, perhaps it is even part of divinity or God's shadow side.[52] There are a few examples in which God

---

saying that "both formulations, that God created the world out of nothing and that there was a formless matter before creation, first occur where Judaism has come under the influence of Greek thought" (*Genesis 1–11*, 110); this is not part of the canonical worldview even though many important Christian thinkers, like Augustine, wrote as though it was (110); cf. Watson, *Chaos Uncreated*, 16.

45. Those who talk about this as the more original meaning of the term in Greek include Hahn, "Tohu Va-Vohu," 45; Küng, *The Beginning of All Things*, 142; Watson, *Chaos Uncreated*, 13; Westermann, *Genesis 1–11*, 103f. Westermann's treatment is the most extensive as it relates to Genesis 1.

46. Levenson is quite adamant about this position; cf. Löning and Zenger, *To Begin with, God Created*, 20.

47. See, e.g., Chandler, "When the World Falls Apart," 467; Keller, *Face of the Deep*, 168ff.

48. See, e.g., Knight, "Cosmogony and Order," 136; Angel, *Chaos and the Son of Man*, 200:206; Batto, *Slaying the Dragon*, 3.

49. See, e.g., Beal, *Religion and Its Monsters*, 15.

50. See, e.g., Gunkel, *Creation and Chaos*, 81–82; Batto, *Slaying the Dragon*, 3, 48, 76, 84ff, 213n19; Beal, *Religion and Its Monsters*, 6; Levenson, *Creation and the Persistence of Evil*, 47. Authors who oppose this position include Tsumura, *Creation and Destruction*, 190; Watson, *Chaos Uncreated*, 3; Westermann, *Genesis 1–11*, 31, 106.

51. See, e.g., Brown, *Structure, Role, and Ideology*, 77; Inch, *Chaos Paradigm*, 71, 77; Keller, *Face of the Deep*, 115, 122ff, 135, 181.

52. See, e.g., Hutchingson, *Pandemonium Tremendum*, 105, 109, 116, 151; Keller, *Face of the Deep*, 142, 191, 226, 231; Bruteau, *God's Ecstasy*, 9.

is said to wield chaos as a weapon or use it to execute judgment.[53] Some metaphors that are helpful for describing other positions are that God is a craftsman who uses chaos as a tool (means) in creation,[54] or God uses it as an artistic medium (substance).[55] Last, God can be viewed as a healer from chaos, understood as an ailment.[56]

7) Depending on one's view of God's relationship to chaos, there are various options proposed for what God does relative to it. It is common since Herman Gunkel to talk about God subduing, mastering, or combating chaos (i.e., *Chaoskampf*).[57] Related to this theme are those who still view chaos as dangerous but talk less in terms of direct divine engagement with it; God's activity is that of limiting, containing, or giving boundaries to chaos.[58] On the other side, a common, less adversarial position includes language of God engaging chaos, but God's engagement is constructive; God's work is to structure, order, or fashion chaos.[59] In

---

53. See, e.g., Hahn, "*Tohu Va-Vohu*," 64; Levenson, *Creation and the Persistence of Evil*, 76. Cf. Tsumura, *Creation and Destruction*, 152ff.

54. See, e.g., Anderson, "The Persistence of Chaos in God's Creation," 44; Bouteneff, *Beginnings*, 13; Inch, *Chaos Paradigm*, 3–4, 78.

55. See, e.g., Batto, *Slaying the Dragon*, 76; Beal, *Religion and Its Monsters*, 14; Hutchingson, *Pandemonium Tremendum*, 151; Inch, *Chaos Paradigm*, 71, 77; Küng, *The Beginning of all Things*, 115; Levenson, *Creation and the Persistence of Evil*, 122; McDonagh, *Between Chaos and New Creation*, 4; Sarna, *Genesis*, 6.

56. See, e.g., McDonagh, *Between Chaos and New Creation*, 51; this is the closest use of the term in the literature to what is being proposed in this project: "Consideration of Jewish-Christian reconciliation should reveal the depths of the chaos, psychological, social and theological, in which we find ourselves and indicate the radical character of the new creation required of humanity and offered by God."

57. See, e.g., Gunkel, *Creation and Chaos*, 81–82; Batto, *Slaying the Dragon*, 3, 76, 84; Levenson, *Creation and the Persistence of Evil*, 47. This position is challenged by Stadelmann, 14, 17–18; Tsumura, *Creation and Destruction*, 190; Watson, *Chaos Uncreated*, 3; Westermann, *Genesis 1–11*, 31, 33–34, 106.

58. See, e.g., Chandler, "When the World Falls Apart," 467; Hahn, "*Tohu Va-Vohu*," 64; Levenson, *Creation and the Persistence of Evil*, 14, 17; Page, *God and the Web of Creation*, 19.

59. See, e.g., Batto, *Slaying the Dragon*, 84; Hahn, "*Tohu Va-Vohu*," 51; Hutchingson, *Pandemonium Tremendum*, 151; Kung, *The Beginning of All Things*, 115; Levenson, *Creation and the Persistence of Evil*, 17; McDonagh, *Between Chaos and New Creation*, 4. David T. Tsumura cautions against such a reading of the ANE and biblical traditions; "Because the idea of creation as establishing 'order out of chaos' cannot be demonstrated as a general feature even in extrabiblical materials, we should be extremely careful not to impose foreign ideas on any biblical text without first placing the text in its immediate literary context and considering the possibility of metaphorical devices" (*Creation and Destruction*, 151).

a related vein are authors who do not necessarily see God's relationship as antagonistic, but write of God's interaction with chaos as separating, dividing, and distinguishing it.[60]

From across the spectrum there are some whose ideas of God's activity toward chaos explicitly talk of reducing chaos or eliminating it from reality; there are representatives, either who view chaos as a force or substantively, who talk about its elimination at the eschaton. However, others who simply view it as an adjective for a state of affairs and not the stuff itself will also talk about God being in the business of eliminating chaos. One group stands out among the others; they suggest that God coaxes or persuades chaos, or in creating elicits its "virtual forms."[61] God does not act on, or over and against chaos, but interpersonally with it. Some of these authors avoid talking about the elimination of chaos.

There is no clearly established definition for "chaos," or agreement on what notions, which have been placed under the heading of "chaos," are represented in Scripture. Even so, there is no shortage of work that argues for Israel's adoption and use of chaos imagery in its Scriptures from a common (equally ambiguous) ANE set of terms and images, as well as Israel adopting the notion of God combating chaos or holding it at bay.

The above group of scholars is content to use "chaos" in various ways and for various purposes. On the other hand, a growing number of scholars are raising cautions about past conclusions and the presuppositions, methods, and logic at work in arriving at them.[62] These dissenters

---

60. See, e.g., Löning and Zenger, *To Begin with, God Created*, 18; Page, *God and the Web of Creation*, 19; Westermann, *Genesis 1–11*, 33–34.

61. The phrase "elicit its virtual forms" comes from Catherine Keller; cf. *Face of the Deep*, 38, 115, 161, 169, 181. Others who feel similarly include Brown, "Divine Act," 21–22, 32; Hutchingson, *Pandemonium Tremendum*, 101; Inch, *Chaos Paradigm*, 3.

62. Questions are not only arising about placing Israel's literary images in a continuum with its neighbors' but also the narrative is being questioned about how in Israel chaos themes were demythologized from a primordial setting into historical settings only later to be projected into an eschatological setting. In his dissertation, Andrew Angel tracked how chaos imagery is used in Israel's writings in the centuries following the writing of its now-canonical books and found that the images remain historical in a vast majority of instances. He states, "Thus these late post-exilic texts used the [imagery] to refer to the establishment of political order within history, the establishment of justice both in history and after death and the creation of the world. Therefore, the idea that a creation mythology was historicized and then eschatologized must be questioned" (*Chaos and the Son of Man*, 205). Few, if any, of the long-presumed-to-be-fact and often repeated frameworks for placing Israel's writings within the broader ANE have

present a very different paradigm for interpreting Israel's theology in its Scriptures, a paradigm in which using the term "chaos" is avoided altogether. They would rather drop the term from biblical studies or explanatory frameworks that appeal to Scripture.

In her research, for example, Rebecca Watson challenges the soundness of chaos being used in respect to any ANE cosmologies. Given the vastly different ways it is used, the common lack of a detailed definition of it, a lack of justification for how it is used, the imprecise practice of grouping disparate terms and images under this catchall category, and the many non-Semitic ideas that have come to accompany this Greek term, Watson believes it leads the current discussions away from a closer understanding of the ANE perspectives. She seeks in her *Chaos Uncreated: A Reassessment of the Theme of "Chaos" in the Hebrew Bible* to show the inappropriateness of the term and an alternative way of reading the images.

David T. Tsumura also does a close study of the terminology, word groupings, and images in Genesis 1 and 2, as well as other biblical texts in *Creation and Destruction: A Reappraisal of the Chaoskampf Theory in the Old Testament*—a revision and expansion of his 1989 book.[63] His study challenges the suitability of "chaos" as a descriptor for the primal conditions.

These recent studies are part of a long-developing trend by some prominent figures in the field who have been taking more cautious stances toward comparative claims. These figures include Alexander Heidel, W. G. Lambert, Claus Westermann, H. W. F. Saggs, and Richard J. Clifford.[64]

---

remained unquestionable under recent investigation.

63. Tsumura, *The Earth and the Waters in Genesis 1 and 2*.

64. Several helpful summaries are available on this cooling trend toward old assumed relationships within the field of ANE comparative studies. See Rebecca Watson's introduction in *Chaos Uncreated*, 1–30; John Seo discusses some of this debate as it relates specifically to Genesis 1, "Creation and Conflict in the Beginning," 122–36; Richard S. Hess has a very helpful history of comparative studies and the lessons in methodology that have been learned along the way in his essay "One Hundred Fifty Years," 3–26. In Hess's study, there have been dissenting voices at least since the 1920s. In 1924 W. F. Albright concluded that the Hebrew cosmology was written in opposition to the Mesopotamian tradition, not in a line with it (8). Benno Landsberger in 1926 raised doubts that any comparisons can be assumed between the western Hebrew tradition and the eastern Babylonian tradition in language, worldview, literary forms, and ideas; any comparisons between the traditions or filling in the blanks of the Hebrew texts with ideas from other ANE texts he believed was projection (9–10). These tensions led to

Even with strong, ongoing dissent, the conclusions of chaos proponents have been presumed to be fact and been repeated as fact in scholarship, at more popular levels, taken up into science-theology dialogues, and used as a foundation for the work of some systematic theologians. This broader context in biblical studies comes into sharp focus in the contrast between Jon D. Levenson's *Creation and the Persistence of Evil: the Jewish Drama of Divine Omnipotence* and David Tsumura's *Creation and Destruction: A Reappraisal of the Chaoskampf Theme in the Old Testament* in how they interpret Genesis 1, especially 1:1–2.

In systematic theology, especially among theologians who are listening to the perspectives of science, work is being done to give an account of creation in ways intelligible within a broader cultural context. Many of these theologians are using chaos frameworks of biblical scholars, such as Levenson, as impetus and warrant for their account of creation. Catherine Keller's reading of Genesis 1, for example, is influenced by appeals such as Levenson's to an ANE chaos framework and undergirds how she builds her creation theology in *Face of the Deep: A Theology of Becoming*. In tracking the broader intellectual developments leading to where we stand, and with the popularity of talk about chaos in biblical and theological accounts of the beginning, it is still an open question of what is the place of "chaos" language in articulating the relationship of God and creation when speaking about *in the beginning*.

---

the separation of Assyriology as an independent discipline from biblical studies in the post-WWI period (8ff.).

2

Shifting Contexts
Theology, Scripture, and Science

MOST OFTEN REFLECTIONS ABOUT THE BEGINNING—PROTOLOGY—AND the relationship of God and creation lie at the center of current uses of "chaos." Notions of chaos are not foreign to these theological foci at various times in the church's history—or within certain Classic philosophical schools. The term is once again in vogue.

In this chapter the rise of the doctrine of *creatio ex nihilo* in church tradition and the theology of creation through the church's history will be presented in a series of brief glimpses. The goal is by no means to be comprehensive; rather, the goal is to provide context for the current project. Within the history of creation theology, a sketch of the development of a scientific worldview in the West will be presented.[1] Next there will also be an evaluation of "chaos" language in present-day science and theology that is based on that use. This glimpse of present day science also will help illuminate part of the broader conceptual context with which theology must dialogue in seeking to express the faith. Lastly, a glimpse will be presented of how the role of Scripture in current theological discourse has changed in recent centuries from what it had been; this has

---

1. Numerous works of historical theology have been written examining the doctrine of creation and God's relationship to creation either at specific points in the tradition or in the writings of certain figures; others look at the relationship of a past worldview to concurrent theological positions (e.g., the relationship of various conceptualizations of creation theology to technology or science). These types of works will be utilized in this chapter instead of retracing the steps of others' scholarship. Along with Gerhard May's *Creatio ex Nihilo* on the rise of the doctrine of *creatio ex nihilo*, one helpful reading of the tradition that will be used extensively in tracking creation theology through history is Christopher Kaiser's *Creational Theology and the History of Physical Science*.

had an affect currently on the open-endedness of theological reflection on creation.

The Creationist Tradition

References to God's creation of the world appear from the beginning of the Christian tradition and continue to the present. There are several basic presuppositions in this creationist tradition that Christopher Kaiser claims can be tracked throughout the Christian tradition even though they have taken form in many ways at various times in that history.[2] The three main points are: 1) the comprehensibility of creation, including its finitude in space and duration;[3] 2) the unity or non-duality of heaven and earth;[4] and 3) the relative autonomy of nature.[5] Kaiser tracks a fourth thread, the ministry of healing and restoration. The presupposition in this thread is that things can change.[6]

Kaiser's interest in the relationship of scientific development and creation theology influences his own interest in this fourth thread. His work in this area is helpful in tracking the changes from the early church in which healing was seen as God working through nature toward the Middle Ages belief in the ordinary operation of God's power (*potentia ordinate*) in sustaining the functions of nature.[7] The healing ministry became more about humans understanding and using the workings of nature.[8] With this growing shift in thinking during the eleventh and twelfth centuries there began to be a split between earthly and heavenly

---

2. The term "creationist" is Kaiser's. It is simply the tradition that affirms God as the creator, who, with the creation of the universe, established a code of law within that universe (19). Remi Brague affirms a similar type of heritage passed into Christianity; "The world of the Old Testament was produced with wisdom (*hokhmah*), but that wisdom did not belong to man. There was indeed a wisdom of the world, but its subject was God, not man" (*The Wisdom of the World*, 48). That divine wisdom, or God's Word, is more stable and enduring than heaven and earth, which will pass away (53).
3. Kaiser, *Creational Theology*, 21, 25.
4. Ibid., 21, 28.
5. Ibid., 21, 32.
6. Ibid., 62.
7. Ibid., 78.
8. Ibid., 80.

callings—those who focused on earthly workings and those who focused on spiritual matters.[9]

The first thread, the belief in the comprehensibility of creation, comes from the belief that humans are created in the image of the same Logos at work in the creation of the world.[10] Even though it is the same Logos at work in the world and in human reason, thus making the world intelligible to humans, there has always been hesitancy, as seen in much of the Old Testament, in claiming that all mysteries can be overcome. There are times, places, and knowledge within the world inaccessible to humans.[11] In addition to the nature of humans relative to the Creator, the notions of limited spatial extent and duration of the visible world have been part of the creation tradition and have added to the sense of creation's comprehensibility.

The spatial and temporal limits of creation, interestingly, were never fully a settled issue—especially the notion of finite duration.[12] Through the first half of the second century, Christian theologians were comfortable in affirming the Platonist assertions of the eternality of matter.[13] Debate over the lack of a certain beginning arose again in certain schools in the twelfth century and in the scholasticism of the thirteenth century. It was raised again in the Enlightenment onward.

The notion of the unity between heaven and earth, the second thread, is a Christian affirmation in contrast to some of its pagan counterparts.[14] Christians de-animated the heavens. The heavens and the earth were both equally created by God according to the same logic/logos.[15] Eventually their underlying belief in the unity of heaven and

9. Ibid., 83.
10. Ibid., 21.
11. Ibid., 22.
12. Ibid., 26.
13. Ibid.; cf. May, *Creatio ex Nihilo*, 1ff.

14. In the Greek concept of cosmos—of there being wisdom *in* the world—humans were excluded from it (Remi Brague, *The Wisdom of the World*, 24). Humans add nothing nor take anything away from the world and its reasonableness. Even more, celestial realities are on a different level from earthly ones (88); those higher realities influence the world below (96). The rule for things is found in the heavens which dwarf the earth in size and significance; evils in the earth are insignificant exceptions to the rule, to reality (108). Imitation of the celestial will help to rightly order human life (130)

15. By claiming *creatio ex nihilo*, Christians broke the Greek chain of effects of the celestial on the earthly, as well as their significance. All creation is equally graced; all creation has equal proximity to God (Brague, *The Wisdom of the World*, 161–62). Also,

earth (e.g., in the way they function) manifested itself in mathematical demonstrations of the similarities between what is seen in the heavens and on earth. It is not until the work of Isaac Newton, however, that such mathematisation comes of age.[16]

Last, the affirmation of the *relative autonomy* of nature has perhaps been the most chameleon-like of the three as the faith has been articulated in various philosophical contexts and in light of an ever-growing body of observations about the natural world. In Kaiser's treatment, he summarizes this creationist notion as follows; "The autonomy of nature is thus 'relative' in the sense of being relational (to God), as well as in the sense of not being self-originated or entirely self-determined."[17] In seeking to find an appropriate place for "chaos" to be used in the relationship between God and creation in this current project, this third thread of the creation tradition is of greatest interest and will be the primary focus as the history of the creation tradition is traced in the following sections. The sections look at the creationist tradition in various eras.

Jewish Heritage

Within the OT, God's initial work of creation is seen to be continuing (or recurring) wherever God acts mightily on behalf of creation.[18] Nature's order is dependent upon God's regular ratification and it is alterable for the sake of fulfilling a good. Thus, nature does not drift into the background of the drama of history or history's resolution.[19] "It is neither

---

human life was no longer a matter of *imitating* the order of the heavens or *inserting* oneself into an order; rather, human life was about *obedience* to God's law/command (155; cf. 175). The effect of this difference in Christianity from its counterparts was that humans were under the direct jurisdiction of God and not the celestial bodies; humans have greater dignity than the world and/or celestial bodies (163–64).

16. Kaiser, *Creational Theology*, 32.

17. Ibid., 33.

18. Ibid.

19. Ibid. Until the "revealed religions" encountered Classic philosophy, for them, the idea of *world* belonged in the realm of history. Outside of those religions, the concept of *world* fell within the realm of nature (Brague, *The Wisdom of the World*, 166). Where *world* is not a matter of history but of nature, the issue of salvation—which happens in history for humans in the attaining of the good (or wisdom)—"has no analogy in nature" (167). Brague believes that Judaism and Christianity—at least in Christianity's early years—historicized cosmology; however, in the gnostic crisis of the second century, Christians began articulating cosmogony in ontic categories instead of historical/narrative paradigms.

impersonal nor amoral; hence it is not to be set over against the freedom and responsibility humans experience in everyday life (Pss. 19; 93; 104)."[20] The primary conceptualization is of God as divine king and creation being a subject living under the king's laws.[21] It is not until the intertestamental period when Judaism was in dialogue with Greek natural philosophy that Judaism developed a more philosophically nuanced idea of the relative autonomy of nature.[22]

Judaism gave to Christianity the notions of God's omnipotence and God being creator.[23] It also passed on the formula "out of nothing" (*ex nihilo*); however, Judaism did not arrive at the doctrine of *creatio ex nihilo* until after Christianity. This was due in part to the fact that they were not engaging philosophical ideas in the way that it became necessary for Christians in the later second century to do so in the midst of tensions with gnostic thinkers. Also, their association of Genesis's early verses with "chaos" did not give them an urgency to reject Platonic notions of world-formation.[24] Thus, the formula "out of nothing" preceded the doctrinal thoughts with which it would later come to designate.[25]

Earliest Church

Like in the OT tradition, for the early Christians creation is not yet separate from history and the story of salvation.[26] Furthermore, the origins of the cosmos, or the "how" of creation, was not yet a problem. It was not until the second half of the second century that these questions arose.[27] Until then, Christians did not confront the Platonic ideas concerning the eternality of matter and the formation of the world from formless matter

---

20. Kaiser, *Creational Theology*, 33–34. The work of H. and H. A. Frankfort ("Myth and Reality," 4ff.) on the ancients' engagement of their world as an active "other" should be kept in mind at this point.

21. Ibid., 108, cf. 109.

22. Ibid., 34. Even so, it is arguable that deep affects of exposure to Greek thinking occurred in many areas of thinking in Judaism, especially in creation theology, even after it did in Christianity (cf. May, *Creatio ex Nihilo*, 22).

23. May, *Creatio ex Nihilo*, 21.

24. Ibid.

25. Ibid.

26. Ibid., 26, 27.

27. Ibid., 26, 35.

(*khora*/chaos).²⁸ Even into the third century, among the philosophically educated Christians the notion of world formation from pre-existent matter was held.²⁹

Appropriating classical philosophy was not conceptually problematic early on.³⁰ There were indeed claims made about Christianity being the true philosophy in contrast to other philosophies.³¹ But even so, attempts were made at melding Christianity with Plato's *Timaeus* as early as Justin Martyr.³² For these early thinkers, there was not a problem in saying both that everything came into being through God and that God formed the world from pre-existent matter.³³ To a certain extent the affirmation that God formed the world from pre-existent matter qualifies what is meant by the statement that everything came into being through God.

Earliest Doctrine of Creatio ex Nihilo

One group of thinkers who was interested in the "how" of creation was the gnostics.³⁴ The writings of Basilides, a gnostic, contain the earliest example of a theology of creation that says God created out of non-being/nothing.³⁵ Even though the formula "out of nothing" had been used before, Basilides was the first to employ it as a conscious rejection of creation as both emanation from God and the formation of preexisting material.³⁶ The purpose was to emphasize the absolute transcendence of God (of whom, for Basilides, there can be no analogies) and the supremacy of God.³⁷ Regardless of Basilides being the first of whom there

---

28. Ibid., 1ff.
29. Ibid., 147.
30. Ibid., 1, 74.
31. Ibid., 118.
32. Ibid., 122.
33. Ibid., 1ff.

34. See M. C. Steenberg's cautions about using uncritically the title of "Gnostics" for those typically classified as such: *Irenaeus on Creation*, 5, 11. It is actually their interest in cosmological speculation, and not *gnosis*, which gives this group any cohesion in the second and third centuries (11).

35. May, *Creatio ex Nihilo*, 76.
36. Ibid., 73.
37. Ibid., 75.

is record of having a version of *creatio ex nihilo*, it is not apparent that his ideas had any lasting historical effect.[38]

For Christians, through Justin and Hermogenes, God's creative activity was viewed in line with Platonism: as world-formation.[39] Hermogenes went the furthest in synthesizing Christianity with philosophy by saying God is *eternally* lord over matter and by interpreting Genesis 1:2 as a chaotic state.[40]

Tatian was the first Christian to say that God produced matter.[41] Then, Theophilus of Antioch added the formula "out of nothing" to the idea of the production of matter. He also contrasted the limitations of the matter-forming demiurge in the *Timaeus* with the omnipotent freedom of a God who creates *ex nihilo*.[42] This gave a new theological sense to the formula "out of nothing." Also, "creation" came to include the production of stuff in addition to the development of the world.[43]

The final components of *creatio ex nihilo* were basically completed in Irenaeus. Irenaeus relied heavily on Theophilus's work. He kept and developed the notion that God's creative activity is free and unconditioned by a pre-existent substance.[44] The world has a beginning in time.[45] Even so, Irenaeus is less concerned with the "how" of creation than the "who."[46] Creation is a gift (not of necessity) through which God expresses God's goodness, which became fully manifest in the

---

38. Ibid., 84.

39. Ibid., 122, 140.

40. Ibid., 141f. For an accessible summary of Plato's idea of formation out of the pre-existent *khora* (i.e., chaos), see William P. Brown's, "Divine Act and the Art of Persuasion in Genesis 1."

41. May, *Creatio ex Nihilo*, 150.

42. Ibid., 161.

43. Steenberg, *Irenaeus on Creation*, 44. It is interesting that the term *creation* was first understood narratively—an unfolding over time; ontic notions were added to the narrative of development; later the definition of *creation* became almost exclusively about coming into *existence* in a *moment, ex nihilo*.

44. May, *Creatio ex Nihilo*, 168, 175.

45. Ibid., 173.

46. Irenaeus does not speculate on the how of creation much beyond the witness of Scripture. It was precisely that type of speculation that Irenaeus believed underlay the gnostic heresies (cf. May, *Creatio ex Nihilo*, 173).

incarnation. The goodness of God, in which creation can participate, is the telos of creation.⁴⁷

The three basic components of Irenaeus's creation theology are that: 1) creation is purposeful and aimed at a telos, with the incarnation being the framework;⁴⁸ 2) creation was begun in infancy and undergoes a process of maturation;⁴⁹ and 3) protology must be understood in terms of eschatology, and vice versa.⁵⁰ Even though Irenaeus relies on Theophilus, and himself believes in a process of maturation for creation, Irenaeus rejects Theophilus's idea of the creation of a material substratum that is then formed by God into the world.⁵¹ Each thing is created *ex nihilo*; there are as many acts of creation *ex nihilo* as there are things. God took from himself the pattern, stuff, and form of creation.⁵² *Creation is at once both generative and formative.*⁵³

The difference between Theophilus and Irenaeus can be seen methodologically in that Theophilus uses Genesis 1:6–25 (days 2–5) extensively and Irenaeus never uses those verses.⁵⁴ Irenaeus wanted to remove any hint of a plurality of agencies in the event of creation; "God must be self-sufficient in the accomplishment of his own creative designs."⁵⁵ There is immediacy in the creative work of God by his hands.⁵⁶ Not only

---

47. Steenberg, *Irenaeus on Creation*, 22, 33.

48. Ibid., 60, 62.

49. Ibid., 60, 96. Irenaeus at least to a small degree can be said to have both components of narrative and concern for being in his understanding of creation; however, by rejecting the idea of the development of a material substratum, he all but eliminates narrative from the idea of the event of creation. For him, creation (coming to be) is in an instant; that which comes to be has a narrative of maturation. Later in the tradition it was understood that creation came into being in a mature, perfected state. A single moment of coming to be is the story of a thing's creation. The history of the world, including the fall, starts after its coming into existence.

50. Ibid., 60.

51. Ibid., 47, 62.

52. May, *Creatio ex Nihilo*, 173.

53. Steenberg, *Irenaeus on Creation*, 47.

54. Ibid., 88. Basil of Caesarea later used these verses and stressed God's statements to the earth to bring forth both vegetation (v. 11) and living creatures (v. 24). Basil spoke of God giving to the earth "fertility and the power to produce fruit for all ages to come" (Kaiser, *Creational Theology*, 38). Narrative versions of God's creative activity did not completely disappear; however, they were largely eclipsed by the dominant idea of *creation* as coming to be, in an instant, *ex nihilo*.

55. Steenberg, *Irenaeus on Creation*, 73; see 72.

56. Ibid., 78, 81.

does Irenaeus eliminate anything being beyond or before God, nothing acts cooperatively with God in his creative activity, because it would, "by their activity, reveal a want in God himself and thereby set up a situation of his inferiority."[57]

The Middle Ages

The thread in the creationist tradition concerning the relative autonomy of the world had several forms even before the Middle Ages. In the OT and even into the early church, God was viewed as a king who, in response to circumstances, decreed laws of operation;[58] the world was seen as a participant/respondent in history and salvation under its Lord. Certain interactions of God with the world and its inhabitants in history, particularly salvific interventions, were depicted as creation events. With Irenaeus, relative autonomy was a matter of ontology in terms of being created distinct from God—a created substance gifted with life. As early as Basil of Caesarea and Augustine, there was another change. Whereas God's activity relative to creation had been viewed primarily as a continual impressed force, there became a greater emphasis on the original, originating act.[59] Basil wrote of an impulse given by the first command.[60] He likened the command to an initial push that sends a ball rolling down a hill.[61] Thus the commands in Genesis 1 for the earth to bring forth both vegetation (v. 11) and living creatures (v. 24) is God giving to the earth a natural and permanent law. From the act of creation, the power to cause germination is present in nature, residing in the element earth.[62] Augustine also had a high view of the beginning. He believed all seminal causes were implanted at creation;[63] they have

---

57. Ibid., 73. This aspect of the creation tradition will be discussed further in a following section.

58. Kaiser, *Creational Theology*, 33.

59. Ibid., 41. One implication of this was mentioned above in Kaiser's fourth thread concerning healing. God was no longer viewed to be acting through the world to heal as much as humans needed to understand the workings of the world God had established and now upholds.

60. Ibid., 38, 39.

61. Ibid., 39.

62. Ibid., 38.

63. Ibid., 41.

their effects at predetermined sequences. This is what he considered to be God's continual creative *activity*.[64]

By the eighth century, for the first time in the West, the relative autonomy of creation—as that autonomy had come to be understood— was seen as a threat to ecclesial authority.[65] There was a concern about intellectual inquiry into the world being pitted against or challenging moral and/or spiritual matters.[66] The unity of creation, heaven and earth—Kaiser's second theme—needed to be reasserted for the church to be seen as presiding over all matters. Nevertheless, by the eleventh and twelfth centuries, there was a much stronger dichotomy between natural and supernatural.[67] Most strongly this appears in the twelfth century in the writings of the Chartrians.

With the Chartrians' rhetorical theory of *integumentum* (wrapping), they sought to peal away outward coverings to find the underlying content, the kernel of truth.[68] They sought to dissect the universe as they would a book to reveal its kernel of truth and then to show the compatibility of its kernel with that of Scripture and Christian doctrine.[69] For example, Theirry of Chartres wrote a two part work in which, in the first part, he describes the physical generation of creation.[70] He does this in such a way that natural processes are nearly mechanical; the events of the six days of creation can be explained according to the principles of physics, "in terms of the natural properties of the four material elements (earth, water, air, and fire)."[71] With the creation of these four elements, creation could unfold from its "central principles."[72] Cosmogony was withdrawn from the realm of the miraculous.[73] It is not until the second

---

64. Ibid., 43.
65. Ibid., 47.
66. Ibid., 48.
67. Ibid., 53.
68. Otten, "Nature and Scripture," 269.
69. José Morales sees this tendency to read creation as a book that reveals its Creator as Platonic itself (*Creation Theology*, 56). This would be consistent with the Platonic influences within this school.
70. Otten, "Nature and Scripture," 272.
71. Kaiser, *Creational Theology*, 50.
72. Otten, "Nature and Scripture," 274.
73. Ibid., 275.

part of Theirry's work, when he describes creation according to the letter of Genesis 1, that he speaks of the activity of the Spirit in creation.[74]

During the eleventh and twelfth centuries two wings emerged within the creation tradition. The Chartrians represented the left wing which, over time, discarded its theological grounding.[75] Those reacting to what would become the left's stress on the regular, upholding power (*potentia ordinata*) of God in the world would come to stress "the *potentia absoluta* ('absolute power') of God to alter the course, or even the existing state, of nature."[76] This right wing within the tradition eventually became disconnected from and/or uninterested in science.[77] It was not until the scholastics after Anselm and Peter Lombard that there was made a systematic distinction between the *potentia ordinata* and the *potentia absoluta* of God.[78]

However, already in the eleventh and twelfth centuries, the normal sequences of nature were viewed as due to a power delegated to nature by God, and the distinction became an opposition that was quite foreign to the sense of Scripture. In place of a relative autonomy of nature based on the efficacy of God's creative Word, one was forced to make a choice: either an autonomous world, created by God but virtually independent of God's continued presence and power; or else a world so utterly dependent on God's will moment by moment that all rational, scientific investigation became impossible.[79]

These centuries mark the beginning of the dissolution of the creationist tradition from within. The process took seven centuries to complete.[80] Unfortunately, as attempts to demonstrate the coherence of Scripture and nature dissipated in the dichotomization between them (along with the dichotomization of God's absolute and ordinary operations) so too did any emphasis in the tradition on the scriptural themes of natural or cosmic salvation dissipate; the scriptural theme of human

---

74. Kaiser, *Creational Theology*, 50.

75. Ibid., 53.

76. Ibid., 52. Representatives of the right wing during these centuries include Damian, Manegold of Lautenbach, and William of St. Thierry.

77. Ibid., 53.

78. Ibid., 53–54.

79. Ibid., 54.

80. Ibid.

salvation became more and more prominent.[81] Thus, a significant soteriological theme within the Bible faded in emphasis within the tradition.

The work of God became set over and against the natural order.[82] The natural order, natural law, became increasingly inflexible and impersonal.[83] *Order* was not as much "upheld by God (through his word, will or power)" or seen *as* the work or vocation of God—as in the works of Aristobulus and Augustine; rather, any employment of God's *potentia absoluta* was seen as upsetting or abolishing that order—an unlikely event.[84] William of Conches (died c. 1154) viewed the ordering of nature to be due to the inherent properties of the elements; nature orders and spawns itself.[85] It brings forth like from like.[86] At the end of the twelfth century the creationist tradition was fraying within the predominantly Platonic paradigms in which it had developed to that point.

With the importation of Aristotle's works into the West in the thirteenth century, Christians were forced to once again defend the faith since it was intolerable to them to have multiple truths. Theologians "had to defend their faith as being true in a thought-world in which their right to specify the criteria for truth was no longer uncontested."[87]

81. Otten, "Nature and Scripture," 282.

82. In Abelard, the split between natural and divine, reason and revelation, shows up in phrases such as "when human reason fails, then the matter should be referred to God" (Kaiser, *Creational Theology*, 55).

83. Ibid., 54. Contrast this with the OT view of a world which, with humans, was both subject to divine decree and included in history's narrative, God's salvific activity, and doxology.

84. Ibid. It would be interesting to investigate whether there is any traceable connection between this trend in cosmology and Luther's views on law (rational paradigm) and grace (irrational).

85. Ibid., 57. By differentiating between methods of knowing about divine and natural orders—through faith and reason, respectively—"William was forced to limit the authority of the fathers (and, by implication, that of Scripture) to matters of religious faith and morals" (ibid., 58). The church and the sciences were each given jurisdiction over their respective areas of moral/spiritual and technological/natural matters. In William's thinking, claims made in Genesis about the ordering of creation must be subjected "to rational scrutiny and could not be accepted as authoritative" (57). Ideas like those of William of Conches showed up centuries later in the work of Spinoza, who reduced the spiritual to the material and claimed that what is attributed to God is what happens naturally based on properties and motions inherent in matter (Israel, *Enlightenment Contested*, 433).

86. Kaiser, *Creational Theology*, 57.

87. Ibid., 89. "Before the thirteenth century, there had not been a sufficiently coherent and autonomous body of scientific knowledge in the Latin West with which theology

Among other things, adaptations were made both in understanding the relationship of revelation to reason and in the conceptualization of God.

In seeking to forge a synthesis between the two bodies of knowledge—the broader heritage of the West and the newly imported Aristotelianism—the popular analogy was used of two books. The Aristotelian methods including observation, abstraction, and reason were placed beside Christianity's emphasis on revelation, illumination, and faith.[88] In terms of truth, it was claimed that these showed two sides of the same coin. As had already been seen in the eleventh and twelfth centuries, however, the distinction between nature and Scripture could backfire. The autonomy of science based on natural reason could be asserted.[89] "In that case, Scripture might be viewed as superfluous or even inferior to human reason."[90] In the attempt to hold the two sides together, it unwittingly placed theology within the province of reason. For example, the claim that God the Father is 'maker of heaven and earth' became a matter of inquiry in natural science.[91] This had numerous effects on the concept of theology and its method.[92]

Thirteenth-century theologians sought to transcend the differences that had developed between the two creationist wings, which stressed either the *potentia absoluta* or the naturally operating world upheld by God (*potentia ordinate*).[93] Even with the efforts of many thirteenth-century theologians, the naturalism of Aristotelianism was intensifying the underlying problems in the tradition. Strong reactions developed against Aristotelianism. For example, in the 1270s, a strong reaction to certain aspects of Aristotelian science surfaced from the supernaturalistic/right wing of the creationist tradition.[94]

---

could interact" (ibid., 121).

88. Ibid., 90.

89. Ibid., 94. See Otten, "Nature and Scripture," 271.

90. Kaiser, ibid. Kaiser sees within the creationist tradition a tendency to undercut its own presuppositions in the way it works out solutions in response to new issues. "Even Bonaventure's more unitive view, it appears, harboured an underlying dichotomy of reason and revelation, or of nature and grace" (ibid., 94).

91. Ibid., 95.

92. Cf. ibid., 95–97.

93. Ibid., 98.

94. Ibid., 99. For example, Bishop Tempier of Paris posted his 1277 Condemnation, much of which was aimed at the Aristotelian notion of the eternity of the world (ibid., 101). Fourteenth-century philosophers afterward concluded that reason shows that it is

Also, Aristotelianism once again brought into debate the early church's debates on the eternality of the world; the regularity and lawfulness of creation under Aristotelianism made a beginning impossible to discover. The possibility of an eternal universe (according to reason) could only be curtailed by an appeal to revelation.

The most significant theological change through interacting with Aristotelianism was in the conceptualization of God and God's relationship to creation. Within Aristotelianism, God is the First Mover located at the boundary of the outermost sphere. God's "very presence was enough to activate the rotation of the outermost sphere of the cosmos."[95] That outermost sphere is "the only object with which God was in any kind of immediate relationship . . . Inner spheres were moved by virtue of their proximity to outer ones."[96] By giving an account of Christianity within such a model, Christians were able to combine the sharpest insights of both theology and science.[97] However, in working with the notion of spheres, "a spatial gap

---

most probable that the world is eternal even though the Catholic Church overruled such a conclusion (ibid., 101–2).

95. Ibid., 102.

96. Ibid. Matter was considered to be purely passive in itself, and cause was completely external to the body. One difference between the medieval theology that arose in response to Aristotle and both biblical and patristic theology is that "in the biblical and patristic literature, the seemingly perpetual motions of nature had their origin in the word or command of God rather than in a mechanical thrust" (ibid., 128–29). Collin Gunton sees personal agency as key in the earlier notion of cause that is changed in the mechanical/physical framework of primary and secondary causation ("The End of Causality?" 63, 67; cf. T. F. Torrance concerning the First Cause "inertially" determining the cosmic order, *Divine and Contingent Order*, 86–87.). Thus, "On the one hand, considerations of God's normal exercise of providence through second causes led to a replacement of the biblical image of God as cosmic legislator by the idea of God as first Mover (the sense of the latter shifting meanwhile from formal to efficient cause of motion)" (Kaiser, *Creational Theology*, 132). God set the cosmos in motion once and for all. On the other hand, however, there was a conservative reaction to the medieval synthesis with Aristotelianism that "led to a renewed emphasis on God's absolute power both in establishing the normal course of nature and in superseding it at any time" (132). It was the conservatives who tried to develop a unified mechanics for heaven and earth to show where indeed God intercedes.

97. Ibid., 103. In Aquinas, the world is the effect of God as primary cause; there is no co-creation (Morales, *Creation Theology*, 113). Secondary causes exist and have effects because they themselves are the effect of God. These lower-order causes cannot make a "preparatory and real contribution to producing the effect of the higher cause" (113). Everything they communicate to another is always ultimately as an effect of God. Cf. T. F. Torrance's summary of this view of contingency and the way it was replaced in the collapse of medieval paradigms (*Divine and Contingent Order*, 86–91).

threatened to open up between the regular activity of God and events on earth."[98] God's providence seemed very remote and God's direct influence on everyday people was thought to be centered in the enlightenment of the soul and infusing grace through the seven sacraments.[99] Either way, God's activity was mediated either through the hierarchy of celestial spheres or through the hierarchy of the church. With the development of mechanical clocks in the late thirteenth and early fourteenth centuries, a new analogy of God as clockmaker was available for use beside God as sphere-mover.[100]

With each instantiation of the creationist tradition in a new context, the basic notion of regularity in the cycles of nature endured; but how those cycles were understood changed, as well as notions of God and God's relation to creation. "From the ancient Near Eastern ideal of divine kingship to the Neoplatonic and Augustinian concept of transcendent Being, to the Aristotelian First Mover, to the late medieval Clockmaker, the idea of God's normal activity became gradually less immediate to the events of the world, leaving the relatively autonomous cycles of nature to take on the appearance of a completely autonomous mechanism."[101]

Kaiser does not believe the adoption of Aristotelianism, in which God's activity was made more remote, could have happened had there not already developed in the eleventh- and twelfth centuries a clear

---

98. Ibid., 104. Both Christopher Kaiser and Willemien Otten credit Aquinas in preventing "the separation of nature and grace from becoming definitive just yet" (Otten, "Nature and Scripture," 282). However, they both recognize that the split between God and world was already set in unstoppable motion in the twelfth century and Thomas's (and even Bonaventure's) holding together of the two sides still rested upon a framework where there are two distinct sides needing to be held together (cf. Kaiser, *Creational Theology*, 93–94.).

99. Ibid., 105. Kaiser proposes that the dichotomy of nature and grace in high medieval thought can be seen partially as an indirect result of Aristotelian science (ibid., 105–6).

100. Ibid., 106. Willemien Otten, when outlining the work of Louis Duprè, notes that late medieval nominalism disconnected the *potentia absoluta* from the *potentia ordinate* in a manner that God's volitional actions were no longer reflected in the workings of nature ("Nature and Scripture," 264). Romans 1:20—"Ever since the creation of the world his eternal power and divine nature, invisible though they are, have been understood and seen through the things he has made" (NRSV)—had been a favorite proof text throughout the Middle Ages. However, the logic of medieval theology that believed God's will was reflected in creation and could be imperfectly grasped by humans became severed (265). The study of nature for purposes of attempting to know God more richly dissipated.

101. Ibid., 109.

distinction between God's normal and miraculous activity.[102] During the Middle Ages the cosmos became mechanical and it was largely believed that "God's direct action and the normal causal connections of nature were mutually exclusive."[103]

The Renaissance Forward

On the one hand, the concepts and methods of the developing natural sciences were largely shaped by the theological tradition out of which they came, even if they became separated from theological reflection.[104] On the other hand, natural science, in turn, was at times a helpful aid to theology. Science helped establish the possibility of a void, which aided in deconstructing the dominant Aristotelian cosmology.[105] Science provided alternative models to the geocentrism of Aristotelian cosmography. And science showed, through mathematical laws and physical models, the unity of earthly and celestial bodies, a connection affirmed in the creationist tradition but made virtually impossible within an Aristotelian worldview.[106] Unfortunately, however, where in the earlier developments of science it was possible to appeal to God's direct action (*potentia absoluta*) where gaps in the natural order presented themselves, it only took about four centuries for mathematics and physics to develop to the point where the gaps were closing in and space for God's direct action in nature was not apparent.[107] Even in dissolving the domi-

102. Ibid.
103. Ibid., 234–35.
104. Ibid., 113–16.
105. Ibid., 122.
106. Ibid., 130.
107. Ibid., 112. Joseph Louis de Lagrange (1763–1813) and Pierre Simon de Laplace (1749–1827) sought to eliminate any recourse to the supernatural (Kaiser, *Creational Theology*, 345). Due to the growing confidence in the scientific method, no one "any longer resorted to Newton's God-of-the-gaps to account for the unresolved problems" (346). Gaps were considered a matter of ignorance and not a place for divine activity. "It was a philosophical commitment on the part of the neomechanists that excluded God, not the result of scientific data themselves, any more than were the earlier arguments in favour of the existence of God" (346). Many of the philosophical commitments "are the product of a particular history and theology, not a necessary concomitant of progressive science" (351). One of Stephen Long's criticisms concerning Modernity's division between fact/value (is/ought), or between natural/moral (reason/faith) is that it forgets its historical contingency and therefore the need for self-critique. Long believes the possibility must remain "that we are frustrated in both our assent to, and our understanding

nant Aristotelian cosmology and once again eliminating any perceived distance between God and the world, God again seemed equally remote from the mechanistic workings of the heavens and the earth.[108]

The transitions brought about within Copernicus's model of the universe were significant. Already before Nicholas Copernicus (1473–1543) there were groups who had been dissatisfied with both Ptolemy and hierarchical views of the cosmos.[109] For example, the Florentine Perspectivists had ceased representing things from a transcendental perspective, in a hierarchical arrangement, which gave spatial location and magnitude to objects based on their intrinsic value. The Perspectivists had a uniform conception of space and portrayed things as they appear from the vantage point of the landscape.[110] Like them, Copernicus was interested in appearances. Also, Copernicus was convinced of the rationality of the world. Without explicitly referring to God or the idea of creation he sought to find the laws of nature that had been infused therein.[111] In opposition to Aristotle's notion that all things (inherently passive) have natural places to which they will go when outside forces cease to act on them, Copernicus believed laws of nature are so implanted by

---

of, the natural. The meaning present in the natural order is not self-evident, and cannot become so by objective human reasoning because such investigation itself participates in the natural. Thus the natural cannot be appealed to without there being at the same time a recognition of those social and historical contexts that make such appeals possible" (*Divine Economy*, 182). See Hans Küng, *The Beginning of All Things*, 25–27, 51–52, on the need for humility concerning science's ability to speak about reality.

108. Ibid., 175. Interestingly the Reformers for the most part preferred the Aristotelian cosmology and its ordered universe, as well as the notion of *potentia ordinata* that was stressed within the Middle Ages in an Aristotelian paradigm (Kaiser, *Creational Theology*, 177). However, whereas the Middle Ages tension was between nature (*potentia ordinata*) and supernature (*potentia absoluta*), the Reformers created a new division in the *potentia ordinata* and focused on the dialectic between creation- and salvation-ordinances (177). Nature and grace were no longer divided respectively between the arenas of *potentia ordinata* and *potentia absoluta*. Instead they were both discussed under two distinct kinds of *potentia ordinata*. Bacon would use this new division to separate nature and grace into two kingdoms both united under God: the kingdom of nature and the kingdom of God (183). The Reformers' shift in focus was significant for their doctrines of revelation and salvation (176)—not to mention divine foreknowledge and predestination.

109. Kaiser, *Creational Theology*, 138.

110. Ibid. This was part of the dissolving of differences between the celestial and terrestrial (Brague, *The Wisdom of the World*, 196).

111. Ibid., 150, 151.

God that it appears they operate automatically.[112] The laws are not intrinsic to creation, but given to it.

In this time period scientists became less interested in the world in an undisturbed, at-rest state, what had been considered to be things in their "natural places" or "contexts." Rather, measurements and observations of things and their parts, as they occur, were made and tables of data were created.[113] The structure and functions of bodies relative to other bodies were examined. "These contributions encouraged a new, more experimental, kind of science in which humans understood nature in terms of the ways they could influence it, rather than in terms of what it was in its undisturbed state."[114]

The scholastics had developed their theology within an Aristotelian worldview in which: 1) the earth was stationary, 2) the universe was finite, and 3) the planetary spheres moved in an effort to match the eternity of

---

112. Ibid., 151.

113. Ibid., 154. "Knowledge that could be experienced empirically and measured now became the only way to explain nature" (Küng, *The Beginning of All Things*, 4). Galileo Galilei (1564–1642) was part of that next wave of more scientific observers of the universe. Through the use of a telescope, he discovered things about the planets in our solar system and that the Milky Way actually consisted of individual stars (ibid.). As was the case in the writings of the more radical thinkers of the Middle Ages, empirically verifiable data was starting to trump biblical claims. According to "the Benedictine B. Castelli in 1613 . . . if scientific knowledge is certain and contradicts what the Bible says, a new interpretation of the Bible is due" (ibid., 4). These challenges were not well received and created more tensions between the ecclesial hierarchy and the sciences; "After the disastrous excommunication of Luther and the Protestants by Rome, the Galileo case was followed by an almost silent emigration of scientists from the Catholic Church and a permanent conflict between science and the dominant theology" (ibid., 6).

114. Kaiser, *Creational Theology*, 160. Cf. T. F. Torrance, *Divine and Contingent Order*, 91ff. In Charles Taylor's account of this transition he speaks of pre-Modern cosmologies having a belief that the cosmos was an embodiment of an underlying organizational structure. In those old outlooks, "the nature of something is the idea it instantiates. And each idea is intelligible against the whole order" (*Philosophy and the Human Sciences*, 256). Every part fit within an interlocking system; it had a logos that fit in that system. In the move toward Modern thinking, the tendency is "to identify the 'nature' of a thing with the forces or factors which make it function as it does, and these can no longer be seen as existing independently of the particulars which function this way. Nature is within" (257). There is no longer meaning in the whole. This transition in thinking was true of objects as well as of humans; humans no longer had a given place/logos due to their lineage relative to an overarching societal and/or cosmic scheme. Brague calls this loss of meaning in the whole—along with a loss of the notion of a bounded whole—within the new, developing cosmography the end of the notion of *world* (*The Wisdom of the World*, 186–89). With the loss of the notion of a bounded world came a change in vocabulary and conception of an infinite "universe" (189).

God.¹¹⁵ During the Renaissance and Reformation, there were developments away from the Aristotelian model even though it was still used extensively by the Reformers. "With the adoption of Copernicus's model of the universe, however, the consistent structure of the scholastic framework crumbled, and in its place there emerged a paradox: all things were now in motion, even the earth, but there was no general mechanism for generating this motion comparable to the role of the *primum mobile* (the outermost celestial sphere) in Aristotle. The entire question of the relation of God to matter and motion had to be rethought."¹¹⁶

During the seventeenth century, many of the themes of the creationist tradition survived. However, the themes were used in drastically different ways among various groups. "Historically it is no longer possible for us to treat the creationist tradition as a unified whole, or even as a spectrum with different wings (as in the Middle Ages). Instead, it must be subdivided into derivative, more specialized traditions that define themselves over against each other as much as in terms of traditional themes."¹¹⁷

Kaiser categorizes the seventeenth-century thinkers into separate, competing groups: the "spiritualist," "mechanist," and "Platonic" traditions. Mechanist philosophy, as seen in Descartes, Gassendi, and Boyle, replaced Aristotelianism in the sciences. The spiritualist approach to nature directly competed against the mechanist. As a middle

---

115. Kaiser, *Creational Theology*, 215.

116. Ibid. Copernicus did not just change ideas about physics and astronomy; his paradigm "had an effect on the whole picture of the world and human 'metaphysics'" (Küng, *The Beginning of all Things*, 3). The changes in worldview brought about by inquiry and observation of the natural world could not be stopped by Rome (6). The harsh criticisms leveled by radical Enlightenment thinkers against the teachings of their present-day clergy may not have been wholly unwarranted in the next century, in this period of rapid ideological and social upheaval. In the face of such changes, "The traditional authorities became increasingly unconvincing" (6). As Jonathan Israel states: "The institutions, social hierarchy, status, and property arrangements on which a given society is based can only remain stable whilst the explanations that society offers in justification command sufficiently wide currency and acceptance, and begin to disintegrate when such general acceptance lapses" (*Enlightenment Contested*, 4–5.).

117. Kaiser, *Creational Theology*, 200.

course the Platonic tradition, centered at Cambridge University, led to the work of Isaac Newton.[118]

The spiritualists integrated to varying degrees matter and spirit(s)/energies.[119] It was difficult to keep a balance in that union. Too little integration could make matter seemingly autonomous and leave little place for the spiritual. Too much integration "could lead to a naturalistic explanation of the spiritual and encourage pantheism or even outright atheism."[120]

Joan Baptista van Helmont (1579-1644) and Gottfried Wilhelm Leibniz (1645-1716) are two of the most significant figures in the spiritualist tradition. For Helmont, nature is simply the effect of God's creative decree; God's Spirit, by an absolute force, gave powers to things to move both themselves and/or others.[121] Leibniz affirmed the perfection of God's initial creative act. All matter, from the initial divine decree, "was invested with an energy that would continue indefinitely and undiminished in quantity."[122] All creation is active in that it receives commands and executes them in a beautiful communal dance.[123]

Leading up to the mechanist tradition—after Thomas Aquinas's modified Aristotelianism was made normative for all Catholics by the Council of Trent (1545-63)[124]—Francesco Suarez, a neoscholastic, tried to get around the seemingly independent operation of the laws of nature (a spin-off of *potentia ordinata*) by saying that the laws were not imposed on creation but were imposed by God on himself.[125] Nature was completely passive and dependent on God's self-ordered activity.

René Descartes (1596-1650), as a mechanist, followed in this line even though he did not follow Aristotelianism. Rather, Descartes was the first to develop a broad natural philosophy to replace Aristotelianism.[126] Matter, for Descartes, was incapable of following God's laws; at every

118. Ibid., 201.
119. Ibid., 202.
120. Ibid.
121. Ibid., 204. The decree is still seen as a divine push or cause.
122. Ibid., 212.
123. Ibid.
124. Ibid., 214.
125. Ibid., 214-15.
126. Ibid., 215. Descartes not only offered a new natural philosophy, but his philosophy started with the human subject instead of God—a drastic change from prior thinking (cf. Küng, *The Beginning of All Things*, 45-46).

moment, matter was dependent on God for its continued existence. At every instant God was creating everything anew.[127] There is no causal relation among events, only passive "material bodies in relative motion sustained by God's continual recreation."[128] The "laws of nature"—Descartes being the one who started the modern version of that idea—were actually an expression of God's attributes.[129] Descartes speculated ways the present world could have evolved out of an original chaos based on the laws of nature: based solely on *potentia ordinata*.

The view of God within this mechanist line transitioned from the medieval view of God being the Prime Mover and Desire of all things to God being the Designer and Lawgiver.[130] When all references to God were eventually eliminated in this tradition, the laws were considered to be a possession of nature rather than a divine prescription for nature.[131] Mechanism became the dominant paradigm in Western science and was a helpful framework in which to construct a program for understanding and controlling nature.[132] It was extremely easy to bracket out the spiritual—including the aesthetic and moral—from the material or natural. In many ways mechanism was intentionally designed to make a clear delineation between the two, leaving the later solely under the jurisdiction of science.[133] This was at least the second notable time in the tradition that spiritual/theological claims were placed under a criteria of truth outside the church's province—the re-introduction of Aristotelianism into the West being the other.

The Platonist tradition—Kaiser's third group—was a reworking of Neoplatonism in response to mechanical philosophy, and yet

127. Kaiser, *Creational Theology*, 215.

128. Ibid., 216.

129. Ibid. In various eras, the notion of laws was different. The biblical notion was that "God ordained laws for all his subjects, even inanimate ones" (Kaiser, *Creational Theology*, 244). This went through adaptations during both the Middle Ages under the notion of *potentia ordinata* and under Suarez's notion of God's legislating of himself. It eventually led to the secularization of "laws of nature" in the eighteenth century (244).

130. Ibid., 234.

131. Ibid., 218. In Kaiser's words, "paradoxically, the assimilation of divine providence to the idea of creation (occasionalism) could thus be turned around into an assimilation of divine creation into universal providence (naturalism)" (*Creational Theology*, 218).

132. Ibid., 234. Interestingly, the theology behind a mechanistic worldview had been worked out as early as the twelfth century (Kaiser, *Creational Theology*, 235).

133. Ibid.

was a different option from spiritualism.¹³⁴ Unlike the spiritualists, the Platonists did not believe motion was inherent in matter. Instead, spirit—which has extension like matter does—can permeate and influence matter; it functions like the Neoplatonic world soul.¹³⁵ Space came to be understood as absolute; matter and God are within it. In the writings of Barrow, for example, he reasoned that space had to be infinite: "or else God would be nowhere . . . space and time were a mathematical representation of the divine omnipresence and eternity."¹³⁶ What the Platonist tradition added that was lacking in the mechanist tradition of Descartes—even though it too affirmed the passivity of matter—were the notions of absolute space and universal active principles operative between individual entities in ways Descartes's occasionalism ignored.

In the universe, more forces were at work than simply inertial motion and the collision of material bodies. Newton sought to explain "inanimate phenomena like gravitation, the diffraction of light, and cohesion."¹³⁷ Newton recognized the dangers—and its unbiblical nature—in the spirit-matter dualism of mechanistic philosophy.¹³⁸ He saw that it could lead to deism or even atheism. Newton, examining alternatives, saw in traditional portrayals of God an utterly transcendent God who was unmoving and absent from history.¹³⁹ Thus, his God—as unbiblical as his opponents'—operated within nature via supramechanical, active principles and in supernatural interventions.¹⁴⁰ Even so, the more the supramechanical principles were studied and summarized mathematically, the more mechanical they appeared: once again leaving little need for God's continued activity. Nature was no longer viewed as *relatively* autonomous; it became *entirely* autonomous.¹⁴¹ As early as a generation after Newton, some even suggested that a nature

---

134. Ibid., 235.

135. Ibid., 237. These ideas can be found in Henry More (1614–1687), one of the early thinkers with John Smith (1618–1652) in this tradition. Many of their ideas of spirit having extension like matter, as well as permeating and influencing matter, are a direct challenge to Descartes's philosophy.

136. Ibid., 240.

137. Ibid., 243.

138. Ibid., 249.

139. Ibid., 250.

140. Ibid. For Newton, "God is the immediate cause of all the effects produced in the material world and spiritual world" (Israel, *Enlightenment Contested*, 214).

141. Kaiser, *Creational Theology*, 251.

that functioned independently from God could also have formed independently of God.[142]

Newton's physics had a profound, even if unforeseen, consequence. "The philosophical effect of Newton's idea was to undermine the very foundation of mechanism and materialism, the notion of the primacy of matter in physics."[143] Two branches formed after him: those minimalizing matter and those emphasizing it. The undermining of traditional notions of and focus on matter within physics is quite interesting given its importance through the centuries philosophically and theologically. This shift happened relatively soon after Newton. For example, in the work of Boscovich (e.g., 1745, 1758), he hypothesized that "atoms were merely mathematical points and that all interactions, even seeming collisions, were the result of forces acting at a distance between those points. In complete contrast to what the Cartesians held, there was no such thing as extension in the material sense: there were only forces acting between dimensionless point-masses."[144] All phenomena of physics and chemistry, he thought as Newton did, were reducible to a single, unified force law.[145]

In spite of the drastic, rapid changes in these centuries, much of what happened through the eighteenth century in physics was connected to theological reflection. "Theologically, the progression was from a clear matter-spirit dualism (Descartes), to matter-spirit symbiosis (Newton), to matter-spirit identity (the later Maupertius and Diderot). The corresponding shift in physics was from a science restricted to geometric quantities (Descartes), to a more comprehensive one of dynamic quantities (Newton), to a science so comprehensive that it could not be quantified at all (Diderot)."[146] The cosmological conversations in these centuries were

142. Ibid., 257. This can be seen in the writings of Samuel Clarke (1675–1729; Kaiser, *Creational Theology*, 257).

143. Ibid., 264. Cf. Prigogine and Stengers, *Order out of Chaos*, 8.

144. Kaiser, *Creational Theology*, 286.

145. Ibid.

146. Ibid., 286–87 Jonathan Israel's portrayal of this era is quite interesting given his methodology of tracking the controversies (cf. *Enlightenment Contested*, 14ff.). He seeks out the issues that were being debated, including who was doing the talking, and about whom they were talking. Israel believes this gives a more accurate picture of an era than simply looking at the works of selected figures, who from a later vantage point seem significant for reasons in hindsight that they should be judged to be significant. In Israel's studies of Enlightenment debates up to the mid-1700s, it is Spinoza and Spinozism that was often at the center in the seventeenth and early eighteenth century (35). Spinoza is often overlooked when giving accounts of this era, and thus the dating of many ideas

still happening among people literate in both theology and the natural sciences. These thinkers were conscious that their ideas in the sciences entailed changes to existing theological accounts of the world.

After the eighteenth century, theology still played a role in the natural sciences. "The main difference from earlier periods was that there was less orthodoxy and more variety—ranging from orthodox trinitarianism to monistic materialism—in the theological stances assumed."[147] The first half of the nineteenth century was the last time that it was commonplace for some members of the Royal Society of London to be clergy.[148] As terms such as "scientist" and "physicist" began to be employed, and the professionalization of each respective field developed, science and theology were further distanced from each other. From the nineteenth century onward it became expected that scientists would suppress personal convictions in their professional work for the sake of objectivity.

A Glimpse of the Present: Chaos in Science

It is difficult, if not impossible, to track the mutual influences of a single dominant (Western) worldview and theology on one another after the Enlightenment. There is neither a homogonous worldview nor unity in theology. Furthermore, after the Enlightenment, with the specialization of each field, science and theology proceeded in a fairly autonomous manner from one another. It cannot even be claimed that in Western thinking one discipline provides the language for secular discourse (even about nature itself) and the other discipline provides language concerning the divine and sacred. Each discipline has become so specialized and technical that they function seemingly independent of the broader cultural milieu; the disciplines not only have languages and perspectives distinct from each other, but also from everyday speech and worldviews of 'laypeople.'[149]

Giving an account of the faith in this context is no longer doing so within the philosophical paradigms of Platonism, Aristotelianism,

---

almost a full century after Spinoza introduced them; e.g., Michael Buckley, *At the Origins of Modern Atheism*, attributes the rise of many radical Enlightenment ideas to Diderot in the mid-1700s for which Spinoza, in the 1600s, should be given credit. Christopher Kaiser's account also all but excludes Spinoza. Thus, what Kaiser describes as a "progression" may in fact be three positions developing in parallel.

147. Kaiser, *Creational Theology*, 252.

148. Ibid., 367.

149. Prigogine and Stengers lament the disconnect between science and culture

Cartesianism, etc. It is not a matter of taking into account the cosmography of Copernicus, Newton, or Einstein—not that it ever was as simple as being confronted with one philosophical or scientific paradigm at a time. There is no single predominant thinker or worldview at this time for Christianity to engage; rather, there are kaleidoscopic views with themes and variations.

In each era of the Western Christian tradition there were those who initially met incoming paradigms with harsh criticism. Yet, the church has managed to endure while adapting to its ever-new surroundings, learning to speak its faith in contexts that raise different questions about familiar issues and new questions about different issues than had ever been in the foreground (or conceived of at all).[150]

Giving an account of God's creative activity and relation to creation at this time in history is challenging. The creationist tradition, especially as it had developed in its conceptualizations, fractured both from within and from external attacks. The past three centuries have been especially taxing on the tradition. As early as the late seventeenth century, the radical Enlightenment thinkers systematically sought to remove all religious "superstitions" within Western culture—perpetuated as they saw it by the power-hungry priestly class. Through reason, they cleared away the theological foundations upon which much of Western culture had once rested and provided new foundations for the newly emerging social structures. They labored to show that there is a *reasonable* explanation for

---

(*Order out of Chaos*, 22). It is dangerous for science to be wielded haphazardly by culture (or its industries) seeking to "man-make" the world or for science to be "a cancerous tumor irresponsibly growing on a substrate society" (ibid., 22). Their concerns about science seem to be equally appropriate for the field of theology.

150. According to Langdon Gilkey, the idea of creation has appeared in every period of Christian history (*Maker of Heaven and Earth*, 41): "And, like a versatile actor, it seems able to don a limitless variety of philosophical costumes; at times it wears the idealism of Platonism (Origen, Augustine); next it appears in the more hardheaded thought of Aristotle (Thomas); then it may forsake these for the simple anthropomorphic categories of the Bible (Luther and Calvin), only to turn up later in the semipantheism of romanticism (Schleiermacher)" (41–42). In Gilkey's view, the doctrine of *creatio ex nihilo*—"that God brought the finite world into being out of nothing through a 'purposive' act of his free will" (43)—is the one central thread giving the whole history consistency (42).

everything.[151] Prior foundations were replaced with ones deduced from universal natural reason.[152]

Under the scrutiny of reason and empirical investigation, many traditional articulations of Christian doctrines suffered.[153] This scrutiny was not simply thrust upon the church by unbelieving radicals; the push toward reasonableness became part of the culture. It became the aim of "every intelligent man to rethink even his most cherished beliefs solely in terms of the available evidence."[154] The result was that "many fundamental ideas which had been long accepted on traditional authority, ecclesiastical or scriptural, were subjected to the cold light of critical reason for really the first time by ordinary Christian laymen."[155] In this intellectual

---

151. Israel, *Enlightenment Contested*, 103, 105, 108, 479, 510, 669, 680. For example, one of the affects of Bayle's thinking was that "instead of theologians declaring what is right and wrong in accordance with God's revelation, universal moral principles based purely on philosophical reason, and wholly detached from theological premises, are made judge of every religious doctrine and ecclesiastical ruling as well as of church history" (Israel, *Enlightenment Contested*, 153; cf. 671); faith was judged inadequate for evaluating justice, morality, and politics; only natural reason would suffice (268). Even those such as Johann Lorenz Schmidt, who were sympathetic to the faith and wanting to eliminate the conflict between philosophy and theology, in giving primacy to reason, did a "systematic and precise reassessment of Scripture and theological doctrine, using scientific criteria to recast theology" (191).

152. E.g., Israel, *Enlightenment Contested*, 252, 254. This trend can be seen in everything from finding rational (i.e., neutral) grounds for a legal system to societal structures to morality itself. See Israel, *Enlightenment Contested*, 194.

153. E.g., along with many traditional ideas of creation and God's interaction with creation, other doctrines such as original sin also were criticized and reworked rationally according to available data. See, e.g., Rousseau's claim that humans are born naturally good and shaped toward good or evil within society; *On Philosophy, Morality, and Religion*, 169ff. Susan Neiman does not intentionally track the history of the doctrine of original sin in her *Evil in Modern Thought*. Nevertheless, she points her readers to progressions in thought in key figures, thus showing how traditional articulations of the doctrine were eroded. Primarily, thoughts concerning the fall, of a one-time ontological change in a past moment, were replaced with historical views of evil's evolution in society, with hopes of its correction in time. What had been a theological doctrine, stated in a more classical paradigm, was transposed in the Enlightenment context into correctible problems, secularly understood, in society, politics, education, psychology, and the like. With everything explained in natural, historical terms, the need for grace was eliminated—as radicals of that age had worked to demonstrate.

154. Gilkey, *Maker of Heaven and Earth*, 12.

155. Ibid.

climate, due to the presence of evil in the world, the reasonableness of the belief in creation was one of the first ideas to be questioned.[156]

Since the Enlightenment, however, there has been a crumbling of confidence in human reason. As early as human reason began being used as the standard, it came under attack. This can be seen in the works of Bayle, Hume, and Sade. These Enlightenment philosophers delighted in embarrassing human reason, if not "torturing it in its folly."[157] After the warfare of the twentieth century, notions of the reasonableness of humanity lay fractured.[158] That which was used to unravel many of the doctrinal formulas in which the Christian faith had been articulated was undone.

From the seventeenth century onward, theological claims were evaluated by and Western society was built upon an appeal to a universal natural reason that itself has been elusive; this reason has failed to transcend context. This does not mean, however, that we can revert to theological language and societal foundations that pre-date the Enlightenment. Those things are no less marked by their context. What this suggests is that the task of reflecting on matters of the faith must be taken up in every context; those reflections should be applied to efforts to reason about societal relations, etc. At the table of human inquiry, theology should not be excluded out of hand as archaic superstition from a bygone era. Every area of inquiry undergoes changes over time. We all can dialogue together to work out articulations to our deep questions in humility about our finitude. There is much that can be gained in dialogue among the humanities and sciences in seeking to venture answers

---

156. Ibid.

157. Neiman, *Evil in Modern Thought*, 164, 168, 195. Thanks to Hume, "the injunction *Be reasonable!* has come to mean *Decrease your expectations*. The demand that we be realistic became a demand that we prepare for disappointment . . . With this conception of reasonableness, Hume sought the overthrow of all notions of reason" (ibid., 168). Even more moderate thinkers like Rousseau claimed that reason is "that great vehicle of all our stupidities" (Rousseau, *On Philosophy, Morality, and Religion*, 43); also, "The art of reasoning is not reason at all; often it is its abuse" (ibid., 80).

158. Neiman, *Evil in Modern Thought*, 327. The horror of World War II's concentration camps "marks a fundamental divide that can almost create nostalgia for the despair which followed World War I" (ibid., 251). Neiman writes further, "What seemed devastated—nay, entirely thwarted—by Auschwitz was the possibility of intellectual response itself . . . The humanistic intellectual skills required to build structures of sense were just the skills that proved treacherous. Seeking meaning and sense in reality could literally be fatal, for both were at odds with those skills required in a place that defied meaning and sense" (ibid., 256, 257).

in this time to pressing human questions. One aim of this project is to be sensitive to some of the emerging views of the world within the sciences when offering a theological account concerning the relationship of God to creation in God's creative activity and an appropriate place for "chaos" language therein.

Listening to Some Shifts in Science's View

Since science parted ways with theology there have been significant shifts in the perspectives of science. The first of these is a change in the optimism of scientific certainty that was based on beliefs in the linearity and simplicity of the universe.[159] It was once thought that if the laws of nature could be calculated, future events could be predicted because everything would proceed in a deterministic manner toward that calculated result.[160] Since the nineteenth century, the universe is not thought to be so wholly predictable. Rather, there is more humility due to the "impossibility of a detailed prognosis."[161]

There are several factors that have led to this position. First, it is not possible to know with exact precision all the initial conditions (e.g., the positions of objects relative to one another). Thus, the inaccuracies in the data entered into formulas will be increased exponentially in the calculations produced.[162] One example: even if the earth's position relative to the sun can be determined within fifteen centimeters, the earth's location in its orbit around the sun cannot be known 120 million years from now.[163]

Second, it is not just the accuracy of the data that stands in the way of certainty. The complexity of the universe continues to be multiplied in ways that stupefy science. It was once hoped within classical science that a fundamental simplicity would be unveiled from beneath the apparent

---

159. Benz, *The Future of the Universe*, 135.

160. According to Jeffrey S. Wicken, "there is of course a long tradition in philosophy of covert mechanical determinism that goes back to Greek atomism and finds paradigmatic expression in the Laplacian notion that if we could but know the positions and momenta of every particle in the universe (its configuration in phase-space), then we could banish entirely uncertainty from time, and blithely predict or retrodict its course of events with complete confidence" ("The Cosmic Breath," 501).

161. Benz, *The Future of the Universe*, 167n4. Cf. Russell, "Entropy and Evil," 450.

162. Benz, *The Future of the Universe*, 132.

163. Ibid., 133.

complexity.[164] However, in something so seemingly simple as calculating the orbits of three bodies that attract one another, the equations are so complex that they cannot be solved.[165] Only linear systems in equilibrium can be calculated with any degree of certainty. They are "the only ones for which a precise description is possible, since they are limited to states of thermodynamic equilibrium and it is only for such states that the bulk parameters are well defined."[166] In nature, however, these are rare, if not non-existent.[167] Laboratory settings are typically where we can create and observe systems in, or close to equilibrium. Finding the key to a universe, once believed to be a determined automaton, is now believed to be a false hope. Notions of simplicity and singularity have been exchanged for complexity and plurality. The idea of a single operating nature has fractured into an array of innumerable, unique participants. Thus, there is a breakdown in the earlier hopes of a controllable order.

Clockwork, mechanistic views of the universe have been replaced with notions of "nonlinear mutual interactions."[168] It is not so much that the parts of the clock are believed to be far greater in number and far smaller in size than once thought. It is that observations about the interactions among parts are not consistent with past views of linear relations of cause and effect.[169] First, the smallest event (e.g., a butterfly flapping its

164. Prigogine and Stengers, *Order Out of Chaos*, 21.
165. Benz, *The Future of the Universe*, 133.
166. Russell, "Entropy and Evil," 452.
167. Ibid.

168. Benz, *The Future of the Universe*, 135. The analogy of the clock changed in the Industrial Revolution to that of an engine running down (Prigogine and Stengers, *Order out of Chaos*, 22). With the unfolding complexities being discovered, Prigogine and Stengers suggest that an analogy of a beautiful sculpture that captures both "stillness and motion, time arrested and time passing" (23) may be appropriate for this age. As an outside observer I would suggest that with the common focus on systems, whether in the natural sciences or social sciences—cf., e.g., Joseph Bracken, *Society and Spirit*—that *community* or *communities* could become a popular analogy; *community* is far more organic than a sculpture and fits the new observations of complexity, plurality, and irreversibility in ways that a sculpture cannot.

169. As much as simplistic notions of cause and effect, entailing either a push or a pull according to linear laws, evoked notions of God being a mover, clockmaker, or designer—perhaps even a meddler—the new thermodynamic models, which must account for 'decisions' by inanimate 'selves,' prompt new conceptualizations of God and God's relationship to creation. On the promise of thermodynamic causality for a new conceptualization of teleology in which development and decision are stressed more than design, see Wicken, "The Cosmic Breath," 502–4.

wings) could have enormous, unintended consequences later on. There is a lack of proportionality or total predictability on how various factors will affect a system. This is due to a second factor of recent interest in science: "communication." "Communication" among entities, especially over distances, is far more complex and mysterious than once imagined. Simply put, "billiard-ball physics has no basis in reality."[170] A few reasons are that, first, to a degree, one of Aristotle's thoughts lives on; the materiality of something "intervenes" in processes; the character of something factors in on how it is shaped by forces and shapes forces. There is "an ingredient of self-determination by a material nature that impresses its own identity on whatever processes proceed through it."[171] Second, things and events cannot be separated or abstracted from their context. "One cannot derive ordered phenomena, the units of individuality, from blind motions . . . they are always conditioned or informed by macroscopic context."[172] In other words, instead of "chance coming-together of brute (i.e., exteriorized) matter," there are now notions of "interdependency of sensation, self-activity, and physical law."[173] Thus, beginnings are not as important as once thought. The beginning does not dictate all that follows. Initial conditions are "not of unique import, for a slight disturbance at any later moment can also alter the path and produce a significantly different outcome."[174] The various contexts and participants therein appear to shape outcomes. There

---

170. Ibid., 501. See Torrance, *Divine and Contingent Order*, 99–100. Essentially there was in science an end to traditional notions of cause. It was replaced by a contingent (relational) order in which all things are intrinsically interdependent; contingence is a notion about relationships. "Such is the vast change effected by relativity physics: classical causal relations are replaced by a dynamic inherent relatedness in the universe, in which space and time are included within the internal connections of all empirical realities and processes and are inseparable from them as space-time. Mechanical laws are discarded along with the rigid structure of classically defined space and time, and field laws are formulated instead, which describe the dynamic invariances of space-time as an orderly open continuum of contingent realities and events" (Torrance, *Divine and Contingent Order*, 100). In other words, in this era of quantum physics there essentially is "an integration of field and particle which requires the abandonment of the classical notion of locality" (ibid., 101). Furthermore, there is "an integration of form and being" (ibid., 102).

171. Wicken, "The Cosmic Breath," 502.

172. Ibid.

173. Ibid.

174. Benz, *The Future of the Universe*, 136. Cf. Polkinghorne, *Quarks, Chaos and Christianity*, 84.

are no gears that can simply be turned back. Complex, context-specific, irreversible interactions are the norm.[175]

Non-linearity and randomness seem to be the rules in nature. Thus, science is now focusing less on substance than on relation, communication, and time.[176] "On every scale self-organization, complexity, and time play a new and unexpected role."[177] Far-from-equilibrium systems may become organized; "New dynamic states of matter may originate, states that reflect the interaction of a given system with its surroundings."[178] Systems close to equilibrium generally follow universal laws in a repetitive way. Outside of equilibrium, it is as though there are mechanisms of communication that can bring the system to various types of structures.

This new view of the world and of time demonstrates differences in inquiry between the Middle Ages and the present. Where the nature of a thing was once studied in an at-rest, out of context state, a new viewpoint is operative in which accidents—in a medieval philosophical meaning—are not added to an enduring existing thing. Currently: "A system is characterized by more than its present state; the path taken also counts, the process is part of the product... This world is one where nature is inherently historical, where matter at even the inanimate level displays an indelible sense of evolution ... The character of the present is dependent on the path from the past: although 'all roads lead to Rome,' the actual journey influences the quality of arrival. It is a world in fluctuation, filled with novelty."[179] Things have changed since Newton and the optimism of the reversibility of time. "In thermodynamics, as time passes the world changes irreversibly; nothing can be done to ever

---

175. In the church's reflections on creation, the beginning gained ever increasing importance. More and more in science, however, subsequent events are constitutive of the present and future system or thing. Beginnings are only just that, beginnings. Contemporary work on creation theology should be sensitive to this matter.

176. Prigogine and Stengers, *Order out of Chaos*, 8.

177. Ibid., 10.

178. Ibid., 12. Benz discusses in a helpful section what science means by "self-organization" when there technically is no "self"; see Benz, *The Future of the Universe*, 136ff. In short, it refers to systems that organize in ways independent of initial conditions (136)—i.e., they do not unfold according to a linear causal chain from initial conditions.

179. Russell, "Entropy and Evil," 451. With these changes in worldview, it is an interesting time for asking the question, what does God's activity of creation entail? Is 'creation' simply the giving of being, or does it entail an ongoing narrative of development/becoming, as was present in the theology of the Bible and the early church prior to the emphasis on the beginning establishing moment.

quite recover the way things were, and nothing can be done to condition entirely the way things will be next."[180]

Due to these kinds of observations in nature, time is no longer seen as completely reversible. When natural laws were seen to be deterministic and thus predictors of the future, it was believed that one could look backward and forward using that same formula. Essentially, at what time and in what place something took place was irrelevant; processes were believed to follow laws irrespective of context-specific factors. Science has moved beyond a pure mechanistic perspective within a generic, absolute space.[181] There is uniqueness to events. Each point in time is not equivalent to another. Thus, time is irreversible (cannot be duplicated). Certainly there are periods of relative equilibrium within systems when they seem to follow laws in a linear, deterministic fashion. However, any fluctuations may lead to bifurcation points (far-from-equilibrium points) where their behavior is unpredictable. There are many possible paths those systems can take at those points and it is unpredictable which it will be.[182] Nature may not be a "self" or "selves" that are doing the "self-organizing." However, nature is far from a dead, determined singularity. Within it there is a great deal of complex activity and "actors."

There are some positive implications for these new views. The older mechanistic views of the universe placed a dichotomy between humans and nature. Nature was viewed atemporally and summarized in universals.[183] "The great founders of Western science stressed the universality and the eternal character of natural laws. They set out to formulate general schemes that would coincide with the very ideal of rationality."[184] When humans engaged nature in science, at first what they encountered seemed to be dead and silent, thus isolating humans from nature.[185] The

180. Ibid.
181. Prigogine and Stengers, *Order out of Chaos*, xxvii.
182. Ibid., xxiii.
183. Ibid., xxviii, xxix.
184. Ibid., 1.
185. Ibid., 6. Neiman in *Evil in Modern Thought* follows the shifts in thinking about the relationship between humans and nature from the Enlightenment into Modernity. She does so through investigating the heightened interest in theodicy in that time period. Each camp of thinkers chose a different combination among possibilities: seeing nature as rational/irrational, good/bad, etc., and seeing humans as rational/irrational, good/bad, etc. What we are left with in the modern era is the "disenchantment of the world" (Brague, *The Wisdom of the World*, 194). It was hoped that humans could be an exception to the cruelty in nature. "Good" became a human endeavor by which they

rationality they thought they could uncover in nature—in this dead and silent realm—excluded much in which humans have a vested interest—for example: life, destiny, freedom, and spontaneity.[186] With the notions of fundamental simplicity, singularity, and linear-determinism dissolving in science, humans are once again being united with their world.

Addressing Uses of "Chaos" in Science

As the field of physics shifted in the late nineteenth and early twentieth centuries from the vision of Newton, of a universe with precise calculable laws, progressively there was a notion of "chaos" that became a regular part of the thinking of scientists. With both the contributions of Einstein's theory of relativity and the introduction of quantum mechanics "the immediate realism, determinism, and reductionism" of previous generations of science was replaced.[187] "Here it became clear that physics

---

could correct nature (203). Neiman points out in stunning clarity how that hope was dashed. Thus, ethics could no longer be seen to have either a cosmological or anthropological foundation; however, "what is more serious is rather the opposite; that, if we may say so, cosmology and anthropology no longer have an ethical foundation" (Brague, *The Wisdom of the World*, 218).

186. Ibid. These notions became possible for the world when, as Russell states, the idea of temporal irreversibility that arose in the nineteenth century led to a view of a world that is "marked by a radical, undeniable difference between past and future, by a statistical quality to its predictions, and by arbitrariness and contingency" ("Entropy and Evil," 451).

187. Küng, *The Beginning of All Things*, 7–8. Even after Einstein things have changed. He was working with the idea of a static universe (ibid., 9). Since him not only has the 1927 notion of Abbé Georges Lemaitre of an expanding universe become accepted, but Edwin P. Hubble empirically showed the science community that there are astrophysical bodies outside the Milky Way and they are moving outward in all directions at great speed. There is no fixed space, and things do not just occupy it (10); space is interwoven with its contents. Torrance describes it in this way: "This four-dimensional continuous indivisible field of space-time relations is far from being merely a scientific 'thought-symbol,' for it constitutes the fundamental continuum of the universe in which energy and matter, field and particle, form and being, are fully integrated, and as such provides the objective dynamic structure ordering all things and events in the universe" (Torrance, *Divine and Contingent Order*, 100). This notion of space-time is linked with the notion that time is irreversible. When something happens in a place it is important because of the uniqueness of that place-time. This also has import to any articulation of *creatio ex nihilo* in the present; "If we are to understand the relation of the Creator to the created order in an integrated and integrative manner it is imperative that God not be thought of as creating objects in space or spatial objects in time. Rather, we are required to think in terms of God's creating the totality of spatio-temporal identities together with their interconnective matrices from absolutely nothing" (Alan Torrance, "Creatio

by no means simply describes the world in itself, independently of the standpoint of the observer, as Newton presupposed."[188]

The pioneering work of Heisenberg in quantum theory unsettled prior thinking, as did theories of relativity and a dynamic, expanding universe. In quantum mechanics relationships are "fuzzy or indeterminate."[189] For example, the Heisenberg Principle entails that "If we know where an electron is (position), we cannot know what it is doing (momentum)."[190] When measuring one, measurements of the other become blurry. Far from the past certainty about the mechanical workings of the universe, scientists are left with statistical probabilities; "The consequence is that if it is impossible precisely to measure the present state of an object (in the classical sense), its future cannot be precisely predicted either."[191] This is precisely where "chaos" gets used in science in a technical way. "In present-day terms, *a process of physics is termed 'chaotic' if its long-term course is not predictable.*"[192] For example, since the location of the earth relative to the sun cannot be precisely determined at any one moment, its location tens of millions of years from now cannot be known. That makes the earth's orbit *deterministically chaotic*.[193]

This incalculable quality of many natural phenomena has changed the course of some of the past claims of "objectivity," "exactness," or

---

ex Nihilo and the Spatio-Temporal Dimensions," 98).

188. Küng, *The Beginning of All Things*, 8.
189. Ibid., 13.
190. Ibid., 13–14.
191. Ibid., 14.
192. Benz, *The Future of the Universe*, 132.
193. Ibid. Stuart Chandler, "When the World Falls Apart," 470, agrees with Robert Poole that chaos theory has only altered Newton's ideas by a degree. In chaos theory it is still believed that the world is "ordered by deterministic laws. These laws are simply a little more difficult to discern than Newton realized: they are nonlinear rather than linear. The only significant difference between the Newtonian and chaos models is that the latter recognizes that the fine details of a deterministic process cannot be precisely known and therefore better accounts for complexity and individuality. Determinism rules; we simply do not have the ability or tools, however, always to recognize it" (470). This criticism may be legitimate. However, not all chaos theorists are trying to prove determinacy. Rather, some argue for just the opposite: freedom, randomness, or chance (cf. Hefner, "God and Chaos," 469–85). The fact is that we do not know which it is, or if either linguistic framing truly conforms to reality. At this point positions of determinacy and chance appear to reflect the prejudices of theorists more than any certainty offered by the available data. This is precisely where dialogue is appropriate between the sciences and the humanities, including theology, in wrestling to articulate answers to these deep

"precision" that was common in some nineteenth-century schools such as the positivists.[194] The inability of science to empirically verify its statements about circumstances has come to the fore; what has been shown in the last century is "the hypothetical character of its laws" and the need not to absolutize its results.[195] "Scientists should reflect that subject and object, method and object, are interwoven, and thus a distinction must be made between the phenomena that can be grasped by science and reality as a whole."[196]

This distinction is rarely kept. It is hard for scientists to ward off of the tendency toward realism. John Polkinghorne admits that "Scientists are realists; they believe that what we know, or what we can't know, shows us what things are really like."[197] In jest his wife bought him a sweatshirt with the motto on it, "Epistemology Models Ontology." The manner in which "chaos" is used in science is an excellent example of this pattern. Observable phenomena in nature most often thwart the certainty that mathematical calculation can provide were it within a deterministic linear system. As unsettling as this may be for those seeking definitive answers, the confounding of their ambitions by systems in nature does not mean that these systems *are* "chaos." Rather, it suggests that, as far as we can tell at this point, systems in nature typically do not exhibit linear, determined characteristics that were once believed to be definitive of a mechanical universe.

Relationships are far more complex than once thought. In a framework of thermodynamics, relativity, and quantum mechanics the world is not believed to be as simple as particles acting externally on one another in space and in time. Rather, "nature is found not to be ultimately

---

human questions and evaluating the implications of the various possibilities.

194. Küng, *The Beginning of All Things*, 25.

195. Ibid., 30. "No method, however certain, no scheme, however adequate, no theory, however precise, may be made absolute" (Küng, *The Beginning of all Things*, 51–52). T. F. Torrance has a similar critique and warning about the language of science that in the end is an abstraction from sense experience: "Regarded from this point of view, scientific theories are logically tautological and can have no claim to bear upon intrinsic relations or structures in being, while scientific laws are devoid of evidential content and are finally no more than freely created sets of conventions for the most effective and economic organization of observational and operational data, yet they are not altogether arbitrary sets of conventions for they have to be consistent with one another" (*Divine and Contingent Order*, 96).

196. Küng, *The Beginning of All Things*, 51.

197. Polkinghorne, *Quarks, Chaos and Christianity*, 85.

divided up like that but, all its particulate properties notwithstanding, is dynamically continuous in space and time, in such a way that all things are what they are through unbroken internal relations with other things, while those inter-relations help to make them what they actually are or become."[198] Things cannot be abstracted from "their natural cohesions in the constituent matter and energy of the universe."[199] In the discovery of the complexity of relationships, new notions of communication, the sensitivity of systems to influence from other systems, and so on, it is no wonder that the world seems *chaotic* in a field that developed under quite different presuppositions of mechanistic determinism. Nevertheless, indeterminacy and statistical probability are not necessarily things that warrant calling systems *chaotic*.[200] The limitations of verifiability on such a label warrant caution in making such a label an absolute statement about the nature of reality.

It was mentioned in chapter 1 that there is much about chaotic systems that is not chaotic and that this label is being questioned as a result, because it is misleading concerning the characteristics that are known about these systems. Thus, it may be convention to use the term "chaos" concerning unpredictable systems. However, based on a theological perspective, which concerns itself with the implications of the language we use about the world, this use of the term should be reconsidered. A more appropriate use for "chaos" should be defined.

It is not just the impossibility of calculating the future of these systems that earns the label of "chaos." Along with using "chaos" in the context of mathematical probability instead of certainty, "chaos" also gets used more casually in science as a synonym for "entropy." For example, one use of "entropy" is for "the thermal motion of molecules or density fluctuations in gases . . . [this] concept of chaos denotes the muddle of immeasurably numerous particles which, on the microscopic level, move in constantly varying interactions and collisions."[201] Essentially the term is being used as it is in more popular conversation as a synonym for "confusion." By linking "chaos" with "entropy," or systems with a high

---

198. Torrance, *Divine and Contingent Order*, 99f.

199. Ibid., 100.

200. This world that defies our attempts at objectification might better be called "thou" or "neighbor."

201. Benz, *The Future of the Universe*, 132. Cf. Russell, Hefner, Wicken, etc. for this type of use.

degree of entropy, it again leads to the same problems of language and meaning as the first, more technical use of "chaos" in science. It shows the bias toward entropy of the speaker and can color future reflections as much as it accurately describes with certainty the nature of reality.

Philip Hefner states that "We can discern at least five different kinds of experience to which scientists have attached the concepts associated with the second law of thermodynamics, with different meanings resulting in each case."[202] These include: "Dissipation of energy—running down," "Change and alternation of a previous order—degeneracy," "The experience of 'one-time-ness'—time's irreversible arrow," "Mixed-up-ness and chaotic disorderliness," and "Alterations that make for possibility."[203] His point is that four out of these five experiences and the meanings attached to them show the dominant (Platonic) Western tradition at work, which dislikes entropy.[204] This anti-entropy/chaos view that pits God against entropy is not the only one. Hefner points to a minority view manifest in Berdyaev that sees these experiences positively.[205] For some within this minority tradition, entropy and God are not in conflict. Rather, entropy is a facet of divinity; it is within God.[206]

Cultural presuppositions about entropy color the meaning given to it; these presuppositions make it quite natural to affix the pejorative label of "chaos" to it. This in turn has influenced theological reflection about it. For example, Sjoerd Bonting connects entropy with chaos and claims that God decreases entropy over the course of the cosmos's evolution. Entropy/chaos was maximal at the big bang and God has been decreasing it since; at the end of time it will be abolished.[207]

This whole framework of demonizing entropy, whether in science or theology, needs to be reconsidered—especially if in theology it leads

202. Hefner, "God and Chaos," 471.

203. Ibid., 472, 473.

204. Ibid., 469.

205. Catherine Keller, whose views are covered in chapter 5, would sympathize with Hefner's treatment, given that she sees the dominant trend in Western thinking in terms of a misogynistic subjugation of the (m)other. Keller sees "on a cosmic level the tendency for order to irrupt from within chaos; to self-organize rather than to depend (like the early Bonhoeffer's 'obedient void') upon an external transcendence to impose it" (*Face of the Deep*, 190).

206. Hefner, "God and Chaos," 469. Although entropy is not demonized in this book, it is not placed within God. The move of placing entropy or chaos within God is not the only alternative to the demonization of entropy.

207. Bonting, *Creation and Double Chaos*, 97.

to the idea that God works against entropy. There is a rule within the second law of thermodynamics that "tells us that all natural processes take place in such a way as to increase the entropy of the whole, that is, the system plus its environment."[208] In fact, in a closed system entropy never decreases;[209] entropy can only decrease in a system if it is part of a larger system into which its entropy can be transferred. Even then, the level of entropy in the larger system does not decrease; entropy has only been shifted around.

If entropy is evil (or an antinomy to God's creative activity), thermodynamic processes themselves are increasing the amount of evil/non-creation within creation and are working against God's ordering of creation. Our own continued existence would be an evil to God's creative endeavors; "Not only individual life, but evolution itself, is like a plague devouring the order of the world; and humankind through its complicated civilization is the most insatiable consumer of all . . . Even the universe in its global expansion seems to grow at the expense of greater entropy."[210] Associating entropy with evil, chaos, or noncreation must be reconsidered given the nature of actual (creative, sustaining) processes within the universe.[211] "Chaos" is a label that colors conceptions of entropic systems and certain outcomes of thermodynamic processes in ways that are not necessarily self-evident. Adopting this way that science uses the term "chaos" should be avoided because of some of the theological implications that have tended to accompany it.

---

208. Russell, "Entropy and Evil," 452.

209. Ibid., 458.

210. Ibid., 460. Entropy is not an evil. In Richard Colling's words, "Without the Second Law [of Thermodynamics] and its inherent quality to make physical matter and energy randomize, nothing in the world would happen. Everything would stop. There would be no chemical reactions, no physics, no connections, no movement, no life—nothing! In a very real sense then, the Second Law is an incredible, unseen, universal driver" (Colling, *Random Designer*, 25; italics removed).

211. In the universe there is constant dying that another might live or be born; stars died that our planet might be born; organisms die that we might be nourished. Christ gifts of himself that others might live; the bread that has been eaten cannot be put back together. Nevertheless, we do not give ourselves away or die as ones without hope; there is the promise of new, resurrected life. "Although life inevitably involves disease and death, the New Testament vision is one of ultimate triumph: the apostle Paul wrote, 'We know that the whole creation has been groaning in travail together until now.' 'The creation itself will be set free from its bondage to decay and obtain the glorious liberty of the children of God' (Rom. 8:22,21)" (Russell, "Entropy and Evil," 462).

The Relationship of the Doctrine of Creation to the Presiding Philosophy or Worldview of the Day

The topics under this section have been mentioned in the treatment on the history of the creationist tradition. Thus, the purpose of this section is simply to bring explicit attention to these issues, not to give full treatment of them. This is important in understanding the nature of the theological task at hand in this project, as well as showing that there is a precedent in the church's history of adjusting the grammar of creation theology so that it is comprehensible in ever-new contexts.

Dependence

One of the primary theses in Gerhard May's *Creatio Ex Nihilo* is that the Christian doctrine of *creatio ex nihilo* arose from Christianity's own presuppositions about God's sovereignty and unlimited freedom. The concept as developed by the Christians, nevertheless, "can only be articulated within the latter's [the Greeks' world formation] frame of reference and by using its terms."[212] Christians used the categories and terminology of the philosophical perspective(s) of the time.[213]

Christopher Kaiser's examination of the creationist tradition through history showed this same trend as May's work. When the philosophical landscape or presiding scientific model changed, Christians found themselves articulating their faith anew in the face of the new paradigm. In just one example: "As in the case of the reception of Aristotle in the thirteenth century, the remarkable thing about the church was not so much its initial resistance to new scientific ideas as its ability to reevaluate and assimilate them in keeping with the historic creationist tradition."[214] Even though many of the same underlying presuppositions remained consistent, these transitions to new contexts rarely came

---

212. May, *Creatio ex Nihilo*, xii; cf. viii.

213. According to the thesis of Michael Buckley in *The Origins of Modern Atheism*, an exactly backward phenomenon took place during the Enlightenment. The atheistic positions were developed according to the categories and terminology of Christianity; their positions were parasitic in many ways.

214. Kaiser, *Creational Theology*, 221.

without changes in the way God, God's activity relative to creation, and creation itself are understood.

Polemical or Reactionary Articulation of the Creationist Tradition

In May's tracking of the development of the doctrine of *creatio ex nihilo*, he demonstrates not only that Christians worked within the frame of reference of their broader philosophical context, but also that the doctrine itself was formulated as an antithesis to that frame of reference.[215] Christians in the second century, such as Justin Martyr, initially harmonized their theology with the cosmology of Plato's *Timaeus*. However, as new questions arose, bringing out inconsistencies in such harmonization, the doctrine of *creatio ex nihilo* was developed as an ontological statement highlighting "the omnipotence, freedom, and uniqueness of God."[216] Other developments, such as affirming God's *potentia ordinata* and *potentia absoluta*, arose as a way of still affirming Christian presuppositions against, yet from within, worldviews that were contradictory to those presuppositions. P*otentia ordinata* and *potentia absoluta* developed within this context beyond what they had been as a substitute for the Aristotelian worldview of *primum mobile* being the source of world's dynamism.[217]

In the midst of the Western theological tradition, many of the catalysts for response have come from within: whether from heretical movements or between parallel wings of the tradition. The point being emphasized, however, is that one's interlocutors contribute significantly to the shape of one's statements and emphases. The way in which doctrines have been articulated within the tradition to a certain degree are molded around both the contexts in which they were developed and that to which they were developed in response. Their forms bear the marks of their history as much as that to which they bear witness.[218]

Transitions in Conceptualizations of God and God's

215. May, *Creatio ex Nihilo*, xii. Cf. May's treatment of Irenaeus's response to the conversations and issues brought up by his counterparts (164ff).

216. Ibid.

217. Kaiser, *Creational Theology*, 234.

218. In just one example, Steven Baldner and William Carroll, in their introduction

Relationship to Creation

As has been mentioned, Christianity's transitions into new frameworks has not happened without adjustments in the analogies it employs concerning God and God's relationship to creation: e.g., King, transcendent Being, First Mover, Clockmaker, Designer, Lawgiver, etc.[219] In the transitions through history in the broader intellectual context and the dominant analogy(ies) employed therein, God was conceived as ever more removed from creation and its ongoing operations. The world, in turn, was viewed as ever more life-less and mechanical; its parts were certainly not viewed as subjects to be addressed in the way they were in Scripture. Kaiser's work ends with the mechanistic worldview in which God is seen as the Designer and Lawgiver.[220] In such a worldview, it is in relation to the beginning, in which everything is set in motion along linear, deterministic laws, that God has significance and according to which God is named; there is less room for the ongoing activity of God.

There are still theologians engaging in dialogue with the sciences and the picture(s) of the cosmos they paint.[221] There are also theologians seeking to articulate the faith in the face of certain philosophical paradigms, such as process thought. The number of various articulations of divine creation and God's relationship to creation is staggering. Each one is in its own way trying to give an account of the faith in the present. Some try to argue for the reasonableness of traditional creationist

---

to their translation of Aquinas's work, *Aquinas on Creation: Writings on the "Sentences" of Peter Lombard* 2.1.1, claim that for Augustine and Aquinas, "what is essential to the Christian faith is the fact of creation, not its manner or mode" (3–4). What they mean by "creation" is explained further in their statement: "The explanation of the six days is really an account of the *formation* of the world, not its *creation*" (4). The first question of philosophy during that era was being—ontological dependence on God. Thus, the age itself shaped the question(s) being answered in theology concerning the topic of creation; "Thus questions such as, how does the first cause give being (existence) to creatures, and how do creatures receive the being that is given to them, are central to such an investigation" (4). In an era where epistemological concerns are paramount, interest in God's "creative" involvement in the six days becomes part of treatments on *creation*. Only secondarily do later thinkers ask if God was necessary to start the causal unfolding that is the object of their observations. Even in the twelfth century scientists had already started taking the beginning of the world for granted and focused on explaining the beauty of the world (Otten, "Reading Creation," 243).

219. Kaiser, *Creational Theology*, 109.

220. Ibid., 234.

221. E.g., Taede Smedes, Arnold Benz, James Huchingson, John Polkinghorne, Sjoerd Bonting, Arthur Peacocke, and the like.

themes or linguistic formulas in the present—for example, that *creatio ex nihilo* should not be dismissed as an irrelevant mythological notion.[222] Some take the liberty of finding new, creative approaches to cosmology. Others look for options that had been jettisoned within the tradition that may at this juncture be of use.[223] Thus, at present there are suggestions about the nature of God's creative activity everywhere from strict instantaneous *creatio ex nihilo* to emanationism to world formation. In the aftermath of the creationist tradition's fracturing, little that was once held as regulative seems to have that force within intellectual inquiry even if it still does ecclesially.

The Relationship of Biblical Interpretation and the Doctrine of Creation

Even though the relationship between biblical interpretation and the church's teachings on creation has not been highlighted to this point, it is, nevertheless, a significant component to the current situation. In Willemien Otten's reading of the tradition, there was a quick transition early in the church from establishing which texts were divinely inspired to concern for the theological content of those texts. A link was established "between biblical interpretation and sound doctrine."[224] Following Augustine's *On Christian Doctrine*, biblical exegesis became the focus "in most intellectual endeavors."[225] By the early medieval period, "theology was on the whole co-extensive with biblical interpretation."[226] In the twelfth century, nevertheless, there were some changes taking place in the Christian-Platonic worldview. "Firstly, the concept of creation was taking on a more dogmatic status as an important locus in the budding

---

222. E.g., Gilkey, *Maker of Heaven and Earth*, 8.

223. As will be seen in chapter 5, Catherine Keller, in part, takes this approach. She believes the ideas of Hermogones, regardless of being conditioned by the Platonism of his day, should be reevaluated in the present; Hermogones, she believes, was fighting for more biblical ideas of world formation (*Face of the Deep*, 48).

224. Otten, "Nature and Scripture," 258. The relation between exegesis and theology has shifted throughout history; for example, "in the church-dominated culture of the Middle Ages, the adequacy of scriptural interpretation—its method, its content, the credentials of its practitioners—often depended on its conformity with an expanding theological tradition" (Otten, "Nature and Scripture," 258).

225. Otten, "Reading Creation," 235. It had, no doubt, been the focus of theological endeavors prior to that.

226. Ibid.

genre of early scholastic theology . . . Secondly, the focus of studying Genesis was shifting. In the twelfth century the primary purpose of reading Genesis was to test and exemplify ideas that one had developed otherwise, serving more as a meta-physical end-goal than a biblical starting-point."[227] Other sources, such as the *Timaeus*, were starting to "encroach on the reading of Genesis."[228]

The relationship of the Bible to extrabiblical literature was being pushed in the twelfth century. At the same time, it was believed that there was "correspondence between the Book of Nature and the Book of Scripture."[229] This century was the high point of this belief.[230] The poetic language in which the themes of the two books were united at times "eclipsed" the scriptural connotations.[231] Eventually the framework for this relationship was eroded from both sides.[232] Both became objects of study in their own right, progressively distanced from theology, instead of bearers of truth about God and/or the nature of reality. Even with authors such as Hugh of St. Victor, for whom the Bible remained

---

227. Ibid., 235–36.

228. Ibid., 236. This can be seen in the writings of Theirry of Chartres and William of Conches. William believed that God created a large chaotic body in which all the elements were mixed. The difference between this and Plato's *khora* was the assertion of the formless mixture being created (Otten, "Reading Creation," 240). He even goes so far as to reject some statements in Genesis, such as there being waters "above," due to the fact that such a claim is *contra rationem* (241). Thus in their works "they aimed at designing their own 'ultra-natural' theology by integrating the physics of Genesis with the metaphysics of the *Timaeus*" (241). The positive side of the union between exegesis and cosmology was that it "forged an alliance between the salvation of humanity and that of the surrounding universe that would permeate much of the tradition of early Christian and medieval theology" (Otten, "Nature and Scripture," 260). Unfortunately, however, "just as science seems to have receded behind the scenes in most contemporary theology, so the cosmos has ceased to play much of a part in contemporary exegesis" (260).

229. Ibid., 225. This analogy of nature and Scripture each being a book to read became quite common. During this time it was presumed that they were complimentary of one another in their "message."

230. Ibid., 225n2.

231. Ibid., 271.

232. It is important to point out that the goal of exegeting both Scripture and nature was not necessarily to connect them with one another, but to give knowledge of the transcendent God or "the interpretation of reality" (Otten, "Nature and Scripture," 283). Baldner and Carroll lament the demise of this type of focus in the study of Scripture: that the text no longer is a word from God pointing the people forward, but that the people look backward to what it meant in their reading (*Aquinas on Creation*, 3).

authoritative, the goal of exegesis became more narrowly focused on explaining the mysteries of the faith; knowledge of creation took second place.[233]

The relationship between the Bible and cosmology (science) was also divided in a context in which theology and the liberal arts were going their separate ways.[234] "With the ongoing development of science along Aristotelian lines in the thirteenth century, not only do we see how the tension between science and exegesis results in separation, but also how the isolation of theology becomes a fact, as it severed not just its intrinsic ties with science, but especially its organic ties with myth."[235]

Baldner and Carroll lay much of the blame for the current methods of biblical studies on the beginning of the sixteenth century when the Reformation controversies led to literalistic readings of biblical texts as propositions.[236] This undermined the reading of Scripture as a unified whole. Looking only at the literalistic signification of words in a historical fashion, and not the unity of the whole, "leads many to question whether the opening line of Genesis can really support the doctrine of creation out of nothing."[237]

On the one hand, there were trends in motion long before the Reformation that were dissolving the place of Scripture in reflecting on the nature of the world. Also, there is question whether it was the voice of Scripture that was being heard prior to the Reformation or whether Scripture was being read less critically through the lens of the current worldview—not that we can ever be rid of this phenomenon. On the other hand, the historical-critical methods under which Scripture is scrutinized today may have had seeds in the work of the Humanists and the Reformers, but are largely an outflow of developments in the early Enlightenment. As the Thirty Years War was finally coming to a close—not before devastating much of Europe—there was "a generally perceived need in the 1650s to revise and adjust the relationship between theology, philosophy, and science."[238] It was broadly felt in intellectual circles that religion had contributed to far too much bloodshed

---

233. Otten, "Reading Creation," 241.
234. Ibid., 243.
235. Ibid.
236. Baldner and Carroll, *Aquinas on Creation*, 3.
237. Ibid.
238. Israel, *Enlightenment Contested*, 65.

and heartache. There were definite changes that arose in response to the perceived problems; "With the philosophies of Hobbes and Spinoza, it became clear that what was being overturned, at least potentially, was all forms of authority and tradition, even Scripture and Man's essentially theological view of the universe itself."[239]

The early thinkers leading into the radical Enlightenment, such as Spinoza and LeClerc, became extremely critical of the Humanists and their handling of texts. "Humanists, . . . were judged largely oblivious to the need to reconstruct the context of beliefs and ideas ancient texts embody and elucidate the assumptions, superstitions, and fears which shaped them, as well as ill equipped to develop the kind of historically based exegesis indispensable for achieving such goals."[240] The aim of the radicals in the 1660s and 1670s was not innocent. For Spinoza, he believed that "the 'true' meaning of biblical as of other texts, and 'truth of fact,' had generally been 'confused.'"[241] Thus, his method was created to keep meanings of texts separate from truth. "Broadly, understanding a text, for Spinoza, is not a question of ascertaining what is 'true' in it or searching for what is authoritative, but rather a historical-critical and linguistic exercise anchored in a wider naturalistic philosophical

---

239. Ibid. The intellectual crises were not stirred up by academics alone. Certainly the intellectual foundations of a society play a significant stabilizing role: "The institutions, social hierarchy, status, and property arrangements on which a given society is based can only remain stable whilst the explanations that society offers in justification command sufficiently wide currency and acceptance, and begin to disintegrate when such general acceptance lapses" (Israel, *Enlightenment Contested*, 4–5). New philosophies such as Descartes's mechanism helped erode old foundations. Yet, there had already to that point been social changes that were demanding new ways of social, political thinking. Old structural views of the cosmos could not account for the cultural plurality and class fluidity spurred by the growing "commercial, imperial, and metropolitan setting evolving in the late seventeenth and early eighteenth centuries" (ibid., 115).

240. Ibid., 416.

241. Ibid., 411.

standpoint."[242] All texts, sacred or otherwise, were subjected to the new techniques. The sacred was secularized.[243]

Theological issues were certainly at the forefront in the century following the Thirty Years War; yet with the changes in science, geography, philosophy, etc., it became increasingly difficult to reconcile the old with the new in theological terms. Finally, there was "by the 1740s, the apparent collapse of all efforts to forge a new general synthesis of theology, philosophy, politics, and science, which destabilized religious belief and values, causing the wholly unprecedented crisis of faith driving the secularization of the modern West."[244] Faith and reason were finally and fully divided, if not seen to be opposed, and the Bible was sidelined in its significance for matters of contemporary theology.

These methods of Bible study, with some of their accompanying consequences, have been passed along to today. With the rise of historical-critical methods, "The scepter of authority passed from the ecclesiastical to the academic hierarchy."[245] Biblical hermeneutics became in the Enlightenment primarily a matter of "accuracy in historical reconstruction,"[246] rather than having a "theological role as source of transcendent meaning"[247] or "contributing to wider theological debates."[248]

These changes in methodology and conceptualization of Scripture within the academy have been troublesome. At the same time in history

242. Ibid. Brague points out in an unrelated treatment on the plurality of worlds that these types of splitting between the fact of something and the good or true began earlier, in the Middle Ages, in the Christian tradition. Wherever there are spatial hierarchies of worlds, temporal succession of worlds, or hypothesizing about possible worlds, it relativizes observations about our world. "The plurality of worlds, even if it remains a pure hypothesis, has an ontological consequence. The real is reduced to being nothing more than the factual. The being and the good are in this way dissociated: the being of this real world which is ours has its source in a good that does not coincide with it but is external to it, namely, the benevolence of God, who chose it among other possible worlds" (*The Wisdom of the World,* 182). Brague applauds theology for being able to dispense with Aristotelianism through undermining the uniqueness of the world (ibid., 178); however, the fact/value (or nature/grace) split has many other consequences.

243. Israel, *Enlightenment Contested,* 421.

244. Ibid., 65.

245. Otten, "Nature and Scripture," 258.

246. Ibid., 259.

247. Ibid., 258.

248. Ibid., 259. Where there are theological claims made based on Scripture, they are often connected to issues of human salvation (ibid.). The "universal referentiality of scripture has been narrowed" within this method (ibid.).

that the creationist tradition was fracturing and all doctrines were being subjected to empirical verification and rational scrutiny, Scripture too was under siege. The union between biblical exegesis and theology had long been dissolving. However, where appeals to the voice of Scripture and its authority may have been helpful to save what was left of the creationist tradition as the presiding general worldview, the church and Scripture were being stripped of being bearers of truth.[249] Natural human reason was given authority. The church and Scripture were being accused of brokering in enslaving-superstitions. Even worse, as Baldner and Carroll suggest, as the biblical texts were subjected to historical-critical investigation, disparities arose between what the texts meant in their contexts and the various formulations of the church's doctrines through the centuries. The scriptural texts were no longer viewed to say all that had come to be affirmed in the tradition.[250] The current spectrum in theological positions being taken in regard to creation is to a certain extent a symptom of both the division between biblical and theological studies—which for centuries had supported one another—and the subsequent undermining of each one of them.

Common Difficulties within the Creationist Tradition

There are two difficulties within the creationist tradition that have been recurring through the centuries in various manifestations; both have to do with the relationship between God and the world; both fall within Kaiser's category of "relative autonomy." The first has been how to navigate between the distinction of God and creation while affirming creation's contingency and dependence upon God for either its initial or

---

249. Even centuries before, their reach had begun to be limited to the realms of morality and spirituality.

250. This issue will come up again in later chapters. However, part of the dilemma is a dilemma of the age in which the problem arose. Where the concerns were epistemology, the biblical texts were treated as an object to be measured and mastered. However, a new era in first questions has arrived: that of language. One of the new approaches to Scripture (or any text) is intertextuality, not empirical accuracy. In this approach, texts are treated more like an "other" than an object; they become a conversation partner more than specimen.

continuing existence and/or growth. The second is the ability to give an account of the respective activities or powers of God and creation.

Both issues arose early on and have been manifest in various forms as Christianity adapted to new intellectual circumstances. The first issue of ontology arose as a question in the second century, first among the gnostics and then among their Christian respondents. Basilides was the first to use the formula *creatio ex nihilo* as a theological statement to avoid the emanation and world-formation models so common at the time; it kept God utterly transcendent and distinct from creation while providing a framework to explain how the world came to exist.[251] On the Christian side, Kaiser claims that in itself

> the creationist tradition does not entail . . . a gulf between God and the world or a de-animation or mechanization of nature in the modern sense. Such an emphasis did begin to enter the tradition with Augustine's separation of the seminal causes from God's consubstantial Word and Spirit, but it was not essential to the tradition itself. The idea of the complete autonomy, or even mechanicity, of nature did not enter until the gulf opened by Augustine widened to the point of suggesting a dichotomy between God's ordering of nature and his absolute power, or even between nature itself and God.[252]

Kaiser defends the biblical and patristic traditions from containing what later became problematic; it is only a distortion of those traditions that opened the way toward determinism, reductionism, and atheism.[253]

Kaiser's reading of the "patristic" tradition, however, may be more charitable than warranted. As soon as the implications of classical metaphysics became a critical issue in the mid-second century and Christians utilized the formula *creatio ex nihilo* in response, a clear ontic distinction between God and creation was made. Where emanation, world-formation (dualism), or *ex nihilo* were the available options for understanding the relationship between God and creation, Christians opted for the distinction of *ex nihilo*. When the world comes into being distinct from God, defining the ongoing relationship, or dependency, of creation with God becomes an issue. The question about God's activity of *creation* at

---

251. May, *Creatio ex Nihilo*, 73.

252. Kaiser, *Creational Theology*, 59–60. That gulf in his account widened significantly in the eleventh and twelfth centuries and continued to do so after the thirteenth century.

253. Ibid., 60.

the time was ontology; that was answered with *creatio ex nihilo*. In other contexts with other questions about divine *creation*, the issue becomes about more than the beginning point, more than about the giving of being. That places a subsequent burden on *creatio ex nihilo* it was not developed to address. In the current scientific view, for example, the history of something is as significant to it as its beginning; this historical view of becoming lies in tension with creation being defined narrowly in terms of a thing coming into being at a beginning point *ex nihilo*. In today's view, it is always being created, but not necessarily *ex nihilo*.

With the distinction between God and the world, there was also a distinction between God's and creation's activity. As can be seen in Irenaeus's theology: since the act of creating became a matter of giving being—where it had once been a matter of forming, establishing, and/or giving life—creating became an activity for God alone, unmediated.[254] Everything having to do with the act of creation, so understood, was God's activity. Any cooperative activity between God and another, even creation itself, "would, by their activity, reveal a want in God himself and thereby set up a situation of his inferiority."[255] Creative activity became a zero-sum notion. Activity had to be placed on one side of the balance sheet or the other. What was given to one party meant the other party could not have that activity. Irenaeus never quotes any part of Genesis 1:6–25 for that reason;[256] nothing but God could be seen to be participating in the creative process, as he understood it.

Even after notions of God's creative activity expanded beyond the scope of beginnings, zero-sum notions were still in play. Whatever was attributed to creation in the unfolding of creation through history was seen as taking away from God—at the least it had to be explained how it was not taking away from God's perfection. Again Kaiser dates the rise of the zero-sum conundrum much later in history when he writes: "The tendency to define the powers of God and matter as mutually

---

254. Steenberg, *Irenaeus on Creation*, 72. Irenaeus made a significant contribution to the way the doctrine of *creatio ex nihilo* was understood. "For God to create out of nothing is for him to create the actual, individualized entities of the cosmos from a state of non-existence. It is specifically to say that the substance of the being of each existing entity has been called into existence from a state of nothingness, of non-being" (ibid., 48). Thus, in Irenaeus's view, "There are as many unique creations *ex nihilo* as there are persons brought into existence" (ibid.).

255. Ibid., 73.

256. Ibid., 74.

exclusive alternatives, as we have seen, dated from at least the twelfth century and had been reinforced by the mechanical philosophers and the Newtonians."[257] As God and world were distinguished in being, it became difficult to give an account of a world that was "relatively autonomous" in activity. Eventually that tension was eased when science parted ways with the theological tradition(s) under which it had earlier developed; "in the seventeenth and eighteenth centuries, a long-range tendency to view the active role of God and the innate properties of matter as alternative modes of explanation gained credence to the extent that the ideals needed for the furtherance of science could not so readily be sustained by positive Christian commitment."[258]

In chapter 6 these issues will be at the forefront as a framework for understanding God's relationship to creation is laid out in which the language of "chaos" can find an appropriate and useful application. At that time the usefulness of Lyle Dabney's work on pneumatology to move beyond some of these classic tensions will be shown. He has developed the language of the Spirit being the Possibility of God for the other and operating as *trans*ject—neither objectifying the other nor becoming the other's subjectivity. In that same chapter a second helpful notion will be developed in speaking about the Word's relationship to creation and operation relative to creation being *trans*carnate. Hopefully this grammar will provide a framework wherein the either/or (or both/and) between God and creation in the tradition will be bypassed.

Summary

One aim of this chapter was to show briefly the history of the doctrine of creation in Christianity. In establishing a framework in which to use the language of "chaos," a significant part of that framework will be God's relationship to creation. However, as has been shown, there was within the West a near total (if not total) breakdown in the ways God and creation had traditionally been understood to be in relation. At the same time, new methods in textual criticism have shifted some of the traditional notions of the Bible's import and/or relevancy for current theological

---

257. Kaiser, *Creational Theology*, 343. Kaiser does not use the notion of "zero-sum." That is what I have chosen to call it.

258. Ibid., 351.

discussion; it became an object of the past rather than a dialogue partner and beacon for the present.

As much as the church has made its home in different milieus in the past, it is still working on that process currently. At each major shift in Christianity's context (or shift in interlocutors) changes occurred in how God was conceptualized and understood in relationship to creation. New ideas and categories were formulated to navigate the new issues and questions facing the church. That process of adaptation and navigating issues has always entailed dialogue within the faith community. The current dialogue is certainly robust, with many widely divergent options being put forward. Nevertheless, some proposals remain stuck on old hurdles; others have not fully transitioned in order to address the questions of the current context; and others are undesirable or perilous proposals—in other words, too compromising on traditional Christian concerns.

Over the next two chapters an example of how this dialogue is unfolding in biblical studies will be given. It was chosen for its relevancy not only to the constructive task at hand, but also on the status concerning language of "chaos" in biblical studies.

3

The Growing Debate around "Chaos" Language in Biblical Studies

Jon D. Levenson's Position

THE AIM OF THE NEXT TWO CHAPTERS IS THREEFOLD. FIRST, THESE chapters show the contrast in opinions on whether "chaos" is appropriate language to use in reference to biblical terms, images, or themes, especially in relation to Genesis 1. Jon D. Levenson is one scholar among many who is in favor of using the term in biblical studies. As with many who use it, he then believes that there are a number of recurring symbols in Scripture that fall within the category of "chaos." In contrast, the position of David T. Tsumura will be given. He is among a growing chorus of scholars challenging the use of "chaos," with accompanying notions of God combating chaos in Scripture.[1] Second, the positions of these two scholars give a glimpse of the divergence of interpretations within biblical studies of divine creation in Genesis 1. In their respective positions they represent two options within the creation tradition. Levenson's position affirms matter as being uncreated, while Tsumura—even though he says Genesis is inconclusive—uses language more commonly associated with *creatio ex nihilo*. Thus, by engaging these two biblical scholars, many of the issues in the creationist tradition can be seen as they are played out

---

1. Rebecca Watson is one of the growing opposition who is challenging the use of "chaos" language. In her view chaos is unclear and inconsistently applied; from the first it was contested as an accurate description of the Genesis 1 situation (*Chaos Uncreated*, 18). The term later moved to the theological arena by default and formed the preconceptions of scholars looking at the Hebrew texts (19).

in current biblical studies. These two authors also bring together the two primary concerns of this project: establishing a framework for understanding God's relationship to creation and establishing an appropriate use of "chaos." Last, the interpretation of Genesis 1 that will be used in this project will be laid out in the next chapter.

In the following treatment of Jon D. Levenson's *Creation and the Persistence of Evil: the Jewish Drama of Divine Omnipotence*[2] his aims, methods, and conclusions will be outlined before being evaluated. In outlining and evaluating Levenson's position it will be shown that some of his aims and observations are insightful and helpful; however, methods such as his have come under fire and recent scholarship has brought the framework in which he works and his resulting conclusions into question.

Levenson's Reasons for Writing *Creation and the Persistence of Evil*

Levenson states three primary reasons for writing his book. The first and primary reason is his conviction that there is no *creatio ex nihilo* in the Hebrew Bible (HB).[3] There is also no concept of a static creation that God made in the past and has continued to exist ever since. Rather, Levenson sees within the HB a drama between God's omnipotence and "the formidability and resilience of the forces counteracting creation."[4] His other two reasons for writing are to examine some connections that become apparent in this drama that Levenson reads within the HB. First, the links between the Genesis 1 account of creation and the Priestly cult need to be explored: how the Priestly cult functions relative to humanity's role described in Genesis 1 "in forming and sustaining the world order."[5] Second, he sees a connection between God as creator and God as lord (in covenant) that needs to be explored.[6] God the creator/suzerain is

---

2. Hereafter the title *Creation and the Persistence of Evil* will be used.

3. During this section on Levenson's position the name Hebrew Bible will be used in continuity with Levenson's own faith tradition and use.

4. Levenson, *Creation and the Persistence of Evil*, xiii.

5. Ibid. As is often done since the introduction of the Documentary Hypothesis, the writings and views associated with the Priestly tradition will at times be abbreviated as P.

6. Ibid., xiv.

dependent upon human beings to ratify God's royal claim; this ratification is the role of humans.

Levenson laments both the need for sophisticated theological reflection on the recent discoveries within biblical scholarship—discoveries based on comparing other ancient Near Eastern (ANE) texts with the Bible—as well as the tendency to miss the continuity between the HB and the writings from Rabbinic Judaism.[7] While addressing his first three concerns, he seeks to show the continuity of biblical and rabbinic perspectives. More importantly he seeks to develop the theological implications of the creation drama. It is this latter aim that is of great interest and relevance to the current project.

Levenson's Presuppositions and Stated Method

Levenson is interested in the historical development of notions concerning creation in the ANE. Dating the various ANE cosmological texts, however, is highly uncertain. This makes any chronologies of texts questionable. Even so, Levenson does not take a completely ahistorical approach to biblical and other ANE texts.[8] At points he makes arguments about texts based on their sequence, which he determines based on either internal features—for example, whether they use a certain name or not[9]—or based on whether one text appears to have another as a source.[10] The constructed sequence of texts and the supposed relations of texts in that sequence do play a role in his observations and claims.

One of his foundational beliefs is that there is a progression in worldview from *Enuma elish*, in which the themes of combat and

---

7. Tracking the biblical themes into their subsequent manifestations is beyond the scope of this project. One recent study by Andrew Angel on that era comes to different conclusions than previous observations (including Levenson's), which claim that the combat myth was located increasingly in eschatology. Angel finds that the combat myth predominantly appears in reference to historical situations within the postcanonical literature. See Angel, *Chaos and the Son of Man*, 205.

8. Levenson, *Creation and the Persistence of Evil*, xv.

9. For example, Levenson reasons that since Psalm 104 uses the name "Leviathan," and since using that name is characteristic of extrabiblical texts from the Bronze Age, and since Genesis 1 does not use that name, then Psalm 104 must be older (ibid., 59).

10. For example, Levenson claims that "The Hymn to the Aten" (Egyptian) influenced Psalm 104, even if it was indirectly mediated through a long unknown line (ibid., 63), since the hymn has "too many resemblances to Ps 104 to be coincidence" (ibid., 61).

creation are linked,[11] to the doctrine of *creatio ex nihilo* in the Abrahamic faiths. The cosmologies in the HB, Levenson believes, represent stages in that progression from creation as *Chaoskampf* to creation out of nothing. Their place in this supposed progression can be seen in the following way. Levenson says that "the Bible offers no connected narrative of primordial divine combat"; there are only "allusions" or "poetic snippets."[12] Because we have literature from other languages, such as Ugaritic and Akkadian, which do have full accounts of combat, it is possible "to get a sense of the full dimensions of the old myth and its continuing vitality in Israel—as well as the failed efforts of some circles to suppress it."[13]

Because we know of those older traditions, we should not assume in the HB that "the *real* theology, the *essential* theology, is one of serene, divine supremacy, only temporarily and inconsequentially interrupted

---

11. It is a matter of interpretation whether the link between these themes is a matter of their close proximity within *Enuma elish* or an actual matter of their integration under a single concept of creation as *Chaoskampf*. Cf. Watson, *Chaos Uncreated*, 20, where she claims that in Babylonian sources there is no intrinsic connection between *Chaoskampf* and creation, and in *Enuma elish* it is only a passing concern.

12. Levenson, *Creation and the Persistence of Evil*, 8.

13. Ibid. For Herman Gunkel, one of the nineteenth-century pioneers of ANE comparative studies, Genesis 1 is a "faded myth" ("The Influence of Babylonian Mythology upon the Biblical Creation Story [1895]," 46). Gunkel believed that Old Testament passages outside Genesis 1 provided a link between Genesis 1 and *Enuma elish* (ibid., 47). The lack of personification or battle in Genesis 1 clearly shows, however, a receding of the mythological (ibid., 49). William P. Brown softens critiques against Gunkel's history-of-religions approach by showing how his interests differed from Welhausenn's (Brown, *Structure, Role, and Ideology*, 220ff). Brown concludes, nevertheless, that regardless of the debates between opposing methodological sides within biblical studies from Gunkel onward, "Given the rational tenor and balanced structure of Genesis 1, the priestly cosmogony is, to say the least, unlike any cosmogonic myth of the ancient Near East" (ibid., 223). Genesis 1 is a *teaching*; it is a 'treatise' (224). Lyle Dabney has a related view: "The opening chapters of Genesis in general, and specifically the first chapter, is, therefore, not to be (mis)taken as a kind of speculation on 'the way things came to be' . . . but rather recognized as a confession of faith concerning the relationship existing between the "God of Abraham, Isaac, and Jacob" (Ex 3:6) and all the world—as well as how that relationship with God determines the nature of the world" (Dabney, "The Nature of the Spirit," 87). Looking at Genesis 1 as a teaching, Brown sees P's conceptual world—in both creation and tabernacle construction—"is preeminently one of harmonious collaboration. P is convinced that only such a 'social' ordering can result in perfect . . . work and order" (Dabney, "The Nature of the Spirit," 225–26). At times the results are better than expected (e.g., Exod 36:5–6; "Such is the unwavering trust of the priestly writer in his conceptual, if not utopian, world" (226). Background (Gunkel) and contextual motivation (Wellhausen) can often cloud the teaching of Genesis 1 as much as it can illuminate it.

by a revolt of underlings of benign origin."[14] For example, the HB has texts that do not speak about the *creation* of God's "aquatic adversaries." These texts should not be harmonized with texts that highlight "the creatureliness and subordination of the monstrous adversaries to YHWH."[15] Rather, to do that would be "to doom ourselves to miss the rich interplay of theologies and the historical dynamics behind the biblical text."[16] This line of reasoning rests upon the sequence of texts and the influence of one ANE worldview and its texts on a neighboring culture and its texts.

Levenson's approach to comparative studies also relies upon his typological or phenomenological method. There are many symbols that he tracks within the HB and other ANE traditions: waters, darkness, death, wilderness, etc. Wherever they appear, Levenson investigates it as a reference to "chaos." As the reasoning in Levenson's above statement entails, the later occurrence of these images can be understood against their oldest known appearance in the old ANE combat myth from which they are thought to descend. In whatever stage of demythologization or historicization the images appear, they still represent the primal enemy "chaos."[17]

14. Ibid.

15. Ibid. Levenson believes that Kaufmann, an influential HB scholar, does this.

16. Ibid. There is no doubt that Levenson is right to speak of *theologies* in the Bible's traditions. What still is under examination is whether the images Levenson points out in the HB function as he says they do in the biblical texts and, thus, if they should be read 1) in conjunction with older combat myths from other cultures; 2) as polemical statements against those other myths; or, rather, 3) in a different framework altogether.

17. In his own words, "My point is that Leviathan, Amalek, Gag, and the like are symbols from different traditional complexes for the same theological concept: the ancient and enduring opposition to the full realization of God's mastery, the opposition destined to be eliminated at the turn of the aeon" (Levenson, *Creation and the Persistence of Evil*, 38). A contrasting presupposition shows up in Frankfort and Frankfort; they state that the ancients "are likely to present various descriptions of identical phenomena side by side even though they are mutually exclusive . . . the ancients' conception of a phenomenon differed according to their approach to it" ("Myth and Reality," 19; cf. Clifford on the ancients' ability to have multiple creation accounts simultaneously, *Creation Accounts*, 199). Since an identical phenomenon, term, or image can function in multiple ways for various explanatory purposes—e.g., a cow being used as a symbol for fertility or as a very strong animal that lifts the sun to the heavens (Frankfort and Frankfort, "Myth and Reality," 19)—attention to specific contexts is crucial; "the procedure of the mythopoeic mind in expressing a phenomenon by manifold images corresponding to unconnected avenues of approach clearly leads away from, rather than toward, our postulate of causality which seeks to discover identical causes for identical effects throughout the phenomenal world" (ibid., 20). Rebecca Watson seeks in her work to look specifically at how images are being used in various contexts in Israel's Scriptures (see *Chaos Uncreated*); it shows the diversity and particularity in the manner and con-

As will be shown, Levenson's view about a historical progression and his typological method play a significant role in how he moves in the argument of the book from examining ANE texts outside of Genesis 1 back to interpreting Genesis 1.

Levenson's Outline and Claims

The three sections of *Creation and the Persistence of Evil* correspond to the three purposes for which Levenson wrote. In the first section he outlines the drama of God's mastery over chaos and the fragility of the resultant state. In this first section he works primarily with non-Genesis texts in the HB.[18] In the second section Levenson examines Genesis 1:1—2:3 against the drama outlined in the first section and he examines the relationship of the Genesis account, as he interprets it, and the Priestly cult—as it would function given such a rendering of Genesis 1. In the final section he argues for the close connection between the notions of creation and covenant in the relational dynamic between God and his creatures.

Levenson's Framework for Understanding Creation

Levenson rejects claims for a *clear* notion of creation out of nothing in the HB.[19] In building his framework, Levenson begins in Genesis 1. The scene in Genesis 1 opens with the primordial, uncreated water.[20] The only way to interpret creation out of nothing within Genesis 1:1-2 is to choose the translation "In the beginning God created the heavens

---

texts in which specific images were employed.

18. Interestingly the outline of Levenson's book to some degree mirrors Gunkel's *Schöpfung und Chaos in Urzeit und Endzeit*. When Westermann outlines Gunkel's work he points out that "Gunkel's starting point is the thesis: 'Gen 1 is not a free construction of the author' (4–16). 'The very ancient elements handed down in Gen 1 demonstrate . . . that Gen 1 goes back to a very ancient tradition' (6–14). 'Certain elements (chaos, stars) point to the Babylonian origin of the tradition' (15f.)" (*Genesis 1–11*, 29). After doing a few comparisons between the traditions, in Gunkel's work (as Levenson does) "a long section has been added entitled 'References to the Myth of the Struggle of Marduk with Tiamat in the Old Testament apart from Gen 1' (29–114)" (Westermann, *Genesis 1–11*, 29); cf. Herman Gunkel, *Creation and Chaos*, 13–77.

19. He is not alone in doing this. Cf., e.g., the positions of David T. Tsumura, Andrew Mayer Hahn, and William P. Brown.

20. Levenson, *Creation and the Persistence of Evil*, 5.

and the earth."[21] This translation, he claims, has been doubted since the Middle Ages and has fallen out of favor with scholars.[22] Thus, he reads in the opening verses of the HB the introduction of both the God of Israel—with no myth of origin or origin to his mastery[23]—and the primordial, uncreated waters. From this starting point, Levenson moves in the rest of part I to other texts within the HB to explain the drama of combat between God and chaos in creation.

As Levenson claims at the start, the waters, a symbol of chaos, have no beginning narrated. They are "the ancient and enduring opposition to the full realization of God's mastery, the opposition destined to be eliminated at the turn of the aeon."[24] Chaos is anarchy;[25] it challenges God's supremacy.[26] This opponent is a real force—or power(s)—that is always a continuing possibility. Chaos is dark, ungodly,[27] malign,[28] and evil.[29] To some of the symbols for chaos Levenson adds descriptors such

21. This verse would then have to be interpreted as a statement about God's creative activity that comes before v. 2.

22. Levenson, *Creation and the Persistence of Evil*, 5. Here Levenson is making reference to the early second-millennium interpretation of Rashi and the trend since E. A. Speiser's translation in his 1964 commentary, which favors Rashi's grammatical points: "When God set about to create heaven and earth—the world being a formless waste, with darkness over the seas and only an awesome wind sweeping over the water—God said, 'Let there be light.'" (ibid., 157n12; cf. Speiser, *Genesis*, 3). Levenson picks this approach over Westermann's (Levenson, *Creation and the Persistence of Evil*, 158n12) or other more traditional interpretations of the grammar. He does not argue his position in detail. Rather, he shows that there is uncertainty about the traditional English translation and that a new translation is in vogue. Levenson himself says that it is probably impossible to resolve the grammatical controversy (ibid., 158n12), as does Hahn ("*Tohu Va-Vohu*," 35ff.). The choice among translations and interpretations of Gen 1:1–3 must be made among several grammatically possible options; the biblical grammar alone is not conclusive. One's own views on theology, as well as one's views on what the theology and worldview of the Priestly writer(s) was, will influence the interpretation chosen.

23. Ibid., 6. There is no myth of God rising out of the primal elements as there is in the Babylonian *Enuma elish* and the Egyptian myths (e.g., Atum rises out of the primal waters; Frankfort and Frankfort, "Myth and Reality," 9). God does not call the waters "mother" as the gods do in *Enuma elish* (e.g., III.23).

24. Ibid., 38.

25. Ibid., 47.

26. Ibid., 135.

27. Ibid., 127. Levenson describes the terms of Genesis 1:2 as "the dark, ungodly forces."

28. Ibid., 46.

29. Ibid., 19, 24–25, 36, 39, 40, 44, 47, 50, 90, 99, 127, 156. Many of these uses of *evil* (including the book title itself) show that Levenson uses *evil* synonymously with "chaos."

as roiling[30] and violent.[31] He even adds personifications such as sinister,[32] hostile,[33] angry,[34] rebellion,[35] and defection.[36]

In one word Levenson defines God's action in creating: mastery.[37] Creation is the "defeating of the forces that interrupt order,"[38] making the chaos into order.[39] God confines these forces in creating, but does not eliminate them.[40] They are subdued and ordered, but they still persist as

---

Levenson offers no justification for equating those two terms, whose definitions are not necessarily mutually inclusive.

30. Ibid., 106, 135. Levenson describes the waters in Psalm 89:10, which he quotes as "You rule the swelling of the sea (*yām*): when its waves surge, You still them" (ibid., 105), as angry and roiling. He also uses Psalm 93:3–4 as an example of angry, roiling waters (*Creation and the Persistence of Evil*, 175n17): "The floods have lifted up, O LORD, the floods have lifted up their voice; the floods lift up their roaring. More majestic than the thunders of mighty waters, more majestic than the waves of the sea, majestic on high is the LORD!" (NRSV). It is not self-evident from these texts that the waters are angry. E.g., in the second, there is a comparison by way of analogy between the magnitude of a known/experienced natural phenomenon and the might of God; the text does not attribute a motivation or emotion of anger to the waters. Such attribution does not seem fitting or congruent with the purpose for which the mighty waters are placed in comparison to God.

31. Ibid., 75. Levenson uses Exod 15:1–19 to talk of "YHWH's ferocious combat against the Pharaonic army at the violent waters."

32. Ibid., 16. Levenson describes the waters of the Genesis flood as "sinister forces of chaos" that would surge forth again if God's command for them to stay back were rescinded. He compares this relation between God and the "sinister forces of chaos" to the situation described in Ps 104:6–9 and Job 38:8–11 (ibid.).

33. Ibid., 48. *Hostile* is used by Levenson in reference to the forces represented by the symbol of Leviathan.

34. Ibid., 106, 108. See n. 30.

35. Ibid., 10, 136.

36. Ibid., 135.

37. Ibid., 3. "The creation narratives, whatever their length, form, or context, are best seen as dramatic visualizations of the uncompromised mastery of YHWH, God of Israel, over all else" (3). Catherine Keller's critique and deconstruction of this type of paradigm should at the least be given an audience before adopting Levenson's position for theological purposes; see Keller, *Face of the Deep*.

38. Ibid., 12.

39. Ibid., 22. In Levenson's account, Israel had a comparable cosmogony with others in the ANE in which there is "a decisive instance of the victory of the forces of order (which are necessarily social and political) over potent opposition: what emerges from creation is a secure and ordered community whose center of authority is unchallenged, effective, and just" (*Creation and the Persistence of Evil*, 69). Cf. Clifford, *Creation Accounts*, 7–9.

40. Levenson, *Creation and the Persistence of Evil*, 17.

chaos/evil. It is the establishment of boundaries by which order is created and it is the maintenance of those boundaries by which it is kept.[41]

Since the chaos-forces are ordered and not eliminated in creation, chaos is inherent in the cosmos, history, and in human beings.[42] There are various symbols used for the manifestation of chaos in these respective realms. "Leviathan is to creation as Amalek is to history and as the Evil Impulse is to the Good in Rabbinic psychology. Each is an ancient or even innate impediment to reality as God, the potentially omnipotent, wishes it to be. Each can be suppressed for the nonce, but will disappear only in the eschatological reversal."[43] With the ever present reality of these forces "The world is not inherently safe; it is inherently unsafe."[44] Until the day God completely conquers chaos/evil, there exists an unsafe tension between creation/life established by God's creative mastery and the forces of chaos/death which threaten God's mastery, and thus, creation/life.[45]

The created world is not a static, secure world; God's activity of creation is not a confined, once-upon-a-time idea.[46] The positive order of creation is not "*intrinsically* irreversible."[47] It is not God's act of creation/mastery that is the ground of security to creation/life against the very real forces of chaos/death. Rather, it is God's covenant faithfulness to keep order that is the only safeguard against the forces of evil. God's covenant faithfulness is the ground of creation's security.[48] God must

41. See ibid., 65: "Order is now a matter of *the maintenance of boundaries*, and even when the forces of chaos pose no threat to the creator, they still persist, and their persistence qualifies—and defines—his world mastery" (italics original).

42. Given that Levenson claims God creates out of the primal chaos, it is unclear, then, how our materiality should not be viewed as evil since the material of creation is simply ordered chaos/evil plotting to reassert itself.

43. Ibid., 41. He says further, "As evil did not originate with history, neither will it disappear altogether *in* history, but rather *beyond* it, at the inauguration of the coming world" (ibid., 50; italics original). This claim would make for an interesting comparison with the views of many Enlightenment/Modern thinkers, who thought that evil arose in history and could/would be solved in history—e.g., Rousseau and Hegel.

44. Ibid., 17. Levenson uses the imagery of the persistence of the sea after God's "combat" with it in texts such as Ps 104:6–9 and Job 38:8–11 in support of his position. This argument works only if "chaos" is employed as a noun and not an adjective that describes a situation.

45. Ibid.

46. Cf. ibid., xiii.

47. Ibid., 12.

48. Ibid., 48. Levenson uses Gen 9:1–17 and Job 41:4—"Will it [Leviathan] make

faithfully continue to act and keep the boundaries since the setting of the boundaries is not permanently effective.

There are times that, in the face of the reality of evil, it appears as though evil is unchecked and/or triumphant.[49] Even so, Israel's liturgy confirms the hope that God indeed is sovereign and it calls out for God, in God's faithfulness, to close the gap between that hope in his sovereignty and their experience of reality.[50] The ultimate hope, nevertheless, is in the forthcoming decisive battle between God and chaos. This will result in a transformation, a process of purgation and eradication, which will establish a new cosmogony, a new creation.[51]

Levenson's Interpretation of Genesis 1

In the first part of his book, Genesis is first examined in comparison and contrast with *Enuma elish*.[52] By way of contrast between the two texts, the gods who remain at the end of *Enuma elish* are not primordial—they come into existence—and those god-like beings who were primordial "fail to transcend nature" and become some of the matter out of which creation was formed.[53] Second, Marduk does not have inherent mastery, but is given his authority by the pantheon of gods. By way of comparison between the two texts, the waters of Genesis 1 "are most likely primordial" as were Apsu and Tiamat.[54] Also, Levenson reads the "Let us make" in v. 26 as an indication that there were other primordial divine beings

---

a covenant with you to be taken as your servant forever?" (NRSV)—to say that God has pledged an eternal covenant for creation's endurance and that God "has, also in an eternal covenant, compelled the obeisance of his great adversary" (ibid., 17).

49. Ibid., 19, 23, 90.

50. Ibid., 19–25. Levenson appeals to Psalm 74 and Isa 51:9–11; 54:7–11 to make his point. "The psalmist refuses to deny the evidence of his senses in the name of faith . . . But he also refuses to abandon the affirmation of God's world-ordering mastery" (ibid., 19).

51. Ibid., 12, 29, 32, 44.

52. Ibid., 3ff.

53. Ibid., 4.

54. Ibid., 5. All the things listed in v. 2 Levenson believes are primordial.

beside God; there was some type of council.⁵⁵ Nevertheless, Genesis 1 affirms that God has no origin and has always been supreme ruler.⁵⁶

In the second part of the book, Levenson returns to his interpretation of Genesis 1 by comparing and contrasting it with the cosmology he developed in Part I based on older texts in the HB.⁵⁷ Levenson recognizes that the placement of the Genesis 1 creation account has theological significance. However, it is not the only creation story in the HB and its significance is not "as the quintessence of ancient Hebrew theology."⁵⁸ He takes an approach that does not subordinate the alleged presence of a combat myth in the HB to the theology of Genesis 1.⁵⁹ Harmonizing other HB cosmologies with Genesis 1 "does violence to the plain sense of the text."⁶⁰ The character of Genesis 1 serves as one point along the progression "that runs from the ancient Near Eastern combat myth to the developed creation theology of the Abrahamic faiths"—in other words, runs to the doctrine of *creatio ex nihilo*.⁶¹ Here there is a distinction in methodologies and investigative interests between, on the one hand, those who give Genesis 1 pride of place in Scripture and subordinate the other biblical cosmologies to it by reading them through

---

55. Ibid. Levenson says that the text does not give us any indicators of the relationship between God and these other alleged beings. Thus, it does not help us know if God's authority is given to him by these others as Marduk's was. Based on other HB texts, it is God who always has the final say, so these divine beings are "subordinate and not very individualized" (5).

56. Ibid., 6.

57. I use the term *cosmology* as Remi Brague does in *The Wisdom of the World*, where he defines it as "an account of the world in which a reflection on the nature of the world as a world must be expressed" (4). *Cosmography* is "the drawing or description (graphein) of the world as it appears at a given moment, with regard to its structure, its possible division into levels, regions, and so on" (ibid., 3). *Cosmogony* is "the story of the emergence of things" (ibid.).

58. Levenson, *Creation and the Persistence of Evil*, 5–6.

59. Ibid., 53.

60. Ibid.

61. Ibid. His framing of the material in terms of a repression of or moving away from the old myth is very different from Rebecca Watson, who argues that Israel was very conscious, deliberate, and consistent in the specific contexts and manner in which it employed certain types of grammar that had long extrabiblical histories; see, e.g., *Chaos Uncreated*, 259ff. It is still an open question whether Israel needed to repress syncretism in its scriptures or whether Israel deliberately tolerated the adoption-with-adaptations of specific images in specific contexts for their own purposes. Were there unwanted, undesirable traditions that the Israelites were unable to fully expunge from their canon or did they intend/desire to say precisely what they said?

the lens of Genesis 1's theology and, on the other hand, those who, like Levenson, try to track the progression of creation theology from sample texts through history.[62]

Levenson uses Psalm 104 as the step in the historical progression just before Genesis 1.[63] In Psalm 104 the sea monster is said to be created and is God's toy.[64] Genesis 1 goes a step further in demythologizing the sea monster(s) because they are not created until the fifth day.[65] Levenson suspects this is for polemical reasons; it eliminates the monsters' prox-

62. If the issue is, as Levenson suggests, which method does more violence to the plain sense of the biblical texts, he has not convincingly demonstrated that using a lens from other ANE cultures, which posits the existence of primordial chaos/evil, an ontology of animosity between the gods and the other, and open combat between the gods and the other, does less violence to the biblical text than assuming a text such as Genesis 1, even though a later text, is a culmination of what had been the creation theology of Israel all along. Levenson's method is not free of a lens through which to interpret the grammar and images of the biblical texts. It does not seek to find the *plain sense* of texts without already assuming a background for the significance and function of the terms and images in that passage. His method undermines his endeavor to find the plain sense of the biblical cosmologies and his claim not to be violating them. The contrasting accounts by scholars such as Watson, Tsumura, and Brown of many of the same texts used by Levenson show how different the meanings of those texts and their images look when not read through a combative lens.

63. Levenson justifies the chronology of the two texts based on the fact that Psalm 104 names Leviathan like many Bronze Age texts would have done, and Genesis 1 does not use the specific name. Also, since Psalm 104 does not have the heptatic structures, it does not show dependency upon the Genesis 1 text (*Creation and the Persistence of Evil*, 59). One question this raises: if Levenson claims that Psalm 104 is adapted from an Egyptian hymn (ibid., 61, 63) and if Genesis 1 is a next step in thought from Psalm 104, why does Levenson use Babylonian theology to compare and contrast with these biblical texts and not Egyptian? The Egyptians and other ANE cultures had different views of the primordial waters than those represented in *Enuma elish*. Also, the Egyptians and Babylonians had very different experiences of the waters in their rivers. It is only speculation how geography and natural phenomenon influenced their myths; however, they do appear to have views of water that reflect either the predictability of the Nile or the unpredictability of the Tigris and Euphrates (cf. Frankfort and Frankfort, "The Emancipation of Thought from Myth," 364-65; cf. Jacobsen, "Mesopotamia," 171-72). Even if there were multiple sources behind Genesis 1, why does Levenson not at least consider the possibility that Egyptian cosmology stands behind Genesis 1:2 instead of Babylon's combat myth?

64. Ibid., 54.

65. Levenson's use of terms such as *demythologized* and *depersonalized* shows his presupposition that Israel's texts are in a line of tradition with an old combat myth. Saying that the waters, darkness, sun, or sea monsters are "not mythologized" or "not personalized" is a different observation with different presuppositions about the possible relationship between Israel's texts and those of its neighbors.

imity to divinity and their role in the creation narrative.[66] "Leviathan is now only one member of a whole species of marine animals, a species that God not only creates, but pronounces good, blesses, and charges 'to be fertile and increase.'"[67] Levenson also interprets patterns in Genesis 1 such as the light being created on the first day and the sun not being made until the fourth day as an instance of demythologization of the sun. [68] In other words, this is one step further away from the combat myth and cosmography of *Enuma elish*.[69]

The terms and images within Genesis 1 have analogues in the broader ANE and thus this text resonates within that context. Levenson makes an argument that even the heptatic structures in Genesis 1, unique among all ANE cosmologies, should not be understood as being completely discontinuous with either its cultural background or the raw material from which the author(s) drew.[70] He traces, for example, the possible cultic influences of the Babylonian *akītu* festival that was a several-days-long New Year's festival in which *Enuma elish* was read on the fourth day. Levenson writes that "As conjectural as any reconstruction of the *akītu* and its meaning must be, its relevance to biblical Israel is even murkier."[71] He is only trying to say that it must not be assumed that the idea of creation across several days within Genesis 1 came about *ex nihilo*.[72] Discussion of this issue of possible inspirations for the heptatic structures in the broader cultural milieu helps serve as a segue for

66. Ibid., 54, 55. Cf. Saggs's thesis about Genesis 1 being polemical against *Enuma elish* in *The Encounter with the Divine in Mesopotamia and Israel*.

67. Ibid., 54.

68. Ibid., 65.

69. In a later section of this chapter I suggest another way of interpreting the subsequent creation of light-giving bodies in Genesis 1.

70. Ibid., 68.

71. Ibid., 69.

72. His strongest arguments for cultural antecedents is in the link between cosmos and temple in the ANE (see Levenson's seventh chapter; also see his *Sinai and Zion*, 138ff.). Since there is a connection between cosmos and temple, and since Israel's temple was built in seven years and was dedicated in the seventh month, during the seven-day-long festival of Tabernacles, there are precedents for linking the number seven with creation. There are possible antecedents in the Canaanite tradition since Baal's temple was built in seven days (Levenson, *Creation and the Persistence of Evil*, 78). Even so, Levenson needs to nuance his claims about some heptatic structures in the Priestly account in light of Brown's subsequent findings that some of them were added later; some do not appear until the MT (Brown, *Structure, Role, and Ideology*, 136).

Levenson for discussing the importance of not separating the interpretation of texts from their setting in the cult.

Levenson does not believe that Psalm 104 or Genesis 1 represent a full demythologization of the waters or the darkness; neither text explicitly states that the waters or darkness were created. In Psalm 104 God only made boundaries for the waters that Leviathan once personified.[73] Likewise, the Genesis 1 account has no explicit statement that the waters or darkness were created. Genesis 1:2 "describes the 'world,' if we may call it that, just before the cosmogony began."[74]

Genesis 1:1–2 shows parallels to *Enuma elish*. The two texts have similar introductory statements. *Enuma elish* begins: "When above [*enuma eliš*] the heaven had not [yet] been named, [and] below the earth had not [yet] been called by a name . . ."[75] Genesis 1:1—"When God set about to create heaven and earth . . ." Second, both texts contain uncreated waters. And third, Marduk uses winds to overcome Tiamat just as a wind from God sweeps over the primordial waters in 1:2.[76]

The two texts are different in two important ways. First, there is no opposition to God's creative activity since the primordial matter is inert. And second, "Genesis 1:1—2:3 begins near the point when the Babylonian poem ends its action, with the primordial waters neutralized and the victorious and unchallengeable deity about to undertake the work of cosmogony."[77]

In Levenson's comparing and contrasting of Genesis with *Enuma elish*, he makes a crucial switch from talking about "inert matter" in

---

73. Ibid., 65. Levenson summarizes: "Order is now a matter of *the maintenance of boundaries*, and even when the forces of chaos pose no threat to the creator, they still persist, and their persistence qualifies—and defines—his world mastery" (*Creation and the Persistence of Evil*, 65).

74. Ibid., 121.

75. Ibid.

76. Ibid. It is at this point that Levenson states: "In spite of some variations, it should now be clear that Genesis 1:1—2:3 is quite close to *Enuma elish*" (*Creation and the Persistence of Evil*, 121). In Levenson's eighth chapter he also makes an argument that God's rest at the end of the Genesis 1 creation narrative has precedents in other biblical texts and ANE texts—e.g., *Enuma elish* and the Egyptian *Memphite Theology* (ibid., 107).

77. Ibid., 122. Levenson never gives an argument for his readers about how the combat between Marduk and Tiamat by which the primordial waters are "neutralized" is connected within *Enuma elish* to Marduk's eventual return to Tiamat's corpse and his subsequent world formation. Thus, it is not clear how Marduk's later formation of the cosmos out of neutralized water is linked with or should be conceptualized in terms of the notion of mastery that marks the earlier narration of the combat. In other words, the

Genesis 1 to talking about "dark, inert chaos."[78] This is not just a change between synonymous terms. It is a change in concepts. He offers no justification for this transition. By making the switch, however, he is able to continue his comparisons between the two documents; "One thing that this primordial chaos shares with Tiamat is that it does not *disappear*, but rather is *transformed* during the act of creation."[79] Order and form are imposed on the chaos.

This transition between vocabulary and concepts brings continuity between Levenson's interpretation of other HB cosmologies and how he interprets Genesis 1. Switching the concepts in the P creation account also colors his depiction of the Priestly cult. It brings Israel's cult into tighter parallel with the cults of its pagan neighbors. In Levenson's chaos-framework, the Priestly cult becomes humanity's kingly participation with God in the building and maintaining of order.[80] "Among the many messages of Gen 1:1—2:3 is this: it is through the cult that we are enabled to cope with evil, for it is the cult that builds and maintains order, transforms chaos into creation, ennobles humanity, and realizes the kingship of God who has ordained the cult and commanded that it be guarded and practiced. It is through obedience to the directives of the divine master that his good world comes into existence."[81] Levenson's transition in concepts introduced into his treatment of the text an antagonistic relationship between God and the raw stuff of creation. It introduced the notion that God's interaction with it in Genesis 1 was about the mastery and control of God's other. Last, it introduced the idea that humanity's relationship to creation in general, but more specifically in the cult, entailed this same relationship of animosity and the need to secure control of the other.[82]

Levenson's Link between Creation and Covenant

Levenson's observations about the link between creation and covenant were mentioned earlier. In short: in the tension that exists within

---

question remains: does the old myth narrate that creation equals mastery?

78. Ibid.
79. Ibid.
80. Ibid., 127.
81. Ibid.
82. These ideas of primordial or innate chaos/evil in creation and the function of

the Priestly cult are irreconcilable with the observations of other scholars such as Jacob Milgrom in (*Leviticus 1-16*, 42-43; *Leviticus*, 8-9). Milgrom pieces together his view of the Priestly worldview and cult from studying the book of Leviticus. At nearly every point, he shows the contrast between Israel's cult and the cults of its neighbors. Milgrom claims that the Priestly cult did not include notions of demonic or evil forces that had to be guarded against or warded off. Rather, the cult itself served to repair the stains of *human* sin and to rightly order the life of the community. In the contrast between pagan cults and Israel's Milgrom says: "The basic premises of pagan religion are (1) that its deities are themselves dependent on and influenced by a metadivine realm, (2) that this realm spawns a multitude of malevolent and benevolent entities, and (3) that if humans can tap into this realm they can acquire the magical power to coerce the gods to do their will. The eminent Assyriologist W. G. Lambert has stated, 'The impression is gained that everyday religion [in Mesopotamia] was dominated by fear of evil powers and black magic rather than a positive worship of the gods . . . the world was conceived to be full of evil demons who might cause trouble in any sphere of life. If they had attacked, the right ritual should effect the cure . . . Humans, as well as devils, might work evil against a person by the black arts, and here too the appropriate ritual was required' [Lambert 1959: 194]. The Priestly theology negates these premises. It posits the existence of one supreme God who contends neither with a higher realm nor with competing peers. The world of demons is abolished; there is no struggle with autonomous foes, because there are none. With the demise of the demons, only one creature remains with 'demonic' power—the human being. Endowed with free will, human power is greater than any attributed to humans by pagan society. Not only can one defy God but, in Priestly imagery, one can drive God out of his sanctuary. In this respect, humans have replaced demons" (*Leviticus 1-16*, 42-43; Milgrom, *Leviticus*, 8-9). In the pagan world, the cult secured the temple "against incursions by malevolent forces from the supernal and infernal worlds" through magic (Milgrom, *Leviticus 1-16*, 43; *Leviticus*, 9). In contrast, "The Priestly theologians make use of the same imagery, except that the demons are replaced by humans. Humans can drive God out of the sanctuary by polluting it with their moral and ritual sins. All that the priests can do is periodically purge the sanctuary of its impurities and influence the people to atone for their wrongs" (Milgrom, *Leviticus 1-16*, 43; Milgrom, *Leviticus*, 9); cf. Milgrom, *Leviticus 1-16*, 44ff. Impurity itself was thus harmless in the Priestly cult, except in regard to the sancta: "The sanctuary symbolized the presence of God; impurity represented the wrongdoing of persons. If persons unremittingly polluted the sanctuary they forced God out of his sanctuary and out of their lives" (*Leviticus 1-16*, 43). Impurity was not a sinister force lying below the surface; it was something to be washed away. The importance of washing is not only to keep God's presence in the Temple; rather, impurity is to death as holiness is to life. Thus, "because the quintessential source of holiness resides with God, Israel is enjoined to control the occurrence of impurity lest it impinge on his realm (see below). The forces pitted against each other in a cosmic struggle are no longer the benevolent and the demonic deities who populate the mythologies of Israel's neighbors, but the forces of life and death set loose by man himself through his obedience to or defiance of God's commandments" (Milgrom, *Leviticus 1-16*, 47). The objective of the Priestly theology with its purity laws was "to sever impurity from the demonic and to reinterpret it as a symbolic system reminding Israel of the divine imperative to reject death and choose life" (ibid.). (This is echoed in the theology of J in Genesis 2 in the command to eat not from the tree of the knowledge of good and evil but from the tree of life.) If one were to work backward in the canon to construct the cosmography

creation between God's mastery and the chaotic forces that challenge God's mastery, it is only God's covenant faithfulness to maintain his ordering mastery that is the foundation of creation's security and not God's mastering/creating activity.

Levenson further develops the connection between creation and covenant in the third part of his book by comparing Israel's faith with *Enuma elish*. In *Enuma elish* there is a movement from plurality to unity, from democracy among the gods to the monarchy of Marduk.[83] Thus, there was no longer a need within the pantheon to deliberate about a course of action. The only resolution before the gods was "whether to accept Marduk's offer, whether to make him king."[84] The alternative was death. There was a suzerain treaty between Marduk and the gods whom he saved from the threat of Tiamat.

Likewise, YHWH saved Israel from Egypt and Israel was then expected to ratify God's resolutions. Because of both God's combat on their behalf and a covenant between God and Israel, now there was to be in Israel "the exclusive enthronement of YHWH and the radical and uncompromising commitment of the House of Israel to carrying out his commands."[85] The only other option would be defection to another god. Israel's monotheism did not necessarily affirm that only one god exists; rather, they were to live in total allegiance to YHWH. "By and large, the texts in the Hebrew Bible that show the most affinities with the suzerainty treaties also regard the other gods as extant, real, and potent."[86] Thus, there is fragility to YHWH's covenantal lordship. Consequently, with God, there was "nervousness and defensiveness with the presence of an alternative to him and his cult."[87] In Levenson's assessment, God

---

of the Priestly tradition—following scholarship such as Milgrom's—Levenson's importation of his notion of chaos into Genesis 1:2 would be indefensible.

83. Levenson, *Creation and the Persistence of Evil*, 131–32. Interestingly Brown argues for an exact opposite movement in the Priestly tradition. Instead of all others being subjected to God's mastery, God invites others to participate with him and decentralizes power as the social order increases in complexity throughout Genesis 1.

84. Levenson, *Creation and the Persistence of Evil*, 132. Levenson hears echoes of this type of subordination of a pantheon to YHWH in the HB (ibid., 133).

85. Ibid., 135.

86. Ibid., 137.

87. Ibid., 139.

needs the witness of Israel and their recognition of his lordship to realize his divinity, to actualize his full potential.[88]

Because Israel must choose between obedience to God and death, Levenson finishes his book with discussing the need to frame humans' relationship to God in terms other than autonomy or heteronomy. Humans cannot be enslaved to the point of becoming controlled objects (utter heteronomy). That would not grant mastery to God. For there to be divine mastery, human subjectivity cannot be assumed by God.[89] They must, rather, be subjects under him, able to choose. On the other hand, there is only one legitimate choice that would not lead to their destruction.[90] Complete autonomy does not define humans' relationship before God. Therefore, neither heteronomy nor autonomy are suitable to describe the covenant relationship among God and Israel/humans.[91]

"Only when the opposition of dichotomy yields to the subtlety of dialectic can we begin to grasp the Jewish dynamics of lordship and submission."[92] Concerning this subtlety of dialectic, Levenson writes: "Israel at Sinai is not "equally free to assent and dissent," but already owes her freedom and her life to the God with whom she has always been in an eternal covenant that was only announced and never negotiated . . . those who stand under covenantal obligation by nature and necessity are continually called upon to adopt that relationship by free decision. Chosen for service, they must choose to serve."[93] With a Creator who commands, the "spiritual politics of the Hebrew Bible begins with duties, not rights."[94] Even so, humans are neither mindless in living in their duties, nor should their thoughts replace the commands of the inscrutable

---

88. Ibid. As I will be arguing, God's rightful lordship does not change, nor does God's relationship to creation *as God* change. It is creation's relating to God as both God and lord that changes. It is the actualization of the full potential of creation, its full realization of its potential for/with God that is at stake. At issue is its choice of life over death. It is this potential toward which Israel's faithfulness bore witness. Also worth noting is that divine sovereignty is the attribute through which Levenson views biblical data and frames his observations. My own theological bias is to see love as God's central, governing attribute highlighted in Scripture and, thus, the attribute through which to read biblical texts and frame observations.

89. Ibid., 140.

90. Ibid., 141. Cf. ibid., 143.

91. Ibid., 144.

92. Ibid.

93. Ibid., 147, 148.

94. Ibid., 148.

God.[95] There is a balance between argument and obedience for humans. Even more insightful is Levenson's observation that this relationship is significant not only in covenant, but also in creation. "The presence of variations of this spiritual dialectic in narrative, covenantal, and cosmogonic texts suggests its centrality and its depth of rootage in the Israelite religious consciousness."[96]

An Evaluation and Critique of Levenson

Presuppositions in Framing the Material

Finding the best explanatory framework in which to give an account of the available data is much of what the scholarly task is about. As history has shown, changing the framework alters how the reality of the same data is understood. When the sun was thought to revolve around the earth, the phenomena of the sun's *rising* and *setting* was interpreted one way—that the sun moves around the earth. When the explanatory framework changed to the earth spinning as it orbits the sun, interpretations about the same observed phenomena changed.

When George Smith and Herman Gunkel first published their comparative studies on *Enuma elish* and biblical creation texts, they thought that *Enuma elish* had been used as a source by the biblical authors. In George Smith's view, the more ancient Babylonian text supplied details for us that are missing in Genesis 1.[97] This type of explanatory

---

95. Ibid., 153.

96. Ibid. When he speaks of narrative, Levenson is referring to his prior contrasting of Abraham's negotiation with God in Genesis 18 and Abraham's unquestioned obedience to God's command in Genesis 22 (ibid., 149ff).

97. Cf. Dobson, *A Chaos of Delight*, 382n147. Smith was not schooled as an Assyriologist; he was an engraver hired by the British Museum to repair cuneiform tablets. In his work on ancient documents at the museum he "discovered" and translated the *Epic of Gilgamesh* in 1872 and *Enuma elish* in 1875. Smith first suggested about the *Epic of Gilgamesh* in 1872: "On reviewing the evidence it is apparent that the events of the Flood narrated in the Bible and the Inscriptions are the same, and occur in the same order" (quoted in Dobson, *A Chaos of Delight*, 39). He suggested when he published *Enuma elish* that "when Genesis was copied from 'the primitive account,' it omits some details, which are included in the Cuneiform narrative" (Hess, "One Hundred Fifty Years," 5; cf. Watson, *Chaos Uncreated*, 15). Smith made suggestions about chaos being in both texts. Gunkel continued in a similar fashion, claiming that *Genesis 1–11* "displayed extensive dependence on the mythological tradition in Babylonia" (ibid., 7). New with Gunkel was that he was the first to bring combat into the discussion of chaos in the Bible (Watson,

framework for the data has undergone revisions and refinements in the subsequent decades.⁹⁸ Traces of Smith and Gunkel can be seen in Levenson's work when he writes that Ugaritic or Akkadian texts help to give us the full sense of the old myth of which the Bible only has allusions and snippets.⁹⁹ Thus Levenson works out of the framework he inherited which presupposes some type of continuum from the old myths of Israel's neighbors through Israel's borrowing of them and demythologizing them to Israel's eventual progression to the doctrine of creation out of nothing. By examining biblical texts as though their use of certain images is in keeping with their use in the old myth (with varying degrees of distance), Levenson believes he is doing the least violence to the biblical text and its meaning.¹⁰⁰

There is now, however, more than one explanatory framework available through which to give an account of the data within extant ANE texts. Those who have developed these variant explanatory frameworks often have done so in reaction to stated weaknesses in methodology of

---

Chaos Uncreated, 16). The notion of chaos and especially connecting it with creation in the Bible were both immediately challenged (ibid., 18).

98. Cf. Hess, "One Hundred Fifty Years," 3–26. Kitchen decades ago criticized biblical scholars for the manner in which they hold on to their theories as though they are doctrinal matters. No matter how appealing the theories may be given one's convictions, or how long it has been the accepted model (e.g., the Documentary Hypothesis), Kitchen encouraged biblical scholars to hold them loosely and let them go freely, as Assyriologists must do when new evidence contradicts their prized theories (Kitchen, *The Ancient Orient and Old Testament*, 18–20, 26–28). It is a growing sentiment that it is time to lay aside making any connections between *Enuma elish* and Genesis 1. Richard Clifford concludes in his studies that "Though its prefatory function is paralleled in Mesopotamia, attempts to show that Genesis 1 is directly dependent on *Enuma elish* cannot be judged successful" (*Creation Accounts*, 140). Heidel's chart of a shared sequence of events between *Enuma elish* and Genesis 1 has been borrowed by Speiser and others as evidence for dependency, even though Heidel "concluded that the parallels were so inexact that the question of actual literary dependency must remain inconclusive" (Batto, *Slaying the Dragon*, 77). Clifford concurs: "Unfortunately, the similarities are misleading" (*Creation Accounts*, 140). They "do not take into account the different structures of the two works . . . The worlds of the two texts are altogether different, in fact" (ibid., 140, 141). Nevertheless, Genesis 1 does have some parallels with other ANE texts; "Given our present knowledge, however, it is difficult to prove that any single work is the source of Genesis 1. The text may well be eclectic" (141). A very helpful account of the development of the various ANE cultures and their myths can be found in Geoffrey Dobson's *A Chaos of Delight*.

99. Levenson, *Creation and the Persistence of Evil*, 8.

100. See Watson's list of scholars who have been challenging the notion of chaos in Genesis 1:2 (*Chaos Uncreated*, 16n27).

those operating within the older framework. When a progression from old myth to *creatio ex nihilo* is not assumed, and when the meaning of biblical images and their function are determined first by their scriptural context and only then compared and contrasted with those of foreign texts, then a radically different picture of Israel's thinking emerges that demands a new framework to explain the relationship of Israel's texts to its neighbors.' Most significantly, in one alternate reading, there is *no combat found in Scripture between God and a part of nature*; far too often theophany is mistaken for combat. There is no depiction of the seas as being angry, rebellious, or evil.[101] No part of creation is innately hostile to God, nor does God meet any part of creation with automatic hostility. Instead, "God's actions toward creation are governed by his good purpose, not automatic hostility to some of its components."[102]

The point here is not to reproduce all of the arguments against Levenson's framework and in favor of alternate frameworks. Rather, the point is that the framework in which one operates is extremely influential in how the data is interpreted. The idea of a mythic evolution out of which Levenson works has been adapted and nuanced over the decades in response to various criticisms against it. Even in its adjusted form, it is still under attack. New readings of the biblical texts and ongoing scholarship in ANE studies challenge the claims made about the biblical texts by Levenson and undermine the adequacy of the framework he uses to explain the data. This will be seen further in the sections that follow.

An ANE Combat-as-Creation Myth or Distinct Combat Myths and Creation Myths in the ANE?

In the work of Rebecca Watson, she claims that in Babylonian sources there is no intrinsic connection between *Chaoskampf* and creation.[103]

---

101. Watson, *Chaos Uncreated*, 4 and 259ff. In relation to Genesis 1:2 specifically, Alster concludes: "Although attempts have been made to find traces in the Old Testament of a combat between God and an alleged monster like Tiāmat (Rahab and Leviathan), there is no evidence that *těhôm* ever was such a personal mythological character. In the relevant passages, *těhôm* refers to the waters of the Reed Sea, and the separation of the waters refers to the exodus rather than to the creation of the world. The scene is Israel's crossing the sea after God had separated its waters (Isa 27:1; 51:9–10; Ps 74:12–17; 89:9–12; Job 9:13–14; 26:12–13)" ("Tiamat," 1638).

102. Watson, *Chaos Uncreated*, 73; cf. ibid., 374.

103. Ibid., 20. She cites N. Forsyth's *The Old Enemy: Satan and the Combat Myth*, in which he too claims that combat is not linked with creation. In the Ugaritic myths of

Even in *Enuma elish*, where the two themes of combat and world formation appear on the same tablet, any connection is of minor or passing concern. Almost without exception—*Enuma elish* being that one possible exception—combat myths "are not concerned with cosmic origins but with theomachic conflicts and the battle for supremacy among the gods."[104] Within these myths the greatness of the struggle is emphasized. There is also a genuine possibility of defeat for both sides.[105] In fact, in many of the myths the champion (or winning side) is defeated in an initial combat before victory is accomplished in the main battle.[106] This can be seen in *Enuma elish* where both Ea and Anu were sent on failed missions to subdue Tiamat before Marduk prevailed.[107]

There are problems in finding a single combat myth tradition. In looking closely at the examples in Ugaritic and Babylonian texts, there are both similarities and glaring differences between them.[108] Presuppositions have often clouded comparative studies in harmonizing these texts.[109] Harmonization also happens between biblical and non-biblical texts. In the biblical examples often cited as combat against chaos, dependence is often assumed more than demonstrated. Thus, differences are overlooked; missing components of ANE combat myths are not highlighted. For example, in Israel's writings waters may flee and dragons may be slain, but there are never two parties in the Scripture locked in *combat*;[110] "there is no mention of the issuing of a challenge,

---

Baal versus Yam or Mot, the battle is at most a struggle for control of the world and its organization; nevertheless, is it El who is the creator, not Baal (Watson, *Chaos Uncreated*, 21). This is in keeping with the scholarly contributions of McCarthy.

104. Ibid., 21. Watson concludes that "a survey of relevant scholarship indicates that, at the least, a causal connection between combat and creation can no longer be presupposed" (Watson, *Chaos Uncreated*, 24).

105. Ibid., 25.

106. Ibid.

107. See Tablet II.53ff and Tablet II.75ff. Interestingly, in *Enuma elish*, the combat of Ea, Anu, and finally Marduk with Tiamat fits precisely with the general purpose for combat myths in the ANE—as a "battle for supremacy among the gods" (Watson, *Chaos Uncreated*, 21). The only thing the battle itself *creates* is the death of the last of the primordial stuff and the enduring fact of the gods being the lone remaining controllers of the destinies within all reality.

108. Tsumura, *Creation and Destruction*, 144ff.

109. Saggs has listed some of the troublesome assumptions made by Gunkel and passed on in the field (*The Encounter with the Divine in Mesopotamia and Israel*, 54–55).

110. Watson, *Chaos Uncreated*, 26.

of any attempt to assault God, or even of acts of self-defiance by these agents. Their active opposition to God is nowhere unequivocally stated; nor is there any indication that God's destruction or 'ordering' of them is a reaction to their behavior."[111] The actual dynamics at work in the biblical texts have been clouded by presupposed "combat" themes.

Thus, in the entire ANE there is one extant text in which a combat has a connection with creation. Even then, the connection has more to do with proximity in the text than with an intentional conceptual integration of the two events. As a general rule, there are distinct combat myths and creation myths in the ANE. Second, the dependence of certain of Israel's writings on the combat myths of its neighbors is commonly assumed. However, even in piecing together all of the biblical texts used as examples, collectively they lack important components of combat myths. Most importantly they lack an opponent fighting against God. Levenson's framework, in which creation is mastery, rests upon a tradition within scholarship that views creation in the ANE as combative. However, as that creation-as-combat tradition is being examined, the evidence once cited in support has been found to be built upon assumptions more than reality. For Levenson to keep his interpretation of Scripture, he would need to rebuild the ANE background and its connections to Scripture from the ground up, in the face of contrary arguments.

Looking Again at the Dynamics in the Narrative of Enuma elish

This section could be considered an excursus. However, since there are many claims made based on *Enuma elish*, it is worth looking at that text itself. Its interpretation is key to Levenson's framework. Reading through the narrative brings to the surface several points of disconnect between the text and how its characters and plot have been depicted. These features of the text bring into question how it has been commonly used.

At the start of *Enuma elish*, the masculine Apsu intermingles with the feminine Tiamat.[112] It is commonly said that Apsu is the subterranean *fresh* water and Tiamat is *salt* water in *Enuma elish*. However, the text does not say this. In V.52–66 the text says Tiamat is the source of

---

111. Ibid.

112. According to B. Alster, *Enuma elish* is the first evidence we have in the history of Babylonian mythology of Apsu being portrayed as a personal mythic character ("Tiamat," 1637).

all fresh water.[113] Apsu, thus, maintains in the text his more traditional place as the "lower part of the cosmos" (IV.144–45). The contrast utilized between Apsu and Tiamat is between masculine and feminine—a generative union—more than between salt water and fresh.[114]

Talking about the initial conditions in *Enuma elish* between Apsu, Tiamat, and the mysterious Mummu as chaos or chaotic is not necessarily in keeping with the tone of Tablet I. In their *intermingling* "the verb does not even indirectly suggest the initial state of the primordial oceans as 'chaotic.' According to Lambert (oral communication), this 'intermingling' of these two waters was orderly in itself, that is, 'as one' (*istenis*)."[115] It was also positive in that it resulted in the generation of the gods. Generation through male-female intermingling (not violence) is the first and most primal mode of creation depicted in *Enuma elish*.[116]

In the movement of *Enuma elish*'s narrative the raw, primal material—which generates the gods and is formed into the creation—exists with no assigned place, established dwelling, or designated purpose. For example, Apsu, the lower part of the cosmos, is one with Tiamat; the traditional layers in Mesopotamian cosmology were not yet established/created. Likewise, the gods when they are birthed have no assigned places or purposes either. Those had not yet been designated for them. They had not yet been called by their names and their destinies had not yet been fixed.[117]

How the young gods are initially related to their primordial parents is ambiguous. The spatial relationships are unclear; in some regards the gods are still enmeshed in their parents. As a result, the aimless gods and the primordial stuff do nothing but disturb one another. The gods act like juvenile delinquents stirring their parents. The gods' motions make ripples in their parents, disturbing them, and their parents' motions in turn disturb the gods.[118] It is only until Apsu is killed and bars are set for

---

113. Ibid., 1636.

114. Ibid.

115. Tsumura, *Creation and Destruction*, 51.

116. Alster, "Tiamat," 1635.

117. In the opening of Tablet I, of all the things mentioned that *were not yet* or *had not been* when the waters of Apsu and Tiamat mingled, the last ones mentioned are about the gods not having come into being, been named, and having their destinies fixed (I.7–8).

118. The young gods were created "within" Apsu and Tiamat (I.9). The gathering together of the divine brothers—their moving and running about in the divine abode

his *place*, and Marduk rises in the assembly, kills Tiamat, and makes a world that the gods and world-stuff are given places. When the primal (now dead) materials are divided up and arranged,[119] the gods are appointed to various realms and given roles. They are given dwellings in which to rest at night—a solution to their disturbing, all-hours antics. Stars are made and put in places, gates and locks ensure the stability of their places.

The angst in the narrative up until the gods and the primordial stuff are assigned places and purposes is deeply felt. The gods seem enmeshed with Tiamat. It had not been established in the relationship between the gods and the primordial stuff, of who controlled whom and who should control the destinies. That was sorted out through combats. Until that hierarchy is established, Tiamat is giving the destinies to her general Kingu, and the gods are giving destinies to Marduk. When Marduk defeats Tiamat and Kingu, he is the only one left holding destinies. One major uncertainty in the narrative is resolved.

It is not Tiamat who was chaos or chaotic by nature; it is not Tiamat who *is* disorder. It is the purposeless gods who stir her up who are as much the problem as Tiamat is by nature or character; after all, it is she who cried out to Apsu in response to his plan to put an end to the gods that she and Apsu should endure the pain inflicted upon them by their offspring "good-naturedly."[120] Mummu is the one who prods Apsu to go on with his plan to kill his offspring, the plan Ea understood causing Ea to kill Apsu and bind Mummu. Furthermore, it is the gods who scheme for their own benefit to convince Tiamat to avenge Apsu. After Apsu is killed and placed, and right after the birth of Marduk, the text says:

> Then Anu begot winds and brought them from the four quarters, to be the van and to command the ranks; and he brought the tornado, a wild surf to worry Tiamat. But now the other gods had no rest any more, tormented by storms, they conspired in

---

(I.24)—disturbed the inner parts of Tiamat (I.23; Heidel, *The Babylonian Genesis*, 19). This was painful to Tiamat and Apsu (I.27); they couldn't sleep (I.38). When Marduk was born, "he caused waves and disturbed Tiamat" (I.107; Heidel, *The Babylonian Genesis*, 22). The gods accused Tiamat's interior of being disturbed so that they cannot rest (I.115).

119. Along with the use of Apsu as a mythical entity and the combining of a combat myth and a creation myth, which both have been noted already, the formation of the sky and earth out of two halves of the corpse of a slain monster within *Enuma elish* is also new to Mesopotamian cosmology (Alster, "Tiamat," 1636–37.).

120. Tablet I. 46; Heidel, *The Babylonian Genesis*, 19.

their secret hearts and brought to Tiamat the matter of their plot. To their own mother they said, "When they killed Apsu you did not stir, you brought no help to him, your husband. Now Anu has called up from the four quarters this abomination of winds to rage in your guts, and we cannot rest for the pain; Remember Apsu in your heart, your husband, remember Mummu who was defeated; now you are all alone, and thrash around in desolation, and we have lost your love, our eyes ache and we long for sleep. Rouse up, our Mother! Pay them back and make them empty like the wind." Tiamat approved it.[121]

In order that they could rest, the young gods convinced Tiamat to fight the major gods on their behalf by pressing her on her personal misery and on her sensibilities as a wife and mother. Tiamat's downfall was in becoming a pawn in the not-yet-destined politics among the gods. Neither Tiamat nor Apsu were chaos in themselves. The not-yet-having-social-order situation among the gods and between the gods and the primal/parental stuff is where the tension lies in the narrative. Thus, there is lacking justification in the text for saying that there was initially creation out of chaos or out of chaotic beings/substances.

It is the entire picture that elicits uncertainty. As the narrative unfolds further, its overall effect gives assurance that it is not the world's matter, the primordial stuff, that controls the destinies but the gods—specifically, Babylon's god Marduk. The arrangements and courses of the cosmic-polis are established by the gods, and not by the stuff of the world. In fact, it gives assurance that there are destinies at all. In the present order of things there is not directionless or purposeless generation. The gods themselves are not purposeless but have places and courses. Humans too have places and courses in the grand picture under the gods. Before this balance is established, there is infancy—literally, newly birthed gods. It is not "*disorder*" or "*anti*-order" because no order or purpose has yet been uttered for it. If any social arrangements were conceived, no one had the recognized authority or power/ability to override the plurality of voices. There is aimlessness—juvenile mixing. There is that which can be cosmos, but it lacks the designs and dictates

---

121. Sproul, *Primal Myths*, 94.

of Marduk, who violently claimed dominance and to whom it is gifted to be the rightful holder of the destinies.

Framing the Reading of Images

Choosing an Interpretive Lens

Levenson does not always make arguments based on the text for why he characterizes the images in the HB in the way that he does in the specific texts he cites: as evil, angry, rebellious, etc. For example, he speaks about the sea in Job 38:8–11 as being a reference to "a somewhat sinister force that, left to its own, would submerge the world and forestall the ordered reality we call creation."[122] The translation he uses of the text is:

> Who closed the sea behind doors
> When it gushed forth out of the womb,
> When I clothed it in clouds,
> Swaddled it in dense clouds,
> When I made breakers My limit for it,
> And set up its bars and doors,
> And said, "You may come so far and no farther;
> Here your surging waves will stop"?

Levenson comments that the only thing to prevent the sinister sea from being left to its own devices is the "mastery of YHWH, whose blast and thunder or whose craftsmanship and commanding word force the Sea into its proper place, apparently without a struggle."[123] Levenson does not justify why he ignores the metaphor in the passage of the sea being birthed, clothed, and swaddled.[124] In the metaphor, the baby gushed out of the womb. Instead of being left naked to spill out all over the place, it was given clothing and a container. Without assuming ahead of time that waters represent a sinister force and that God's action in the text should be understood as opposition to the sea, this passage sounds grace-full and is a touching image of God's parenting of a child—though be it a *large, mighty* child.

The significance of references to bars and doors should not *automatically* be assumed to be an antagonistic relationship. It is possible to

---

122. Levenson, *Creation and the Persistence of Evil*, 15.

123. Ibid.

124. Cf. Watson's treatment of this passage (*Chaos Uncreated*, 275ff) as a contrasting view to Levenson's.

find a *background* for that popular interpretation by looking narrowly at two places in *Enuma elish*. The first is where Ea killed Apsu and then took Mummu[125] and "shut in (and) barred (the door) against him."[126] Narrowly, this can be understood as an overpowering and limiting of Mummu. In the metaphor in this context, nevertheless, Marduk domesticates Mummu; Marduk puts him in a holding pen, places a ring in his nose, and then leads him around.

The whole work viewed widely narrates a movement from there being no structure and purposes among the gods and the primal elements to every element having a place, as well as the gods having assigned places and roles. This reference to Mummu being limited and no longer being anyplace (or everyplace) can be understood as a mythic explanation both for how and why the cosmos is as it is and for the gods' lordly relationship to the stuff of the cosmos.

The second reference in *Enuma elish* to hardware such as bars, gates, or doors is on Tablet IV lines 137–140 and is in a similar category to the first. After Marduk killed Tiamat, he "vanquished (and) subdued" his other enemies.[127] He then came back to her dead body, smashed her skull and severed her arteries. All the gods rejoiced, Marduk received gifts, and he rested. Finally he decided "to create ingenious things" out of the carnage:[128] "He split her like a shellfish into two parts: half of her he set up and ceiled it as the sky, pulled down the bar and posted guards. He bade them to allow not her waters to escape."[129] Here the metaphor is one of a prison.[130] However, just as with Apsu after he was killed, Tiamat's corpse was made into a recognizable part of the cosmos. She—or rather, her matter—finally was assigned to a place instead of having no place (or everyplace). There is also a transition here, as there was with Apsu, that she is now talked about less as a character, but as water, a component of the cosmos. It is her waters that the guards are not to allow to leak, not

---

125. It is unknown who or what Mummu is; he *may* be some form of mist (Jacobsen, "Mesopotamia," 170). Mummu is the only other primal character with Tiamat and Apsu at the opening of *Enuma elish*.

126. Tablet I.70; Heidel, *The Babylonian Genesis*, 20.

127. Tablet IV.123; Heidel, ibid., 42.

128. Tablet IV.136; Heidel, ibid., 42.

129. Brandon, *Creation Legends*, 100; cf. the translations in Sproul, *Primal Myths*, 102; and Heidel, *The Babylonian Genesis*, 42.

130. This follows the theme in the tablet of locking up those who had sided with Tiamat (IV.111–20, 127).

her.[131] The concern is the maintenance of the place of her waters in the cosmos being newly established. The purpose and place toward which Marduk decided to use half of her corpse is as the sky. He put up a bar and guards to make sure his cosmos stays as he places it. Notice that no bar or guards are posted for the half of Tiamat's corpse left below.

The security of the upper waters is good news for the readers of the myth who know that a huge volume of water is suspended over their heads. This was also good news in that Anu, Enlil, and Ea now had their corresponding *fixed* residences, or stations.[132] The fourth tablet starts with Marduk being given a throne among the gods as their lord in a time when no hierarchy of the gods over matter had yet been established. That lack of established hierarchy is resolved when Marduk slays Tiamat and takes the destinies away from Tiamat's general Kingu. The tablet ends with not only the first lack being addressed (no hierarchy) but also with Marduk having formed the beginnings of a cosmos, thereby establishing residences and stations for the other three great gods.

The last significant reference to containing hardware in *Enuma elish* is on Tablet V in which Marduk has created stations for the great gods and is setting up the astrological entities as their likenesses. Marduk "opened gates on both sides, and made strong lock(s) to the left and to the right. In the very center thereof he fixed the zenith."[133] The point of the tablet is

---

131. I should at least mention that in the ANE part of someone was considered to be linked with that very person and their presence. Doing harm to someone's shadow, name, or the like was considered to be doing real damage to the person him-/herself. The argument being made here, however, is that the bar and guards secure the place and purpose for which Tiamat's corpse was being used in Marduk's cosmos making. There is a transition of concern in the narrative from whether any power is greater than the raging Tiamat to concern for the fixed nature of the sky being made out of the waters of the now slain Tiamat. Just as Levenson himself says of Apsu and Tiamat, "One never forgets their physical basis, water, and each of them dies, so that the primordial gods are no more, and Tiamat is now at best only the matter out of which Marduk has shaped the world" (*Creation and the Persistence of Evil*, 4).

132. Tablet? IV.146; Heidel, *The Babylonian Genesis*, 43. The lower half of Tiamat's body does not become the subterranean waters. Apsu had already been made into that. The lower half became the earth—the place to which Marduk (formerly Enlil) was assigned (Jacobsen, "Mesopotamia: The Cosmos as a State," 169; cf. Tsumura, *Creation and Destruction*, 134). Only her upper half was fashioned into the waters at the opposite pole of the cosmos from Apsu, the subterranean waters.

133. Tablet V.9–11; Heidel, *The Babylonian Genesis*, 44.

the assurance that the gods and their likenesses, the stars, all have duties and places, and that "none might go wrong (and) be remiss."[134]

The point of looking at these three references in *Enuma elish* is only to show that all references to gates and/or bars in the ANE do not necessarily designate an adversarial relationship, especially not an ongoing one. In two of the references they do elicit notions of either a pen or prison that holds in what had been Marduk's adversary. In a third reference they keep the courses of the newly made astrological entities. Nevertheless, in all cases the adversary (if there was one) was already neutralized, even killed, at the time the securing hardware was used. Its function was to enduringly fix some facet of the newly placed cosmological arrangement. In all of the references, their inclusion offers assurance of the constancy and surety of Marduk's ordering of the cosmos out of a previously pathless and place-less cast of characters. Because gates and bars serve this broader function in the text, and not always in reference to a persisting adversarial relationship, no more should be claimed about them than that they reassure the reader that there is a strong, steady boundary for that which exists and would be aimless otherwise.

In Job, the birth imagery bears closer resemblance to Marduk's ordering of his newly made stars. In other words, the birthed seas are neither a prisoner of war nor the dismembered corpse of his vanquished foe. In Job, a baby lacking viscosity receives the type of creative care Marduk's stars receive: the gift of a steady place that is for the good of all.

A second issue related to interpretive perspective is that Levenson's use of *Enuma elish* is nearly to the exclusion of considering other possible ANE interlocutors. In the twenty years since Levenson published his book, comparisons between Genesis 1 and *Enuma elish* have been undermined even further than they had been previously.[135] Also, by ignoring the way the primal waters are treated in Egyptian or Sumerian

---

134. Tablet V.7; Heidel, ibid., 44. Also: "In the *Atra-Hasīs* epic, I i 15, S v 1, x rev. i 6, etc., Enki (Ea), the god of the sweet-water Apsu, is mentioned as having 'the bolt, the bar of the sea' . . . This 'bolt' may have kept Tiam(a)t(um) out—that is, kept its waters from mixing with the waters of Apsu, as they did at the beginning of *Enuma elish*. Thus, in the cosmological traditions of Mesopotamia, there seems to have existed a distinction between the domain or area of the 'sea' and that of the subterranean ocean" (Tsumura, *Creation and Destruction*, 51).

135. Cf., e.g., Clifford, *Creation Accounts*, 140; Tsumura, *Creation and Destruction*, 143; Watson, *Chaos Uncreated*, 271n20, 376, etc. See also Ouro, "The Earth of Genesis 1:2," 259–76.

cosmology, for example, Levenson does not consider as a source for Genesis 1:2 the moral neutrality of the waters, their generative power, or the non-combative relationship the gods have with them in much of the ANE literature. Instead he chooses to view the waters within the notion of chaos that he constructed in comparison to a specific interpretation of one ANE text.

William Brown has studied the role of waters in Greek, Egyptian, Ugaritic, Sumerian, and Akkadian cosmologies and found in the MT's precursors that the closest parallels to the way waters function in Genesis 1—with a generative function for land, fish and birds—are found in certain cosmogonic traditions in Egyptian, Sumerian, and Akkadian. In Sumerian mythology, the originations of birds and fish are conjoined.[136] The Sumerian god Enki, the god of the watery abyss, represents the power of fertility. As that tradition was brought into Akkadian, Enki was cast "as the water god who provides, in addition to fish, birds from the waters above."[137]

In Egyptian literature, Nun was the primeval ocean deity. "Nun was often pictured as a stagnant primeval ocean that the air churned in order to bring about the appearance of the 'hillock.' . . . Nun functioned only in a generally creative sense in that the primordial god was considered the ultimate theogonic source."[138] The gods, such as Ptah, would seize into themselves the power of the potential for being within the primal material into themselves in order to create. "Water, as personified by Nun, exhibited a generally creative potency in Egyptian mythology . . . In short, water is often described in Egyptian cosmogonies as having a creative link not only with aquatic creatures such as fish, but also with birds."[139] Thus, within Genesis 1, with the way waters come to participate in God's creative activity at God's exhortation—particularly with fish and birds—the more likely ANE background for the waters are the positive, generative perspectives from Sumerian, Akkadian, and Egyptian sources.

---

136. Brown, *Structure, Role, and Ideology*, 179.
137. Ibid., 178.
138. Ibid., 180. Cf. the generative potency of Tiamat in *Enuma elish*.
139. Ibid., 181.

Looking for the Function of Images in the Context of the Whole Work

Why does Levenson insist that the Flood narrative and the Exodus narrative manifest "the same pattern of a cosmogonic victory over lethal waters" as a combat myth?[140] Regarding the Flood narrative, it does not personify the waters and only shows God as the one in control. The only way to read the waters in that narrative as anything other than a large volume of water used as a tool of judgment and purification by God is to import those ideas into the text from combat traditions. The problem with that importation is that the antagonists in ANE combat myths are nowhere described by the term "flood."[141]

Similarly, Levenson states that the Exodus is a combat *at* the sea in which the "enemy is not the sea (which is totally under YHWH's control), but Pharaoh."[142] If there is a combat myth underlying Exodus 14–15 that has been fully historicized, and if the adversary is Pharaoh (as in the case of the Flood narrative it was the wickedness of humanity), why does Levenson color his descriptions of the waters in these accounts as though they represent the watery chaos-adversary from another culture's combat myths? Why does he import concepts found in myths about a hand-to-hand *combat* between a god and waters into biblical texts about a *conflict* between God and humans in which God uses waters? Levenson does not clearly or convincingly show the logic of how an ancient myth about cosmic combat underlies a story with characters of a different nature (humans instead of a natural element), in an historical setting (instead of a primordial, a-historical setting), and with waters having a different role (as instrument instead of living adversary). Most puzzling, if the antagonist becomes humans instead of waters, how is Levenson's vilification of the waters justified, as well as the continuation of the chaos motif in regard to these waters?

In looking at the importance of context, it is questionable whether the author of Exodus meant for the events at the sea to be read as *combat*,

---

140. Levenson, *Creation and the Persistence of Evil*, 75.

141. Tsumura, *Creation and Destruction*, 154–55. More will be said about this in the chapter on Tsumura's position. For now it is enough to say that Tsumura finds in other traditions where the flood is an instrument of destruction employed by certain gods. It is a tool, never an adversary. See Tsumura's examination of floodwaters in both the Bible and other ANE texts (*Creation and Destruction*, 152–55).

142. Levenson, *Creation and the Persistence of Evil*, 76.

although this interpretation has certainly been in vogue.[143] Another way to read the entire narrative of Exodus 1–14, which results in Israel's celebration in chapter 15, is that God orchestrates a series of events whereby Israel and Egypt come to know that he is YHWH.[144]

The author writes the narrative in such a way that readers, unlike the characters in the narrative, get to see what God is up to. The reader is let in on the irony that it is God who must harden Pharaoh's heart during the onslaught of the plagues. Pharaoh is not nearly as strong or god-like as those in the story presume him to be. God holds Pharaoh up so that, at Pharaoh's letting go of the Israelites, it appears God has achieved a hard won victory over a strong foe. This played on people's beliefs concerning the might of Pharaoh and Egypt in order for them to have some comprehension (by analogy) of the greatness of God's power.

After God, by means of a crushed Pharaoh, lets the people go, God positions Israel in a precise place by the sea from where they cannot flee (14:2). God then sends poor Pharaoh after them by once again hardening his heart, and the hearts of any of his advisors who may have wisely at that point counseled otherwise. The Israelites, who still at this point fear the Egyptians and not YHWH,[145] think they would have been better off staying in Egypt under the superpower that God is manipulating to come after them. God *saves* Israel from his puppet-Egypt by letting them cross the sea, and then God drowns the Egyptians in the waters. Egypt comes to know that YHWH is God. Israel also comes to know that YHWH is God and they fear him more than the world-superpower they watched

---

143. See, e.g., Gowan, *Theology in Exodus*, 134ff.

144. On the significance of the theme of knowing in Exodus, see Nahum M. Sarna, *Exodus: the Traditional Hebrew Text with the New JPS Translation*, 5. Statements throughout Exodus 1–14 indicate that knowledge for both Egypt and Israel that YHWH is God is God's aim: that Israel will know the Lord see Exod 6:7; 10:2; that Egypt will know the Lord see 7:5, 17; 8:10, 22; 9:14, 29; 11:7; 14:4, 18 (Gowan, *Theology in Exodus*, 134, 137). Last, the following reading of the Exodus 1–14 narrative is heavily influenced by Eslinger, "Freedom or Knowledge?")."

145. Contrast the way they refer to Egypt and going back to serve the Egyptians as they are crying out *in fear* (Exod 14:10–12) with the statement about Shiphrah and Puah in Exod 1:17 where it says that since they *feared* God, they disobeyed Pharaoh's order to kill the Israelite babies. God needed to orchestrate an event by which Israel's erroneous fear of the Egyptians would be replaced with fear of YHWH. This whole narrative from its early account of the midwives makes clear that people will work in service to that which they fear.

YHWH crush. This transfer of fear is a prerequisite for Israel following God (Exod 13:21–22; 1:17) and not the Egyptians (Exod 14:10–12).

Levenson calls this a "combat" at the sea. However, the term *combat* is only justifiable from the perspective of the human characters in the narrative. The author lets the reader see that the "combat" is a sham. Pharaoh is not a god who can combat with YHWH; so Pharaoh must be propped up (hardened) so that the "combat" looks convincing to both sides. But never does Exodus's author let the reader think Pharaoh or Egypt can engage YHWH in true two-sided combat as the old combat myths reported among divine/primordial beings. If the author of Exodus imports imagery from old combat myths and every presupposition in the ANE about the divinity of Pharaoh, it is only to make a mockery of them and expose their hollowness before almighty YHWH. In the worldview within which the Exodus narrative is told, God alone is in the category of cosmic forces.

Thus, it is not enough to be able to say that vestiges of an old combat myth are present in a biblical text and then interpret terms and images in the biblical text as though they still function the way they did in the other ANE texts. The meaning and significance of terms and images must be determined by their use and function in their context: i.e., in the immediate sentence, passage, work, other works of that genre or theological tradition, and the extant texts of that people group. Only then should comparisons and contrasts be made among the ways those images function in other cultures. Neither the Flood nor Sea Crossing narratives stand as examples in the Pentateuch giving warrant for linking the waters of Genesis 1 with "chaos."[146]

Reading Chaos into the Priestly Cosmography: Genesis 1:1—2:3

Genesis 1:2 is not overly generous with its descriptions. It introduces a *tohu wabohu* earth, darkness, the waters, and the presence of the Spirit of God. The verse does not say how to view these things. It does not say

---

146. If anything, they support Milgrom's view of the Priestly theology in which the (symbolic) impurity wrought in human sin replaces the (real) demonic in the traditions of its neighbors (see n82).

that some represent chaos, evil, or anything other than matter. Context helps determine what to do.

Levenson observes that there is no combat, no struggle, or resistance in the text. In Gen 1:1—2:3, the primal stuff is inert. God orders it. Even so, Levenson presumes that the text is in line with *Enuma elish* so that the stuff of v. 2 is a symbol for chaos—that it is evil.[147] The Priestly account represents for Levenson a new step in the demythologization of the primordial stuff away from the myth of combat/mastery. This explains the inertness of the chaos and the absence of resistance to God's ordering in the text.

The question is, however, whether reading notions of chaos/evil within the text is an accurate reading of the Priestly cosmography. William Brown has studied the MT, LXX, and the Hebrew *Vorlage* behind the LXX. He makes a strong case that the tradition represented by the LXX and the Hebrew VorLXX (itself of Palestinian origin) represents an older textual tradition that lies closer to the "Priestly" source. In both the LXX and the VorLXX the waters play a generative role. They begin as inert, but by vv. 9 and 10 they are named and are elicited to participate with God in creating.

Analysis of the texts shows that the MT is a redaction of this older textual tradition. From that older tradition, the Masoretic tradition added many heptatic features. Also, even though the earth retains its generative role in the MT, certain transition formulas were moved or removed to downplay the generative role of the waters.[148] Thus, in looking at the text tradition from which the Masoretes drew, one sees there is a social/collaborative structure throughout in which "God assumes the role as the 'total' subject, the earth and the waters are depicted as agents and occasionally subjects in the process of creation, and the remaining objects of creation are commanded to be agents in the maintenance of order, all within a rigorously consistent structure."[149] In this social structure, "God is not set *over and against* the created order; rather God is portrayed as

---

147. In the reading of *Enuma elish* offered above, it is questionable to read the primal waters as chaos/evil, especially prior to Tiamat being brought into the conflict among the other characters. Therefore, even if there were a connection between this ANE text and Genesis 1, it still would not necessarily be correct to label the primal waters as chaos or evil.

148. Brown, *Structure, Role, and Ideology*, 98ff.

149. Ibid., 208–209.

acting fundamentally *with* the created and creating order."¹⁵⁰ The divine "commands" should be interpreted as *jussive* commands to "connote a sense of collaboration among the agents."¹⁵¹ God's rule is *with* creation.

Thus in the conceptual world of P, the picture "is preeminently one of harmonious collaboration. P is convinced that only such a 'social' ordering can result in perfect (*ṭôb*) work and order."¹⁵² According to Brown this is the ideology, or *teaching*, of P's cosmogony. It "offers a cosmic prolegomenon for the realization of a clearly differentiated community, for the inauguration of a new age in the cultural history of the exilic/post-exilic community, as well as a utopian ideal by which anything less than perfect cooperation and order can be critically assessed."¹⁵³ Such an ideology is "characterized by collaboration in which all segments of the cosmic/social order are incorporated according to their respective abilities."¹⁵⁴

Undesirable Theological Implications

In the categories of the classic framework for the doctrine of creation the three options were creation out of nothing, emanation, or dualism: in other words, creation—distinct from or out of God—as a total act of God alone or some type of interaction between God and a preexistent other. Levenson outright rejects a notion of creation out of nothing within the HB and chooses to read the cosmologies through the framework of a preexisting, uncreated chaos. Not only is there this uncreated

---

150. Ibid., 214. In Remi Brague's assessment of Israel's faith, "they imagined a creation that was not the result of the work of God, let alone the result of a combat between God and some primitive monster, but of speech" (*The Wisdom of the World*, 47). Creation is certainly a production; "And yet creation is also the instilling of a meaning through a word and the attachment of a value: the creative word is the word of justice" (ibid.). Brague's equating of the creative word with justice works well with Brown's view of Genesis 1 if *justice* is taken to mean what Sharon Baker describes in "The Repetition of Reconciliation." Therein biblical justice is depicted as a reconciling move, equated with right action, mercy, the removal of blindness (i.e., with light), being satisfying to God, and an absence of violence (Baker, "The Repetition of Reconciliation," 229–32). It is restorative and builds relationships (229). If that is biblical justice, then God's creative call in Genesis 1 is certainly just and gives both meaning and value to what God is doing.

151. Brown, *Structure, Role, and Ideology*, 225.

152. Ibid., 225–26.

153. Ibid., 232.

154. Ibid.

chaos, it is neither morally good nor neutral. He classifies it as evil. Thus, God's most fundamental relationship to the only thing that is primally *other* to God is antagonistic. These two forces, the good-God and evil-stuff, are in open conflict with each other. Levenson does not give the powers of chaos intellect or give them personhood beyond personifying their manifestations. Nevertheless, chaos works against God and God's cosmogonic efforts.

With Levenson's starting foundation of tension between God and the other, God's action toward the other is (dis)colored accordingly. The impetus and end of God's action is to gain mastery so that God would reach the fullness of God's lordship over all others. This happens in *opposition* to the other and ultimately at a cost of the complete *nihil*-ation of the primal other. God will truly gain alpha position when not only all else is subjected to his ordering mastery, but also when that fundamental, primal chaos/evil within all else is conquered and eradicated. When God's own coming to be is described relative to sovereignty, lordship, and mastery, it results in an incomplete view of God's motive, work, and aim in creating and in relating to creation itself.[155] God's foundational relationship to the other is not opposition. God's first act toward the other

---

155. Since Levenson is influenced by process thought, he entertains the idea that the relationship between God and creation is not a settled matter in the HB; cf. Matthew Levering—*Scripture and Metaphysics*, 77ff—on Levenson's background and for a critique of his position from a position of classical theism. For Levenson, since authority is established in relationship (*Creation and the Persistence of Evil*, xvii), God's authority is something that comes to be perfected, or ratified by creation, or it is frustrated and challenged by the forces of evil operative within creation. For example, "the utterly benevolent God of creation will be himself only when humanity, male and female, created in his image, is able to be itself, without the interference of the malign forces. In this theology divine and human integrity are neither identical nor separable. Both are *ultimately* real, but *proximately* frustrated" (ibid., 46; italics original). Levenson does not claim there is a coming to be of God's authority in Genesis 1; it is a given in the text. I would argue that it is possible to talk about the fixed nature of God's authority in relation to creation from God's side on the basis of God being Creator and creation being contingent upon God's creative activity. God is by nature God; in relation to this creation God is Creator. These do not change regardless of creation's response. However, whether creation relates back to God as God is subject to fluctuation. I readily concur with Levenson, nevertheless, that Genesis 1 stands in contrast to *Enuma elish* on the fact that there is no combat in Genesis 1 in which God must gain or establish his position of authority in relation to the stuff of his creation.

is not mastery by way of combat, force, or even command. Rather, God is love; God's first act is self-gift by the Spirit (Gen 1:2).

Levenson's starting point of tension has implications for God's relationship not only with creation, but also for humans in how Levenson depicts the function of Israel's cult and in how their covenant relationship is defined. Within the cult, humanity's relationship to creation mirrors God's. The cult is a matter of holding back and holding together; it is a tool for engaging the enemy. Only insofar as that is accomplished can and does the good order that is creation come into being. The cult (and God's creating) is not first and primarily about the unfolding of the good and the beautiful. It is not first about the expression of the good among a people in relation to God. It is not first loving God and neighbor. It is first a battle. The cult (and creating) is defined first by what it negates.

In Jacob Milgrom's years of studying Leviticus, he concluded that in the Priestly cosmography there was no notion of the demonic.[156] The demonic that had to be fended off and guarded against in neighboring cults was eliminated in Israel's Priestly cult and replaced with human sin. Humans were the problem; nothing else.[157] Humans did not start as a universal problem. Rather, insofar as they did not live out the goodness of God's calling—i.e., follow after God's walking before them—they *became* impure. Within the cult, there was a solution for the polluting effects of human sin. The solution was not a warding off or holding back the effects of human sin. The solution was a positive (creative) life-giving restoration into the goodness of the covenant community.[158] The cultic/

---

156. See n82. Douglas Knight has observed this as well. He concludes that for Israel "what is primordial is the goodness of this world and of humanity; what is radically intrusive is the evil which humanity does . . . In the idyll of this world, humans interject discord" ("Cosmogony and Order in the Hebrew Tradition," 147). It is key to keep in mind that "evil in the Hebrew tradition is assigned no ontological value. It has no essence, no independent existence. It is something which is done by humans, deleterious acts directed against other humans and against God" (ibid., 147).

157. Levenson even says when commenting on Psalm 104: "In a worldview in which even Leviathan was formed for benign purposes and continues to delight his creator, only humanity is capable of posing a challenge to God . . . The great struggle for the altogether good world has moved from cosmogonic myth into the human community and perhaps the human heart as well" (Levenson, *Creation and the Persistence of Evil*, 58). Levenson unfortunately neglects this observation when outlining his claims that the Priestly cult was a participation in God's cosmic mastery of chaos.

158. Cf. Milgrom, *Leviticus 1–16*, 49–50. According to the Priestly view, "while sin may not scar the face of the sinner it does scar the face of the sanctuary" (ibid., 49). Because of this, there is collective responsibility within a society to not allow the wicked

religious *way of life* of the people also needs to be stressed with, if not above, the reparative practices provided for in the Priestly literature. Living in holiness, in the sacredness of life, is of key significance in many of the obscure prescriptions for daily life in the Levitical code.

In regard to the covenant between God and Israel, Levenson wrestles between humanity's autonomy and complete heteronomy.[159] Humans cannot be completely mastered and lose their subjectivity. For God to be lord over humans, all hints of autonomy cannot be erased; that would undermine God being lord over a *them*. On the other hand, if humans are utterly autonomous, then God lacks mastery. In Levenson's zero sum framework, for God to win, the other must lose some of the freedom it possesses by nature;[160] it must lose some of its

---

to flourish (50). There is extra responsibility on the high priest and leaders to "bring special sacrifices (4:9, 23), for their errors cause harm to their people" (50). "Thus, in the Priestly scheme, the sanctuary is polluted (read: society is corrupted) by brazen sins (read: the rapacity of the leaders) and also by inadvertent sins (read: the acquiescence of the 'silent majority'), with the result that God is driven out of his sanctuary (read: the nation is destroyed)" (50). In the Day of Purgation, the purification of the sanctuary was extended to the people; it was a day "for the collective catharsis of Israel. God would continue to reside with Israel because his temple and people were once again pure" (ibid., 51). On blood as life—and living within/according to either life or death—in the Priestly theology, as well as the *symbolism* (versus magic) of the cult, see Milgrom, *Leviticus 1-16*, 254-58, 711-12, 1000-1004; in brief, "Sacrifice, in their view, means returning life to its creator . . . Because the concept of holiness represents the forces of life . . . , the sacrificial system enables Israel to enter the sanctuary—the realm of holiness—and receive, via the sacrifices, the divine blessing (cf. Exod 20:24) of life-giving procreation and life-sustaining produce (19:25; 23:11; Ezek 44:30; Prov 3:9-10). Simultaneously, Israel must guard against the occurrence and incursion of impurity, the symbol of death" (*Leviticus 1-16*, 1003).

159. Arguably the gap between these two options lies in the doctrine of creation—in the gap opened between God and the world in their existence and operations. Levenson rightly sees that theology of creation and covenant are linked. Unfortunately, because he works within the traditional polarity of creation theology—especially by choosing to start with a duality—this polarity shapes and limits how he portrays covenant relationship.

160. See Charles Taylor's treatment of differing notions of freedom in part 2 of *Philosophy and the Human Sciences*. Levenson's use of the term *freedom* in this portion is a modern use because freedom belongs to the person instead of being ascribed based on having a certain place in a society (ibid., 319). Levenson's view would also be an example of a negative theory of freedom; freedom is individual independence from others (ibid., 213). Levenson says that there is a divine command prior to humans having freedom. Thus, there is a duty to use freedom according to the command. This is not using a positive theory of freedom, however, because in the using of freedom, the person has not "effectively determined oneself and the shape of one's life" (ibid., 213). The person

personhood.[161] Both God and the other cannot both, at the same time, come to the fullness of personal expression. Covenant and creation both entail a gain for God and a loss for the other. The other is subjected under the command of God.

Levenson seeks to find a way through the insufficiency of saying covenant (and creation) is both autonomy and heteronomy by an appeal to dialectic. Nevertheless, in the framing of the dialectic, God's prior commanding and imposition of duties still remains over-and-against the free ones who must choose the place of servanthood. Thus, recognizing "God's inscrutable yet unimpugnable mastery is always *painfully* difficult—God has made things that way."[162] The consolation for submitting against one's grain is that "it does result in the good life in which God reinstates his justice and renews his generosity . . . the good order that is creation comes into being."[163] This willful subjection is the precondition for the good order to come about. In addition, for creation to be willfully subjected, then, is also a facet of the *good* order.[164]

Levenson hypostatizes chaos/evil and makes it innate within creation. Because God is against chaos/evil, God is against creation insofar as chaos/evil is innate to it. God can only be unreservedly for creation at the eschaton when chaos/evil is purged. In the Christian tradition, evil has been defined commonly as a lack. Even though that lack is manifest within creation with real, negative consequences, evil is still not hypostasized. Thus, God does not suppress *it*; that would be logically absurd. Rather, evil can be eliminated through God's abundant gifting. God's response to evil is not *against* creation.[165] It is *for* creation and creation's fulfillment.

---

is submitting to another's designs instead of seeking self-realization. The person freely truncates their freedom, a part of him-/herself.

161. Levenson did not invent this dilemma or zero-sum framework. It is an ongoing issue in the classic framing of the doctrine of creation. He simply starts on the side of dualism (autonomy) and works toward divine mastery, instead of starting with divine fiat alone (heteronomy) and explaining the otherness of creation. One aim of this project is to move beyond the dilemma of these approaches in the doctrine of creation.

162. Levenson, *Creation and the Persistence of Evil*, 156; italics added.

163. Ibid.

164. It is remarkable that Brown, looking at the exact same text, comes to the exact opposite conclusion. It is cooperation and collaboration—full participation by all according to ability—that is a requirement for and part of the good order.

165. This claim is certainly not a settled matter in biblical theology. Divine justice in the Bible has been interpreted as punitive for centuries. The challenges raised against

Levenson's Laudable Ideas

First, Levenson rejects the presence of a notion within the HB of a creation that was established in a fixed state at God's decree. He has observed in the HB the dynamism of the relationship between God and creation, which includes humans.[166] He also understands that covenant is not fixed by divine decree and irrevocable.[167] It too is relational and dynamic; it is ongoingly honored and chosen. His observations about the dynamism of the relationship between God and creation/humans in creating and covenant will be affirmed.

Second, Levenson is right to reject the dichotomy between autonomy and heteronomy in the divine-human relationship. Nevertheless, in building his creation theology, he has simply chosen the opposite of creation out of nothing; the tension between choosing God as sole source or there being an autonomously-existing other remains. He is to be applauded for wanting to get beyond that tension between the two polarities. His creation paradigm simply does not enable him to describe his dialectic outside of the language of "command" and "freedom," "obedience" and "argument" that is rooted at the poles in the dichotomy. Even so, his insight and intention to go beyond the dichotomy will be preserved.

Third, connecting covenant and creation together is a brilliant observation and Levenson is right in making it. However, the way in which Levenson frames the two components is not the only justifiable viewpoint. He assumes, even in the Genesis 1 account, that the waters, darkness, and *tohu-wabohu*-earth are symbols of chaos/evil. Thus, God's interaction with them is command and mastery. If notions of evil were eliminated from his interpretation, the relationship of God to the other in creation and covenant would change drastically. Also, if more attention were paid to the divine speech of "Let there be . . ." it could be interpreted as *call* and *response* instead of *command* and *obedience*. God's utterance becomes a positive proposition toward fullness, goodness, and beauty for the other instead of mastery, limitation, and subjugation.

---

this interpretation have been increasing in recent years by those who see God's justice as restorative; see Sharon Baker's "The Repetition of Reconciliation." The notion of evil as a lack is not universally accepted and has not been free of criticisms; see Torrance, "Contingency and Disorder," 87–92; also see Russell, "Entropy and Evil," 449–68.

166. See, e.g., Levenson, *Creation and the Persistence of Evil*, 12.

167. Ibid., 138.

God's speech becomes abundant gift for that which is addressed instead of a curse leading ultimately to God's own good.[168]

If anything Levenson does not make the connection between creation and covenant strong enough. He should have interpreted creation in light of both covenant and the "spiritual politics" of the biblical narratives. He observes that there is a similar politic at work in narratives, covenant, and cosmological texts. However, he does not speak about God's relationship with matter in cosmogony in the same ways he tries to nuance his treatment of God's interactions with Abraham, and later with Israel. Levenson speaks of creation more in terms of combat and establishing forcefully an order *against* the primeval chaos. The goal is heteronomy in regard to the primal chaos/evil. Levenson does not talk about *consent* of the chaos/evil—the dynamic at work in the related narrative and covenant texts. The fact that the waters, darkness, and desert-earth are called chaos/evil precludes such a notion. Because Israel's creation texts share the same dynamic as both narrative and covenant texts and because of the lack of human heteronomy before God in those non-creation texts, Levenson should have re-evaluated how he portrayed God's relationship with the primal substances in God's creative activity.

By identifying the stuff of Genesis 1:2 as symbols of chaos/evil, the way he described God's relationship with it was affected. This then pushed his view of the cosmology of the Pentateuch in a theological direction that the non-creation texts therein show us not to move. Regardless, Levenson's observations about the connection between narrative, covenantal, and cosmological texts in the Pentateuch and their themes are valuable and will be supported, even if his framing of the texts will not be.

Fourth, the work that Levenson has done linking the temple and cosmos is significant. The temple is a microcosm of the world—the world as it should be[169]—and the world is a macro-temple.[170] "Collectively, the function of these correspondences is to underscore the depiction of the

---

168. See Brown's suggestions for interpreting these divine speeches as more indirect, jussive commands, *Structure, Role, and Ideology*, 122, 225.

169. Levenson, *Creation and the Persistence of Evil*, 100.

170. If other ANE gods build a temple after creating, or one is built, and they rest in it (ibid., 107), what theological statement does the Priestly writer(s) make about God's abode/temple by saying that God created the heavens and earth (2:1) and God rested (2:2)? The absence of a reference to temple seems to be the exact type of statement Levenson makes: that the whole of creation is—or is to become—God's macrotemple.

sanctuary as a world, that is, an ordered, supportive, and obedient environment, and the depiction of the world as a sanctuary, that is, a place in which the reign of God is visible and unchallenged, and his holiness is palpable, unthreatened, and pervasive."[171] Even though a different framework for understanding God's creative activity and God's relationship to creation would change Levenson's language about temple and world, it is a significant connection, nevertheless, that Levenson offers.

William Brown has already done some of the work to place Levenson's connection between temple and cosmos in a non-mastery framework by focusing not only on the finished products as Levenson does, but by comparing the *processes* by which creation and tabernacle-construction are described.[172] Both processes have 1) a social hierarchy marked by collaboration, 2) respective roles for each group suitable to differing abilities, and 3) progressions free of resistance or opposition.[173] In fact, in Exodus, the response of the 'generous of heart'[174] is so great in bringing forth raw goods for the tabernacle that some had to be turned away. Levenson's work of connecting cosmos and temple has been invaluable and has led to helpful insights in connecting the *processes* by which they were established.

Fifth, Levenson's claims concerning the type of transformation/new creation that will take place at the eschaton are good.[175] Even so, his framing of history as a movement between the varying levels of divine mastery over the primordial, innate chaos/evil in the world, humans, and history is not necessary or desirable. Where chaos is manifest within

---

171. Ibid., 86. In Milgrom's work on the significance of animal sacrifice for the cleansing of the temple and altar from the impurity of inadvertent sin—not the purification of the sinner—he says: "The inadvertent offender needs forgiveness not because of his act per se—as indicated above, his act is forgiven because of the offender's inadvertence and remorse—but because of the consequence of his act. His inadvertence has contaminated the sanctuary, and it is his responsibility to purge it with a $ḥaṭṭā't$" (*Leviticus 1–16*, 256). Given Jacob Milgrom's work on sacrifice, Christ's spilt blood on the cross would take on a different, yet significant, cleansing function within the macrotemple, the world. Although, in an important theological point, God's people (also called God's temple) are given Christ's blood to ingest. The joining of Levenson's and Milgrom's scholarship on temple and sacrifice has far-reaching implications for how Christ's sacrificial death can be understood, as well as for the Eucharist.

172. Brown, *Structure, Role, and Ideology*, 212.

173. Cf. ibid., 213–14.

174. Ibid., 213.

175. See, e.g., ibid., 39ff.

creation, it will certainly be eradicated. However, the way "chaos" is defined makes all the difference in what that means. Levenson's hopes for the future are laudable, but they will be given a different meaning as a new framework is proposed and the terms are redefined.

Conclusion

Levenson's position represents one side of the discussion within biblical studies. This side has a long history, and its perspectives continue to be repeated often. Even so, there are good reasons to employ caution before adopting this view of ANE thinking about creation. In the following chapter the other side of the discussion will be presented by examining the work of David T. Tsumura. In addition, an interpretation of Genesis 1 will be proposed.

4

The Growing Debate around "Chaos" Language in Biblical Studies

David T. Tsumura's Position

DAVID T. TSUMURA NOT ONLY TAKES A DIFFERENT POSITION THAN JON D. Levenson in interpreting Genesis 1, the character of their writing reflects their methods. Levenson's writing is much more colorful and dramatic than Tsumura's technical, yet still engaging, writing.

In this chapter Tsumura's side of the conversation and an analysis of his position will be offered. The intent in engaging Tsumura's work is to show that it is not only possible to give an account of creation in Genesis 1 without reference to chaos, but that it provides a way to a more plausible and richer reading of the Priestly teachings. Following an exploration of Tsumura's interpretation of Genesis 1, the interpretation being utilized in this project will be offered.

The Questions Tsumura Seeks to Answer in *Creation and Destruction*[1]

There are many assertions about links between the Genesis 1 account and other ANE traditions. Tsumura in his work seeks to weigh the claims concerning connections between various ANE traditions within surviving texts based on detailed examination of the texts in question. Specifically he

---

1. Hereafter, *Creation and Destruction*.

wants to examine the notions of preexisting chaos that have been associated with Genesis 1.

Tsumura is greatly concerned with methodology. He, with others before him, believes "a synchronic and structural study should have priority over a diachronic and comparative one."[2] Many errors in comparative studies are made because texts and the images in them are not understood properly. There are also many erroneous links being perpetuated based upon faulty etymology.[3] Thus, in this revision and expansion of his 1989 book[4] he investigates not only Genesis 1 and 2, but also "the functions of 'waters' and 'flood' in biblical poetry" as well as whether "the so-called chaos dragons such as Leviathan, Rahab, and Yam have anything to do with the creation motif in the biblical tradition."[5]

Distinguishing Tsumura's Methodology from Those Whom He Critiques

Tsumura's Synchronic Approach

In Tsumura's methodology the first question to ask about a text is its genre and purpose. Not enough attention has been given to the contrasts between the nature and function of the literature in the various ANE cultures. For example, "Ugaritic has no prophetic poetry, no psalmody, no extensive examples of literary narrative prose."[6] It has very different genres than the Bible. Thus, in making comparisons across cultures, there has

---

2. Tsumura, *Creation and Destruction*, 4. See Kitchen, *The Ancient Orient and Old Testament*, 87–88; see also Richard S. Hess's outlining of the development of methods and his suggestions for methodology in his essay "One Hundred Fifty Years," n. 63. Similar to Tsumura, in Rebecca Watson's view it is a problematic methodology to first go to outside sources to interpret Scripture (*Chaos Uncreated*, 3n7).

3. Tsumura, *Creation and Destruction*, 4.

4. Tsumura, *The Earth and the Waters in Genesis 1 and 2*.

5. Tsumura, *Creation and Destruction*, 4–5.

6. Ibid., 146. Cf. Craigie, "Ugarit and the Bible," 107.

been a tendency to "biblicize" other ANE documents and interpret biblical documents mythologically.[7]

In determining the meaning of terms or images in these various texts, literary context is of greatest import.[8] The structure of the text shows the relationship of the terms in the text or literary devices at play: i.e., merism, hyponym, antonym, synonym, simile, metaphor, etc. Seeing the terms' relationships to others in the text often indicates the nuances of a term being highlighted. By noting these nuances as well as noting trends in specific word pairings across texts it enables one to see that certain terms and pairings are often reserved for specific applications within cultures.[9]

One brief example of looking at structure is Tsumura's look at Psalm 46 where the presence of a fight between God and the sea has been proposed.[10] The structure shows, however, that there is a comparison in the psalm between the destructive capacities of the sea against the mountains or earth (vv. 2–3), and the destruction God can bring on the

---

7. Ibid. There has also been the tendency to harmonize the differing purposes for the combat motifs in the Ugaritic and Babylonian traditions even though the nature of the conquest in each is different. On the one hand, Baal was establishing his kingship among the gods. On the other hand, Marduk was already enthroned among the gods and was sent to deal with the agitated Tiamat (Tsumura, *Creation and Destruction*, 151). I have mentioned, nevertheless, that the superiority of the gods as a whole to the primordial stuff had not been established in the politics of the narrative at the point when Marduk engages Tiamat. For this reason there is some parallel between the function of the combat in the two traditions; Tiamat is simply not part of the pantheon of gods, even though Marduk needs to establish his superiority over her.

8. See, e.g., Tsumura, *Creation and Destruction*, 151.

9. E.g., as will be shown later, certain terms for water are used in reference to certain parts of the world in both Israel's writings and those of its neighbors. Also, depending on the context, whether a bipartite cosmos (heaven-earth) or tripartite cosmos (heaven-earth-under the earth) is being described, different terms will be used consistently for the various parts. There are also contexts in which the three levels of earth (i.e., everything under the heavens) are being mentioned: the human abode, waters beneath, the underworld. Careful attention to the cosmography used in a text and the terms used in reference to its parts is crucial, or mistakes can be made in comparing the texts of a single culture—let alone in comparing across cultures.

10. This link has been made since Gunkel's influential work. It can be seen in the work of scholars such as Mowinckel, Weiser, Neve, and Day. Their positions can be contrasted with those of Saggs and McCarthy (Tsumura, *Creation and Destruction*, 156).

nations or earth in judgment (v. 6). The psalm never places God and the seas in tension with one another.[11]

Last, Tsumura questions the logic and accuracy of some of the prior etymological connections made between Israel's terms and those in the myths of its neighbors, especially divine names in the myths. The logic had once been that a Hebrew term such as *tehom* in Genesis 1:2 was derived from Tiamat;[12] therefore, the presence of *tehom* shows that *Enuma elish* is a source for Genesis 1, and *tehom* should be interpreted mythically as a symbol for the notion of chaos, even if it is much more toned down than was once represented by Tiamat. However, more recent etymological analysis shows that it "is almost impossible to conclude that Akkadian *Tiamat* was borrowed by Hebrew as *tĕhôm*."[13] Looking at the trend in Mesopotamia and Canaan to take common nouns and *later* make them into divine names in limited mythological settings, it is more likely the seeming similarity between *tehom* and Tiamat is a shared Semitic root *thm*.[14] A simpler, logical explanation for *tehom* is that Israel never deified its word from the root *thm* as its neighbors did their words in select contexts.

Tsumura's View of Gunkel's Legacy of Diachronic and Typological Methods

Given the technical nature of Tsumura's methodology, he is critical of diachronic methodologies that draw upon typology and allusions between texts. Much of what he does is to clear away the conclusions of those types of studies by analyzing the method by which they were reached, critiquing the logic of the arguments, and dissolving the evidence through careful study of the texts in question. Tsumura denies that there is any evidence "that the entire myth of ancient Canaan was

---

11. Ibid., 160. See his ch. 9 for the full treatment of Psalm 46.

12. Ibid., 36. This was Gunkel's suggestion.

13. Ibid., 37. William Brown has a similar position (*Structure, Role, and Ideology*, 103n15); cf. Westermann, *Genesis 1–11*, 104.

14. In Tsumura's words, "It should be pointed out that the Akkadian term *ti'āmtum* > *tâmtum* normally means 'sea' or 'ocean' in an ordinary sense and is sometimes *personified* as a divine being in mythological contexts. Therefore, the fact that *tĕhôm* is etymologically related to Tiamat as a cognate should not be taken as evidence for the mythological dependence of the former on the latter" (Tsumura, *Creation and Destruction*, 38); see 43–53 for a detailed treatment of the various Semitic languages.

transferred to the Bible by means of so-called historicization. It is virtually only in the poetic texts that the 'similar' materials appear, and they usually constitute just a group of words or phrases, never sentences or discourses."[15] His synchronic approach shows that similarity of phrases does not mean similarity of subject matter across texts with different genres or purposes, and from different cultural perspectives. Showing the "similarity or the 'fact' of sameness in form" between ANE texts shows only that;[16] the hard work of synchronic investigation still needs to be done before comparing and contrasting terms, images, and ideas between the texts. Comparing forms has not been distinguished enough from a synchronic approach.[17]

The Contrasts in Observations of ANE Traditions Based on These Methodologies

Against the backdrop of the picture that has been typically painted about ANE mythology and the Bible's relationship to it, Tsumura offers evidence for a drastically different account. First, there is more than one combat myth in the ANE. In some—for example, in the Baal myths—neither the creation nor arranging of the cosmos is ever associated with the myth, only the cosmos's maintenance.[18] In fact, in the Baal myths the creator god El is not even involved in the combat.[19] Scholarship suggests that if there was an early combat myth, it started along the Mediterranean or to the North.[20] *Enuma elish* is a later tradition in which a conflict between a storm-god and the sea is woven into a story of the creation of the cosmos;[21] "a combination of these two themes appears only in *Enuma*

---

15. Ibid., 149. Although this quotation is specifically about Canaanite texts, he also takes issue with comparisons between Babylonian mythology and biblical texts throughout the work.

16. Ibid., 148.

17. Ibid., 149.

18. Ibid., 40, 145. There are even Mesopotamian combat myths that have nothing to do with creation (ibid., 145). H. W. F. Saggs concludes that "in Mesopotamian thought cosmic creation did not of necessity involve a divine combat" (Saggs, *The Encounter with the Divine in Mesopotamia and Israel*, 59; quoted in Tsumura, *Creation and Destruction*, 145).

19. Tsumura, *Creation and Destruction*, 41.

20. Ibid., 39.

21. Ibid., 41.

elish out of all the ancient Near Eastern literature discovered thus far."[22] Thus, these two mythical themes represent divergent traditions with different purposes in their cultures.

Second, there are several types of creation accounts in ANE literature. For example, within Mesopotamia, one tradition, only extant in *Enuma elish*, links the themes of combat and creation. A second tradition—for example, seen in *Creation of the world by Marduk*, from the Neo-Babylonian period—describes creation without either conflict or personified waters.[23] A third common tradition spoke of creation in terms of a birth from "Sky" (An) and "Earth" (Ki).[24] This is a tradition wherein the process of creation is clearly not establishing order out of chaos.[25] Thus, not all ANE (even Mesopotamian) creation traditions link combat with creation or speak of creation as the ordering of primal, chaotic stuff. The broader ANE context is far less homogenous than has been presented in some comparative studies.

Tsumura's Interpretation of Genesis 1:1—2:3

Tohu Wabohu

Even within the early centuries of Christian interpretation, the words *tohu* and *bohu* were understood as "formlessness."[26] This has been continued in many modern translations. These translations use, for example, "confusion," "unreality," "emptiness," or "nothingness."[27] Many modern scholars follow in the line of Albright, who suggested that the phrase *tohu wabohu* means something like "chaos" and the word *tohu* itself refers to

22. Ibid., 190.
23. Ibid., 40.
24. Ibid., 151.
25. A tradition of *bringing forth* is present in some Egyptian myths where the waters are not ordered; rather, a god comes forth out of the waters and creation as well is drawn out of them. In other Egyptian myths creation is the ejaculation of the creator god (see "Theology from Memphis" in Sproul, *Primal Myths*, 77, 79).
26. Ibid., 9. Tsumura notes that the interpretation of Gen 1:2 as "formlessness" appears in the writings of significant Christian figures. Even though Augustine was not referencing the Hebrew, in *Confessions* 12.22 he considers a starting point of formlessness. Arguably this early interpretation reflects more the Platonic philosophical surroundings and less any special insight into the Priestly worldview due to closer temporal proximity than we have today.
27. Ibid., 12.

"chaos as a watery deep, or *tehom*, in the Mesopotamian sense."[28] As was seen in Levenson's work, in cases where these terms in Genesis 1:2 are thought to symbolize chaos, chaos means "'disorder' or 'disorganization' and stands in direct opposition to 'creation.'"[29] In contrast, Tsumura argues that the sense of the words originally was more concrete.[30]

Tohu

Tohu is found twenty times in the OT—eleven of those instances being in Isaiah.[31] Westermann's three categories for *tohu*'s appearances have become a standard and Tsumura interacts with them. Westermann's three classifications are: 1) a desert, 2) a desert-like state, and 3) emptiness.[32] The first category of an actual desert is not controversial.[33] Tsumura agrees with Westermann. In instances such as Deuteronomy 32:10, *tohu* simply means desert. Ugaritic's *thw*, which is probably a cognate of Hebrew's *tohu*, also means "a desert."[34]

Tsumura first addresses the abstract third category saying that "a lack" or a nuanced notion of "emptiness" is closer than notions of "nothingness" for these references. It is important to note when trying to find *tohu*'s meaning in Genesis 1:2 that instances of *tohu* fitting in this third category are never in reference to earth or a city. If *tohu* in Genesis 1:2 is interpreted in terms of Westermann's "emptiness" or Tsumura's "lack" it would be the only place in Scripture where *tohu* has such a meaning where 'earth' is being described.

The second category—a desert-like state—is used to describe the condition of places like land, earth, or cities.[35] Westermann views references in this category as either a desert-state that is threatened against a people/place or as a reference to "the state that is opposed to and precedes creation."[36] One text where Westermann believes *tohu* is the

---

28. Ibid., quoting Albright.
29. Ibid., 13.
30. Ibid., 10.
31. Ibid., 22.
32. Westermann, *Genesis 1–11*, 102–3. See Tsumura, *Creation and Destruction*, 22.
33. Tsumura, *Creation and Destruction*, 23.
34. Ibid., 12.
35. Ibid., 23.
36. Ibid., 22.

opposite of creation is Job 26:7. However, Tsumura notes that *tohu* is in parallel with "a *place* where there is nothing" (emphasis added). Thus, a corresponding concrete translation of "a desert-like place" or "an empty place" better fits the context.[37] In Isaiah 45:18 Westermann again takes *tohu* as "chaos," the opposite of creation. In the structure of the verse, however, the first line is contrasted with the second. That would contrast *tohu* with "to be inhabited." Here again it is a desert-like or uninhabited place.[38] The translation is more appropriately: "He created it not to be a desert-like place; he formed it to be inhabited."[39]

Westermann's second grouping of occurrences is not necessarily wrong. It is more a matter that his comments and translations of the texts do not adhere strictly enough to the more concrete notions implied by the texts themselves and the category heading given them—"a desert-like place."[40]

Bohu

This word only appears three times in the Bible and it is always with *tohu*.[41] Its etymology is not certain, but it "seems to be a Semitic term based on the root *bhw*, possibly a cognate of Arabic *bahiya* 'to be empty.'"[42] The Arabic term is known to have the concrete meaning of a tent being *empty* rather than an abstract meaning like "nothingness" or "emptiness."

In *bohu*'s three uses it is parallel to *tohu* in Isaiah 34:11 and juxtaposed with *tohu* in Genesis 1:2 and Jeremiah 4:23.[43] The uses are only "in reference to 'earth' (Gen 1:2; Jer 4:23) or the 'land' of Edom (Is 34:11)."[44]

De Moor, when studying the Ugaritic phrase *tu-a-bi-[ú(?)]*, suggested it signifies "the state of chaos" in light of Akkadian *nabalkutu* and

---

37. Ibid., 25. Tsumura translates the verse: "He stretches out the high mountains over *an empty place*, he suspends the earth over a place where there is nothing" (*Creation and Destruction*, 25; emphasis added).

38. See similar terms in this type of construction in Jer 4:27; Isa 24:12 (Tsumura, *Creation and Destruction*, 25).

39. Ibid.

40. Ibid., 22.

41. Ibid., 13.

42. Ibid., 15.

43. Ibid.

44. Ibid., 18.

Hebrew *tohu wabohu*.⁴⁵ Tsumura follows the possibility of a link between these words by looking at instances when Akkadian *nabalkutu* appears in reference to earth, as *tohu wabohu* is used in the Bible. There are only a few such instances in versions of the *Atra-Hasis Epic* and *The Ritual of Kalû*. In all of these instances, which point toward a development of an idiomatic meaning in Akkadian, they speak of the Earth's womb or the earth itself being "out of order," "not bearing," or being "unproductive."⁴⁶ Just as with a human womb that has no children when it is barren or unproductive, the earth (or its womb) is said to be 'out of order' when there is a state of "no vegetables, no cereals."⁴⁷ Tsumura concludes that this use of *nabalkutu* "has nothing to do with 'the state of chaos.'"⁴⁸ If the Ugaritic phrase and Akkadian idiom are compared, as de Moor proposes they should be, their uses in reference to earth undermine claims about being references to chaos. This undermines the claim for reading *tohu wabohu* as chaos in light of them. Tsumura also questions the linking of *tu-a-bi-[ú(?)]* with *tohu wabohu* due to the possibility that the damaged symbols on the Ugaritic tablet are being misread, and thus the Ugaritic in that context may not have any correlation to *tohu wabohu*.⁴⁹

Tohu Wabohu

The view that Jeremiah 4:23–26 depicts a return to primeval chaos is strongly influenced by reading *tohu wabohu* in Genesis 1:2 as chaos; it is "not based on contextual analysis of Jeremiah 4:23ff. itself."⁵⁰ The two texts at least both describe the "earth" with the phrase *tohu wabohu*, although overall the components of the earth are listed in different orders and different terms/components are listed in the two texts. They also have different subject matter; "in the Genesis passage it is 'earth' // *tĕhôm* that is described; in Jeremiah, 'earth' // 'heavens.'"⁵¹ In Jeremiah the two parts, earth and heavens, represent the whole which is the topic of concern. In

---

45. Ibid.
46. See Tsumura's full treatment, *Creation and Destruction*, 19–21.
47. Ibid., 19.
48. Ibid., 22.
49. Ibid.
50. Ibid., 28.
51. Ibid., 30.

Genesis, *tehom* is part of "earth" and completely covers the earth/land—much like the floodwaters covering the land in Genesis 6–9.[52]

In Jeremiah 4:23–28, the words "earth" and "heavens" appear in v. 23 and v. 28 forming a frame for the section; the descriptions of the heavens and the earth in the two verses correspond to each other.[53] The passage says in v. 23 "(the earth) *tōhû wā bōhû*" // "(the heavens) are without light" and in v. 28 "(the earth) will dry up" // "(the heavens) will be dark."[54] *Tohu wabohu* corresponds with "will dry up" just as "are without light" corresponds with "will be dark." This means *tohu wabohu* in v. 23 means something like "aridness or unproductiveness," a consistent picture with v. 27: "the whole earth will become a desolation."[55] The threat in Jeremiah 4:23–28 is thus destruction due to a lack of water.

Isaiah 34:11 places *tohu* and *bohu* in parallel. The NASB translates the verse:

> And He shall stretch over it the line of desolation
> And the plumb line of emptiness.[56]

In connecting the vocabulary of this verse with Genesis 1:2, some have said the land is reduced to chaos. However, Tsumura sides with Wildberger when Wildberger claims this verse simply speaks of the land becoming desolate and a waste so that it cannot support inhabitants.

Given Tsumura's examination of *tohu* appearances and concluding that there are three types of uses that are similar to Westermann's analysis—desert, desert-like/desolate/empty place, or emptiness—and given that the uses of *tohu* with *bohu* in Jeremiah 4:23 and Isaiah 34:11 remain consistent with the second category of *tohu*, "it would be very reasonable to understand the phrase *tōhû wābōhû* in Gen 1:2 as also describing a state of 'desolation and emptiness,' though the context suggests that this was the initial state of the created earth rather than a state brought about as a result of God's judgment on the earth or land (cf. Jer 4:23, Isa 34:11)."[57] In other words, "*tōhû wābōhû* signifies the earth in a 'bare'

---

52. Tsumura concludes that these two texts could not have been patterned after each other with so many differences on so many levels (ibid.).
53. Ibid., 31.
54. Ibid.
55. Ibid.
56. Ibid., 32.
57. Ibid., 33.

state, without vegetation and animals as well as without man . . . the earth as being 'not yet' normal."[58]

Tsumura believes his literal translation of these words for the condition of the "earth" as "desert-like and empty" or "desolate and uninhabited" fits the literary structure of the entire chapter. A discourse analysis of Genesis 1:1–3 shows that vv. 1–2 are the setting for the event that begins in v. 3.[59] Verse 1 is a summary statement of the whole—using the merism "heavens and earth"—and v. 2 focuses on the "earth." The author uses in v. 2 a grammatically positive statement—*tohu wabohu*—instead of negations like in 2:5–6 ("no shrub . . . no plant . . . no rain . . . no man"[60]).

In looking further at the literary structure, the climax days, days three and six on which vegetation, animals, and humans are created, are fitting for a *tohu wabohu* "earth." In Tsumura's words, "the 'not-yet-productive' earth becomes productive when God says, . . . 'let the land produce vegetation' (v. 11) on the third day and . . . 'let the land produce living creatures' (v. 24) on the sixth day. Then, the 'not-yet-inhabited' earth becomes inhabited when God says, . . . 'let us make man as our image, in our likeness' (v. 26)."[61] Tsumura calls these three creative events "God's fiats."[62]

Regarding the issue of whether v. 2 tells us about the pre-existence of the stuff mentioned in it, Tsumura gives a short treatment. He says the narrator's concern was not one of ontology. The text does not say that the earth and water had pre-existed, that there existed an earth in this state, or that there was *nothing* there. "Rather, he simply provides the audience with the preparatory information that the 'earth' was *not yet normal*—that is, 'not yet' the earth as it was known to them."[63] In other

---

58. Ibid. Watson suggests that the Bible is silent about the "what" from which the universe was formed (*Chaos Uncreated*, 18n30). She concurs with Tsumura that the language in Genesis 1 is equivalent to "wilderness," "uninhabited," "desolation following judgment," or "empty" (16).

59. Tsumura, *Creation and Destruction*, 33.

60. Ibid., 34.

61. Ibid. Tsumura could also have noted that the many kinds of vegetation, land animals, and swarms of fish and birds are in stark contrast to a barren desolation (vv. 11, 20, 24). God's blessings to be fruitful and multiply and to fill the earth (vv. 22, 28) are also an important addition to the conditions of v. 2.

62. See below a critique of Tsumura's position on divine fiat.

63. Ibid., 35.

words, Tsumura stops at saying it is a scene of 'not yet' instead of saying it is either a scene of 'not yet there' or a scene of always there. It is a scene of "universal readiness," with "God's spirit hovering in anticipation."[64]

Tehom and Other Terms for Waters

Since Gunkel suggested that *tehom* derived directly from Tiamat, many scholars have assumed some type of direct or indirect connection.[65] Etymological studies since then have shown that it "is almost impossible to conclude that Akkadian *Tiamat* was borrowed by Hebrew as *těhôm*."[66] This has not deterred some scholars from still claiming that there is at

64. Ibid.

65. Ibid., 36. For several decades "some Assyriologists have been questioning the alleged connection between Gen 1 and *Enuma elish*" (ibid., 38)—e.g., J. V. K. Wilson, A. W. Sjoberg, W. G. Lambert, T. Jacobsen, etc. (ibid., 38–39nn15–19). Hess outlines the split between Assyriology and biblical studies following World War I. For instance, Landsberger in 1926 stated that studies are not supporting the assumption "of an originally common Semitic world view for East and West Semitic" that underlay comparative studies (Hess, "One Hundred Fifty Years," 9); the strong distinctions between Akkadian and Hebrew were losing all color and shape in the superficial comparisons that had been practiced (10). "Henceforth greater restraint would be exercised in making parallels, and although many would not observe the cautions set forth by these and other scholars, the optimistic use of ancient Near Eastern materials to fill 'gaps' in the biblical texts and virtually to reinterpret them would no longer find acceptance in either field" (10). Biblical scholars are the ones who "continued to stress shared features" (Hess, "One Hundred Fifty Years," 10). Some of the reasons given specifically against relating *Enuma elish* and Genesis 1 are that the idea of a battle between a storm god and the sea originated either on the Mediterranean coast or in northern Mesopotamia. This myth was later incorporated within the creation account of *Enuma elish*, a connection not made in any other extant work. In fact, it was probably a relatively late incorporation made "during the reign of Nebuchadnezzar I (1124–1103 BCE . . .)" (Alster, "Tiamat," 1636). Nevertheless, several other more common creation frameworks (even within Mesopotamia) do not have any combat and do not personify the waters. For those interested in tracking a progression in notions of creation in the ANE, "there is no reason to assume that the older stage without the conflict-creation connection necessarily developed to a stage with this connection," even in texts subsequent to *Enuma elish* (Tsumura, *Creation and Destruction*, 40). The extant texts do not show the connection being made anywhere outside of *Enuma elish*. In an excursus Tsumura also examines the possibility of a connection between Genesis 1:2 and a "Canaanite" dragon myth, that itself was not connected to creation. He concludes that such a myth was not behind Genesis 1:2. Since neither a Canaanite nor a Babylonian combat myth can be shown to be behind Genesis 1:2, Tsumura concludes that "there is no relation between the Genesis account and the so-called *Chaoskampf* mythology" (56–57).

66. Ibid., 37. Morphologically, the Hebrew term corresponds to the Ugaritic *thm* (Tsumura, *Creation and Destruction*, 42).

least a "mythological" connection between the terms.⁶⁷ A distinction between two words having a common Semitic root (*thm) and one word coming from the other has not been kept. Akkadian's common noun *ti'āmtum > tâmtum* ("sea," "ocean") from which the divine name Tiamat was formed, also came from this shared Semitic root. Hebrew's *tehom* should not be assumed to be a depersonification of an Akkadian divine name since there is a shared Semitic root that lies behind both languages.⁶⁸ Furthermore, even the common nouns in Ugaritic, Akkadian, and Eblaite appear in some mythological texts without personification, with the ordinary meaning of "sea" or "ocean." These cultures had the grammatical means to distinguish between the ordinary, nonpersonified thing and the deity.⁶⁹ The missing definite article with *tehom* in Genesis 1:2 is only one instance among several in the chapter where the definite article is missing with a common noun.⁷⁰ Given the abundance of counter evidence, its absence "has nothing to do with personification or depersonalization of the original term."⁷¹ *Tehom* is a Hebrew common noun from the Semitic root *thm* and is not a *de*-personified or *de*-mythologized loanword.

Common nouns based on the root *thm* appear in West Semitic languages, but it is the term *ym* or *yam* that typically is used to denote the sea in these languages. Even so, it often depends on what type of cosmography that is being used for which term will be employed. In Hebrew, if a three-part universe is being discussed—heaven/earth/sea—*tehom* is never used; it is *yam* that is the third part, the sea.⁷² Hebrew *yam*, then, was used in circumstances that correspond to the Akkadian *apsu* and *tiamtum, tamtum*, even though the correspondence is not exact between the Hebrew heaven/earth/*yam* tripartite division and the

---

67. Ibid.
68. Ibid., 43; see 47.
69. Ibid., 47–48.
70. Ibid., 48–49.
71. Ibid., 49.
72. Ibid., 50; see 63–64. Cf. Gen 1:26, 28; 9:2; Ps 8:8–9; Ezek 38:20; Hos 4:3. Since each of the three parts is distinct in this three-tiered structure and together constitute the whole, it is *yam* that is used in contrast to *ereṣ* (earth) in Gen 1:10. The *hammayim* (waters) over which the Spirit of God broods at the end of Gen 1:2 also never appear in a tripartite division (Tsumura, *Creation and Destruction*, 69). Genesis 1 is consistent with other Hebrew cosmographies in the appropriate employment of terms for the waters.

Babylonian heaven/earth/*Apsu* division.⁷³ "On the other hand, in the relationship with the term '*ereṣ* 'earth,' Hebrew *tĕhôm(ôt)* is hyponymous (Ps 71:20, 148:7; Prov 3:19–20; Gen 1:2) and, hence, what *tĕhôm(ôt)* refers to is included in what '*ereṣ* refers to—that is, the *tĕhôm*-water is part of the earth."⁷⁴ If a three-part earth is described—or as the Babylonians had the three earths: the abode of humans, Apsu, and the underworld—*tehom(ot)* is the term used for the subterranean waters that corresponds to the Babylonian Apsu.⁷⁵ In Ugaritic, their terms *thm(t)* and *ym* function very similarly to their Hebrew cognates.⁷⁶ In sum, "tehom" in its uses in the various Hebrew cosmographies never parallels the place of "Tiamat" and its cognates in Akkadian cosmographies.

If there is a bipartite division of the cosmos—heaven(s) and earth—*eres* "earth" is everything under heaven, including the sea.⁷⁷ Thus, if a bipartite division is being used in a Hebrew text, *tehom(ot)* is a part of the *eres*, the everything-under-heaven. Since Genesis 1 opens with a bipartite division of the cosmos, since elsewhere *tehom(ot)* is hyponymous with *eres* in bipartite cosmographies, and since *tehom(ot)* is never used elsewhere in tripartite descriptions of the cosmos, *tehom* is best understood in Genesis 1:2 as being part of the "earth."⁷⁸ The earth and its *tehom* are described as *tohu wabohu* and *hosek*: "not yet productive and inhabitable and without light."⁷⁹

In this picture within v. 2, "the water (*hammāyim*) of *tĕhôm* seemingly covered all the 'earth' like the Deluge, as vv. 6ff. suggest."⁸⁰ Since,

73. Ibid., 65.
74. Ibid., 50.
75. Ibid.; cf. 65.
76. Ibid., 51. Tsumura concludes: "In other words, the Akkadian *tiāmtum, tâmtum* probably has a much wider semantic field than its West Semitic cognate terms, Hebrew *tĕhôm(ôt)* and Ugaritic *thm(t)*, which became hyponymous to '*ereṣ/arṣ* as noted above. Thus Hebrew *tĕhôm* semantically corresponds more closely to *apsû* than to *tiāmtum*, though it corresponds morphologically to the latter" (Tsumura, *Creation and Destruction*, 53).
77. Ibid., 66. E.g., see Ps 148:1, 7.
78. Ibid., 69.
79. Ibid. The first two descriptions certainly make sense. It is curious that Tsumura trades the notion of darkness being over the face of the deep for the earth being "without light." The latter notion sounds more Greek—darkness being a lack of light—than the idea of the text, especially with the comment in v. 4 that God separated the light and the darkness.
80. Ibid., 70.

"earth" in this verse is everything under the heavens, "land" is not being placed "in opposition to the seas (*yammîm*; see v. 10)."[81] Rather, the situation is viewed from above, similar to Psalm 104:6—"You covered it with the deep as with a garment; the waters stood above the mountains."[82] The topmost/visible part of the earth of Genesis 1:2 is the covering of *tehom*-waters, darkness, and the Spirit.

"[The] dry land was 'not yet' formed (*or* seen) until v. 9, where God said: 'Let the waters from under the heaven be gathered to one place and let the dry land appear.' Unlike the cosmology in *Enuma elish* and other ancient myths, the land in Gen 1:9–10 was not a product of the primeval water, hence a part of the water; it was a product of divine fiat by which God gathered the waters from under the heaven 'to one place,' that is, as 'seas,' which are a part of the earth.[83]

It is relatively common for the conditions brought about by the Flood to be compared with Genesis 1:2. Claims have been made about the flood waters being linked with chaos or chaotic forces. The Hebrew term *mabbul* (flood) appears thirteen times in Scripture: twelve in Genesis 6—11 and once in Psalm 29:10 where God sits enthroned over the flood.[84] Tsumura refers to P. C. Craigie's belief that the Psalm reference symbolized God's subjugation of chaotic forces, just as Baal was enthroned over the conquered flood.[85] However, the Ugaritic term *mdb* "flood" is never used to describe Baal's enemy, Yam/Nahar. The term *mdb* does not refer to a conquered foe in any extant Ugaritic mythology.[86] Also, Baal never sat enthroned over his conquered enemy, the sea-dragon Yam.[87] Likewise in Hebrew *mabbul* does not refer to a conquered

---

81. Ibid.
82. Ibid. Tsumura is quoting the NIV here.
83. Ibid., 74.
84. Ibid., 154n67.
85. Ibid., 153.
86. Ibid., 154. In one place it does describe the sexual power of El; it is "like a flood" (ibid.).
87. Ibid. This means Craigie's statement about Baal being enthroned over the "flood" is false on two points and, thus, is misleading.

foe. It "always refers to the 'Deluge.'"[88] The Deluge was the mighty power used by YHWH to totally destroy the world.

In the Mesopotamian traditions, Marduk never sits enthroned over Tiamat.[89] However, Marduk does use *abūbu* "the Deluge" as a weapon when attacking Tiamat.[90] Thus, the Deluge in Hebrew and Akkadian is not a chaos-enemy. It is a divine instrument. Several ANE gods such as Adad, Nergal, Asshur, and Marduk are said to be the "holder of the lightning, lord of the Deluge."[91] In Psalm 29 God's voice is compared with lightning seven times in vv. 3–9. In v. 10 God is enthroned from "before the Deluge," eternally.[92] If there is a connection in thought and/or imagery between Genesis 1:2 and the Flood narrative, the scriptural and possible ANE background behind the use of *mabbul* undermines thinking of the covering waters as a symbol of chaos, or God's once-upon-a-time adversary. The floodwaters are a divine instrument in Genesis 6–9 as they were in other ANE cultures.

Ruach and Elohim

Tsumura does not treat the *ruach elohim* in great detail. Earlier it was mentioned that Tsumura treats Genesis 1:2 as a scene of "universal" readiness, with "God's spirit hovering in anticipation."[93] He cites William Brown's analysis of the debate on whether to translate *ruach elohim* as "the wind of God" or "the spirit of God."[94] Those who choose "the wind of God" often do so because they view *ruach* as the final description of chaos in v. 2. Those favoring "spirit" see 1:2c as a reference to "divine creative potency."[95] Tsumura, with Brown, favors the evidence for "spirit." "Contextually, *'ĕlōhîm* of *rûaḥ ĕlōhîm* (2c) refers to God, who created the

---

88. Ibid.

89. Ibid. Ea does establish his abode over Apsu, but Apsu is the subterranean water in *Enuma elish* and not a Deluge.

90. Ibid.; see *Enuma elish* IV.49.

91. Ibid., 155.

92. Tsumura takes the phrase temporally instead of locatively (ibid.).

93. Ibid., 35. This general notion of readiness and anticipation is related, yet is in contrast to the pneumatology of Lyle Dabney that will be used later in which the Spirit specifically *is* the Possibility of God for creation.

94. Cf. Brown, *Structure, Role, and Ideology*, 75–77.

95. Brown, *Structure, Role, and Ideology*, 75; Tsumura, *Creation and Destruction*, 74.

universe ("the heavens and the earth" as merismus) in v. 1. In v. 2c he is about to get involved positively in the universe as *rûaḥ*."[96]

God's creative action was accomplished by his speech in v. 3, according to Tsumura. Verse 2c "seems to describe a situation in which God's words were not yet uttered; in other words, God's breath was not articulated as a voice to pronounce his creative word but was ready to get involved in such creative actions."[97]

This "breath of God" is not without a creative function. In other biblical texts, there is a close relationship between God's breath and God's creative action: Ezekiel 37:1–14; Psalms 104:30; 33:6; Genesis 2:7.[98] God's breath is said to either create (Pss 33:6; 104:30) or animate (Ezek 37:14; Gen 2:7). In Genesis 1:2 God's breath is "ready to become engaged in his creative action."[99] It happened in v. 3 when God uttered his word.

Critique

The most significant critique of Tsumura concerning his interpretation of the text is his insistence on creation being by *divine fiat* within the Priestly creation account.[100] His claim is that God alone acts; there is no other *actively* involved. The creation itself is passive. He cites the work of William Brown concerning *ruach elohim* but does not interact with Brown's study of the MT, LXX, and VorLXX. Even if Tsumura uses only the MT and not earlier available texts, he still cannot avoid dealing with God's speeches being addressed to water and earth. In v. 11 God says, "Let the earth cause wild vegetation to sprout."[101] The report in v. 12 states, "the earth brought forth wild vegetation." Even though the MT minimizes the waters' creative role, it still contains remnants of the older tradition. In v. 20 God says, "Let the waters produce . . ."[102] Verse 21 reports: "So God created the great sea monsters and every living creature that moves, *of which the waters produced* swarms, according to their

---

96. Tsumura, *Creation and Destruction*, 75.
97. Ibid.
98. Ibid., 76.
99. Ibid.
100. See, e.g., ibid., 33n126; 34; 34, n132; 74.
101. Brown, *Structure, Role, and Ideology*, 60.
102. Ibid., 61.

kinds..."¹⁰³ The LXX and the VorLXX are even more explicit in making these claims about the activity of the earth and waters.

Tsumura shows that in v. 2 the "earth," everything under heaven, is nonproductive and empty. However, the text moves beyond this initial not-yet-familiar, "passive" stage; it lasts only until v. 9.¹⁰⁴ "In short, both 'land' and 'water' are transformed from passive to active participants in the creative process when they are conferred their respective names in v 10."¹⁰⁵ Earth and its waters are brought beyond that initial infancy to be active participants according to what suits them in the cosmic community. Through the process of God's early ministrations, the lack in v. 2 was reconciled; they are brought into producing, filled entities.

Related to this critique is the way Tsumura finished his analysis of De Moor's connecting of the Ugaritic phrase *tu-a-bi-[ú(?)]*, Akkadian *nabalkutu*, and Hebrew *tohu wabohu*. Tsumura finds that *nabalkutu* and *tu-a-bi-[ú(?)]* are used similarly when used in reference to "earth." In the oldest Akkadian text there was a reference to the "earth's womb" being "unproductive/not bearing/out of order." Later in Akkadian, when "womb" was no longer included, it meant an "out of order" earth that had no plants or cereals. Even though Tsumura believes, based on the other occurrences of *tohu* and *bohu* in Scripture, that they mean something like arid/unproductive and empty/uninhabited, he tries to distance the Hebrew phrase from any connection to the Ugaritic *tu-a-bi-[ú(?)]* by citing Lambert and Huehnergard on whether *tu-a-pí-[ku]* and not *tu-a-bi-[ú(?)]* is the word to be read in the damaged Ugaritic. Given, however, the generative roles of the waters and earth later in the Priestly account, the possible notion of the earth "not bearing" or being "barren" makes a great deal of sense. Even if a morphological connection is uncertain or questionable, there seems to be resonance between the ways these phrases functioned respectively in these cultures.

Tsumura works to sever any ANE connections whereby biblical creation can be interpreted in such a way that it is not completely by God's operation/fiat.¹⁰⁶ He wants *tohu* and *bohu* to be adjectives about

103. Ibid.; italics added. Translations that say "to swarm with" or "teem with" erase "the transitive force of the Hebrew verb. There is no evidence that the Hebrew verb functions in any fashion similar to the typical English translations" (Brown, *Structure, Role, and Ideology*, 106n25). The force of the verb is that the waters "bring forth."

104. Ibid., 45.

105. Ibid.

106. He rejects in a footnote B. Otzen's suggestion that the background of Genesis

ongoingly inanimate matter. He does not want to consider the possibility that in ANE worldviews, including that of Israel, they encountered their world as an *other*, not inert stuff.[107] Tsumura chooses not to speak of God's creative activity through/by the Spirit and Word being the possibility for an abundantly *productive* earth/creation. The theological framework that will be developed in chapter 6 will try to move beyond the zero-sum spectrum between divine fiat alone and the conflict of dualism in which theology of creation for so long has been placed, and in which Tsumura operates.

Tsumura's Laudable Ideas

Given the precision with which Tsumura investigates texts, his work as a whole is of great value. He does not assume as fact many of the claims made by those employing diachronic and typological methods, but rather weighs them against the available data. In so doing, he clears the way for a new picture of ANE cosmologies.

The connection between violence and creation is far less widespread than had once been thought; in the extant texts it is limited to *Enuma elish* alone. Cosmologies in which the primal waters are not personified are common. Also, cosmologies in which the primal waters are generative or

---

1:11–12 is a mythological idea of an Earth Mother who gives birth to the products of the soil; this in itself is not a highly controversial position. Additionally, he rejects this because no ancient myth says that both plants and animals are the products of the earth; and, second, the existence of these things in Genesis 1 is by divine fiat and not by a Mother Earth (Tsumura, *Creation and Destruction*, 34n132). Otzen's position can be found in "The Use of Myth in Genesis," 39. Where Levenson takes the side of dualism in his doctrine of creation, making God's activity an intrusion upon or addition to the raw chaos-stuff, Tsumura takes the opposite approach. He does not speak of any actor other than God. Even though he avoids the question of ontology/genesis because he believes it is not a question the text seeks to answer, his repeated use of "divine fiat" through his work is consistent with a *creatio ex nihilo* position. I would claim that neither zero-sum position can do justice to the fullness of the dynamic within the text. Cf. Michael Welker's article, "What Is Creation?" 63–71, as an attempt to look with fresh eyes at the theology of Genesis 1.

107. Frankfort and Frankfort, "Myth and Reality," 4ff. In Brague's analysis, the ancients did not have an overarching word such as *world* or *cosmos* (*The Wisdom of the World*, 11); instead, parts are named—e.g., "heavens and the earth." Nevertheless, what was there Brague does not call a "thou"; rather he says "it unfolds before a subject" (13). Even more, the ancients did not look at their surroundings (i.e., *cosmos*) as the Greeks did in order to learn of its inherent wisdom and imitate it; rather, it is wisdom that produces the world as such (16).

creation takes place by way of procreation between two entities are more commonplace. There were many different cosmologies within the ANE. As the work of H. and H. A. Frankfort shows, some cultures simultaneously held contradictory accounts because each account was for a different purpose; they were specialized to answer different questions.[108]

Tsumura shows that the connection between Israel's cosmologies, especially Genesis 1, and *Enuma elish*, or Ugaritic combat myths (that are not about creation), should not be made.[109] Eliminating the prior presupposition of a combat influence and reading the biblical texts synchronically undermines previously held notions of combat within them. The voices of the biblical texts themselves undermine frameworks such as Levenson's built on the idea of combat and mastery. God is shown not to be fundamentally at odds with creation or any part(s) therein.[110]

Tsumura shows that interpreting *tohu* and *bohu* in Genesis 1:2 in a manner consistent with their other occurrences in the Bible is itself consistent with the direction the rest of Genesis 1 takes.[111] The climactic days are fitting for a world unproductive and uninhabited.

If Genesis 1:2 is a chaos that must be ordered and mastered, as Levenson suggests, that ordering of chaos only stands as a backdrop or

---

108. Frankfort and Frankfort, "Myth and Reality," 19–20. This is another reason to use caution in making typological comparisons between texts.

109. Brown shows that the use of water(s) in the Priestly account more closely mirrors Sumerian, Akkadian, and Egyptian traditions in which the waters are viewed as a positive, generative, and sometimes passive entity (*Structure, Role, and Ideology*, 184).

110. See Watson, *Chaos Uncreated*, 369–76.

111. It is alarming how many scholars agree that *tohu* and *bohu* have something to do with "desert" and "empty" but go on to talk about chaos anyway. E.g., Hahn agrees that *tohu* means "desert" ("Tohu Va-Vohu," 28) and the *tohu-wabohu* draws on a tradition that sees the conditions as very dry (28n82). Even so, Hahn talks about reasons for importing the nonbiblical term "chaos" ("*Tohu Va-Vohu*," 46) and eventually follows Levenson's use of the term (61, 64); chaos becomes something that is "eager" to return. Brown's handling of these terms also is lacking. He claims they are a *farrago*: two alliterative words that together have a different meaning than they do separately. He thinks the English farrago *hodge-podge* is an appropriate translation. Thus, he claims that the text depicts a "process of differentiation and incorporation of powers" (*Structure, Role, and Ideology*, 230). His last claim is true. However, on the one hand, if Tsumura's definitions are used, the lack of differentiation still stands in v. 2 if one notes that the *tehom* waters are not in the right place according to their normal place in a tripartite division of the earth. Their being not yet normal tells the audience there is a hodge-podge that will be differentiated in the narrative. On the other hand, Brown notes the progressive incorporation of powers in the text. Brown claims that the earth and waters move from being inactive to active in the chapter. If Tsumura's conclusions about *tohu* and *bohu* are

condition for the vegetation, animals, and humans of days three and six. Levenson's account lends itself to viewing the history of creation being about the pinnacle creation—humans—and their drama that unfolds *on* the earth. Such an interpretive view of the natural world is not out of line with the development of anthropocentric thinking in the West during the past millennium.

If, on the other hand, Genesis 1:2 is about *everything under heaven* being unproductive and uninhabited, then God's creative activity is about and for the whole of creation. There is a singularity to the text's theme and a unity of destiny shared by all. The text is about the "earth" no longer being a barren waste and empty. The "earth" is coming to maturity; humans enter as *part* of the growing complexity of related/relating participants. Humans are one character, undoubtedly an important one, in the grand narrative of everything under heaven with a divine calling in relation to God and the rest of the "earth." All are developed into and participate in a single community.

Moving Forward: Interpreting Genesis 1

When looking at the broader literary unit in which Genesis 1 is located, Claus Westermann has an intriguing perspective on the many points of resonance between *Genesis 1–11* and other ANE texts. He takes a step back from trying to link specific biblical texts with a specific ANE precursor. Throughout his commentary on these chapters, he accepts that there are many points of comparison between *Genesis 1–11* and the texts of *all* of Israel's neighbors. Westermann is just as quick, nevertheless, to point out how the biblical texts are different in the details. The texts' authors were able to integrate many points of contact with Israel's neighbors while still speaking in the unique theological voice of the Priestly

---

allowed to stand, the nature of the lack of activity comes into sharper focus. The inactivity equals not producing and empty. It then stands in juxtaposition to a bountifully productive and full earth; an earth participating in the goodness of what God created it to become. Tsumura's interpretation of v. 2 opens up Brown's observation about differentiation and suitable incorporation into the cosmic community's unfolding in even more vibrant terms. Brown need not have rejected Tsumura's interpretation of v. 2, only his claims about creation by divine fiat alone.

tradition. These contrasts with other ANE texts actually help to bring into focus the points being made in the biblical texts.[112]

In Westermann's view the theological point of these chapters is to point in two different directions. First, in looking back, these texts share in the circle of human tradition.[113] There is a moment that Israel shares with its neighbors; the authors "wanted their audience to hear something that belonged to the prehistory of Israel."[114] After all, the very content of the chapters is the story of all creation and humanity. Westermann does not say this, but the artistic genius of these chapters is that as they speak about everyone's story through the theological lenses of Israel, they do so in the vernacular of everyone's stories. Second, the stories "look forward to the history of Israel and of the people of God."[115] Unique to Israel's primeval story is that it is linked to history. As the *shared* stories come into greater focus, with ever increasing detail, God calls to Abram to leave his home and become one through whom all families will be blessed (Gen 12:1:3).[116] Again, in the artistry of Genesis, Abram is called out from among the people in whose vernacular the story thus far had been told.

Thus, any allusions to other ANE traditions that may be present in Genesis 1 will not be examined as though they fit in a progression of religious belief. Rather, it will be assumed that the myriad of images are part of the genius of the artistry of Genesis employed for theological purposes. The very medium through which the story is told serves to underline the theological points being made. There are not remnants of a tradition (or traditions) that could not fully be suppressed in Israel,

---

112. This notion of bringing Israel's thought into focus through comparative studies is similar to Clifford's position already cited.

113. Westermann, *Genesis 1–11*, 65.

114. Ibid.

115. Ibid.

116. Westermann's interpretation of this point runs against the cultic claims of Levenson. Westermann states, "When the primeval story is seen as a prologue to the history of God acting with Israel, then each narrative and each genealogy is affected, and each individual text takes a new direction. The texts no longer speak to Israel in the context of the action of the primeval period on the present—there is no cultic actualization—but through the medium of history. The created cosmos is not created and ordered anew in Israel with the recitation of the creation story; rather, God's action, which Israel has experienced in its history, is extended to the whole of history and to the whole world" (*Genesis 1–11*, 65). Westermann later says quite clearly, "When the creation narrative [generically understood] lost its setting in life, it also lost its original function which served to maintain and secure the present state of the world and of life" (92).

but rather, there were images that were consciously and deliberately employed for the author's own purposes.

Of interest in looking at Genesis 1 is its own history of development. William Brown's strong arguments about the MT being a later development of the textual tradition contained in the VorLXX indicate that the VorLXX would then lie at least one redaction closer to the original Priestly tradition than the MT.[117] The theology of that VorLXX is distinct from both Levenson's and Tsumura's positions.[118] That Priestly worldview resonates quite strongly in the current theological milieu. Its significance will be seen in the theological framework being constructed in this project.[119] For now, what that Priestly perspective will be presumed to entail will be summarized briefly.

A few points about the biblical text will be noted in moving forward from the positions of Levenson and Tsumura. First, the "double creation" in the LXX has been an attractive option within the tradition for interpreting Genesis 1.[120] The LXX clearly makes v. 1 a creation statement;

117. It is interesting, given the likelihood of the MT being a redaction of the earlier theology represented in the Vor LXX, that the LXX is often dismissed by scholars or treated as dangerous. For example, Westermann notes when commenting on Genesis 1:20, "the Gk, like other versions, understands the first sentence of v. 20 as a command directed to the waters to spawn fish . . . , by analogy with v. 11" (*Genesis 1–11*, 136). Since the version in the LXX tends to systemize these links between days, Westermann warns that "we must be on our guard against this and note that P was careful to preserve the unique character of each work of creation knowing full well that they were once independent" (ibid., 137). However, Brown has shown that this common dismissal of the LXX is unmerited, given that this same "systemization" appears in the Qumran texts (*Structure, Role, and Ideology*, 129). For those working subsequent to Brown's work, just the opposite concern should be operative. It is the MT that moves to separate the days once structurally paired.

118. Arguably the theology of the MT is different from their positions as well.

119. See chapter 6.

120. Brown uses the phrase "double creation" to mean: "Heaven and earth are the created 'aformal' substances from which the entities named 'heaven' and 'earth' are fashioned in vv 6–8 and 9–10, respectively, within the formal creation account of six days" (*Structure, Role, and Ideology*, 35). Theophilus of Antioch had a similar type of idea about creation; God created a formless material substratum *ex nihilo* and then formed it (Gerhard May, *Creatio ex Nihilo*, 161). William of Conches also had such an idea of double creation (Christopher Kaiser, *Creational Theology and the History of Physical Science*, 57; Otten, "Reading Creation," 240). In Genesis, verse 1 is silent about the *what* from which God created everything. In the Christian tradition, Tertullian argued based on that silence for *creatio ex nihilo*. From Ambrose to the Middle Ages, that verse was thought to be sufficient by itself to refute Platonic notions of the eternality of matter (Brown, *Structure, Role, and Ideology*, 35). Cf. Westermann, *Genesis 1–11*, 95, for a

God made everything. Verse 2 is then a description of what was first made and then v. 3 begins the formal process of creation. The LXX is one example of an early step in unequivocally precluding the eternality of the stuff in v. 2. Even so, the VorLXX and MT do not try to give a clear answer to the question of genesis.

Tsumura and Levenson are correct that there is no definitive way to answer from the grammar of the text whether the earth, waters, and darkness are created or uncreated.[121] Even so, there are other factors that can be considered in deciding the relationship of the first three verses to one another, and thus, how to interpret the statements of v. 2.

One consideration for deciding how to arrange vv. 1:3 is the stylistic tendency of P to employ staccato, punchy sentences.[122] It would be quite out of character within P to have a long, complex sentence that includes all of vv. 1–3.[123] If v. 1 functions independently as a short heading or description for all that is to follow—the creation of the heavens and the earth (i.e., everything)—it does not create a problem in the relationship between v. 1 and v. 2. Verse 1 is simply a summary statement and v. 2 is the start of the narrative.[124]

Claiming that v. 2 is the start of the creation narrative is a reading consistent with the content of the verse and its similarity to other ANE stories of creation. When narrating creation it was common to look

---

critique of more contemporary appearances of a double creation position.

121. Cf. Hahn, "*Tohu Va-Vohu*," 35ff for a discussion on the various grammatical options concerning the relationship between vv. 1, 2, and 3; he also mentions the theological motivations for why the various choices are often emphasized. Hahn himself opts for translating v. 1 as a summary or title statement, v. 2 as a "once upon a time" or "when-there-was-not-yet" clause (a statement of "before"), and v. 3 as the beginning of the action proper (44).

122. This has been noted as far back as Wellhausen (Westermann, *Genesis 1–11*, 97).

123. Westermann, *Genesis 1–11*, 97.

124. Westermann cites H. Strack, H. Gunkel, O. Procksch, W. Zimmerli, G. von Rad, W. Eichrodt, W. H. Schmidt, H. A. Brongers, and U. Cassuto as fellow supporters of this position (*Genesis 1–11*, 95). Hahn also concurs with this position in his dissertation ("*Tohu Va-Vohu*," 44). Claiming that v. 1 is a summary is different from claiming double-creation—that v. 1 is a statement that God created a hodge-podge that he then fixes in the rest of the chapter. Rather, it leaves any possible pre-v. 2 events unspecified as the VorLXX and MT do. Also, by resisting the temptation to make v. 1 a report about God's first creative act, it respects the progression of the narrative. The narrative opens with a *tohu wabohu* earth. It is not until God creates a dome in the waters that separated some below and above it, that there is a sky/heaven(s) (v. 9); see both the Greek and the Hebrew. Since the creation of the heavens does not come until v. 9 in the narrative, this undermines claims that v. 1 narrates the first creative act.

at the present and narrate its opposite. "This state and all that is taken for granted with it is, as it were, abolished for a moment; the present and apparently permanent state of the world is taken back to a moment when an event is taking place in which the present state is in a process of becoming; the event starts from a 'not yet,' from a state of nothingness of chaos."[125] This is the way creation is *narrated*, instead of being stated *propositionally*: e.g., *creatio ex nihilo*.[126] It sets up the "flash point" in a sequence by which to narrate creative activity.[127] The intent of such statements in cosmologies "is not to describe a state that preceded creation, but to mark off God's act of creation from a 'before' which is beyond words and can only be described in negative terms";[128] its primary purpose "is to delimit and not to describe, even where a positive expression such as 'darkness and night' or . . . [*tohu wabohu*] has replaced the negative sentence."[129]

Verse 2 is a statement of "not-yet"—a not yet that is yet full of anticipation. Little more should be read into v. 2 about if or how the stuff narrated therein got there. Also, the language of "matter" and "formless matter" had not yet passed from Greek philosophy into Hebrew thought at the time of P's composition.[130] "Both formulations, that God created

125. Ibid., 43. As careful as Westermann is with deconstructing many facets of Gunkel's tradition, he still uses "chaos" and some accompanying notions unapologetically.

126. Ibid., 46.

127. Ibid., 44.

128. Ibid., 46.

129. Ibid. Westermann states later: "It is much easier to exegete the verses when we can presume that the intention of the writer is not really to give a picture of the situation that preceded creation, but to present the act of creation as an event, corresponding to the 'When not yet' of the older narratives (similar explanations are given by G. von Rad and K. Galling)" (ibid., 102). It is worth noting that it is from Egyptian texts that Westermann finds a parallel to the "not yet" being stated in the positive and not the negative, as is most common in ANE cosmologies (46).

130. Ibid., 109–10. There are some scholars like Kitchen and Milgrom who believe the Priestly materials were composed much earlier than the exilic, post exilic time period. Milgrom's strongest argument about the antiquity of P is that whole sections of D reflect the language of P, but D is never used within P (*Leviticus 1–16*, 10, 12–13). He believes P was redacted in the time of the first Temple, prior to exile. Kitchen points out that the features of Genesis 1 are consistent with other second millennium ANE cosmologies. Thus, if it were to be dated according to ANE studies and not by the documentary hypothesis, it would be dated much earlier than the second half of the first millennium. This makes a roughly nine-hundred year spectrum in suggested dating among scholars for the composition of the Priestly cosmology—from the fourth to thirteenth centuries BCE.

the world out of nothing and that there was a formless matter before creation, first occur where Judaism has come under the influence of Greek thought."[131] Thus, the questions of pre-existent matter and *ex nihilo* are later questions that v. 2 does not address. It cannot be said that one or the other is *intended* in the text.[132] In Westermann's (and Tsumura's) view, Genesis simply says "God created the heavens and the earth."[133]

Even if it is allowed that v. 2 was not written to answer the later question concerning creation happening either *ex nihilo* or from uncreated pre-existent matter, and if its primary purpose was to provide an entry point into which God's creative activity could be narrated, how the Priestly author(s) chose to begin the narrative and what to call it is still significant. The 'not-yet' description of v. 2 is informative concerning the nature of God's creative activity that is narrated, even if the question concerning the origin of the 'not-yet-as-we-know-it' stuff of v. 2 is not answered.[134] It says what was imagined within the Priestly tradition to be the opposite to the results of God's creative activity. Because it has implications for what God's creative activities entail, the interpretation of the not-yet is important.

The Priestly cosmology opens with positive statements instead of statements of negation. From the point where the Priestly cosmology begins its narrative there is no place where the two most basic components of the earth—the *tehom* waters and the land (as well as the darkness)— are said to come in to existence. The darkness is present in the report of vv. 4–5;[135] the prior presence of the waters is implied in the wording of

---

131. Ibid., 110.

132. Ibid. In Westermann's words: "It is meaningless then to ask whether P thought if there was or was not matter before creation" (ibid., 109).

133. Ibid. For the sake of doing theology in today's context, however, more must be said than that there is an apparent absence of the question of genesis, and thus the absence of an answer, in the text. Saying that "God created" begs the question of what is meant by "created." In giving an account of God's *creative* activity in this book, the Hebrew text will have to be allowed to reverberate beyond its own bounds.

134. It is common to view the "Let there be . . ." statement of v. 3 as the initial instance of creation. I would suggest that the movement of the Spirit at the end of v. 2 should not be overlooked as being a necessary component to God's creative activity. Both Spirit hovering and speech are narrated as activities of God in the Priestly cosmology. Claims concerning creation by Word alone are an insufficient commentary on the text.

135. "And God saw that the light was good; and God separated the light from the darkness. God called the light Day, and the darkness he called Night. And there was evening and there was morning, the first day" (NRSV).

the command of v. 6;[136] and the "appearance" of land at the gathering of the waters in v. 7 suggests it had simply been covered to that point.[137] But the language of what to call the introductory, 'not-yet' condition of v. 2 still needs to be determined.

Many have imported the Greek term "chaos" to either describe the condition of the first components or emphasize that the stuff itself *is* chaos.[138] Both uses of the term presume that what is described—created or not—is present and is not just an elaborate way of saying *nihil*. In the Christian tradition there have been thinkers who have followed Greek ideas that v. 2 is a description of raw matter lacking everything but material causation, a situation akin to the *khora* in Plato's *Timaeus*.[139]

As the narrative unfolds, however, it shows that there is not a complete confusion or mixture of materials. Rather, as Tsumura suggests, there is a layering of the earth's components (land, *tehom*, and darkness) that is assessed as *tohu wabohu*—unproductive and empty. The not-yet circumstances of v. 2 could just as easily be called "infancy" or "immaturity"—a trope used elsewhere in Scripture (e.g., Job 38:8–11) and within the Christian tradition (e.g., Irenaeus).

The option selected has many implications for how to understand in the text God's initial relationship to creation and the nature of God's creative activity, as well as what kind of world is coming into existence: a passive or obstinate stuff receiving forms or a subject being nurtured into maturity. Claims concerning the nature of the stuff are just as important as claims concerning its condition. Concerning the former: the narrative of Genesis 1 points toward the subjectivity of the land and waters.[140] They are guided and/or enlisted as much as they are formed and/or coerced.

---

136. "And God said, 'Let there be a dome in the midst of the waters, and let it separate the waters from the waters'" (NRSV).

137. "And God said, 'Let the waters under the sky be gathered together into one place, and let the dry land appear.' And it was so" (NRSV).

138. Westermann uses this language too, going back and forth between "chaos" and "nothingness." Or he will use the phrase "the nothingness of chaos" (*Genesis 1–11*, 43).

139. Watson provides a helpful list of references in the writings of early thinkers who either supported or criticized such a position (*Chaos Uncreated*, 13). Critics included Hippolytus, Methodius, and Clement of Alexandria.

140. Brown suggests this in "Divine Act and Persuasion," when he says that "what is described in Gen. 1.2 is not malevolent, autonomous chaos, but the earth and the waters as living 'elements' that are enlisted by divine command to participate positively in the creative process" (32).

They are neither utterly inert nor recalcitrant.[141] Thus, the subjectivity of the v. 2 components will be affirmed.[142]

Concerning the condition of this subject: the narrative of Genesis 1 opens with basic infantile stuff, which God addresses. It is not "chaos," obstinate, or in a chaotic condition. It is *tohu wabohu*: "barren/desolate" and "empty." God's dedication to the young creation leads to the forming-as-we-know-it of heaven and earth on days 2 and 3 respectively. This can be interpreted as formation for the sake of ordering (to be a stage for history) or the nurturing of that infant into life in the community. The earth, waters, and other parts of creation mature in their active participation under God's guidance in cosmogony; they progress from moving about at God's request to the production and support of other parts of creation.

Holistically viewed God's creative activity is more community development than the formation or establishment of particular objects or a cosmos. Each part is related to others and has responsibilities relative to others, or, in turn, has responsibilities that contribute to the fulfillment of the whole. More than establishing a fixed structure out of inanimate matter, God develops a community.

This trajectory is foreshadowed in the statements made in v. 2 at the opening of the narrative. Tsumura's arguments about *tohu*, *bohu*, and *tehom* are compelling, yet moving forward from his findings has not gained traction. Brown thinks Tsumura was too concrete in arriving at his interpretations. However, as noted above, if the terms are taken as "arid/unproductive" and "empty/uninhabited," this functions very well in the direction the entire passage moves. Brown characterizes this direction as "a movement from constituent bases (light, water, and green earth) to the particular 'social' forms they help produce and sustain."[143] He does not see the story of those particular "constituent bases" beginning in v. 2, but only, rather, as they are called to and named in vv. 3, 9–10. Those verses are a significant dividing line for him in the text.[144]

---

141. It should be recalled that people in the ANE did not perceive natural things as lifeless matter. Later Greek or scientific views should not be put on the text.

142. This is consistent with the observations of Christopher Kaiser (in chapter 2 of this volume), who noted that the biblical view of God is as a king who legislates for his subjects, including the earth.

143. Brown, *Structure, Role, and Ideology*, 217.

144. Perhaps his interest in the parts/individuals in the text over the whole is a reflection of our times more than the interest of the text. Clifford points out that "perhaps the

But prior to Brown's reading of the parts, however, the text introduces itself as a story about the whole (v. 1) and begins its telling with the not-yet description of the whole 'earth'—that which would become an organic community.[145] When the first narrated divine act has come to pass through the operations of God's *ruach* and speech in vv. 2c–3, there is no reason based on the text to exclude from the whole the presence of any of the parts in which Brown initially takes interest: light, waters, and land.[146] The infant whole of which they are part, nevertheless, even this side of that creative act, is not yet beyond the *tohu wabohu* description of the not-yet earth in v. 2. The descriptions of v. 2 are fitting descriptions about the community (or lack thereof) into which the parts would come to participate. Before (or in the absence of) God's community-nurturing creative activity, there is only a dead emptiness.[147] Even after the Priestly cosmology begins to narrate God's creative ministrations the *earth* does not immediately cease being barren (literally), empty, undifferentiated,

---

single most important feature of ancient Near Eastern cosmogonies is that they generally issued in a peopled universe, a world, a system. Even when focusing on a single item . . . they put that item in the context of the whole . . . Any dichotomous distinction between creation of the whole and creation of the individual is not warranted for the ancient Near East" (*Creation Accounts in the Ancient Near East and the Bible*, 199).

145. Interestingly, in v. 2 God is included, by the Spirit, as a participating agent in this growing-up community—not that God needs maturing, but that the community with which he is joining himself needs to grow into his goodness.

146. Just as the narrative of all creation's story in *Genesis 1–11* is Israel's story, because they are within it but not yet called to the specific place and purpose for which God chooses them, so too the story in Genesis 1 is from vv. 2–3 the story of the whole, inclusive of the light, waters, and land, which have not yet been called to specific places and purposes—i.e., to mature in expressing goodness according to what is suitable to them.

147. In the Priestly cosmology there is the same dynamic that Jacob Milgrom has found in Leviticus: God's creative activity is life for the community just as the cult affirms, protects, and nurtures life and holiness. In the cult, death is the opposite experience for the community just as in Genesis 1:2 the opposite circumstance from the realization of God's creative activity is a dead waste. In the cult, apart from walking in God's ways, the people of God would experience a deadly destruction upon God's departure from the Temple (Milgrom, *Leviticus 1–16*, 50); Tsumura finds that *tohu* and *bohu* together are used to describe such a destruction; "it would be very reasonable to understand the phrase *tōhû wābōhû* in Gen 1:2 as also describing a state of 'desolation and emptiness,' though the context suggests that this was the initial state of the created earth rather than a state brought about as a result of God's judgment on the earth or land (cf. Jer 4:23, Isa 34:11)" (*Creation and Destruction*, 33). *The point of creation is not a movement from disorder/chaos to order. The whole point of the Priestly thinking about creation and the cult is the development of a vibrant community that affirms, protects, and nurtures life/holiness!*

and dark; but even there (or precisely there), the Spirit of God was present.[148]

God's "ordering" of creation in Genesis 1—or establishing "constituent bases"—is not a highly debated notion; the narrative moves from the general to the particular. In that movement, it also moves progressively to greater multiplicity and complexity in the social forms established among the parts.[149] As has been mentioned, after the parts are named— e.g., the "land" is named "earth" and the "waters" are named "seas" in v. 10[150]—the various parts are each invited to participate in the unfolding community; all parts are called upon to contribute in the community according to what is suitable to them.[151] The land/earth and waters/seas become "collaborative agents" in creating under God, the Creator and "Commander."[152]

One of the progressions in these callings is significant. In calling the land and waters "to the particular 'social' forms they help produce and sustain"[153] God was essentially addressing environments in which the produced things were to thrive. God first addresses the land, telling

---

148. As will be suggested in chapter 6, it is precisely there that the Spirit is present because the Spirit of God is the Possibility of God for the o/Other. It is this Spirit that operates inseparably with God's Word to make possible the coming to be of creation. On another topic, noting this movement in the text from emptiness and unproductiveness marks a significant departure from Levenson's framework, in which he interprets patterns in Genesis 1 such as the light being created on the first day and the sun not being made until the fourth day as an instance of demythologization of the sun: in other words, his view is that Genesis 1 is one step further away from the combat myth and cosmography of *Enuma elish* (Levenson, *Creation and the Persistence of Evil*, 65). Rather, there is continued growth and development unto being a productive, full community narrated in the text.

149. Brown, *Structure, Role, and Ideology*, 217.

150. Ibid., 37.

151. In Brown's words, "the etymological eloquence characteristic of the divine commands addressed to the waters and the earth have the effect of underscoring their respective abilities in the formation of products suitable for the divine creative scheme" (*Structure, Role, and Ideology*, 214). All of this is part of the "social dimension of the priestly cosmogony" as seen in both Genesis 1 and the building of the tabernacle; it "is most evident in the respective roles of the earth and the waters in relation to God. The earth and the waters are treated as active creators in Genesis 1 and work in collaboration with God. Hence, each bears a social function in relation to ['*elohim*]" (ibid., 213). Important is that the respective contributions of the earth and waters "in the process are made in the context of service" (ibid., 213–14).

152. Ibid., 212.

153. Ibid., 217.

it to "grass grass" (v. 11). This is only one of two places in the whole Bible where the verb "to grass" is used.[154] God's intention is that the thing which is produced is to be dependant upon and united with the continued activity of the actor. It is like the action of singing a song, where the song ceases when the singing ceases. This is different from an action where the thing produced is distinct from the thing producing it or the very action of producing it (e.g., a chair being built by a carpenter).[155] Following this first divine address for land to grass grass, God addresses the waters telling them to "flying flyers" and to "swimming swimmers" (v. 20).[156]

The pattern is very clear and very important. Before each thing comes into existence, the environment is addressed to which the thing produced is related. The environment itself is supposed to play a part, to be in sustaining, nurturing relationship with that which lives in it;[157] the nature/character of its existence is dependent upon and united to the continued activity of the environment. Those within the cosmic community shape both one another and the resulting dynamics of the community by their nurturing activity.

After addressing both the land and seas, God then addresses God's self and says "let us create man in our image, male and female" (v. 26). God is the final 'environment' introduced in the narrative. The "let us" is not as

154. Sacks, *A Commentary on the Book of Genesis*, 7. Cf. Joel 2:22 where it is used within a description of a harmonious (eschatological) time. Westermann translates Genesis 1:11, 12 as follows: "v. 11: 'Let the earth green forth fresh green'; v. 12: 'And the earth greened forth'" (*Genesis 1–11*, 142).

155. Sacks, *A Commentary on the Book of Genesis*, 7.

156. It is certainly odd that God would address the waters in regard to birds. However, Brown has searched other ancient writings and found that Israel is not alone in linking the creation of birds with water. This link can be seen in the ANE as far back as Egyptian and Sumerian sources (*Structure, Role, and Ideology*, 184). "Such a tradition casts a generally positive light upon the role of water in creation, in contrast to other traditions that highlight the negative, resistant role water often assumes in mythological texts (e.g., *Tiamat* in *Enuma Elish*, *Yam* in Ugaritic literature)" (184).

157. Without having to accept that these environments are addressed as characters and that they have any participation in bringing about their inhabitants, it can at least be conceded that the environments are named. Although the work conducted in contemporary science is discovering the "self-organization" of systems (or "active" matter) and the effects of one system on neighboring systems (cf. Prigogine and Stengers, *Order out of Chaos*, 8–13). Joseph A. Bracken has also done a great deal of theological reflection on systems, including on the effects subsystems have on larger systems of which they are part; see *Society and Spirit*. The movements in Genesis 1 toward complexity, multiplicity, and interrelationships have a great deal of resonance with work being done in science.

much a theological assertion in the narrative, as it is often treated, as it is an anthropological assertion.[158] The writer distinctly separates humans from other animals—from all other created things—by the unique environment in which humans exist. To be human is to exist in God. God is addressed as humanity's environment. By God's breathing, they live. "In him we live and move and have our being" (Acts 17:28). Brown notes the structure in the LXX also helps give both light and humans a special, more unmediated, relationship to God.[159] There are three groupings in the LXX structure: 1) Heaven, firmament, luminaries; 2) Water, seas and land, marine and winged creatures; and 3) Earth, plants, land animals.[160] Structurally light and humans are associated with heaven and earth respectively; however, they are unique in their creation. God is the one called to relate to this creature who is dependent upon his continued breathing into them, as that which lives within and out of the very life of the Triune God. Humans are to be the song God sings, imaging their creator.[161]

The details of the biblical narrative continue to illustrate that relationship. For example, God breathed *neshama* (breath) into the

158. Others have made related statements. E.g., Phyllis A. Bird has noted that "the verb '*āśâ* ['do, make'], which has heretofore been used only in the execution reports, to emphasize the divine activity, is now taken up into the announcement itself. The becoming of *adam* is inconceivable apart from God's own direct action and involvement; the willing of this creature requires divine commitment" ("'Male and Female He Created Them,'" 346). Not only does Bird note the nature of God's statement, but she notices its relation to the prior commands: "each order is referred to an already existing element of earth (land and water) and its locus and proximate source. In contrast, *adam* is assigned a function or task by the very word of announcement, a task defined in relation to the other creatures and to the earth, which is its habitat but not its source. Humanity is also distinguished from other orders of life by its direct and unmediated dependence upon God. For *adam*, habitat is neither source of life nor source of identity" (ibid.). See n.157 concerning Brown's position.

159. Brown, *Structure, Role, and Ideology*, 40. "As noted above, only in the sections dealing with the creation of light and human beings does one find the transition marker (*kai egeneto houtōs*) enigmatically missing from its typical location. Thus a tighter connection is forged between command and fulfillment without the formal intermediate step" (ibid.). With humans, first, the command is directed at God. Second, humans are not distinguished by species/kinds (their likenesses to one another), but in their being created in the image and likeness of God. And third, humans are to rule over specific things within the three domains of the community: "'over the fish of the *sea* and the winged creatures of *heaven* and the herds and all the wild animals of the *earth* and all the reptiles that crawl upon the *earth*' (vv 26, 28)" (ibid., 41).

160. Ibid.

161. In the very way humans were made to exist relative to God, God was creating a creature that he could become. Human is not something that is outside of or

nostrils of *adam* (2:7). Only God and humans have *neshama* in the Old Testament.[162] Human beings, as ones who share breath with God, live in a dynamic, dependent relationship with God; "when you take away their breath, they die and return to their dust. When you send forth your spirit, they are created" (Ps 104:29–30).[163] Human life is God's song. Furthermore, humans' desires for the good and their kingly-status do not proceed from themselves but from this intimate relationship;[164] these come from God. It was necessary for Adam to go regularly to the center of the garden for sustenance and guidance from God, from the tree of life.[165]

Summary

There have been proposals since very early in the tradition of equating Genesis 1:2 with "chaos." Whereas these comparisons were originally a conscious effort to harmonize Christianity and Greek philosophy, the comparisons in the past century have been driven primarily by ANE comparative studies. While, as Watson points out, this choice of terminology was immediately challenged in the nineteenth century as being inappropriate for Genesis 1, it has become widely used. It is still being challenged by those employing synchronic methods to the biblical text. Yet the term with its accompanying notions is still being applied to the text.

Links between ANE texts have been asserted often on the basis of shared notions of chaos. These typological connections are often repeated from one scholar to the next as fact even though dependence is not demonstrated between the texts and detailed synchronic methods have

---

disconnected from God, and in that way not foreign to God.

162. Hamilton, *The Book of Genesis*, 158ff. Isaiah 42:5 and Job 27:3 show that this word is closely related to *ruach* (ibid., 158).

163. It is verses such as this one that makes the statement about God's Spirit being present with the *tohu wabohu* earth in Genesis 1:2 so interesting; the Spirit is for all creation what humans experience in a special way.

164. Hans Walter Wolff makes these assertions particularly in relation to a study of *ruach*: *Anthropology of the Old Testament*, 39. Hamilton has argued that these two words have a very close function in the Old Testament.

165. It will be developed in chapter 6 that the Spirit breathed into *adam* is the same Spirit that is the Possibility for all creation. God gifts himself within the cosmic community as the good into which it is called to mature. That good is God's own self-emptying love at work for others, for their growth and flourishing.

not been applied to verify kindred thinking.[166] Recent studies have raised flags about many of the cross cultural links that have long been asserted. Some of the assertions are about links between terms, images, or myths across cultures, as well as about the conflation of divergent mythological themes. For example, creation has often been asserted as having a connection to chaos in the ANE. However, chaos-talk in reference to creation has been more challenged than affirming the use of chaos imagery within other mythical or historical contexts, for other theological/rhetorical purposes.[167] Brown's examination of many of the ANE creation myths shows how diverse their accounts of the beginning are. There is little ground in ANE literature for connecting *Chaoskampf* and creation.

By clearing away many of these long perpetuated assertions through the work of scholars such as Tsumura, Watson, and Brown, it opens up a view of Genesis 1 (as well as other cosmological texts) that is quite powerful and much more in line with the tone of the rest of Scripture. The Priestly creation account as a whole moves from a not-yet-productive, dark, and uninhabited infancy, into a nurtured and nurturing social network in which all are called according to what is suitable to them into the service of the o/Other.[168] The Priestly account is a teaching concerning God's creative call against which the responsiveness of the whole community is measured throughout history. It is a picture of the beginning, the end, and God's calling at every moment between—as the narrative about the Tabernacle's construction showed. This will be developed in chapter 6.

In the next chapter, an example will be investigated of the way "chaos" language has been used by a systematic theologian. Catherine Keller adopts the terminology from biblical studies—as well as science and philosophy—while at the same time, taking it in a different direction in her reading of Genesis 1 than suggested by Levenson or his opponents.

---

166. Watson, *Chaos Uncreated*, 24.

167. Ibid., 19.

168. It does not move between the antinomies of chaos and order, but between the Priestly antinomies of death/life, profane/holy.

5

Catherine Keller's Tehomic Theology
A Theology of Becoming

IN THE PREVIOUS CHAPTERS THE MANNER IN WHICH "CHAOS" HAS been used in science and in biblical studies has been critiqued. It was noted in the introductory chapter that the uses of "chaos" in these fields have been taken up into theological reflections. The aim of this chapter is to show an example of how "chaos" language has been borrowed out of science and biblical studies into systematic theology. Any number of examples could have been chosen.[1] Along with the sophistication of Keller's thoughts on chaos, her work was chosen due to the number of useful cautions and suggestions she has for doing theology in our present context. Also, Catherine Keller's tehomic theology, as she lays it out in *Face of the Deep: A Theology of Becoming*, has been selected because her position varies from those already seen in the previous chapters. Although influenced by exposure to science and ANE comparative studies, she takes the opposite approach of Levenson and does not demonize the stuff of Genesis 1:2.

Keller has both a different perspective and a different approach than Levenson. In her approach to interpreting scriptural images, she does not select an ANE lens as Levenson does, and interpret Scripture through that matrix. On the other hand, she does not represent the side of Tsumura or Brown who either denounce "chaos" language or propose other sources from the ANE with which to compare the

---

1. E.g., Inch, *Chaos Paradigm*; McDonough, *Between Chaos and New Creation*; Hutcheson, *Pandemonium Tremendum*; Bruteau, *God's Ecstasy*; Cupitt, *Creation out of Nothing*; Page, *God and the Web of Creation*; Neiman, "The Myth of Chaos."

images of the Bible. She does not try to make any direct claim for an interpretation of the text based on what she believes is the most appropriate reconstructed ANE perspective. Rather, Keller's approach is to deconstruct what she sees as the Babylonian and biblical tendencies toward masculine domination of the tehomic feminine. She shows briefly how this is a recurring theme throughout history that rises out of tehomo*phobia*. By deconstructing instances of domination and by folding in layers of voices from less dominant traditions throughout the centuries, she both opens up the possibility of a new reading and legitimizes it with a myriad of past witnesses. These marginalized voices become permissive and instructive in reading creation in Genesis 1 in non-*ex nihilo* ways, wherein *tehom* plays a significant, positive roll. In short, they help Keller weave a tehomo*philic* tapestry.

In this chapter, first Keller's tehomic theology will be outlined. Second, there will be an assessment of which aspects of her theology are useful and which aspects are not useful (or would benefit from revision according to the alternative approach being developed). In general, the dynamic aspects of creation's relationship with God within her theology are applauded. On the other hand, the lack of a more conventional trinitarian paradigm in her theology will be questioned; it need not have been excluded. Further, in her theology concerning the relationship of God to creation, Keller moves too far in her grammar of *in*wardness, thus, in the end, blurring together God's and the world's becoming.

Keller's Tehomic Hermeneutic in *Face of the Deep*

Genesis 1:1—2:3, especially 1:1–3, is the biblical text of primary focus in *Face of the Deep*. Throughout her work, Keller focuses on specific terms in these first verses through her tehomic hermeneutic[2] in which understanding is not about knowing the object from a fixed perspective.[3] Rather, there is a dynamic relationship between the text and the interpreter. Understanding is "a relational, therefore relativizing, effect

2. See Keller, *Face of the Deep*, 103ff.

3. Ibid., 104. Keller shows a familiarity with several postfoundationalist thinkers in her work and follows in that vein. It is interesting to see the resonance between this hermeneutic philosophy and new views of the universe since Einstein; there is no absolute space within which things are plotted, but things are understood relative to one another. Notions of relativity and intertextuality function similarly in their respective fields of the sciences and the arts.

of interpretation."[4] The task of understanding is never complete; the subject, the text, is never mastered. The interpretive relation is forever ongoing, with "infinite perspectives of knowledge."[5]

The complexity of hermeneutics is not multiplied only by the factor of the multiple contexts and theological perspectives of the interpreters but also by the factor of interdimensional folds[6] and gaps[7] within the text, in the layers of positive and negative relations of biblical texts with one another and with other ANE texts.[8] Thus, texts have fields of effects.[9] In this relativizing relation with a text, interpreters creatively negotiate with the history of a text's effects.[10] "Thus the text cannot mirror an original, transparent—and apparently nonexistent—meaning. It will make meaning through a cooperative interaction in history—meaning not from nothing but from everything preceding. That meaning lives only in the relationships constituting the present signifying process."[11]

---

4. Ibid., 105.

5. Ibid.

6. Ibid., 109.

7. Ibid., 118. Gaps make room for dialogical relationship with the text. Gaps "invite the filling of them by citing other passages in the canon" (118).

8. Ibid., 108–9. See ibid., 5 on her goal of soliciting a "chaotic multiplicity of biblical writings, genres, voices and potentials" in order to achieve an "algorithmic expansion of a hyper-familiar old text." She does not explicitly confess here, but she also uses extra-biblical texts and images to expand familiar biblical texts. In outlining her hermeneutic with its fields of effects, Keller does not address if it is possible that some effects go too far afield from the text.

Texts can certainly have many effects; but not all of them are righteous (doing justice to the text). Effects can be as disordered as the people doing the reading (and their contexts); thus some effects stand in need of recapitulation. In her postfoundationalism, Keller does not talk about what to do with disordered or ill effects—effects that are not rightly related to the text. Keller dismisses any moderating point of view and thus leaves her audience no ground for assessing whether the effects she describes from the biblical text in her work are rightly related to the text. In the context of the tapestry she weaves, any claims against her perspective would be considered dominating and repressive. Perhaps the only option is to weave a different tapestry and let the readers of this present work choose which work in the gallery to take home with them.

9. Ibid., 109.

10. Ibid., 106, 109.

11. Ibid., 119. Much like in process thought where all that becomes does so out of the milieu that precedes (plus options offered by new aims/lures), Keller's ongoing hermeneutic is in conversation/relation with what has preceded.

Tehom: The Site of Becoming

Within her work *tehom* (the deep) itself—from Genesis 1:2—folds and unfolds in its meaning(s). Most basically it is the site of becoming.[12] She uses many synonyms for *tehom*: "matrix of possibilities," "chaoid," "milieu," etc.; most commonly, however, she uses "chaos" and "deep." Tehom is not the creator or a creature. In other words, it is not created.[13] This milieu, this "unformed future,"[14] is "neither being nor nonbeing."[15] It is tempting to reduce tehom to a signifier for an idea, but Keller rejects making this site of becoming a nothing; she will not let it go away.

Tehom is "*always already there*," and thus, both creator and creature always already have a prior relation to it.[16] However, instead of considering it as a place *before* beginning, it is better understood as *of* beginning.[17] It is a "between-space" in the "feedback loop of the new and the given"[18] fraught with potentiality/possibility. With Deleuze, Keller affirms that this "depth is not 'a dimension' but the dimensionality out of which the spatiotemporal dimensions unfold."[19]

It is not until the fourth and final part of her work that Keller brings "creativity," a well known process-thought term, to the foreground of her treatment of tehom. "The creativity is not a cause, not even the First Cause, but rather the condition that conditions all causal processes. The creativity itself does not become; *it makes becoming possible*. We imagine it therefore as the matrix of possibilities."[20] Since, for Keller, all is *in* God, tehom becomes the depth of God (and of world)[21] that gives birth to God;[22] it is "Ocean of divinity, womb and place-holder of beginnings, it is not Elohim but the first place or *capacity* of genesis."[23] Both God and

---

12. Ibid., 12.
13. Ibid., 10, 28, 181.
14. Ibid., 29.
15. Ibid., 12.
16. Ibid., 163; italics original.
17. Ibid., 161.
18. Ibid.
19. Ibid., 168; cf. 35.
20. Ibid., 181.
21. Ibid., 231.
22. Ibid., 180.
23. Ibid., 231.

world "arise as effects of the primal creativity."[24] God (Elohim) *as effect* is the one through whom *all causes arise*.

Keller is careful to clarify that tehom/creativity is not nothing; it is not a vacuum.[25] She rejects any *creatio ex nihilo* reading of the Bible. The Bible "knows only of the divine formation of the world out of a chaotic something: not *creatio ex nihilo*, but *ex nihilo nihil fit* ('from nothing comes nothing'), the common sense of the ancient world."[26] From an *ex nihilo* worldview, if a primordial chaos is considered, the autonomy of this chaotic something is often assumed.[27] However, this presupposes the logical opposite of *creatio ex nihilo* as the only option. It presupposes a "dualism of Creator/creature or Creator/chaos."[28] Keller chooses a third option of dialogical cooperation, which precedes that Creator/creature dualism—a *creatio cooperationis*: "non-linear interactions between Elohim and Tehom."[29]

Becoming

Throughout the entire work, Keller critiques the theological tradition of *creatio ex nihilo*. One of her first critiques is the lack of biblical warrant for *creatio ex nihilo*.[30] In the history of Christian and Jewish thought, through the second century C.E., "creation" referred to the formation of the world from unformed stuff.[31] This idea did not disappear immediately. The biblical and philosophical notions of primordial stuff were still at issue when Augustine was writing the last three books of his *Confessions* at the end of the fourth century.[32] Even though the *creatio ex nihilo* position rose quickly in dominance, Genesis 1:2 remained problematic for

    24. Ibid., 181.
    25. Cf., e.g., ibid., 115.
    26. Ibid., 4.
    27. Ibid., 116. Augustine called this chaotic something a nothingsomething (*nihil aliquid*); cf. Keller, *Face of the Deep*, 75 and Augustine, *Confessions*, XII.6.
    28. Keller, *Face of the Deep*, 117.
    29. Ibid. Cf. ibid., 98, 116ff. This dialogical cooperation will be explained further when her panentheism is outlined.
    30. Ibid., 6.
    31. Ibid., 15. Keller relies heavily on Gerhard May's *Creatio ex Nihilo: The Doctrine of "Creation out of Nothing" in Early Christian Thought* for her information on the history of this doctrine.
    32. Ibid., 16.

its proponents—everything that comes between "in the beginning" and "God said." For example, Athanasius skips over the verse altogether in his polemic support of *creatio ex nihilo*.[33]

It was widely known in the fourth century that Genesis 1:2 was compatible with "pagan mythologies and the platonic *khora*."[34] Keller exploits this quandary for the *creatio ex nihilo* proponents. In Genesis 1:2 and within the imagery of the Old Testament, "This interstitial darkness refuses to disappear. It refuses to appear as nothing, as vacuum, as mere absence highlighting the Presence of the Creator, as nonentity limning all the created entities . . . this void evinces fullness, its waters, viscosity."[35] In the previous section it has already been laid out what Keller does with the tehom, how she treats it positively in contrast to the tehomophobic tendencies of the West.[36] She uses v. 2 in her theology instead of skipping over it or doing hermeneutical acrobatics to make its contents into *nihil*.

In taking v. 2 seriously Keller rejects any idea of creation as a unilateral act, whether it is understood as an act of domination, repression, or even making—if "making" is meant as either "forming" or "creation from nothing."[37] She dislikes notions of origin because of their characteristic

33. Ibid., 57.
34. Ibid., 58.
35. Ibid., 9.
36. Keller not only critiques the phobia of chaos in the theological tradition (especially Barth: ibid., 84ff.), but she even deconstructs it in Scripture and other ANE traditions (26ff). She blames this tehomophobia on a culture of (male) dominance and its exultation of "order," *Chaoskampf*, mastery, and the like (cf., e.g., 31ff., 95ff.)—i.e., creation as order (20). Chaos in literature, art, and culture is often feminine—e.g., Tiamat in *Enuma elish*, or *tehom* in Genesis 1:2 (28). Order is then woman being "behind and subordinate to man, ordered, related, directed to man . . . In other words in the subordination of woman to man lies the social template of chaos-control: the very bottom line of the Creator's dominance and defeat of tehom." (ibid., 95; cf. Julie Galambush, "*Ādām* from *Ādāmâ*, *'Iššâ* from *'Îš*: Derivation and Subordination in Genesis 2.4b—3.24," 33, nn2 and 3 for a bibliography of differing positions on order among God, Adam, Eve, and animals in the garden). In this matrix of power and dominance, creation takes place by battle, not by procreation/birth (Keller, *Face of the Deep*, 18ff, 28, 60ff, 82, 130); the waters are sterilized. The problem is that in this matrix of dominance (whether in the divine realm or the human) "it must produce the monsters that at once justify its control and mock its mastery" (ibid., 97; cf. Beal, *Religion and Its Monsters*, 4–10). The "monsters" (e.g., Tiamat) may never have been monsters to begin with. They only were reacting to threats and/or attack. Keller uses the demonizing by the Nazis of the Jews as a human example.
37. Ibid., 17.

of being absolute.[38] She also wants to avoid totalizing origins because they are prey to accusations of *onto*theology.[39] The idea of divine origin has been privileged in most traditions in their myths.[40] The notion of origin "classically subordinates and ontologically precedes 'beginning.'"[41] On the other hand, however, the notion of beginning is a relative, historical notion. It developed as a secular counterpoint to the notion of origin.[42] Just as Keller rejects the polarity of *ex nihilo* versus autonomous co-eternal stuff that is conquered and/or formed, she rejects the polarity of origin versus beginning. Both ideas of beginning and origin, in the end, come from or function as a myth of origin.[43] In contrast, in the matrix of tehom there are no totalizing origins. There is beginning and beginning again, which "are historical-secular and *therefore also* mythical/theological."[44] The topos of the deep is "a place not *before* but *of* beginning."[45] There are the possibilities of the deep and all that has pre-existed with which all that is becoming already is related. Even God, through whom all causes arise, is first an effect. In the process of becoming there is no absolute origin.

Early in *Face of the Deep* Keller's focus is on the issue of creation's becoming. She juxtaposes her position against the familiar *creatio ex nihilo*. The doctrine of *creatio ex nihilo* entails in it a metanarrative that is a single line from beginning to end,[46] origin to goal.[47] God's ultimate dominion is unquestionable in that metanarrative in that he established it *ex nihilo*. Further, time and space serve only as the arena of salvation—salvation history.[48] Nature is a matter of fact—a given that is of little consequence—wherein the drama unfolds. It is not an actor in the drama or a key recipient of God's creative-salvific ends. Keller addresses this in

38. Ibid., 5.
39. Ibid., 160.
40. On this issue she draws from Edward Said and his treatment of *origin* versus *beginning*.
41. Ibid., 159.
42. Ibid., 5, 159.
43. Ibid., 159–60.
44. Ibid., 160.
45. Ibid., 161.
46. Ibid., 43.
47. Ibid., 50. Keller is just as concerned about *creatio ex nihilo*'s absolute future "beyond time and transience" as she is about an absolute origin (ibid., 20).
48. Ibid., 43; cf. 50, 58, 89.

her reading of Genesis 1. One way is through the unpacking of v. 2 and treating all its terms, including the waters, respectfully, not making them nothing or making them evil.[49] Another is in taking seriously the repeated phrase: "let there be . . ."[50] In answer to any interlocutors who might point toward "making" or "creating" in Genesis 1:1—2:3, Keller asserts: "For a theology of becoming, it is precisely the dichotomy of 'making' and 'letting be' that Genesis precludes. How else does Elohim *make*—but *by* letting be: 'And God said: *let* there *be* . . .'?"[51] In her view of there being dialogical cooperation—*creatio cooperationis*—between Elohim and Tehom (and between God and creation) she reads the "let there be" less "in the monotone of command than in the whisper of desire."[52] In the divine address of Tehom, "create is not *to master the formless but to solicit its virtual forms.*"[53] It is at God's invitation in v. 11 that the earth produces vegetation and in v. 20 that the seas creatively produce sea creatures.[54] Keller welcomes, in direct opposition to Barth, the idea of

49. Cf. ibid., 115. The final section of *Face of the Deep* is a step-by-step "algorithmic expansion" of all the key terms in v. 2, not just *tehom*.

50. "Let there be" appears in Genesis 1:3, 6, 14. Other phrases with "let" appear in Genesis 1:9, 11, 15, 20, 22, 24, 26.

51. Ibid., 17; italics original. Keller draws from William P. Brown's reading of the divine commands of Genesis 1 in *Structure, Role, and Ideology*.

52. Keller, *Face of the Deep*, 116. She agrees with Speiser's reading of Genesis 1 in that "he finds P repudiating *not* the assumption of a preexistent chaos, but rather the belligerent and politically oppressive *chaoskampf itself*" (ibid., 115). Cf. Speiser, *Genesis*, 11, where he places the positions of Genesis 1 and *Enuma Elish* "poles apart." Genesis 1 has a "critical position" toward what he believes are its sources. H. W. E. Saggs also views Genesis 1 as written in opposition to Mesopotamian mythology (*The Encounter with the Divine in Mesopotamia and Israel*, 53).

53. Keller, *Face of the Deep*, 115 (italics original). In this way Keller argues that Genesis 1 shows neither a "simple dependence nor simple opposition" to other ANE cosmologies; rather, Keller believes Genesis 1 is a "parodic divergence" (ibid., 268n47). For Brown, Genesis 1 should be read in the spirit of the *Timaeus*, in which god/Demiurge uses the random/chance causes of Khora. In Genesis, God takes what-there-is to work with and persuades it toward the good. The nonoppressive method of creating has as much to do with the good of the creation as the form taken (Brown, "Divine Act and the Art of Persuasion," 19:32). Elsewhere, Brown finds much more similarity between the waters in Genesis 1 and other ANE sources than with those of Apsu and/or Tiamat in *Enuma elish* (*Structure, Role, and Ideology*, 184).

54. Keller, *Face of the Deep*, 26; see also ibid., 82, 195, 217. Keller relies on Brown and his treatment of the alliteration in these two verses: "produces" (*tadse*) vegetation (*dese*) in v. 11, and "produce" (*yisresu*) sea creatures (*seres*) in v. 20. Cf. Sacks, *A Commentary on the Book of Genesis*, 7–12 for his treatment on this alliteration and the two other places these verbs are used in the Old Testament: in Exodus's plagues and in an eschatological

the maternity of the spirit or its waters that makes room for "more evolutionary theories of emergence, theories that might now emphasize the self-organizing complexity of creation."[55] In Keller's view it was many of the church fathers who "nihilified the (m)others of the narrative."[56] And many recent theologians simply follow in this tradition.

Keller's theology of becoming turns away from a logocentric doctrine of creation. Instead of eliminating tehom and inserting the divine Logos into nothing, she sees the incarnation of the Logos derived within "the chaosmic width of the creation."[57] In the feedback loop of beginning and beginning-again, of new and old, a "chaosmic Christ would represent the flow of a word that was always already materialized, more and less and endlessly, a flow that unblocks the hope of an incarnation, in which all flesh takes part."[58] Thus instead of *ex nihilo*'s linear history, Keller opts for an Irenaean "helical, recapitulatory sense of history."[59] In the recapitulatory loops, the new creation of all things is forever hoped for and possible. This is a material eschatology wherein incarnation, creation/new creation, is always going on in "redemptive recapitulations."[60]

In the last chapters of *Face of the Deep*, where Keller goes more fully into God's becoming, she addresses the notion of panentheism, of which she is a proponent.[61] This is where her idea of creation and new-creation as incarnation becomes not only a matter of the world being *capax dei* but

---

image in Joel. Sacks uses the following English translations: "to grass grass," "to swarm swarms," and "to flying fliers." Keller does not use the skies as an example as Sacks does. Brown says this wordplay concerning the birds and the sky would rely on a Hebrew Vorlage from which a LXX version was made that is at variance with the MT (Brown, "Divine Act and the Art of Persuasion," 26).

55. Keller, *Face of the Deep*, 94.
56. Ibid., 44.
57. Ibid., 19.
58. Ibid.
59. Ibid., 56.
60. Ibid., 56, 220. It should not be assumed however, that Keller means by the ongoing incarnation that God "consummates his loving control" by it or achieves complete lordship, understood as the subjection of his subjects (Keller, *Face of the Deep*, 90). She rejects this Barthian "*intimacy of domination*," wherein there is "*intimacy without reciprocity*" (90; emphasis original). She rejects Barth's "He-God" who "penetrates but is not penetrated" (90). Thus, for Keller, in the *incarnation* that is creation, God is taking form/body *and* is being affected.
61. Cf. Keller, *Face of the Deep*, 218ff.

God being *capax mundi*.[62] For Keller creation *is* incarnation[63] to the point that "the incarnation is coextensive with the body of the creation."[64] In her words, the *en* ("in") of pan*en*theism "does not as one might think designate some clearly lineated space of intersecting substances, let alone of mutual containment—as though the mutual immanence of divinity and world resembles Chinese boxes or intersecting circles. The *en* designates an active indeterminacy, a commingling of unpredictable, and yet recapitulatory, self-organizing relations. The '*en*' asserts the difference of divine and cosmic, but at the same time makes it impossible to draw the line."[65]

There is flux, or overlap, "of divinity with world, of world with divinity."[66] The relations are recapitulatory for God as they are for the world. The relationship of grace is no longer one of unilateral dependency of creation upon its Creator.[67] Rather, the becoming of creation constitutes God's embodiment/incarnation.

In the interplay of Tehom and Elohim, there is the capacitation of creation's becoming; it is in this capacitated relationship of creature with creator that the world is *capax dei* and God is *capax mundi*. Thus, "Any event, every spacetime of the capacious process of creation, might become readable as a unique, holy and temporary embodiment of the infinite."[68] In this ongoing process of creation "there takes place always, in endless quantities and qualities of difference, deformation and transformation, the *incarnation*."[69] This *in*carnation results in carnage. Only some of what is possible is materialized, actualized in the decision of becoming.[70] With the deformations and transformations in the incarnation there is always the hope of redemption, that the scars of creation/incarnation "may fade into gentler wrinkles."[71]

This highlights the reality that becoming does not always go according to divine aims. In her move away from creation out of nothing to

62. Ibid., 219.
63. Ibid., 219, 226.
64. Ibid., 221.
65. Ibid., 219.
66. Ibid.
67. Ibid., 89.
68. Ibid., 219ff.
69. Ibid., 220.
70. Ibid., 220, 221.
71. Ibid., 221.

creation (becoming) out of chaos Keller works to replace the idea of sin that has been passed down from Augustine. In Augustine sin is "understood as the *internal* resistance to the ordained order," which "requires *external* dominance"[72] as a corrective, containing corollary. Augustine's definition, Keller claims, represented a shift from "socially framed guilt"[73] to *personal shame about the darkness of each human's disordered nature.*[74] For example, sin for the psalmist "meant a deforming injustice for which members of a community stand responsible before each other and therefore God."[75] They are guilty for their unjust relations.

Keller revives a communal, relational way of looking at sin in her theology of becoming. Tehom—which is neither good nor evil, but the potential for good or evil[76]—is the medium of human sin. Within it / out of it is the freedom to actualize good or evil.[77] Since we are not created from nothing but from preconditions, that which precedes us constitutes us; for good or ill, preconditions *in*fect us; they "have shaped, privileged and deformed" us.[78] This originating sin (not a one-time original sin) is part of the mix (the good and the bad) that co-originates us. "If one earthling falls into alienation, into greed, into domination—that sin will infect its relations and thus *in part* constitute all who follow . . . I stand *not guilty* for the patterned chaos of relations performing me—but *responsible*. I become guilty if I do not take responsibility for the effects of past relations upon me now, as I affect the future."[79] In this way, Keller calls sin, as Augustine did, a "force of habit";[80] "We go along, we do not resist, we seek to secure our existence. The repetitions become habitual,

72. Ibid., 70.
73. Ibid., 71.
74. Ibid., 70.
75. Ibid., 70–71.
76. Ibid., 81.
77. Ibid., 80.
78. Ibid.
79. Ibid. Even if the notion of being *constituted* by relations may be a stretch for the reader, it is possible to accept that one person being oriented perversely in a population affects the relations of the rest of the population with that person; others may take a defensive, closed posture toward that person. Thus all the others will not be rightly related to *all* their neighbors; they will not have the openness of "drawing nigh" to all others. If each person lives in myriads of disoriented ways, even if only by fractions, this compounds and multiplies the unrighteous ways in which all persons within a community are related to one another and to other communities.
80. Ibid.; cf. Augustine, *Confessions*, VIII.5.12.

often compulsive, carried along by global patterns of assumption—economic, sexual, racial, religious. Amidst these structures, our agency may be unconscious. But it is never simply absent—we slip 'by our will.'"[81]

This force of habit is "the habit of discreation."[82] Instances where this discreative habit is blocked are conduits for chaos, the potential for good or ill. In that place a decision for a new good or a new ill is made.[83] "The habit of discreation is healed, inasmuch as it can be healed, not by a one-time, unmoved incarnational solid, but by the *capacitating* flux of what for us mammals is an ever carnal grace. Which we may address. *As you*."[84] It is in these recapitulatory loops that new creation happens from what is available, not *ex nihilo*.[85] New creation is the aim, the lure, of the word[86] perpetually incarnating itself, perpetually becoming.[87] Salvation is this new creation.[88]

---

81. Keller, *Face of the Deep*, 80. Her suggestion that "we seek to secure our existence" reminds me of Isaiah 28:15—"Because you have said, 'We have made a covenant with death, and with Sheol we have an agreement; when the overwhelming scourge passes through it will not come to us; for we have made lies our refuge, and in falsehood we have taken shelter.'" God's response to this behavior is as follows: "therefore thus says the Lord God, See, I am laying in Zion a foundation stone, a tested stone, a precious cornerstone, a sure foundation: 'One who trusts will not panic.' And I will make justice the line, and righteousness the plummet; hail will sweep away the refuge of lies, and waters will overwhelm the shelter. Then your covenant with death will be annulled, and your agreement with Sheol will not stand; when the overwhelming scourge passes through you will be beaten down by it" (vv. 16–18, NRSV).

82. Ibid., 81.

83. For the importance of decision in 'creation' see Keller, *Face of the Deep*, 160, 181.

84. Ibid., 81; emphasis original. Keller does not unfold what she means by "ever carnal grace." Perhaps it is related to the flow of the always already incarnate Word that becomes incarnate anew in every moment of becoming. There is that which is incarnated and the carnage of that which is not (*Face of the Deep*, 220, 221).

85. Ibid., 55ff.; cf. *Face of the Deep*, 298n32. This is consistent with Brown's perspective and why he argues for a reading of Genesis 1 that runs parallel to the *Timaeus* (see n53).

86. Keller oscillates throughout her work between capitalizing terms and not capitalizing them. I try to stay consistent with what she does within the context of the idea I am outlining.

87. Ibid., 220ff. There is little distinction between the location/instance of God's incarnation/becoming and creation's becoming. Keller certainly wants to distinguish between God and creation. However, it is at times difficult to differentiate their becomings in the flux between them.

88. Ibid., 56; cf. 227.

The Divine

Elohim and God

Elohim and *God* are two common terms that are broadly opened up within the final part of Keller's *Face of the Deep*. By deconstructing them within Genesis 1—or opening up their field of meaning—she makes room for tehom and her theology of becoming. It helps her avoid any hint of ontotheology by placing the divine within the origin-less process of becoming. "Clearly a tehomic theology does not use 'God' as the founding word, 'God creates' as its original act and fact."[89] In questioning 'God' as a something or "some One," her tehomic theology relocates the "identifiable *subject* of theology."[90]

"Elohim" itself is a plural word, which Keller takes to have theological significance.[91] It is not a personal name and can be used of any deity. Keller asks what to do with the word's impersonal plurality given that "Elohim" is "a common name for the object of the Bible's monotheism."[92] She answers through her panentheistic framework. Normally "Elohim" takes a singular verb, but in *bara*'s second use in the Bible, in v. 20 at the creation of humans, it is in the plural.[93] She takes this plural "let us create" as the democratic voice within the heavenly court of the "angelic multiplicity *of God him / her / it / themself.*"[94]

In her unfolding of angelology it enables Keller to affirm, "'Even "in the beginning" there is God and not-God, thus enabling God, as concept, to be.' The not-God within God reinscribes at the same time the many within the one."[95] Thus, the complexity of "Elohim" in Genesis 1 is read as a "plurisingularity";[96] as in the whirlwind of Job—which Keller reads as a midrash on the Genesis creation—"with its chaotic swarms of star, angel and beast," there is a hint of multiplicity

---

89. Ibid., 172.
90. Ibid.
91. Ibid., 173.
92. Ibid.
93. Ibid., 174.
94. Ibid., 175. See Hamilton, *The Book of Genesis*, 133ff. for the six categories in which this "let us create" typically has been interpreted through the years.
95. Ibid., 175; Keller is quoting personal correspondence she received from Stephen Moore.
96. Ibid., 177.

of the divine in the Genesis creation.[97] Or, with Norbert Samuelson, Keller reads "the Elohimic multiple: as angels and as energies."[98] Angels embody, not just bring, messages as the multiple.[99] Angels both hide and reveal God.[100] In short, "angels" becomes a way for Keller to talk about God's embodiment in the world while keeping some notion of distinction between God and world.

There is no way to grasp this plurisingularity; when "our thought habits press toward unity and division, the multiple is reduced to an aggregate of ones, contained within, adding up or reducing down to a single One . . . but these sub- and super-unities keep dissolving as we approach them."[101] Elohim/God is "not just anyone. And not just the One. We hear the Manyone . . . the turbulent swarm of godhood has always transgressed any possible boundaries between the One Original Creator and the many derivative creatures."[102]

Elohim is a created *space*. There is no way to name the subject of the verb *created*. Elohim too is an object—effect—of "created."[103] The "creation has no substantial subject."[104] Creator and creation are both effects of primal creativity—tehom/depth/chaos—even though creativity does not cause anything.[105] Tehom/creativity is the depth of God that gives birth to God.[106] Creativity is only "the condition that conditions all causal processes."[107] It is Elohim that/who is "the effect through whom all causes arise."[108] "All that becomes is *in* God, but not as apples are *in* a basket; perhaps more as they grow *in* a tree. Because all that becomes, becomes *within* God—as *part* of God—God is also becoming. So a primal Other not separate from but within God . . . produces the elohimic

---

97. Cf. ibid., 176–77.

98. Ibid., 177; Keller draws from Samuelson's *Judaism and the Doctrine of Creation* in her thoughts on angels.

99. Ibid.

100. Ibid., 176.

101. Ibid., 177.

102. Ibid., 177–78.

103. Ibid., 178; cf. 180.

104. Ibid.

105. Ibid., 181.

106. Ibid., 180. Cf. Hefner, "God and Chaos," 469.

107. Ibid., 181.

108. Ibid.

effect within language."[109] In the "chaosmic committee work" it is up to creation/the creature to respond with sensitivity to "the cosmic desire"— the lure or initial aim of elohim—and not block its own becoming.[110]

Ruach and the Tehomic Trinity

There is pneumatic space in between the divine and the world, between the spirit (divine) and the waters (deep). It is in this space that "the intimacy of the infinite begins to open," always looking/moving to the future.[111] This space is an erotic field, a rhythmic drumbeat pulsing all forward. The ruach deposits "the wad of writing in the next abyss." The "writing" is the opening of the deep and the unfolding of the divine manyone;[112] it is their intimacy that opens. It is the deep and manyone together that is capacitating of creation.

The Spirit/Ruach is the third in Keller's tehomic trinity: Tehom, Elohim, Ruach.[113] Tehom/Chaos, the topos of Deep, if "it were a person or a god it could signify the trinitarian 'first person.'"[114] It is not God but the *depth of God*; "Ocean of divinity, womb and place-holder of beginnings, it is not Elohim but the first place or *capacity* of genesis."[115] Because all is in God, Chaos is "the heterogeneous depth of divinity and of world," the *complicatio*.[116] It "anonymously gives birth to another, 'not separate but different,'"[117] the *explicatio*. This *explicatio* which is not separate but different from Tehom is what is *realized*, which means at once to be *divinized* and to be *actualized*.[118] In short, God-world is/

---

109. Ibid., 180.
110. Ibid., 181.
111. Ibid., 230.
112. Ibid., 231.
113. Ibid.
114. Ibid.
115. Ibid.
116. Ibid.
117. Ibid.; Keller is using a phrase from Tertullian here.
118. Ibid., 232. Again, this blurring and uniting of God's and the world's becoming in Keller's pan*en*theism is a facet of her work that will not be affirmed.

are birthed on the face of this depth. The *explicatio* "enters language as Word, Wisdom, Torah."[119]

The oscillation between "tehom and elohim," the first two "persons," creates.[120] "Creation begins—continually—in this relation, this incipient incarnation, at the edge of the waters."[121] The relation between tehom and elohim, "the 'relation of relations,' may be called by *implication* the *spirit of God*."[122] This pulsing force, this relation, opens a "third space," an *implicatio*, "where Tehom could flow into language and Elohim."[123] As the pneumatic space between God and either world[124] or tehom, the Spirit is "the differentiator which relates them one to another."[125] Thus the Spirit is differentiator and connector; "this spirit will not transcend or obliterate differences; rather differences are intensified precisely by being brought into relation."[126] "Spirit" signifies the relationality itself. Keller relates her treatment of Spirit to Augustine's in which the Spirit is the Love shared between the Father and Son; it binds them together "as lover and beloved."[127] "God the Spirit would then signify not only the "immanent" trinitarian relations, but also an 'economic' interdependence of creator and creation, and as such the interrelation of all creatures . . .

---

119. Ibid., 231.

120. Ibid., 232.

121. Ibid. In her discussion of panentheism, Keller says that "the names Tehom and Elohim may henceforth designate, if not 'persons,' two capacities of an infinite becoming" (ibid., 219). What this means can be defined by her statement: "If the godhead, or rather the goodness, *'in' whom unfolds* the universe can be theologized as Tehom, the ocean of divinity, the divinity *who unfolds 'in'* the all is called by such biblical names as Elohim, Sophia, Logos, Christ. The all in the divine, the divine in the all: this rhythm of appellations does not name two Gods, or even two Persons. Yet it does echo the trinitarian intuition of complex relationality *immanent* to an impersonal Godhead and personalized in the *oikonomia* of the creation" (ibid.; italics original).

122. Ibid., 232.

123. Ibid.

124. There is a complication within Keller's work of knowing what to do with the world in the relationship between *tehom* and *elohim*. Her treatment of the terms in Genesis 1 gives the only insight in how to navigate this complicated milieu. The early appearances of some terms in Genesis 1 are interpreted as tehom/chaos to which the *explicatio* is related. As creation unfolds, Keller interprets some terms as literal earth and seas to which God is in panentheistic relation—in which realization is at once both divination and actualization.

125. Ibid.; Keller draws on Deleuze for this idea.

126. Ibid.

127. Ibid.

The 'differentiator' can be said to connect divergent forces to their shared potentiality—i.e. the possibilities that can be realized only in relation: the 'I' who cannot become apart from 'you.'"[128]

Chaos and God must be held in relation to one another.

> Apart from the spirit 'brooding o'er the chaos,' Tehom remains a sterile possibility and 'God' remains mere Word, fleshless abstraction and power code. Only through pneumatology does theology have a prayer. For if the life and breath of divinity is the life and breath of the universe, then only in the "Spirit of Life" can our God-words *address* the mystery. Without this Spirit all our words circulate in a disembodied vacuum. For only in Spirit does Logos have *body*: that of creation. The universe becomes Sacred Body there where genesis takes *place*. No wonder the Spirit . . . vibrates at the edge of chaos.[129]

The Spirit also "connects our depths to our differences. It is of course *our* spirit—not as a possession or a self-possession but as the rhythmic life of all creatures, and only as such the *spiritus creator*."[130] The erotic field, the rhythmic beat of the Spirit ensures that there is creation, that incarnation takes place on the face of the Deep.[131]

In her theology of becoming, then, the "persons" of Keller's tehomic trinity go by many names. The first "person" may be called Tehom, Deep, Womb, Tiamat, depth of God. The second may be called Manyone, Difference, Elohim, Word, Wisdom, Torah. The last, the relation between the first two, is the Spirit, wind, Shekhinah, or Ruach.[132] Thus, in her triune formulation she concludes that "In beginning: a plurisingularity of universe, earth echoing chaos, dark deep vibrating with spirit, creates."[133]

Keller's Laudable Ideas

Many of Keller's ideas are noteworthy and will serve as helpful building blocks when they are placed in an alternative framework in the next chapter. Many of them will work with little change. However, within

---

128. Ibid., 232, 233.
129. Ibid., 233.
130. Ibid., 238.
131. Ibid., 232.
132. Cf. ibid., 231–35.
133. Ibid., 238.

a non-panentheistic theology, certain parts will need to be adjusted or left out.

First, in contrast to Levenson's perspective, her tehomic theology demonstrates what a theology employing "chaos" would look like that views the watery deep in a positive light. She tries to make tehom neutral. Tehom is not good or evil; it is the possibility for either. In her reading of Psalm 104:24–26, she says that the sea monster can be affirmed as good, just as such monsters were in Genesis 1:21. Nevertheless, affirming the goodness (or moral neutrality) or playfulness of the chaos monster does not mean it is "safe" or "cute."[134] Her treatments of the book of Job and Herman Melville's *Moby Dick* caution against such assumptions. In other words, as was claimed in the previous chapter, the Priestly cosmology does not demonize any part of creation and Keller is right in rejecting tehomophobic positions.

Second, Keller's tehomic theology presses on many of the weaknesses of traditional formulations of *creatio ex nihilo*, with accompanying notions of an absolute origin and end. Her treatment exposes the fact that salvation history and any other linear metanarrative about history is a constructed idea; it is not a given. In this linear construction, ideas about original sin or a fall have been articulated. She joins the chorus of thinkers in the past few centuries who find this doctrine of a one-time change in the past to be troublesome.[135] Also, linear notions of history easily serve as a breeding ground for visions of endless growth, development, and advancement of human beings in not only their social arrangements, human capacities, and collective knowledge, but also in their conquest, utilization, and consumption of creation.[136] There is no end to human hunger and hope for more ad infinitum.

Keller's work exposes a related problem concerning the traits of dominance and power that are asserted about God in traditional *ex nihilo* formulations. Any such claims about God have drastic effects on (or are the effect of) how people will seek to live in the image of that God.

---

134. Ibid., 27–28.

135. See chapter 2n153.

136. Even though the world wars supposedly dashed these hopes of the Enlightenment(s) and Modernity, these lessons have been quickly forgotten; hopes of endless increase still run deep. It should be noted, in all fairness, that Irenaeus himself—the one who championed recapitulation—taught that to be human is to grow in knowledge (by grace) for the entirety of this life and beyond. Neither a linear nor cyclical view of history is free of the danger of endless advance. Construction in Babel has yet to cease.

The subjecting of the (m)other is just one outcome of the unquestionable might of the God who creates order from nothing at his very command/ word, or even the God who crushes instantiations of chaos by *his* mighty arm. Keller prefers the ethical implications of a nonabsolutizing, originless becoming.

While Keller's jettisoning of the *creatio ex nihilo* doctrine will not be followed in this book, her attention to dangerous issues surrounding the doctrine makes her work laudable and worth listening to. There is a need to re-articulate this significant doctrine in a manner that integrates well with context-appropriate articulations of Original Sin. There also needs to be attention given to her concerns about linear growth and a God who interacts with creation one-sidedly.

Third, Keller's tehomic theology helps to resolve those same accompanying problems of traditional formulations of *creatio ex nihilo* that her theology presses against. In bringing many past voices into her tapestry, Keller sides with a non-chronological treatment of Genesis 1:1—2:3. She, like Levenson, cites the interpretations of an eleventh-century Jewish commentator, Rashi, which have been gaining popularity in recent years. Keller draws on E. A. Speiser's revival of Rashi's views.[137] Key among them is the breaking down of the presupposition that Genesis 1 intends to communicate a precise chronology of events. This paradigm shift away from the subject being about a serial listing of acts begins in the first verses where Rashi shows that the first sentence, which begins with, "When Elohim began to create heaven and earth," is more the subject matter of the first chapter; it is about the whole together, and not chronology or steps.[138] Chronology contradicts the first sentence;[139] through the lens of vv.1–3, the chapter serves more as a panoramic view than a turning of the pages of a cosmic scrapbook. An implication in this change is that creation is not a one-time, back then act. The "When Elohim began to create..." becomes the clue not only for reading Genesis 1, but it then prefaces the reading of all of Scripture: the unfolding of God's creative activity that will come to fullness in a/the Sabbath rest.[140]

By Keller changing the "when" of creation to *always* (instead of *then*) she also changes the character of creation. She lets the "let there

137. Cf. Keller, *Face of the Deep*, 114ff.
138. Ibid., 115.
139. Ibid.; see Keller for the detail of her argument and Speiser, *Genesis*.
140. Keller sees this rest not as a stopping of all activity or as all creation freezing

be . . ." of Genesis 1 hang in the chaos. She rejects God being completely separable from creation and, with it, God's utter dominance, or any reading of Genesis 1 that includes notions of mastery. God solicits creation's forms.[141] The earth and the waters are invited "into the grand creative sweep of God's designs."[142] Just as important to the notion of divine invitation is the accompanying notion of creation's response, the *response-ability* of creation.[143] In the next chapter a nonpanentheistic framework will be outlined in which this address and response could take place. In so doing, the distinctions made will preclude some of Keller's statements about the *self-organizing* complexities within creation or spontaneous natality. She does not endorse the autonomy of the cosmos, but, nevertheless, by *en*-meshing creation and divinity, creation is often attributed with divine capacities. Even so, her ideas about the ongoing nature of God's creative activity, God's soliciting invitation to creation, and the responsibility of creation are all positive.

With Keller's deconstruction of creation from nothing and its accompanying linear metanarrative, comes her suggestion of a helical view of history. There is beginning and beginning-again. Each entails a decision from among possibilities, from preconditions.[144] These loops of decision from preconditions not only hold promise for an account of God's ongoing work of new creation, but they also are equally promising in giving an account of sin. These two sides of Keller's treatment on becoming were already outlined in detail in this chapter so that will not be repeated. However, there are some benefits to this type of paradigm that should be pointed out, some of which Keller herself neither makes explicit nor draws upon in *Face of the Deep*.

The following benefits are related to Keller's description of disordered becoming. Before listing the benefits, however, it should be noted

---

in final changeless perfection. Rather, it is God and creation finally being at home with one another: "divinity at home within the rhythmic structures of natural/historical time, even as it structures human work within a sustaining cycle of refreshment" (ibid., 195).

141. Ibid.

142. Ibid., 116; Keller is quoting William Brown here.

143. Cf. Randy Maddox's book *Responsible Grace*, 19, for the importance of response within a Wesleyan theological perspective.

144. Keller pays attention to developments in science. Her elimination of a linear metanarrative and downplaying the Beginning (as though history deterministically unfolds out of it) in favor of beginnings can, in part, be attributed to voices beyond religious studies.

that Keller limits her discussion of discreative habits to humans. Her theology of becoming encompasses all creation, yet she does not expand sin—discreative habits that hinder or destroy the fullness of becoming—to all creation.[145] This is a loss within her account. The idea of chaos being developed in this project will treat all discreative "sins" uniformly, whether they are "committed" within matter itself or by thinking beings.[146] Thus, the benefits of taking her thoughts on "sin" and applying them universally within all creation will be the following.

First, that which God is saving creation from can be defined uniformly for material creation and for living beings. It is no longer multiple problems of creation's fallenness and humanity's fallenness and sin.

Second, within Keller's paradigm, it is the existence of specific disordered decisions of becoming and their consequent disordering effects that is of greatest concern. The decision is certainly willed; becoming cannot be otherwise. However, her theology does not lose itself in discussions of intent. Within most western judicial thought there is a necessity of mal-intent for there to be a crime, or sin.[147] All creation

---

145. One possible reason is her desire to celebrate the abundance of life within creation. She does not want to demonize circumstances where humans are harmed by nature. I imagine her response to such harm is, who are we to blame nature and its explosive, frolicking life when we are in its world? This guess is based on chapters 7 and 8 of *Face of the Deep*, in which she treats respectively the book of Job and Melville's *Moby Dick*. In her treatment of Job, Keller believes the point of God's final response is to tell Job to look at the magnificence of the wild things—their frolic and animal energy; we wander in their midst at our own peril. By interpreting *Moby Dick* as a midrash on Job, Keller sees Moby Dick—the leviathan—as a character content to swim along in its domain but also as an unbreakable rock against which all who battle it will be dashed. Thus, Keller protects creation from her discussion of becoming-gone-wrong. She wants to embrace the explosive force of creation's becoming and to deconstruct any prior labels of its evils.

146. The expectations of human beings for themselves and for the rest of creation have gone through cycles since the Enlightenment. Various thinkers have had perspectives: from positive expectations for humanity and creation to positive expectations for humanity and negative ones for creation to negative expectations for both (see Neiman, *Evil in Modern Thought*). William Brown suggests that the central lesson of Job is that only when Job is stripped of his constructed societal notions of what is right—by watching the grace of God at work among the *wild* animals—can he begin to find a proper perspective of right relation as a human to God and creation. If Neiman's (and to a degree Brown's) research teaches anything, it is in showing the complicated history of humanity understanding and finding its place in the world. Depending on one's perspective, instances of chaos may be an infinitely large set; or they may be a surprisingly small set.

147. Cf. Neiman, *Evil in Modern Thought*. This will be developed further in chapter 7 when I define *chaos*.

and creatures are responsible for (guilty of) their discreative decisions; the consequences stand in need of recapitulation regardless of what was intended when making those decisions. Keller's framework cuts through to this most basic problem.

Third, Keller revives a communal (relational) paradigm for understanding sin in juxtaposition to most post-Augustinian formulations. The relational definition of sin—or the more comprehensive idea of chaos that is being developed—works for both individuals and communities. It is individuals in relation making decisions of becoming that effect the subsequent relations within the whole. Both individuals and communities need healing.

Fourth, Keller defines the problem of sin in a dynamic and historic way. Each event happens in relation to that which preceded it. She does not depend upon a one time, once upon a time, mythical account of a fall, which has for centuries now been a liability when presenting Christianity to an audience who thinks in post-Enlightenment ways.[148]

Lastly, Keller's description of sin—within her framework of becoming—takes embodiment seriously; she says it cleverly: matter matters. Sin arises in the process of embodiment/becoming. It will be fixed in the process of embodiment/becoming, as new creation takes place within the recapitulatory loops. This is our salvation.

The last benefit of Keller's description of sin naturally leads into discussing the benefits of her position on salvific recapitulations. The benefit of taking our embodiment seriously has already been mentioned. If Keller were to keep together creation and creatures more closely in defining sin—or as is being developed, the idea of chaos—other benefits are, first, that recapitulation addresses uniformly the process by which discreative occurrences within material creation and living beings are rectified. Secondly, the process of new creation is not only the same for all creation, but it is equally for all creation. God's creative and redemptive activity involves the material world as much as it involves all living beings. The world becomes a significant character in the drama instead of the background. Lastly, salvific recapitulation is just as dynamic and relational as Keller's treatment of sin. It requires unending, ongoing cooperation—response—from creation.

---

148. Cf. Neiman, Buckley, and the like. For an excellent article that summarizes the issues and a way of moving forward in biblically faithful manner, see Harlow, "After Adam."

Critique

Two major critiques of Keller's tehomic theology will be given here. Each one is related to significant facets of the theological position being developed in this project. The first critique relates to the relation of God within creation. The second critique relates specifically to the use of "chaos" in Keller's work.

First, on the ontological spectrum between pantheism and divine transcendence—such that everything is in a reality distinct from God's own[149]—Keller proposes her pan*en*theism as a third, middle option. Her position does not hold God as ultimately being the only subject, with the world being reducible to God and God's activity (pantheism): nor does it hold a stark distinction between God and a world-bereft-of-God. She affirms that God is "Thou" to the world as theism desires. However, at the same time, the "en" in panentheism "makes it impossible to draw the line" between God and world.[150] Keller's full position will not be repeated here. In it, however, the boundary between God and world is so blurred, it is in such flux, that God and world are inextricably caught up with one another. The "*en*" affirms this relation. The *manyone* cannot be defined apart from the inclusion, within its array, of a *concretizing angelic host*—embodying messages; nor can *creation* be defined apart from the inclusion of *divine embodiment*. Within Tehom, the creator and creature "create, effect, *each other*."[151]

She further strengthens the indistinguishable *in*-ness of God and world in her use of *in*carnation. Creation *is* the incarnation of the manyone on the face of the Deep (which should not be separated from the becoming of the manyone itself/themselves). Creation is where God is

---

149. Keller, *Face of the Deep*, 88. Keller primarily has her eye on Barth and his notion of transcendence throughout her work. A God that exists apart from creation can touch but not be touched, penetrate but not be penetrated. Such a world external to God can only have instrumental value to God (see ibid., 89).

150. Ibid., 219.

151. Ibid., 218.

embodied. Incarnation becomes coextensive with *all* realization: both divinization and actualization.[152]

Even Keller's thoughts on Spirit end up confusing divine Spirit with human/cosmic spirit.[153] She is right to recognize the need for both differentiation and relation between God and the other, whether that other is creation or Tehom. However, "spirit" becomes little more than a term that describes that *space* of separation and relation. Keller does no better in her pneumatology than the Western tradition—which in line with Augustine defines the Spirit in terms of the relation between the Father and Son, the love shared between them—in objectifying (and thus minimalizing) the Spirit. As will be shown in the next chapter, the pneumatology of Lyle Dabney affirms distinction and relation between God and creation, but "Spirit" is abundantly more than a name for that *space* of distinction-relation. Keller's pneumatology has hints of connection with Dabney's in that she sees the pulsing, erotic field of the Ruach as the rhythm of life that moves all creating forward by keeping all in her tehomic trinity in relation. Nevertheless, Dabney keeps the Spirit as Divine Spirit, the third person of the Trinity, who is the Possibility of God for the other and who operates transjectively through creation, opening it up to the possibility for the o/Other. This means the Divine Spirit is less likely to be reduced to or confused as being the human spirit (as Keller can be interpreted to do in her framework of "in"), nor does the Spirit make objects out of human subjects (as Keller reacts against in the *creatio ex nihilo* paradigm, especially as it is in Barth).

Folding God into the process of becoming in ways that gives God little differentiation from the world and its becoming is not the only option between pantheism and a world devoid of God, or a world *made* by God. She claims to be teasing out suppressed minority positions within the tradition. Even so, it is questionable whether any of her predecessors would recognize their sentiments in her theology. For example, even those who did not renounce the eternality of matter affirmed a start to

---

152. As Keller says: "The action of God is its *relation*—by *feeling and so being felt*, the divine invites the *becoming* of the other; by feeling the becoming of the other, the *divine itself becomes*" (ibid., 198; italics original). There is oscillation between divine attraction and divine reception, invitation and Sabbath.

153. It was mentioned earlier that the Spirit signifies the interrelation of Keller's trinity and all creatures with others. Thus, the Spirit "connects our depths to our differences. It is of course *our* spirit—not as a possession or a self-possession but as the rhythmic life of all creatures, and only as such *spiritus creator*" (ibid., 238; italics original).

Catherine Keller's Tehomic Theology 179

God's formative/creative activity. There are other ways of speaking about the relation between God and the world that affirm dynamic relationality between them, and yet still are located within more prevalent currents of the Christian tradition. Due to their familiar landmarks, these options can more broadly resonate within the Church as it wrestles with understanding the mystery of its faith in certain of the Church's current contexts. It can also serve Christians in those contexts as a vehicle for articulating the Gospel in a way that may be comprehensible to their unbelieving neighbors.

As has already been noted, many of the ideas in Keller's theology of becoming are useful as they relate to creation. However, on the other hand, where God is concerned, there is no sufficient reason that a more recognizably Christian view of the triune God *must* be abandoned. In the next chapter it will be demonstrated that it is possible to give an account for the becoming of the world in response to the call of the triune God: Father, Son, and Holy Spirit. The contrasting difference between this account and Keller's will be the contrast between the use of "trans" versus "in." The operation of the Spirit in creation will be spoken of as *trans*jective. And the operation of the Word in creation will be spoken of as *trans*carnate. By setting up this relational dynamic, it will open a very specific place in which "chaos" can be used theologically. This use of "chaos" will have many benefits within the realm of theology, some of which have already been mentioned.

Second, Keller uses the term "chaos" most often as a synonym for *tehom* and "deep." She uses many other terms as synonyms to these three words; however, "chaos," *tehom*, and "deep" are her three most commonly used terms. Her use of "chaos" in that manner should be avoided. The term "chaos" has a long history within biblical studies. All of them are tehomophobic uses, which is exactly what Keller works to deconstruct. Keller certainly does not want tehom to be mistaken as a cute or safe space; perhaps this is why she might want to draw on the connotations of "chaos." Nevertheless, she does not want to present a position wherein *ordering* and *forming* are the default assumptions about what is needed within the primordial stuff, the milieu of milieus.[154] "Tehom" and "deep" work well as terms that evoke a boundless well of unrealized

154. Keller does not speak of a *primordial* stuff/situation because in her framework there is no time prior to the process of becoming. If there were, there would be an absolute origin. Thus, in her theology, there is the site of becoming, the realm of possibilities, but it is not *before* becoming; it is *of* becoming.

futures. Even though Keller wants to weave in some angst about the wiliness of becoming on the face, "chaos" is not the best term to use for that purpose—given its history and connotations. Keller herself outlines the deep-rooted tradition in western culture to try to fix or solve instances of chaos. At worst, it needs to be conquered and mastered. Keller could have developed a term such as *profundus* to bring in that sense of angst, instead of working upstream against the history of "chaos" in the realms of biblical and ANE studies, as well as its cultural history.

The connotations of "chaos" work against her development of a tehomophilic framework. If "chaos" popularly evokes something in need of solution, why not reserve it theologically for that type of function? Within this project, that is precisely what is being suggested; "chaos" should be used as the overarching category for instances where discreative decisions take place within all creation. Keller's discussions of human sin would be a subset within this broader category.[155] Developing this account of chaos within a more recognizably trinitarian paradigm is the direction we now turn.

Last, concerning chaos, as was shown in the previous chapter, recent biblical scholarship questions the validity of applying it to Genesis 1:2. Without critiquing Keller's use of "chaos" within her postfoundationalist hermeneutic based on an historical-critical approach, it can at least be pointed out that she adopts the use of "chaos" in reference to Tiamat and Genesis 1:2 based on scholarship such as Levenson's—even if she critiques what he and the masculine tradition(s) do with the (feminine) chaos.[156] Arguably, she should not have adopted their use of "chaos," given its questionability.

Summary

Keller's work has as many folds as the deep of which she writes. The complexity of the process thought in which she positions herself aids in the mystery. Nevertheless, there are gems in her work that do resonate not

---

155. One danger with this use is precisely what Keller is working against. She is concerned about any instances when one group makes monsters out of another in order to justify mastery. The definition of *chaos* being developed does not go without the problem of *who* gets to name *what* is chaos. Keller has a postfoundationalist framework in which making any one position absolute is avoided. Without going that route, this problem will need to be addressed in the following chapter.

156. Keller, *Face of the Deep*, 26.

only with the Priestly perspective outlined in chapters 3 and 4, but also with contemporary audiences.

By looking at the history of the doctrine of creation, entering the biblical studies debates, and by showing how a contemporary theologian uses "chaos" language, hopefully it has been shown that this terminology has been used in a myriad of different ways, few if any of them in desirable ways. Even if Levenson and Keller are to be applauded for the underlying impulses that pushed their thinking in the directions they did, there is another way forward in our context that seeks to listen both to the voice of Scripture and the intentions of the tradition. It is now time to turn to the work of laying out that alternate framework in which "chaos" language can serve an appropriate and useful purpose.

6

A New *Creatio ex Nihilo* Framework

CONCERNING THE ISSUE OF CREATION, THE FOLLOWING HAS BEEN noted. First, although the intent of those wrestling to articulate the faith in ever changing thought-worlds has been honorable, it was noted in chapter 2 that there were at times undesirable and unintentional consequences to the paths chosen. Among those highlighted, the physio-spatial divide (for lack of a better term) between God and the world, such that the activity of one was seen to be mutually exclusive of the other, has been quite problematic. This tension will be eased in the framework being proposed by expanding key ideas from Lyle Dabney's pneumatology. Second, there has been much debate in biblical studies concerning what the Priestly creation account says theologically. While being faithful to the movement of the text, the text will be allowed to reverberate in answer to questions that postdate its composition for the sake of informing theology in the present. While what follows is not biblical theology—in that it does not attempt to summarize the theology of a biblical text, book, or author—it does seek to be informed by Scripture and in return serve as a framework for the present through which to read and engage Scripture.[1]

---

1. This circularity between theological affirmations, rules of faith, and the biblical text has been part of the church's practices since the early centuries; cf., e.g., David S. Yeago's essay, "The New Testament and the Nicene Dogma."

Proposed Framework in Which to Define "Chaos"

Borrowing Some Key Features of Lyle Dabney's Pneumatology

Lyle Dabney seeks to complete in his pneumatology the theological turn begun in Luther.[2] Whereas there had been, in Luther's eyes, a theology of glory—a theology of human ascent (graced nature)—Luther proposed a theology of God's descent, understanding God in relation to the incarnation and the cross. Within this Lutheran tradition, the Father and Son had been defined in relation to the cross. However, the Spirit was defined in terms of bringing humans to what had been accomplished in the cross. Dabney seeks to finish Luther's turn by defining the Trinity, including the Spirit, in terms of the cross.[3] To that end, in an examination of Mark's narrative, he concludes that the Spirit is

> *the possibility of God even in the midst of every impossibility that God could be present and active, the divine possibility that the living God might be found even in the midst of chaos and death, indeed, precisely in the midst of chaos and death, the possibility that God might yet be for us and we might yet be for God, and thus the possibility that even those who suffer that deadly estrangement might beyond death be raised to new life, transformed life, a life in which the crushed and broken and incoherent bits and pieces of a life are taken up anew and made whole.*[4]

Because the Spirit is the one who is the possibility of God in every impossibility, the Spirit is integrally part of the life, death, and resurrection of the Son—not just the subsequent application of that which was accomplished by the Father and Son on the cross and mediated by the Son.[5]

---

2. Dabney's pneumatology is laid out in an accessible manner in a series of lectures published together in *Starting with the Spirit*, edited by Gordon Preece and Stephen Pickard; several of them were later published in other forms after their original appearance (see the bibliography).

3. See Dabney, "*Pneumatologia Crucis*," 511–24, esp. 513–15.

4. Dabney, "Naming the Spirit," 58—italics original; cf. Dabney, "*Pneumatologia Crusis*," 524.

5. Cf., e.g., Wolfhart Pannenberg's pneumatology. His typical formula is to talk of an activity of the Father by the Son and the Spirit. He clarifies the "by" as the obedience of the Son to the Father and the glorification of the Father and Son through the consummation of their work by the Spirit (*Systematic Theology*, 3:134–36). This is true in the case of creation and redemption. In redemption the Spirit reveals and teaches about what the Father and Son accomplished and moves us to faith, hope, and love (5); the "basic saving works of the Spirit" are summed up in the gifts of faith, hope, love, and adoption

The Spirit is the presence and possibility of God in Christ's Passion—the possibility that creation might still be for God and the possibility of God to be for/in impossibility. "Indeed, it is precisely the kenotic work of the Spirit of life to plunge himself into death, hell and the grave, to 'empty himself' into the abyss of death and raise the one who, by virtue of that self-same Spirit, gave himself to death on the cross to gain new life for all creation."[6] Simply, in the cross, which is centrally definitive of God, the Spirit is seen to be *the possibility of God* and "is not to be identified simply as 'power' or as 'life' or as a 'relationship' or as 'gendered,' male or female—as is so often the case."[7] If the Spirit is to be named, the primary name should be Possibility of God.

The use of the word "possibility" can be misleading for those who are accustomed to its philosophical use, in the distinction between possible and actual. The term is not being used in this technical sense. That would make the Spirit something not-yet-realized in God (a potential) that could not, then, have agency or be in a give and take loving relationship.[8] That would also make the Spirit very similar to the Tehom in Keller's trinity.

Nevertheless, there are certainly philosophical issues in the background of Dabney's pneumatology. His pneumatology "*develops its understanding of creation in terms of the priority of possibility, not in terms of the priority of being or the real* . . . As Eberhard Jüngel has pointed out, it was an act whose consequences for the history of the western intellectual tradition are almost impossible to overestimate, when Aristotle declared in his Metaphysics that the real was necessarily prior to the possible (*Met* Q, 1049 b 5; cp L, 1072 a 9), which had as its logical correlate that the real defines the parameters of the possible in thought and deed."[9] *Possibility* is

---

(cf. 136–236). Thus, "the work of the Spirit is simply to glorify the Son by teaching us to know the Father in the Son through whom we have access to him . . . Because the Spirit, as Creator of a new life with no death, is himself an eschatological reality, he can also make manifest the eschatological significance of the coming and history of Jesus" (ibid., 16, 17). The Son gifts the Spirit to us as an anticipation or pledge of the future (7, 11). Until then, the Spirit ecstatically raptures believers into union with Christ (ibid., 16, cf. ibid., 134).

6. Dabney, "*Pneumatologia Crucis*," 524.

7. Dabney, "Naming the Spirit," 58.

8. I thank Thomas Oord for reminding me that this term has other technical uses that may create misunderstandings of the pneumatology being advocated.

9. Dabney, "The Nature of the Spirit," 101–2 (italics original). The implications of the priority of the Real and some of the ways this has shifted in Western thinking has been

being used in the sense of the Spirit, as an agent, a person of the Trinity, "making possible." This framework "does not begin with a metaphysical claim for the ontologically real, it starts rather with the Spirit of God who in the death and resurrection of Jesus Christ is identified as the possibility of God that brings the real into emergent being."[10] The Spirit being the Possibility *of God* should not be understood that the Spirit is "making possible" God. Instead, it is that which is other to God for whom the Spirit is the Possibility of God. As Dabney's work shows, this operation of the Spirit, demonstrated powerfully in Christ, is a work of God *for us*.

This turning around of the deeply engrained order of possible and real merits brief illustration beyond what Dabney offers in his lectures. Since the Spirit is the first creative move of God as possibility for the other, the Spirit is not making or giving "possibilities" or a "set of possibilities." Such a use would be more in keeping with Aristotle's legacy. Also, such a use is common in those who speak about creation organizing, or being organized, from randomness and disorder, from a realm of possibilities. However, the word is not used in the plural. Such notions are being excluded. Instead, the Spirit is the possibility for the other. There is the openness of God-making-possible the other, the other's expression. By such open-endedness to the making-possible activity, it provides space (possibility) for the agency and ingenuity of God's other to be operative with God in creatively moving forward.[11] By the Spirit, God makes possible the stepping forward into what is not, rather than the making actual one of the not-yets (possibilities).[12] There is no capacity that nature or

---

outlined in helpful ways in Remi Brague's *The Wisdom of the World*.

10. Dabney, "The Nature of the Spirit," 102.

11. See, ibid., 104. In looking at the focus of creation theology through the eras of the church, there has been a progression in the focus on the Father (the first article) to the Son/Word (the second article). This has had its effects. "As we saw above, a theology of the first article thinks of the act of creation as that state of emanation of necessary being down the ladder of contingent being from divine to angelic to human to animate to inanimate. The theology of the second article, on the other hand, emphasizes the personal and purposeful nature of the act of creation and likens it to the speaking of the Word of Law and Gospel—so Luther—or to the carrying out of a providential plan—as in Calvin. But perhaps a theology of the third article should conceive of creation in a different way entirely: as an act of discovery" (Dabney, "The Nature of the Spirit," 104).

12. One possible objection needs to be addressed. The finitude of creation is still being affirmed. In the Spirit being the Possibility of God, a human cannot decide in the next moment to be a bird. However, instead of seeing our finitude as a limited set of possibilities given to us by God (the Real), another option is being proposed. God has not calculated from the beginning all possible outcomes based on every possible

creation possesses to move forward, but the life-giving breath of God blowing through makes possible the 'new' or the 'further.'[13]

Moving forward: in the relationship between God and creation, the Spirit, as an operating agent, is the possibility that there can be an other for God, one that is both related and distinct.[14] It is this "relationship in the Spirit as the breath of God that gives breath to all creation, which is the possibility of God for the world and the possibility of the world for God, a relationship that even permits the speaking of a/the w/Word to an o/Other and the hearing of the w/Word of the o/Other."[15] The Spirit is not the relationship between God and the other—neither a space giving distinction between God and creation nor a glue that keeps them related, or interacting in proximity. Another way of stating this: the Spirit is *other* from creation, but being *other* implies relatedness.[16] We are not identical with the Spirit, the Giver of Life, who is the very Breath of God breathed through us; but being *other* means that we can be, indeed are,

---

combination of choices made among the provided possibilities. God is not waiting to see which option among all possible outcomes becomes reality. The question for God is far more interesting than which horse entered in the race will get around the oval first. God certainly is more knowledgeable than creation about the precise ripples that each action has on the relational dynamics within the cosmic community. However, the beauty of God joining with the cosmic community, of making possible that which is other, that which truly has agency, is being surprised by the activity, the word, of an other. The great mystery in God's relationship with creation is where these agents whom God makes possible will take this thing. How often must God reflect, "That certainly is not how I would have thought to do that, but that works," in response to the positive inventive responses of creation? God makes possible that creation can participate in creating the nonexistent future, rather than creation picking and choosing among not-yet futures that God provides.

13. Dabney, "The Nature of the Spirit," 103–4.

14. Recall the tension within the tradition—affirming a distinction between God and creation while still articulating a relation of God to (or need for God in) creation. Catherine Keller's pneumatology defined the Spirit as the space that gives separation/distinction and relation to God and creativity/*tehom*. Her approach reflects the trend in Western pneumatology to define the Spirit in terms of the relation between the Father and Son, the love shared between them. Dabney cuts through identifying the Spirit *as* the relation in favor of identifying the Spirit as the relating one. The Spirit is the Third Person of the Trinity, who is not merely passive, but acts, with the Father and Son, relative to creation.

15. Dabney, "The Nature of the Spirit," 100.

16. In Dabney's words, "only that which is both different and related is 'other.' That with which we are identical is not 'other,' it is simply a repetition of ourselves. That to which we have no relation, on the other hand, is likewise no 'other,' it is as far as we are concerned, simply 'not'" (ibid., 97).

defined relative to the Spirit. It is in the Spirit "that we are established and maintained in relationship with the One who is truly Other, the Wholly Other, with whom we are not identical and yet with whom we are always related. And in that difference in relationship we are at one and the same time related to one another and to the entirety of God's creation."[17]

From the first page of the Bible there is no part of creation devoid of the Spirit's presence. God is other than creation, but creation is not "autonomous from its Creator."[18] In the Spirit, God is with and for creation, even where it seems most unlikely or impossible. Even in the imagery of Genesis 1:2, what elsewhere may be a catastrophic destruction for God's people and the land is, because of the Spirit's presence, a picture of "the possibility and promise of creation."[19] In all that takes place in the narrative, "there is woven the presupposition of the presence of the Spirit."[20]

By the Spirit's presence in human beings, they can be and were created to be *for* the o/Other: God and the-rest-of-God's-creation (i.e., neighbor). "By virtue of the Spirit as the ubiquitous and life-giving presence of God in the world, we might say then that, from the very first, we—indeed all creation—are 'otherwise engaged in the Spirit' and are thus ever and again encompassed in events of emergent commonality . . . For the Spirit of God," writes Dabney, "is that which relates us to God and to one another ever and again at each moment of our existence."[21]

This o/Other orienting Spirit, as Dabney points out, is not the same as human subjectivity, the human spirit seeking out God, nor is the Spirit God's subjectivity meeting us face-to-face or making objects out of humans to control them. The Spirit does not operate in the categories of *sub*ject or *ob*ject within God's creation, but rather *trans*ject. This means that "from the very inception of our lives we live 'out of' the presence of God's spiritual breath, borne away from ourselves on the winds of the Spirit to the 'other' of our neighbor and to the 'Wholly Other' of our Creator."[22]

This grammar of "trans" is helpful in shaping the imagination concerning God's relationship to and operation relative to creation. "Trans"

17. Ibid., 97–98.
18. Ibid., 98.
19. Ibid.
20. Ibid., 99.
21. Ibid.
22. Ibid., 99–100.

dances between seeing the Spirit either as an outside causative force intruding on creation or being conflated as part of creation. In blowing through/across creation, the Spirit orients those whom the Spirit inhabits outward toward others. That which is the Possibility of God *for us* is not generic in its operation; the Spirit is o/Other pointed. In the Spirit we live "eccentric" lives that have their center in an o/Other.[23] The Spirit is the possibility of God for the other and the possibility that the other might be and live for the o/Other. All created things, especially humans, "are, from the first, social in nature."[24] They are to live eccentric lives by the very possibility of God by which they were created to do so. The Spirit operates "trans"-creation to that end. Love of God and neighbor is the orientation according to which creation exists by the Spirit. The Spirit is not present to creation that the Spirit might be ours, but it blows where it will that we too might be for others.[25] "Thus, just as the 'east wind' drives the various waters westwards or bend the many different plants of the field in a *common* direction, thereby effecting in the many a *common* result without in any way reducing their individual differences, so in like manner the divine wind of God's Spirit can move upon the waters of chaos at the first or among a people at a certain time and place and bend their lives to a *common* purpose and a distinctive social existence."[26]

It is in this way that the Spirit is the possibility that there can be an other for God that is both related and distinct. The new category of God relating to creation by the Spirit transjectively affirms simultaneously distinction and relation; it does not try to balance between the two separately-stated antinomies of transcendence and immanence, but rather offers a grammar that moves beyond the prior tension.

In terms of God's creative (and redemptive) mission, the Spirit is the possibility of God for all creation, for that which is not yet "son/daughter" to the Father. For example, upon Jesus's anointing with the Spirit at his baptism he is cast by the Spirit into the desert and eventually to the cross. It is precisely in the impossibility of these places that the Spirit is the possibility or presence of God in the not-yet of the Father. This mission is manifest in God's others by the Spirit. The outwardly-oriented/

---

23. Ibid., 100.

24. Ibid.

25. Ibid., 101.

26. Ibid., 100. This quotation shows that Dabney is willing to use "chaos" in reference to Genesis 1:2, unlike what is proposed herein.

orienting Spirit takes God's children into all that is not yet child of the Father so that new, transformed life might be found there. More than gracing nature unto salvation or making a favorable judgment concerning a dead, rejected nature, salvation is a transformation of that nature by the possibility of the divine Spirit that we might truly be children of the Father.

An Adaptation to Dabney's Proposal: Looking Again at the Second Person

By the fourth century, a method typically employed against those who claimed either that the Son or Spirit were creatures, or that three Gods were being taught within Christianity, was to demonstrate the inseparable operations of the Trinity.[27] With this method Christians sought to establish not only the divinity of the three persons, but also the unity of the distinct persons in being, power, presence, and activity. Even though orthodoxy on these trinitarian issues has been worked out in that early context and inseparable operations is not needed for the purpose of *establishing* right doctrine, it is still a helpful theological affirmation both supported by Scripture and through which to read Scripture.

Dabney originally sought to finish the turn begun in Luther by defining the third person of the Trinity, with the Father and Son, relative to God's work in Christ and the cross. This aim can be seen as a move toward inseparable operations in a context where it had been insufficiently affirmed. This facet of his work on pneumatology is especially laudable. Nevertheless, in seeking to define the Spirit based on the activity of the Spirit relative to Christ, the West's traditionally-passive Spirit was depicted as active almost to the detriment of the second person. The second Person, especially in Christ, became the one whose *activity* was a matter of *consent* to the Spirit.[28] The traditionally active and passive qualities assigned in the West to the Son and Spirit respectively were nearly reversed. In moving forward, a more robust manner of speaking about the inseparable operations of all the persons, including the Word will be suggested.

As with the tensions noted in Dabney's work concerning traditional positions about the Spirit's relation to creation, finding a way to talk about

---

27. Cf., e.g., Hilary of Poitiers, *De Trin.* 7; Augustine, "Sermon 52."
28. See, e.g., Dabney, "Naming the Spirit," 47.

the Word relative to creation has been equally difficult. The options have tended to vary between either the Word being a distinct, external command given to or acting upon creation, or the Word being imbedded to some degree within creation. Keller's theology is an example of the latter in which creation is coextensive with the *in*carnation of the divine word. There is indistinctiveness in subjectivity of who is expressing whom. In chapter 2 it was noted that problems arose later in the tradition when God either was conceived as existing and acting as an external force to creation or was confused with creation in pantheistic or pan*en*theistic paradigms. With the growth of scientific inquiry, in the first option God became unnecessary and in the second the spiritual became subject to natural observation and eventually superfluous as well.[29]

Those are not the only options. Just as the Spirit operates transjectively to creation, the Word operates in a *trans*carnate manner—through, across. God is certainly distinct in this framework, but not solely exterior to creation or spatially separated from creation. God is not conflated with creation or embodied therein, save in the *in*carnation of the Second Person in Jesus. *In*carnation is the self-revelation, self-expression of God living enfleshed. On the other hand, in the coming to be of creation, made possible by the inseparable operations of the Triune God, it is not God's self-revelation, self-expression (i.e., incarnation). It is our self-expression of God's self-gifted goodness trans-creation. We are imaging divinity, but God is not self-expressing God in us. Preserving respectively the subjectivity of creation and God at work is key in affirming the Word operating relative to creation transcarnately versus incarnately.

The coming to be creation is also not plucking out from the intersecting Word what to embody of the Word. Just as the Spirit does not become our possession, creation does not capture snapshots of the Word as the form it takes on. There is a movement and orientation of the Word; it is a song of love to/for the other. Initially it is in the Possibility of the Spirit that the operation of the Word makes possible a word to be spoken by an other in relation to the Godhead.[30] In God's subsequent creative activity, it is the rub of the Word/call of God transcreation—with the always present Possibility of the Spirit—in relationship to which

---

29. It was also noted that there were struggles with what to do with laws of nature. Were they intrinsic to matter, applied to matter, or followed by God, who is the cause behind the workings of nature?

30. See Dabney, "The Nature of the Spirit," 102.

creation can respond with a word. Creation does not speak the Word, but its own—its own word sparked and made possible by the God who speaks first. The friction of the expressed love of God—the Word transcarnate—in creating is the possibility of creation having a voice, and a vocalization relative to which creation makes its tones. Creation can come to self-express, in orchestral array, the divine love/goodness God self-gifts trans-creation. The Word is the possibility for that expression, any expression, in creation's becoming.

Thus, the invisible God is not seen in creation. Creation is not God's body such that disharmonious response implies a disfigurement of God in God's embodiment or in what other's describe as God's becoming. At the same time, creation was not created to subsist distinct from God in such a way that God's activity or presence is an addition to it or a disruption of it (e.g., with *potentia absoluta*). Creation lives, moves, and has its being by the moment by moment transcarnate, transjective operations of the Word and Spirit respectively from the Father, whose creative work by the Spirit and Son is the possibility that creation might be embraced as an other by the Father and self-express that he is Father; it is his child. He searches creation, knowing it and delighting in it. The language of a self-operating, self-existing nature that receives grace as a possession does not make sense in the framework of God's existence and operation relative to creation by the Spirit and Word. Neither does language that enmeshes God with creation through an emphasis on *in*carnation have a place. All concerning creation takes place/is possible by the inseparable operations of God transcreation.[31]

In developing the grammar of this new framework it certainly would be helpful to have a new preposition: for example, *throughin*. *Through* by itself can carry too much the notion of a passing intersection with little or no interaction, unless it is taken in the sense of "by means of." *Throughout* can carry too much the notion of extension versus dynamic relation. Using *in* can be confusing in that either creation

---

31. It should be noted explicitly that classical theism is not being proposed or defended here. God interacts in history with his creations. However, this does not mean that God is becoming creation, maturing, or changing in character. In God's calling and responding to others' responses, it can be said that God is getting to know the others he makes possible. Still a great deal of reservation is exercised, nevertheless, in avoiding process notions of God's becoming; those are paths that I do not affirm. God would have been God irrespective of there ever having been a creation (Lodahl, *The Story of God*, 65).

would be a container for God or there could be misunderstanding that the Word *in*carnates as the substance or form of creation or the Spirit is creation's subjectivity and/or expressed by creation. With the word *throughin* there would be both the movement of intersection between God and creation—thus avoiding pantheism or panentheism—as well as the friction of inwardness that circumvents a clean duality in terms of creation's utter separation from God. There is no creation apart from the acting presence of God *throughin* it.

Clarifying the Relationship of the Proposed Position with Panentheism

Within this project, the *in* of panentheism has been criticized, especially the way it can be interpreted to function in Catherine Keller's work in her language of incarnation and divine embodiment. There are, nevertheless, many forms of panentheism. In some ways, positions that lie on the spectrum "between an acosmic theism, which separates God and world (G / W), and a pantheism which identifies God with the universe as a whole (G = W),"[32] can all be labeled as panentheistic positions—very loosely defined with the formula G > W. These moderating positions want to embrace both the self-identity of God and God's intimacy with creation, the two poles of the spectrum.[33] To the extent that the position outlined herein has been forged out of those same sympathies, it could be labeled as panentheistic. However, differences in understanding the "in" of panentheism typically become the splintering issue among panentheisms. Such is the reason the position of this project bears little affinity with the traditional markers of panentheistic positions[34] or with one of the positions in a typology of major Western panentheistic positions.[35]

The framework developed herein moves against the manner in which many—if not all—of the eight common themes in panentheistic positions, as outlined by Michael Brierley, are articulated. Those themes include the cosmos as God's body, the language of "in and through," the cosmos as sacrament, language of inextricable intertwining, God's

---

32. Gregersen, "Three Varieties of Panentheism," 19.
33. Ibid.
34. See Brierley, "Naming a Quiet Revolution," 5–12.
35. See Gregersen, "Three Varieties of Panentheism," 20:34.

dependence on the cosmos, the intrinsic, positive value of the cosmos, divine passibility, and degree Christology.[36]

The grammar of "trans" has been adopted and developed specifically to preclude many of these panentheistic markers. The cosmos is not God's body, divine incarnation. Also, the cosmos does not become sacrament "under, in, through which God comes;"[37] there is not a general sacramental principle being affirmed, which claims "that any and every thing has the potential to become a full vehicle of the divine."[38] God is fully present throughin creation at all times; but God is not "graspable within finitude" or "to be discovered in the miniatures of life."[39] The move away from "in" to "trans" means that God is not present *in* creation by degrees, only to be fully realized in Christ or at the eschaton.[40] God is always fully present and operative trans-creation; but God is present so that creation itself can express its own word in relation to God's manner of relating to others, not a portion of God's Word or a lesser-quality version thereof. Our word is expressed relative to the plumb-line of God's relating to others in love, goodness, truth, beauty, etc. Our word is expressed relative to the very Possibility of God that our word can be expressed at all.

The claim that God suffers in and with creation where and when creation suffers, because of being embodied therein, does not translate in the grammar of a "trans" relationship. The reality that God can suffer emotional wounds as a lover, suffer the blasphemy and quenching of his operations, or suffer in the Son's incarnation is not being rejected. However, God is not suffering by being embodied throughout the cosmos.[41] Also, God is not "inextricably intertwined with creation" or "dependent on the cosmos" by some necessity of divine nature or even by choice in the ways panentheists tend to talk.[42] God has chosen to join with and gift himself throughin the cosmic community, for which God is its possibility, according to his steadfast love for and covenants with the community. It is true that the community cannot be defined apart

---

36. Brierley, "Naming a Quiet Revolution," 5–12.

37. Ibid., 8.

38. Ibid.

39. Gregersen, "Three Varieties of Panentheism," 35.

40. See Brierley, "Naming a Quiet Revolution," 12 and Gregersen, "Three Varieties of Panentheism," 27.

41. Cf., Brierley, "Naming a Quiet Revolution," 11.

42. Cf., ibid., 10–11.

from an inclusion of the present activity of God throughin, meaning that "*nature – God = 0*."[43] However, this relationship of God to creation is not eternally or necessarily part of *God*.

Even though avowed panentheists both identify with and deny certain themes common among panentheist positions, the language of "trans" places the position of this project at odds with nearly every one of them, at least the manner in which "in" colors them. It also places the present position at odds with Gregersen's taxonomy of positions. The language of possibility and *trans* means that God can be, indeed is present, everywhere. The Spirit is possibility in every circumstance, including impossibility. Thus, the proposed framework is not a soteriological panentheism in which creation is not-yet "in God" while awaiting such a conversion/movement.[44] This position also does not fit either the cycle of "alienation of finitude" from God and return to God within German Idealism or the God-World relationship in dipolar (Whiteheadian) panentheism.[45] The world is neither a self-expression of God nor a journey of self-experience by God; and our "misdeeds" do not become the "misfortunes"[46] of the God who is at the same time both "the universal cause and the all-inclusive reality."[47]

Thus, even though the position offered in this project shares the aims of panentheist positions to affirm together the self-identity of God and God's intimacy with the world, there are few ways in which the grammar of "possibility" and "trans" place this project in agreement with the predominant types of panentheism or common markers of panentheistic frameworks. The *in* of pan*en*theism far too much governs the articulations of various issues for the label of panentheism to be embraced as suitable for this framework. At the most this framework sympathizes with the common themes and intentions of panentheism in general while proposing a significant revision of much of the grammar, including the label itself.

---

43. Gregersen, "Three Varieties of Panentheism," 35.

44. See ibid., 27.

45. See, ibid., 28, 31.

46. This language comes from a statement written by Charles Hartshorne that is quoted in Gregersen, "Three Varieties of Panentheism," 32.

47. Gregersen, "Three Varieties of Panentheism," 31.

Describing God's Creative Activity in Conversation with Genesis 1

By applying the proposed framework to the reading of Genesis 1, it gives the text a fresh flavor. The presence of the Spirit in v. 2 is precisely in character. It is the *eccentric* character of the Spirit to be always present no matter the scene. The Spirit is the Possibility of God in every circumstance. The Spirit is also the Possibility of God that there be an other, one characterized both by distinction to God while at the same time itself being eccentrically oriented to the o/Other. God's other is a response-able other.[48] The Spirit's eccentricity is also a kenotic drive into every impossibility for God.[49] Just as the Spirit drove Christ into the wilderness and even to the grave in Mark's Gospel that the Kingdom might come even there, the Spirit in Genesis 1 was actively nurturing the infant creation that was yet desolate and empty; it was not-yet unfolded into a fully expressive agent of God's goodness (loving care for the o/Other) in God's developing cosmic community. Its responses had not yet matured into productive/reproductive fertility, the abundance of life.

In responding both relative to and by the transcarnate Word according to the eccentrically orienting Spirit, creation was growing not only into the goodness and beauty of its relationship with God, it was in turn maturing into ever more numerous creation(s) spawning and nurturing others. All the characters in the cosmic community develop in Genesis 1 into ones operating in service to the growth/good of others.[50] The result is that we are not just *related* to God and others by the Spirit, but, by the cooperative response of others to God's call in our coming to be, we are *dependent* on the activities of both God and others in our

---

48. For the importance of response to God's initiating grace (i.e., prevenient grace) in Wesleyan theology, see Maddox, *Responsible Grace*, 19, 44, 55, 83, 86, 87–90, 259n21.

49. See Dabney, "Naming the Spirit," 46–50.

50. Keller criticizes *creatio ex nihilo* because ultimately the creation that is established by a unilateral use of divine power then has only instrumental value to God; it glorifies God. This *creatio ex nihilo* framework does not accept creation as a work of God alone. Even in creating, God both speaks and listens. God has an other to listen to, not a scripted other. With Genesis 1, this framework looks forward to God being able to be at home with creation (God's other) and enjoying that ultimate Sabbath. God does not create so that creation can be an instrument glorifying God—that it can work for God. In Genesis 1, God does not need any part of creation to take care of God. However, the story does culminate in God delighting in creation and resting in it.

becoming. In Genesis 1, God elicits that which exists to support the coming to be of others.

In the Godhead, so moved according to the manner seen in the operations of the Spirit, it comes as no surprise that the Word's involvement in creation would be oriented in a like fashion.[51] The Word too is spoken as both the possibility for expression by the other and as care for the unfolding of the other.

The divine speech of Genesis 1 has often been labeled as "command." Technically the grammatical force of the verbs makes the statements commands, even if that is nuanced by saying they are jussive.[52] However, if the Word operates transcarnately in creation, the commands must be considered differently than they have been. They cannot be an object/force acting upon God's creation—moving it about as a pawn. They cannot take shape *as* creation, becoming *in*carnate. Nor can they be thought to establish/create *ex nihilo* by divine fiat, monergistically.[53] Rather, *as the Spirit and Word operate inseparably, there is the possibility for an other enabled to become/respond in concert with the goodness of God's self-gifting for it in the Spirit and Word.* The divine speech would be more appropriately labeled as "call." As God's Word operates transcarnately with the transjective Spirit, it is both message for and possibility by which the other responds. It is both the call for self-expression and the possibility for it. The call is being issued such that creation can speak

---

51. In Irenaeus's framework of creation by God alone, he still makes statements worth pondering. In the working of God's hands it is the Word who "'establishes,' that is, works bodily and confers existence, while the Spirit arranges and forms the various 'powers,' so rightly is the Son called Word and the Spirit the Wisdom of God" (*Epideixis* 5; quoted in Steenberg, *Irenaeus on Creation*, 64). In essence, in the operations of God's hands the Spirit demonstrates the Word while the Word articulates the Spirit (ibid., 64). This dynamic between the Spirit and Word appears to be a fitting way to talk about their operations in the proposed framework. Throughout this chapter there will be references made to Irenaeus's theology by way of comparison or contrast. The hope is that this will provide more illumination to what is being proposed. Some of Irenaeus's thoughts transfer well. Also, some of Irenaeus's ideas and patterns of thinking have been regrettably overshadowed in the intervening centuries. By making note of his positions, this chapter will hopefully show how the ideas herein are to some extent congruent with certain aspects of Irenaeus's thinking and facilitate a recovery of those facets in the present.

52. Cf. Brown, *Structure, Role, and Ideology*, 122–23, 225.

53. This statement does not deny *ex nihilo*. It only denies a certain notion of *creatio ex nihilo*.

out in its own voice ongoingly, moment by moment. For creation movement/becoming is always taking place.[54]

A *Creatio Ex Nihilo* through the Possibility of Creation's Self-Expression Rather Than Divine Fiat

Genesis 1 does not answer the question whether God created out of nothing or began with a pre-existent stuff. The narrative opens with a non-productive, empty *earth*—a not-yet-as-we-know-it earth, over which the Spirit hovers. It narrates the earth as opposite of what the Priestly theology believed creation to be about (except, even then, the absence of God's presence in the Spirit could not be affirmed). In spite of the ancient method employed to narrate creation in Genesis 1, the grammar of creation being developed here affirms with the tradition the doctrine of *creatio ex nihilo*.

In the present framework, the nature of God and God's creative activity makes *possible* the *inclusion* of a *word from the other* in the creative event, an other who *does not preexist* the very creative activity of God itself. It is the grammar of divine *possibility* that makes room for saying simultaneously both that prior to creation there is nothing—non-preexistence of any other—and that the event of creation itself entails a synergism between the activity of God and an expression from an other

---

54. This framework draws on Irenaeus's general affirmation that "God is Creator, and he creates as the trinity of Father with Son and Spirit" (Steenberg, *Irenaeus on Creation*, 67. Two outcomes of this are that creation is a "communal act of Father, Son and Spirit, working in harmony and with singular purpose" (ibid., 64) and that everything God creates is in communion with the triune God (ibid., 67). Even with these Trinitarian claims, Irenaeus does not always carry them out well. For example, with humans it is the Trinity in whom they are brought to life and are to be perfected. However, Irenaeus repeatedly states that it is the physical form of the Son's future incarnation after which humans are made (ibid., 137). This helps to give many of Irenaeus's claims a more christological than Trinitarian focus. The roles of the three persons that are emphasized also keep the focus on the Father and Son; the Spirit, except in reference to being an ongoing vivifying principle through the human soul, is not as essential to the creative process: "the Father is creator, the Word the means by which the Father creates, and the Spirit is the adorner of that creation wrought by the Father through the Word" (ibid., 64–65). In one location Irenaeus explicitly calls the Spirit "creator," a term usually reserved for the Father and Son (*Haer.* 4.31.2; Steenberg, *Irenaeus on Creation*, 70). To Irenaeus's credit, it was rarely claimed that the Spirit was "creator" for over two centuries after Irenaeus. Even Augustine did not press that claim until some of his latest writings (cf., e.g., his *Contra Maximus* from 426, in which he utilizes Ps 33:6). It is Irenaeus's general affirmation of Trinitarian participation that resonates with the current framework.

made possible by God. The active ingredients in the very first coming to be of creation included, to the Father's delight, the Possibility of God, the Word of God, and the non-preexistent word whose expression was/is creation's coming to be. While this makes a positive statement, it is still a humble one; there is a great deal that remains unasserted about the mystery of creation in the grammar.

By speaking about the Spirit's relation to creation as transject and the Word's relationship to creation as being transcarnate, it enables different language about coming to be. This language honors *creatio ex nihilo* and intends to communicate its spirit while employing a different grammar. With the very Call of God for the other is the present Possibility of God; it is their activity together which is the possibility that the response of a non-preexistent other be included in the dynamic of the creative event. Joining the Spirit, who is everywhere always present as possibility in impossibility, the reverberation of the transcarnate Word gifts the possibility of our coming to be, that we speak as other. There is no sequence to the call and the expressed word of becoming a related creation that the call makes possible; it is with/upon the call that creation's self-expression is possible. There is no capacity of either life or expression possessed by creation; there is no autonomously existing creation, but only a creation whose coming to be is possible by the Spirit and Word presently operating throughin. There is simultaneity in the other being related to God the Father (established by the inseparable operation of the Spirit and Word) with the very establishment that there is the other by the synergism of Spirit, Call, and self-expression/word. By the Spirit and Word the Father calls "let there be" and by the same Spirit and Word there is with/upon the call the self-declaration of an other, "here I am."

There is no entity that is made that is subsequently addressed and/or empowered for response; there is not a thing created that is turned on or enlivened. There is not a second act of God by which the created other is then addressed or by which it can respond. God does not act on creation or as creation, but trans-creation. There is only the creative act of God by the eccentric Spirit and Word. In the very act of making possible an other, creation expresses itself as a responsible other.[55] It does

---

55. The notion of response is quite important in Wesleyan theology. In the proposed framework its use requires great care. The grammar of the Word being transcarnate precludes a notion of creation receiving any type of objective call to which it in turn responds. Instead of seeing the Word as something received or a coercive force, it is more of a friction throughin creation that gives rise to the possibility of self-vocalization

not pre-exist the initiation of God's creative operation while at the same time participates with God in the creative event due to the nature of God and God's creative activity making such synergism possible.

Because of the nature of the inseparable operations—the character of which are fitting of the God who is love—creation does not take place by divine fiat. God's creative activity is the very possibility that there is a word from another to that activity. God's operations trans that coming-to-be creation ensure that it is not God establishing a creation with possibilities, but being the possibility for the self-expression of an other relative to God. In the creative event there is that which is truly other whom God loves. In creating, God's operations in respect to that other demonstrate the nature of divine love. It self-gifts for the good of the other while exposing itself to the unknown of whether the free other will openly, outwardly self-express itself in kind.

The coming to be of creation is no longer a matter of zero-sum accounting. God's creative activity is synergistic with the very other who is being created. Without being preexistent to the call, the being-created-one speaks with/upon it. The coming-to-be creation comes to be in relation to the Triune God. The Call, with the Spirit, is the possibility for the expression, the becoming, of the other. That which is creation is the response(s) to—word's expressed relative to—God's call(s). Creation's coming-to-be is not necessarily saying the same thing as the call; it does not incarnate the Call. Creation cannot express via its subjectivity divine subjectivity and God does not express God's subjectivity in the other. Rather, God's call(s) make possible the self-expression of the other; it allows for ingenuity in response.[56] Thus, God's creative activity is in itself a kenotic act. It is a joining of and a joining with the cosmic community being created; it is in total respect and care for the others therein.[57] In

---

of an other. There is the possibility in/by that operation that the word of the other is a self-expression of God's self-gifted goodness. To some degree creation's coming to be is responsive to God's call throughin, insofar as creation's becoming is made possible and in relation to that divine operation; righteous expression requires sensitivity and attunement to God's orienting activity trans-creation. This framework places a new flavor on what *response* would mean.

56. More will be said about this later.

57. In the words of Michael Lodahl, "The very fact that Christ, the Word become flesh, was nailed to a cross by other men reveals a vulnerability on God's part, a willingness to suffer our abuses of freedom. God the omnipotent One does not hoard power but shares power. In the very act of creation, the God who is self-giving Love has shared with the creature the power to be. Anglican theologian John Macquarrie has written,

making possible the other, God self-gifts himself as the possibility for the other. Nevertheless, the shape creation comes to be is the word it speaks.

In the earliest image of creation in Scripture God is present with it. The introduction of the theme that God is creating the whole (v. 1) is met subsequently with an affirmation of God's abiding presence throughin. The Priestly tradition cannot narrate for its pupils a *world* devoid of God, to which God or God's activity is foreign or an "external" addition. The first definition (by way of an image) of God as Creator is God *with* creation. The earliest notion of creation—in all its dimensionality and historicity—includes within *creation/world* a statement of God being *with* it.

God is not just *with* creation, a participating member of the newly begun and emerging community, God is *for* creation. With the newly becoming creation in Genesis 1:2 God is seen as relating positively with it in offering himself in gift. Self-gifting is precisely the first movement of God's *creation* of the heavens and the earth; God, by the Spirit, gifts himself as the possibility for the other (Gen 1:2). The Spirit broods over the waters.

In chapter 4 the structural analysis of Genesis 1 in the work of William Brown was used to highlight the way God calls to various parts of creation to participate with God in the increasing unfolding of the community. Looking at the text through the proposed framework, their participation is by the transjective Spirit and transcarnate Word. In asking the land "to grass grass" (v. 11) and the waters "to swimming swimmers" (v. 20) God's intention is that the thing which is produced is to be dependant upon and united with the continued activity of the actor. It is not as though God creates alone or that there is such a thing as an independently-existing creation that can create alone. Creating is cooperative and the result is collaborative, not only between God and the part of creation beckoned to act—beckoned to nurture the new other—but also with that which comes to be. Ever since the first creative gesture there

---

'His creation was also a self-emptying ... His love and generosity led him to share existence with his creatures. [This is not simply] a limitation of power but also God's making himself vulnerable, for there cannot be this love and sharing and conferring of freedom without the possibility of suffering on the part of him who loves and shares and confers.' The God we call omnipotent does not exercise all power, if indeed power has been shared with us" (Lodahl, *The Story of God*, 62 [Lodahl's brackets]; cf. ibid., 63).

have been three parties in each creative event: God, existing creation responding to the call to nurture another, and the new responding other.

In chapter 2 Irenaeus was criticized for making a clean distinction between God and creation in being, power, and operation.[58] He made creation a zero-sum enterprise with God having the entire operation. Even so, the intention was laudable. Irenaeus wanted to stress the immediacy of God to every part of creation through the respective operations of the persons; there is no mediation.[59] Since each thing has a creation *ex nihilo* by none other than God alone, everything in the cosmos has a direct connection to the incarnate Christ (rather than to a generic material substrate). Creating is a 'hands-on' affair for God that true-to-character went to the extreme intimacy of the Incarnation and the Pentecostal indwelling.[60] "With creation itself as the act by which the economy is initiated, God's immediacy to and direct contact with the creation—established by this image of the Father with his two hands—becomes the basis by which it can be declared a reality established in and moving towards his goodness in his work of redemption."[61]

Even though the immediacy of God to creation, for the purpose of creation's perfection in God, is laudable, by eliminating God's creative work within creation such that creation is also called to become by and for the *other* as it is called to become by and for the *Other*, Irenaeus thereby defines creation's, especially humanity's, perfection relative to God alone and not relative to God and neighbor.[62] By including in our

58. This does need to be tempered by the fact that spatially and temporally, for Irenaeus, there was no place beyond or outside of the infinite God. Nothing falls before or outside of God's creative activity. Also, when the Father creates *with Son and Spirit* they are not extended outside of or beyond the Father; cf. Steenberg, *Irenaeus on Creation*, 114. (Irenaeus has the seeds of all that would eventually fall under the inseparability of the Godhead.) More than spatial separation, it is the clear distinction in being of creation from God that becomes conceptually problematic (see n. 3). In the proposed framework, it is not possible to talk of a creation at all apart from the transjective and transcarnate operations of the Spirit and Word therein. Irenaeus was able to speak of material bodies that endure after God's formative activity—bodies upon which God could act and breathe life; cf. Steenberg, *Irenaeus on Creation*, 132–34. In contrast to Irenaeus's view, in the proposed framework, God does not act upon a distinct, enduring creation; God enduringly acts throughin, being the very possibility that there is a responding other.

59. Steenberg, *Irenaeus on Creation*, 78–79.

60. Ibid., 81.

61. Ibid.

62. This can be seen, for instance, in Steenberg's statement: "This is of the utmost

coming to be the participation of God *and* others, our telos is defined by the perfection of those constituting relationships—the love of God and neighbor.

What is being affirmed in the present framework is that God's goodness is directly present throughin an o/Other oriented community. It is the goodness of God in which and toward which creation moves, to the delight and glory of God; God makes possible for creation to self-express the divine manner of relating to others. Nevertheless, the complex expressiveness of the community in relation to the newly becoming creature—which is intrinsic to the synergism of the creative event—is also significant, and not just God's creative activity with isolated individuals. In such a communal synergism, God's goodness can still directly be the "substance" of all created reality—understood in terms of it being the provided possibility and the end of God's call.[63]

This sharing with creation (operating and dwelling throughin it) defines God as Creator and Lord. In creation, God is certainly Lord among the many; but that lordship is defined by way of being the possibility for *good* (self) expression by others and nurturing them into the fullness of *good* (self) expression. Even as the Lord and Creator, God interacts with the world and his creatures in a way that suggests partnership, not an over-against relationship. God's lordship is not the subjugation of the other. There is no cosmic struggle to subdue the infant creation. God reaches out with the possibility of establishing a relationship with an other by the Spirit. The Spirit and Word make possible a responding,

---

importance when Irenaeus comes to consider the perfection of this human creation, which is ultimately the perfected communion of the human being created by the triune God, with the life and glory of the Father, Son and Spirit" (*Irenaeus on Creation*, 107; cf. ibid., 108).

63. This use of *substance* plays on its use in the work of Irenaeus. He states that God's will and power are the substance of all created reality (Steenberg, *Irenaeus on Creation*, 45, 49). It is crucial to attend to the point in Irenaeus making such statements. He is not talking about *how* at this point. "In stating that 'God's will is the substance of all things,' he speaks not of a definition of ontological essence, but of formative generation by the one thus capable of redemption" (ibid., 45). It is more helpful to view "*the character* of that will as the substance of the fashioned handiwork" (ibid., 104; italics added). This is easily translatable into the framework being developed here, in which the self-gift of God for the other as possibility is not only according to the character of God's goodness but is a self-gifting of the possibility of the other to express divine goodness in relation to the o/Other. Irenaeus's work can be interpreted that the character of God is the form for creation. In the present framework, it is a matter of creation, with ingenuity, expressing itself in harmony with the pitch of God's creative activity trans-creation.

relating other, whose very response, with God's creative operation, is the creative event.[64]

In terms of further growth and development, God acts and the situation once marked by indeterminacy, nonproductiveness, and emptiness is enlivened. It expresses itself for the community, the o/Other. Creation does not move to fulfillment immediately, all at once. God nurtures this one into maturity and participation in the discovery and expression of good, loving interrelations in the community—the community in which God has chosen to participate integrally and ultimately unite/incarnate himself. This type of kenotic creative-activity that nurtures the other defines the character of God. The activity is according to the nature of the loving God and the manner of the inseparable operations of the Godhead.

Certainly God exercises authority over his creation. He is the Master Craftsman who initiates, enables, and leads the formation of a good world. He, as the loving, good God, gifts himself to that end. He is simultaneously impetus, possibility, and plumb-line. He alone is worthy of our worship. Nevertheless, God's lordship is not an end in itself but a means of loving relationship for all within creation. It cultivates and governs community to and into the glory of God the Father.[65]

Birth and Maturation

Using the tropes of birth, infancy, and maturation in regard to creation is not foreign to Scripture or the Christian tradition. For example, important to Irenaeus's theology is his idea of maturation and growth.

---

64. Biblical notions of righteousness and justice typically follow in these lines of care for other; cf. Baker, "The Repetition of Reconciliation: Satisfying Justice, Mercy, and Forgiveness." Care for the least of these was a key measure of justice. The *rule* of Israel's kings was often measured by the treatment of the widows, orphans, and poor—not just that they might not suffer, but that they might have fullness of life. In the life of the community, God in his activity of creation and dominion was to be imaged.

65. It has become more common since Luther to define God's character and activity in the world relative to God's self-revelation in Christ, particularly the cross. In the cruciform pattern of Christ's life (e.g., Phil 2:1–11) and in his teachings, there is consistently the message of God's self-giving, self-emptying love on behalf of others (the term *cruciform* with the accompanying notions is taken from Michael Gorman's *Cruciformity*. This provides a lens through which to read Scripture. Jesus says that the Law (which includes Genesis) and the Prophets can be summarized by the command to love God and to love one's neighbor as oneself (Matt 22:34–40; Luke 10:47; see Lodahl, *All Things Necessary to Our Salvation*, 46–50, esp. 48).

Creation, for him, was called forth to move toward a telos and not to stay forever as it was in the beginning. "Creation is not stagnant, but ever maturing and advancing towards that *telos* which since the genesis has been its intended point of fulfillment, and which is fully revealed in the incarnate Christ's promise of an eternal kingdom."[66] The narrative of Genesis 1 concerning the beginning itself pointed for Irenaeus to the reality of eras of growth through history.[67] Even creation's restoration at Christ's second coming (new creation) is not an end, but a means for further growth throughout eternity.[68]

Thus, the beginning is not the end to which we seek to return nor was it ever an end in itself. Rather, the "genesis of the cosmos is the picture, painted in unfinished outline yet of significant descriptive value, of its future and, ultimately, of its end."[69] God creates in goodness that creation might grow to participate in the glory of God, God's goodness, shared by the Father, Son, and Spirit for all eternity.[70]

Irenaeus clearly stated that humans, as well as creation, were created as "children" or "infants."[71] Adam and Eve did not start in perfect adulthood; rather, humanity "must begin with the other terminus of human growth, that of the babe, the infant, who needs be suckled on milk before it can graduate to firmer food, which Irenaeus calls the 'bread of immortality—the Spirit of the Father.'"[72] The incarnation was planned from the beginning; it was a planned step in the movement toward the adulthood/perfection of creation to be entered in the eschaton. Until the

---

66. Ibid., 52. Gregory of Nyssa believed that creatures were always in motion, developing either toward or away from God. There is no such thing as being stationary (Douglass, *Theology of the Gap*, 189).

67. Irenaeus read the "days" in Genesis 1 as "phases in the economy of salvation" (Steenberg, *Irenaeus on Creation*, 86). Thus, on day 6 Adam ate the fruit and died, and Christ came to recapitulate human death. "There is demonstrated in Gen 1 chiefly a chronology of salvation, framed in a timeline of creation, significant both historically and eschatologically" (Steenberg, *Irenaeus on Creation*, 87; cf. *Haer.* 1.18.2).

68. Irenaeus often said that to be a creature, to be human, is to grow in grace for all eternity; cf., e.g., *Haer.* 2.25.3; 2.28.3; 4.11.1. Cf. Steenberg, *Irenaeus on Creation*, 58.

69. Steenberg, *Irenaeus on Creation*, 21.

70. Ibid., 36.

71. Steenberg, *Irenaeus on Creation*, 142.

72. Ibid., 143.

Incarnation and Pentecost, God and humanity were getting accustomed to one another.

Irenaeus did not read Genesis 1:3 as a narrative of perfection then fall. Rather, it was a narrative "of imperfection, growing and maturing into the fullness of life, which is ultimately the life of Christ."[73] Christ reveals that the telos of history is congruent with "the protological witness of all scripture. . .namely, the eventual perfection of full participation in the divine life."[74] The garden was created as "a nursery for newly-fashioned human race."[75]

Congruent with this Irenaean tradition, it was suggested in chapter 4 that the imagery of Genesis 1:2 be viewed as *infancy* instead of within notions of chaos. Whether we are speaking of God's initiatory creative act *ex nihilo* or the synergism of creative activity between God, existing creation, and the things coming to be, that which God makes possible begins in infancy when it 'bursts out of the womb' (Job 38:8–11).

In a previous section it was mentioned that the birth of creation, its initial coming to be, is the word it speaks that is made possible by the Spirit and Word. The non-preexistent creation comes to be in the creative event as a self-expression made possible through God's creative activity. This goes beyond the questions being answered in Genesis 1. It seeks to answer a question that probes into that which happens before the opening of the narrative, or a question that demands a different kind

---

73. Ibid. Reading Genesis in terms of a sin-and-fall lens is being challenged based on the text itself. See, e.g., Bechtel, "Rethinking the Interpretation of Genesis 2:4b—3:24," and Bechtel, "Genesis 2.4b—3.24." See also Harlow, "After Adam."

74. Steenberg, *Irenaeus on Creation*, 9.

75. Ibid., 147. One of the notions this project works against is seeing the creation of nature simply as background for humanity's story. Because of Irenaeus's strong anthropological focus, he often saw creation as being made for humanity's benefit; the earth's creation is really just the first step in the narrative about humans. Even so, as emphasized in the current project, he did at times mention that "the service of Creation to the human race is to advance both parties fully into their *teloi* at the fulfillment of the economy" (ibid., 149). In the end, regardless of the garden's formation for the young Adam, it was human community that was ultimately needed to help in his growth into perfection; only Eve was suitable for Adam (ibid., 151).

of answer than starting with a Genesis 1:2 reply. Within such a framework, Genesis 1:2 would be the just-birthed creation.

Infancy

With the infant creation in Genesis 1:2 God is seen as relating positively with it in continuing to offer himself in gift. As was mentioned, self-gifting is the first movement of God's creative activity. By the Spirit, God gifts himself as the possibility for the other (as seen in Gen 1:2). As a mother hen broods over her chicks, the Spirit broods over the waters.

In the initial scene of Scripture there is all the anticipation of what the infant creation will become. The divine Parent holds a young, at-this-point barren and empty creation, knowing the character of expression into which God desires to nurture it and that there are more creatures God wants to introduce into the community. In addition, God has greater insight into the interconnectedness of the community and his own yearning that love be expressed in those relationships to the benefit of all, whom God loves. The specifics of what creation will *do* in response are the greatest part of the anticipation. The hope is that in doing it that creation will come to self-express the goodness that God gifts to it in himself. In the teaching of the Priestly tradition, whether in narrating cosmology or tabernacle construction, abundantly good response is the ideal and indeed possible.[76]

In this initial condition, creation—the "earth"—bears nothing. What it lacks, God makes possible. Creation is gifted with the Possibility of God. God is the perfect Possibility to the extreme youthfulness of his creation. It is not that God makes a chaos, a *dis*order, an *anti*-order. God makes an other with whom he is related positively, in favor of whom God acts. He is for and on behalf of this other, as the One into whom/to whom the other is drawn by the very offering of God's self throughin.

By the Spirit and Word, God is womb to the unfolding of the promise of this child. Names are given. These creations/creatures are called to express themselves in ways 1) fitting to them, 2) nurturing to others, and 3) beneficial to the whole created community. God by his boundless wisdom begins to parent, counseling and collaborating in the way creation

---

76. See Brown, *Structure, Role, and Ideology*, 209–15.

should go (e.g., Exod 13:21–22)—all the while, being the very Possibility for creation's expression, creation's relation to the o/Other.

Growing Up(s)

Creation does not move linearly, forever forward, from not-yet to arriving at a pre-envisioned order, a static point of fulfillment. There is no precise, determined form into which all parts will lock into place when they perfectly align one-day. Rather than a linear movement toward an ideal picture, there is continual oscillation between becoming in relation to God's call to the manifesting of good and the making room for something new. There is conversation and respiration of creation with the Father in and by the Word and Spirit.

Through the Possibility of God for the other and by the Word a divine call is uttered *throughin* creation. Creation comes to be in relation to the very transjective and transcarnate presence of the Spirit and Word who make it possible. Creation's response is a joining with the enlivening self-expression of God. God's expression is not as much an object received as it is something that moves throughin creation. Creation's response is a tune creation sings with God's song. The response is not merely a matter of *repetition*. Creation's response is an imaginative *self-expression* of (God-natured) goodness by God's-other made possible by God's self-gift throughin creation. In voicing its word, there is the 'exhale' and the 'listening again' to God's call. Creation must exhale to breath anew or say anything else that is both new and good.

Creation's becoming is moment by moment and season by season. We do not live in a fixed state. There is no single perfect or harmonious condition toward which creation is moving and into which it will be frozen for all eternity. There is no eternal summer. God is not accumulating perfect things or perfection within creation as if it were a museum. Perfection cannot be collected since creation does not establish something at one point that then endures through time in that initially created state. Rather, creation exists in dynamic relationship to God and others, a relationship of endless possibility for discovering manifestations of good. In that relationship of joyful discovery, humanity and all creation breathes.

Fall and winter are as much about God's design as spring and summer. Rest is as much about God's design as work. Decay, dissolution, and erosion are not evil. Having responded in beauty and goodness to God's prompting, there is a letting go of that for the conversation to continue. There is a making room for discovering new manifestations of beauty, life, and love. There is no idolizing of or resting on past accomplishments. There is celebration in the exhale of what has been and anticipation of the possibility of the future—including the resurrection of the dead and the life of the world to come.

God did not design us to be built up into one thing, the greatest, the best possible thing that is then maintained for all eternity. Rather this horizon toward ultimate perfection is stood on end in this paradigm. The aim of every cycle, every expression, is perfect love of the o/Other. All history is not building in and towards a single perfection. With the passage of time the people of God certainly have a more extensive collection of interactions with God in which to understand God's character. Those living today have the advantage (or disadvantage) of what has preceded them. Nevertheless, all creation, with humanity, is not being built into some super manifestation of itself. Rather, each participant needs maturation in every now.[77] Manifestations of the good are enjoyed here for what they are as they occur; they are encouraged and nurtured in *this* place and in *this* time. The Good One delights in the respirations of his creation and creatures, in their inventive words.[78] There is the enjoyment

---

77. It is not enough to say that God was encountered or divine goodness was expressed at some point in the past and that we are adding on to it. God must be encountered, known, and properly related to in every present. For example, because Gregory of Nyssa understood this, he wrote his own account of the life of Moses, even though Philo and Clement had already done so (Douglass, *Theology of the Gap*, 209). He believed every generation must imagine themselves in that ancient context and wrestle with its significance in the present. "By standing within the opening of revelation, Gregory was committed to a certain type of transformative knowing, a *metanoetic* knowing that 'does not consist in mere information and notions'" (ibid., 214). Also, the Cappadocians fought Eunomius because they understood that everything revealed was revealed in a context—the *adiastemic* God was revealed in and through a *diastemic* context/medium (ibid., 79–87). Language is unable to transcend itself and speak absolutely, as Eunomius failed to recognize (ibid., 83). Because of the limitations of language and the reality that it is always on the move, there is always need for reexpression (ibid., 109). Thus, rather than absolutizing the past and building upon it, we must seek to experience that to which it faithfully points; we must seek to know God in the present and express that reality. The notion of linear progression needs to be stood on end. The church is no more holy or loving now than it was at Pentecost, in spite of the many intervening instances of holy living or loving acts. Rather, in every new expression or cycle we must seek to relate in the goodness made possible to us by God's self-gifting.

78. Any parent experiences this by analogy as their children experiment with

of building, the enjoyment of tinkering and watching it for a season, and the anticipation in the making room for the next thing. In response to and out of God's making possible activity, there is an open-endedness to creation's ingenuity for manifesting goodness, truth, and beauty each moment and season of creation's becoming. There is limitless opportunity for discovery.

Another important point to make in regard to God's creative activity is that conversations do not happen all at once. In Genesis 1 God began a cosmic community that unfolded in sequence, over time. From barren infancy the 'earth' grew in diversity, complexity, productivity, and fullness. All of history is a collage of actors in diverse contexts whom God calls to collaborate and cooperate in imaginatively relating in goodness.[79] Growth and discovery takes time. Creation does not happen in a flash, but in ongoing exchange.

---

positive activities and expressions.

79. In talking about history Michael Lodahl states: "Stories do not happen all at once; they go somewhere and take time getting there. To recognize that, in the Bible, God appears in time-full narrative is to understand God as willingly related to time, to the very history of creation itself. This Actor in the Story truly does graciously dwell with the world, acting within creation's own time-full sequence . . . Time and duration, direction and goal are inevitable factors in the Story of God, for that matter, in the way God's Story gets told" (*The Story of God*, 15; cf. ibid., 97).

7

The Place for "Chaos" in Theological Discourse

SEVERAL ISSUES HAVE BEEN NOTED CONCERNING "CHAOS" UP TO THIS point. First, in the introductory chapter, it was noted that the term "chaos" lacks a precise definition according to which it is consistently used in theological studies. In general it is used to designate various notions of pre-creation conditions and problems arising subsequent to creation; some authors link the two uses in an attempt to account for evil based on the endurance of (or recurrence of) precreation chaos. Clarity and consistency in using the term is needed. Second, using the term "chaos" for differing notions of pre-creation conditions has a long, contentious history within Christianity. Through that history, the notions to which the term has been applied are varied. Even with the uniqueness of each one, some of the notions in various eras show similarities. Regardless of any novelties, they wisely have been challenged.

The term "chaos" itself is not the problem, only the notions within the various frameworks to which it has been applied. "Chaos" has strong connotations, and certainly a more suitable application for it can be found in which its strength can be put to use.

The Uses of "Chaos" That Are Avoided

The many types of "chaos" uses in theological studies were outlined in the first chapter. Most all of those uses are being avoided for various reasons.[1] The following is a listing of notions that are being excluded in the present formulation of "chaos."

First, any notion of there being anything that pre-exists God's creative activity is being rejected; such a dualism creates more problems than it answers. There is no pre-existent matter in any form (or lack of form). There is no preexistent force, power, or entity that is other to God or even part of God that should be called chaos. The wisdom of the Christian tradition in affirming *creatio ex nihilo* is being embraced.[2] Second, along with notions of preexistence, Catherine Keller's notion of *tehom*/creativity is also being excluded. Even though "chaos" for her is neither before nor after creation, neither existent nor nonexistent, but rather of creation, her framework and the hermeneutic she employs pushes into categories less prevalent within the major currents of the tradition. The issues she wants to address can be met within frameworks bearing stronger resemblances to more familiar voices in the Christian tradition.[3]

The third type of notion being avoided is linking "chaos" with "disorder," either pre- or postcreation. Authors who use the term in this

---

1. One of the ways Enda McDonagh uses the term is the closest any current uses come to the way it will be defined in this project. Even though he uses "chaos" in many ways being rejected, in one place he says: "Consideration of Jewish-Christian reconciliation should reveal the depths of the chaos, psychological, social and theological, in which we find ourselves and indicate the radical character of the new creation required of humanity and offered by God" (McDonagh, *Between Chaos and New Creation*, 51).

2. It has already been noted that the move to *creatio ex nihilo* did not come without accompanying difficulties through the centuries. In some regards, it too introduced a new kind of dualism between God and creation subsequent to the affirmation of *creatio ex nihilo*; "For in that idea, God, as the external, self-sufficient and eternal Artificer, is separated by an impassable gulf from the temporal, finite world He creates" (Gilkey, *Maker of Heaven and Earth*, 10). As José Morales states: "Christian theology has always had great methodological difficulty in finding the right place for the world alongside a God who stands in no need of that world" (*Creation Theology*, 71). The affirmation of the tradition that nothing preexists God's initiating creative act will be preserved while at the same time a grammar that finds a closer relationship between God and the world without melding God with the world will be sought.

3. Process thought, within which Keller works, is often criticized for its dualism of two divine-like components: God and creativity. Langdon Gilkey believes process thought is in line with the *Timaeus* and gnostic thought as historical examples of dualism (*Maker of Heaven and Earth*, 45). He defines dualism as any view in which there are, on the one hand, principles of organization that provide form or structure (e.g., God) and, on the other hand, something that is structured (e.g., *khora*; or for Keller, *tehom*; Gilkey, *Maker of Heaven and Earth*, 46). Christians who try to articulate the faith in a process framework do many things to smooth over the dualism of God and creativity.

way often, in turn, link God's creative activity with ordering; the work of creating is primarily about achieving and sustaining a comprehensible structural arrangement. This suggests that order/structure is the telos of God's creative activity. Or it suggests that the aim, nature, and character of God's creative activity are distinct from and/or secondary to God's greater aims relative to creation through history. The undesirable implications of these options can be illustrated by using Irenaeus's suggestion that the destiny of creation is the Glory of God. On the one hand, if creating is about developing an order and if creation's destiny is also said to be the Glory of God, then somehow order becomes definitive of the Glory of God. On the other hand, if ordering is not definitive of God's Glory, to which creation is destined, then God's creative (ordering) activity simply becomes background or secondary to a divine activity far more definitive of God and creation's relationship to God. In other words, if creating equals ordering, the creation of the world becomes disconnected from its history and telos.

Keeping "chaos" distinct from "disorder," especially if disorder is believed to be the opposite of creation, will be helpful in the framework that is being proposed. Thus, in a similar vein, "chaos" should not be used to describe systems with a high degree of entropy. The Second Law of Thermodynamics does not govern the movement between "chaos" and "order"—between non- or pre-creation and creation—in the universe. That language colors conceptions of the nature of the world in which we live and does not appear to be most fitting for what is revealed in Scripture concerning our world and God's work therein. It assumes that the universe is made to be a cosmos/structure, a lifeless arrangement of cogs, instead of being an organism/community of interrelating participants and systems. It also contradicts the reality that life/living requires the release of energy that accompanies the shift to a higher level of entropy. Similarly scientists and theologians interfacing science have used "chaos" as a descriptor for systems or phenomena that appear, based on their current epistemic abilities, unpredictable or random. Again, the

---

Some equate the Spirit with creativity. Keller makes a similar move by also bringing creativity within the divine. However, her "trinity," then, does not have the traditional three persons. Her trinity is Elohim, Creativity, and Spirit.

witness of Scripture does not concur with such conclusions that the universe *is* chaotic.

Fourth, "chaos" should not be used concerning that within creation that has not-yet reached fullness. Infancy or immaturity should not be demonized or called chaos. It certainly does not exhibit fully all that we hope for it in the future. However, its potential to be nurtured into further growth and learning is not properly called chaos. For someone or something to operate in an "age-appropriate" manner in itself is not "chaos." Even with a need to mature, God's creations are called to participate in goodness within the community according to their ability.[4] Such a contribution can help mature creation so that in the next response, a new, higher expression of goodness would be appropriate.[5]

Lastly, as with rejecting the use of "chaos" as a synonym of "disorder"—as the opposite of "order"—the notion of "chaos" being developed in this project avoids using "chaos" in reference to things or persons being anti-"order." Such uses assume that the measure of *creation* and the completion of God's efforts is order. Notions of a particular, fixed societal and natural *order* are being excluded as the goal of creation in favor of relational notions—relationships of love. "Chaos" will be defined relative to goodness, truth, and beauty being expressed within relationships rather than the presence of order. Not just any arrangement will suffice. Order (structures) can be beautiful, but order itself is neither the impetus nor end of creation. This better reflects theological assertions that the One who is Creator is love. God is not defined as order. Thus, "chaos" is not anti-order, but juxtaposed with love of God and neighbor. Relating in love defines the divinely-gifted hum of the cosmic community.

Defining "Chaos": Growing Pains

Now that a theological framework has been set out in the previous chapter in which the grammar of *possibility* is used in regard to God's creative operations and God's relationship to creation has been defined as being

---

4. Recall from chapter 3 Brown's examination of P's account of the manner in which creation and the construction of the tabernacle took place. The calls given were for all to respond according to what is suitable to their gifts and abilities.

5. More will be said about this later.

trans-creation, it is possible to proceed to a definition and explication of "chaos."

Very simply, *chaos is coming to be that is in disharmony with the Possibility of and Call for our becoming in love for the o/Other*. Creation does not always express itself in tune with God's eccentric call. In its otherness it makes ventures out of kilter with what is gifted (blessed) to it according to the goodness of the self-gifting Triune God. These chaotic expressions are *possible* because of the nature of God's transjective, transcarnate operations of the Sprit and Word, but they are not what God lovingly self-gifts to creation.[6] This coming to be of creation in *dis*cord with or in a manner antagonistic to others is "chaos."

That discord in the community makes us recoil away from embracing others (and possibly the Other). We want to shield our eyes, cover our ears, silence our communication, and pull away from proximity. These expressions of chaos tear at our relating to others in the community in love. They inspire us to draw in and hold our breath instead of being moved by the Spirit; in response we leach that life-affirming flow from the community. Chaos makes us painfully aware of our nakedness and in desire of defenses from the very ones with whom we are called into nurturing relationship.

On the one hand, chaos can come about in numerous ways: for example, by a misjudgment of the currents of the Spirit and Word of God throughin creation, by being inattentive to the currents, by a limitation of understanding concerning the ramifications of one's actions, or a lack of thoughtfulness concerning one's actions. The result is that an appropriate way of relating to God and others, which is opened up to creation by the transjective Spirit and transcarnate Word, is not expressed.[7] This would

---

6. Because of the stress on possibility over the real—seeing God's activity as our possibility instead of seeing God as giving us possibilities—any negative expressions of creation in coming to be are not in God or among divine possibilities. Rather, they are the word creation speaks in relation to God's loving self-expression, God's making-possible-activity throughin creation.

7. Up front it needs to be mentioned that the nature of intent in expressions disharmonious with God's creative operations is not at issue here. As Susan Neiman points out, in the bewildering testimonies of those who assisted with the Holocaust, the actions of those with the most benign intentions can facilitate incomprehensible horror. While at other times, those with the most tortured consciences can be the least guilty (*Evil in Modern Thought*, 275). What is at issue is the occurrence of any expression that brings about chaotic dynamics in the community.

qualify as "many halting, stuttering, mis-spoken words."[8] Creation is still getting to know its Creator; it still sees as though through a dark glass. Having been born in immaturity, there is much each part of creation must learn; there are many ways it can grow up in its practices of (self) expressing what God makes possible by his self-gifting trans-creation.

There is, on the other hand, an even more profound "frustration and nullification of the work of the Spirit"[9] and Word. There is a word of blasphemy against the Spirit and quenching of the Spirit.[10] There is a saying of something across-the-grain of the good intentions of God's calling unto righteous/just expression.

Whether creation's responsive expression is disharmonious or antagonistic—maliciously or not—such a word of becoming is *malcreative*; it establishes a *chaos*. Because the response is a coming to be, in that it establishes something, even if it is defined by being chaotically related instead of lovingly, it is still creative. Even a *discreative act* that defaces or nihilates another creates a circumstance.[11] Instead of always manifesting beauty and goodness, creation at times manifests tangible chaotic circumstances. Chaotic, dissonant expressions and the consequent chaotic relations lie in contrast to the array of harmonies that righteous responses make with God's self-gifted goodness. It is not that God's creative activity has gone awry; it is that the partner(s) with whom God works in creating falter(s).

Just as hate is not the opposite of love in the New Testament, so chaos is not the opposite of creation/new creation. The opposite of love—fear—is a condition of not having yet blossomed under and into the fullness of love.[12] Hate is something different altogether. Hate is a murderous act; it de-faces and nihilates the other. So with creation/new creation, its opposite polarity is not chaos, but rather the earth *tohu wabohu*—a yet-to-unfold, barren infancy. The movement is from *tohu wabohu* to the creative (self) expression of God's goodness or to the

---

8. Dabney, "The Nature of the Spirit: Creation as a Premonition of God," 110.

9. Dabney, "Naming the Spirit," 56.

10. Ibid.

11. I thank Catherine Keller for the phrase "discreative act" and for many of the concepts that underlie her use of it (see chapter 5). Other possible phrases could be used as well: e.g., "creation-dissolving activity" or "community-killing activity."

12. E.g., 1 John 4:18–19a—"There is no fear in love, but perfect love casts out fear; for fear has to do with punishment, and whoever fears has not reached perfection in love" (NRSV).

creative self expression of chaos, a creaturely invention—an invention that is a quenching or blasphemy of the Spirit and Call who are the very possibility of our response.

Creation's opposite is a condition of not yet having blossomed under and into the fullness of God's glory. Chaos is something different altogether from *tohu wabohu*. Chaos is a response of creation; and as such, it is that which, in part, constitutes what is creation. Even so, chaotic response is a mal-creative activity; it is counter-nurturing. It harms others and the relationships within the community. In other words, *"chaos" is defined as instances when any part of creation (organic or inorganic) holds its breath and/or says something in disharmony with the inseparably operating Spirit and Word, who would have something more beautiful, abundantly life affirming, and rightly related to God and all creation for it.*

Instances of chaos are present throughout all creation—whether in the physical universe (timing, energy, matter: organic and inorganic) or in the animal kingdom (instincts, habits, perceptions, attitudes, ideas, societal relations, etc.). Those circumstances themselves can give rise to further instances of chaos—thus growing and compounding subsequent un-*right*eousness. Where there has been distortion, where perversion is the frame of reference or is habitual, responding in harmony with God fully becomes all the more difficult (and possibly dangerous); it takes even more imagination to envision the good that is possible. Circumstances condition the shape or extent of what can be expressed next—whether that next expression is good or chaotic. We respond to God harmoniously or discordantly within the confines of our current circumstances. The finitude of our embodiment, to whatever advantage or disadvantage, tempers what can be done next in creative expression.

Nevertheless, even though the discord of chaos is embodied throughout creation, that does not *determine* future expressions that God makes possible. There is not a lone linear progression of cause and effect at work from the Beginning to the End. History is full of complex nonlinear interactions and bifurcation points. Righteous response to the Father can happen through the work of the Spirit and Word; this provides, to some extent, a recapitulation of what was marked with chaos. It is a coming of the Kingdom in the midst of a creation marred by chaos.

With this use of "chaos," all discreative acts within creation are treated the same way. Human sin is a subset of chaos, the umbrella category. Chaos equally needs to be recapitulated whether it appears in sentient or insentient creation, with malicious intent or not.

Chaos in Nature

"Chaos" itself is used as the broadest category for improperly related becoming. It covers all of creation, even the physical world, which speaks upon God's call(s)—as in Genesis 1. Much of the work that it would require to fully identify all that would constitute improperly related expression (chaos) in nature will have to be left to those more knowledgeable and qualified to make those judgments. Important to distinguish in assessing nature, however, are the differences between immaturity, processes involving the second law of thermodynamics, and chaos. For example, it was noted in chapter 2 that Sjoerd Bonting at times blurs those distinctions when he says that during cosmic evolution "entropy"/"chaos" decreases and order increases until God abolishes "chaos" at the end of time.[13] It was mentioned in response that entropy is essential for the sustaining of life as we know it. Life processes require the energy released at the breakdown of structures. New life depends on there being entropy in the system—that not everything is crystallized. For example, without the birth and death of stars there would have been few of the elements that make up our planet. If food cannot be broken down in digestion, every animal dies.

Movement back and forth between order and entropy cannot be defined as inherently bad or evil. Talking about all entropy/chaos being abolished sounds good, but must be reconsidered. Cycles and seasons are a part of the good creation (Gen 1:14). God's goal and work in creation must be something other than battling, subduing, or abolishing that which makes movement, life, and newness in the world possible. It is one thing to say that God's creative work is continual, and another thing to define "creating" in terms of what would be a life-ending endeavor, in negative terms as the abolishment of entropy.

Chaos is a type of coming to be—becoming in the synergism between God, existing creation, and the new other in the creative event—in a manner discordant with God and neighbor.[14] Thus, in naming exam-

---

13. Bonting, *Creation and Double Chaos*, 97.

14. Logically it would not be possible to be in discord relative to God's self-gifting operation and not, then, be in discord with others. Likewise, it would not be possible to

ples of chaos in nature, it is important only to name that which comes to be such that it lacks the characteristic love and nurture of the other seen in God's operations. Some examples in need of consideration are the improper copying and division of DNA and chromosomes resulting in birth defects, health problems, or even death. Cancers, along with certain bacteria, molds, and viruses, could be examined as possible examples of chaotic, discreative becoming in relation to God and neighbor. Certainly there are many other possibilities, possibly even ones concerning inorganic matter, which could be named by those with knowledge of such things.

The important rule is not to use "chaos" as though the universe *is* chaotic by nature. Just because many of the responses in the universe are unpredictable, does not mean it should be called chaotic. Part of the fascination and mystery of others is that they do things differently than we would have done them; or, they come up with something completely unexpected or imagined by us.[15] God makes creation possible with the openness that it may speak a word as other. Nevertheless, by the very operation of its Creator relative to creation, it is created/called to in goodness and self-gifted with divine goodness. It is enabled to speak in the calling activity of God. It is only the expressions of nature that are not congruent with the possibility of the call that are "chaotic," not the unpredictability of the expressions themselves. It is also important to stress that the participating others made possible in God's creative operations are not necessarily evil or recalcitrant. They are enabled to speak freely. Even so, as immature, unknowledgeable, and unwise as they are, only a word spoken in concert with the self-gifting of God is a prudent, divinely intended type of response—a response which is expressive of God's goodness/love throughin.

One topic of which it is difficult to give an account is natural disasters. Historically there have been answers given about them: 1) that affirm the overall goodness of creation and its telos to the extent that

---

be out of kilter in regard to being lovingly related to others and not be crosswise to God transcreation.

15. Scientists are discovering new mysteries and complexities within the universe that make it all the more difficult to make calculations in the linear way it was once hoped in past centuries. It is worth pondering that it might be that they are uncovering, much like the ancients in relationship to their environment, the otherness of the universe made possible by God. Scientists went looking for the inner workings of a mechanism and have found instead a co-creature, a bewildering other.

natural disasters are simply a necessary part (although how and why they are is unknowable) to the progression toward ultimate goodness; 2) that speak of them as a design flaw; 3) that point to them as evidence for the absence of a design and/or designer; 4) that argue that God and creation are not in fact good, but cruel.[16] It is difficult in the current paradigm to determine whether an avalanche is infancy, chaotic response, or decay. Are volcanoes and earthquakes improperly related to God's good creative call to become, are they halting, stuttering speech or murderous acts? In incrementally relieving earth's pressures, thereby saving us all from more widespread destruction, is the earth's crust doing so in the manner in which it is called? In a system such as Bonting's where chaos is anything that is not yet perfected order (thus something that is not yet fully abolished), there is a way to explain these events away. At least God could be excused, to a certain degree, from culpability.

Irenaeus did not point to the root of the problem being either in embedded effects of sin or in improper choice; it was an issue of the passibility, weakness, and finitude of materiality.[17] Matter and materiality was not considered evil; Irenaeus's hope was not in escaping materiality. He also rejected Greek notions that matter is stubborn or fickle in its relationship to God.[18] Rather, matter was simply yet to be perfected. Recapitulation/new creation was a solution for the problems (or limitations) of materiality; it was a refashioning of the material, making it fit for incorruptibility, for eternity.[19] Such perfection/maturation is made possible through the *in*carnation of the Word. Thus, in an Irenaean framework, issues such as natural disasters would have been an issue of immaturity, not yet having come to the fullness of the goodness God, which God both planned for creation from the beginning and is working on in the incarnation. There is more work to be done at the second coming. Natural disasters can also

---

16. Susan Neiman's work is a helpful history of many positions on this matter developed during the Enlightenment and beyond; see *Evil in Modern Thought*.

17. Cf. Steenberg, *Irenaeus on Creation*, 55, 123; *Haer.* 5.3.1.

18. This idea was not uncommon in Greek thinking. E.g., Aristotle thought that matter was resistant to imposed forms (Torrance, *Divine and Contingent Order*, 88). Ultimately matter could be blamed for disturbing the order of the cosmos (ibid., 88).

19. In such a view (though not in Irenaeus himself), death itself has a sacramental character. We are not passively victimized by death. Rather, we entrust ourselves to the Father that by his hands this preparatory work for eternity would be achieved in our death and resurrection. Our baptism is a foretaste and a seal of what is to come in our death and resurrection. We look forward to the raising of our bodies in incorruptibility (whatever that may mean). In living and dying it is all unto the glory of God.

be a consequence of prior chaotic responses to which a not-yet perfected creation was susceptible. Excluding conversation about the incarnation, God's creative call throughin creation has yet to be answered in perfect, ongoing harmony with the o/Other to the Glory of God (to the exclusion and eradication of chaos). The incarnation was another step toward the fulfillment of full, mature response. Creation still awaits participation in the work to be done at Christ's return.

God did not initiate creation (create) for the 'earth' to remain immature. The call itself is nothing short of complete (divine) goodness self-gifted as possibility for self-expression by the other. Creation's immaturity is not "chaos"; being immature is not evil. However, there are dangers in immaturity. There are pains in growing up: stumbling, stuttering, etc. The susceptibility of the immature to respond chaotically is great. Being both immature and marked by chaos increases that susceptibility. Being not-yet perfected also means that there are significant consequences (shaping effects) to any responses within the community. As we continue to look for the resurrection of the dead and the life of the world to come, we attune ourselves to God with utmost attention and creatively seek to self-express the good even at this time, under these conditions. Prior chaos clouds our imagination and we are vulnerable to being marked by our neighbors in ways that shape our responses for good or ill. We do not have to be determined by our marks; but acting according to them does come 'naturally' even if we will be held accountable for not following in God's ways.

Creation's (a) exhaling and infancy and (b) malcreative acts may at times be difficult, if not impossible, to distinguish—especially when so much of creation is marked by chaotic interrelationships. Nevertheless, theologically these groups should remain distinct. If this distinction is maintained: 1) God's relationship with creation is not defined first as antagonistic; God does not approach creating as problem solving, or creation itself as a problem to be addressed; God's creative activity is not first negation, but (self) gift; 2) God's point of beginning in Genesis 1:2—creating a *tohu wabohu* earth—is not an evil or a disaster; it is the start of a relationship with a responsible other; 3) theologically there is room for Genesis 1:2 and the movement in Genesis 1 from a barren natality to an o/Other-affirming community without falling into some of the problems with double creation; 4) there is room for seasons and the second law of thermodynamics—without which all in creation would halt immediately; 5) the trajectory of creation is not seen as being toward a fixed, static state; there continues to be dynamism for exploring expressions of goodness; 6) there is no endless/upward progression of creation—there will forever be seasons for rest and for work; 7) the dynamism of God's creation can be affirmed as good without confusing that dynamism with the evil of chaotic acts; 8) "chaos" is then defined such that it is truly a problem that needs to be addressed and the effects of which need eradication; 9) the eradication of chaos does not entail the nihilation of an other—on the contrary it would be the nurturing of the other; and 10) the eradication of chaos entails the same self-gifting of God for the other as God's creative activity.

Chaos in Humanity

Under the umbrella category of chaos, being argued as a fitting label throughout all creation for coming to be out of sync with God's self-gifting throughin, traditional discussions of human sin and sinfulness are a subset. In order to get a more detailed sense of what chaos in humanity entails, the intended relationship between God and humanity will be sketched. This will bring into relief, in the portion that will follow the sketch, the nature of chaotically expressing oneself in relation to God and neighbor.

First is God's creative intention. It was pointed out in chapter 4 that in Genesis 1 humans have a different pattern to their creation. For the first and only time in Genesis 1, at the creation of humans God addresses God's-self. In a way, God is the 'environment' solicited upon which humans are to be dependent and united; they live out of/in/upon God's continued action throughin. They are the ones called to image God as they mature into the gift of God's goodness. It was suggested, as with Paul's statement to the Athenians, that to be human is to exist in God: "In him we live and move and have our being" (Acts 17:28).[20]

A similar theme is present in Genesis 2. In the Yahwist (J) tradition YHWH God is said to cause trees to grow out of the ground. Two particular trees have names: the tree of life and the tree of the knowledge

---

20. Cf. Augustine, *De Trin* XIV.12.16; see also 1 Cor 3:16 and 6:19 along with Augustine's treatment of these texts in *Con. Max.* II.XXI.1. First John 4:7–21 also has a wonderful passage about humans living in the love of God which is manifest most perfectly in God's actions in Christ's death on the cross. Cf. Steenberg on Irenaeus's interpretation of the *imago dei* (*Irenaeus on Creation*, 67, 102, 134–37).

of good and evil. These two trees *in the middle of the garden* undoubtedly have God as their source.[21] If God is the source of these trees, the tree of the knowledge of good and evil is a natural, God-made feature of the garden. The story does not tell us one tree is good and the other is a menacing evil or a carrot God cruelly dangles in front of Adam and Eve. One tree does have the word "evil" in its name, but its symbolism must be something other than being from the very pit of hell if its source is God. The narrative puts them both *together* and so any interpretation must account for that. In God's design, this tree belongs being planted right next to the tree of life; it should be planted in the center of the garden next to that tree from which they *are* told to eat.

"The knowledge of good and evil" has received several predominant interpretations. Most common among them historically is a form of sexual knowledge.[22] There are two other places in the Old Testament where "the knowledge of good and evil" appears. Deuteronomy 1:39 speaks about young children not yet having the knowledge of good and evil. It could be that they do not yet have sexual knowledge. However, it has been suggested that a better interpretation is that they do not yet have the discernment for making their own choices. This later interpretation makes sense in the other occurrence of the phrase in the Old Testament where Solomon prays for this discernment, this knowledge of good and evil (1 Kgs 3:9). Surely he is not praying for sexual knowledge at the dedication of the Temple. Hamilton concludes that "what is forbidden to man is the power to decide for himself what is in his best interests and what is not. This is a decision God has not delegated to the earthling . . . Man has indeed become a god whenever he makes his own self the center, the springboard, and the only frame of reference for moral guidelines."[23] It then makes sense why one who *eats* of that tree of the knowledge of good

---

21. It has been suggested that the central location is a parallel to the central location of the tabernacle in the Israelites' camp; cf. Brodie, *Genesis as Dialogue*, 124.

22. Jacob Milgrom is one who takes a more classic interpretation of "knowledge" as being sexual knowledge (*Leviticus*, 188). The original temptation Adam and Eve faced was the urge to procreative creativity. However, Milgrom claims that this urge toward procreative creativity translates into other realms of humanity making a good or evil world (ibid., 189). Even Lyn Bechtel sees this tree as a metaphor for human maturation specifically having to do with sexual self-awareness—a natural, non-evil step in human development; see her "Genesis 2.4b—3.24."

23. Hamilton, *The Book of Genesis*, 166.

and evil would be straying down the path of dying. Literally the text says, "eating, you will eat and dying, you will die" (Gen 2:17).[24]

The tree of the knowledge of good and evil—i.e., charting our own course into the open-ended possibility provided us by our Creator—is designed to be planted next to the tree of life from which we should eat—i.e., to be in dynamic, constant relationship with God, speaking congruent to the goodness of the o/Other orientation made possible from God in order to image him in all we do.[25] Speaking forth our own word without being tightly related to God's abundantly life affirming self-gifting is to speak life-leaching chaos for us and the community.

This was even true in the wisdom tradition. From the wisdom tradition, Hans Wolff demonstrates that the Hebrews understood human speech to be done correctly when it is in concert with God. The right word is the word that comes from hearing (Prov 18:13; 19:20); is at the right time (Prov 25:11); is quietly thought out (Prov 29:20); is temperate and kind (Prov 25:15); and requires the fear of God (Prov 1:7; 9:10; 15:33).[26] "God is at work even between the word which the wisdom of

---

24. Sacks, *A Commentary on the Book of Genesis*, 24. In the framework of St. Thomas Aquinas, as outlined by David Burrell, the distinction between creator and creature allows this freedom of the creature; "Creatures are indeed capable of an utterly initiatory role, but it will not be one of acting but of failing to act, of 'refusing' to enter into the process initiated by actively willing 'the good.' In that sense, we can be 'like unto God,' but only in a self-destructive manner . . . the only absolute beginning available to human willing is self-destructive. And even this absolute beginning will not be absolute, but the result of prior vices arising from a particular context. For human beings generally, sin is not so much an exercise of radical autonomy as it is wandering down treacherous paths with the wrong set of companions. So the exercise of autonomy, even of the self-destructive sort, is rare; the will is in fact much more moved than mover." (Burrell, *Freedom and Creation in Three Traditions*, 91, 92). This issue of "failing to act" will be addressed in the concluding chapter. There is a need to examine the relation of "improper relation/expression" suggested in this project with Aquinas's position of nonaction.

25. God's design is echoed throughout the Bible: "I am God Almighty, walk before me, and be blameless" (Gen 17:1); "In all your ways acknowledge him and he will direct your paths" (Prov 3:6); "But blessed is the man who trusts in the LORD, whose confidence is in him. He will be like a tree planted by the water that sends out its roots by the stream" (Jer 17:7–8; cf. Ps 1); "Pray continually" (1 Thess 5:17). Zachary Hayes based on more recent scholarship on Genesis 2–3, states that there is now a "tendency to measure the 'guilty lack' with which sin is concerned not in terms of a 'lost possession,' but in terms of the failure to move toward the only future which God intends for us. Grace is not something we once possessed and then lost. On the contrary, it is a gift to which God has called us throughout history, but we have always failed in our response" (Hayes, *What Are They Saying about Creation?*, 89).

26. Wolff, *Anthropology of the Old Testament*, 78.

man conceives in secret and that which then proceeds from his tongue (Prov 16:1) . . . Thus if man does not want to fall short of his real being, either in hubris or in laziness, he remains dependent on the God who in Israel began to speak with him in a human way."[27]

That humans would continually be attuned to God is the intent of God's self-gifting in his creative operations. However, humans do not always respond congruent with the dynamic of God's creative self-gifting. They do not have their tree, their frame of reference, planted next to the tree of life, but, rather, take 'nourishment' from their own tree, to their peril.

In the course of Christianity's history, the reason for this phenomenon came to be addressed under the doctrine of original sin. For much of the doctrine's history it has been understood that there was a fall of human nature in the sin of the first parents—that this fallen nature has been transmitted to all subsequent generations. Thus, the consequences of that first sin are universal to all humans. By appealing to the notions that have traditionally been part of the doctrine of original sin, it would be easy to account for chaotic responses among humans. For example, it could be claimed that they act according to their damaged nature. However, just because humans are capable of unspeakable evil—or even to point to the historical fact that we are guilty for doing it—does not necessarily entail that human nature is inherently, enduringly evil.

Within the notions of creation developed here, they preclude any idea of a fixed, fallen human nature with which every offspring of Adam and Eve is born. In the present framework of creation and chaos, original sin would have to be adjusted accordingly in its articulation. First, chaos has a history, an evolution; it is not fixed. Second, the context in which we become, inclusive of its instantiations of chaos, shapes and gives parameters to our responses, but it does not determine them. Inherent in God's ongoing creative activity is the possibility of good response. This leads to a third difference. Because the instances of chaos that are passed on are specific to each place and time, and because the future is not linearly determined by the past in each moment of creation, the manner in which each expression is shaped by prior instances of chaos varies by

---

27. Ibid., 79. Cf. James 3:2—"Anyone who makes no mistakes in speaking is perfect, able to keep the whole body in check with a bridle."

degree and kind. There is not a homogeneous, fixed fallen nature transmitted since our first parents.

More needs to be said about the differences of this new framework of creation and chaos in how to understand human sin or sinfulness, especially since the traditional notion of a common fallen nature is being adjusted. It is not as though every human responds disharmoniously in their conception (i.e., in their initial coming to be), entailing that we subsequently express ourselves chaotically based on a common fault in each of our own beginnings. It is not as though a better first step could have been possible in relation to all others in the community. Rather, humans come to be in the cosmic community in which the expressions of others, good or bad, affect others in the community. If, for example, the molecules in that infant-creation misbehave, it can have far reaching ripples for not only that newly conceived life, but also into the systems that person is a part (his/her family, neighborhood, town, etc.). A chaotic act in the smallest of systems can have increasingly bigger effects on the larger systems of which it is part. Those effects are not necessarily linear (deterministic) all the time.

There are choices to become by all in God's creation. However, those choices are certainly shaped/directed by the choices of others. For better or worse, our coming to be is not only a cooperative, collaborative operation between God and us, it includes the eccentric call of God to the stuff of the world to support and nurture us, an other. The very stuff of which we are made participates with us in the cosmic community.[28] The actions of our matter can be a good to us or malcreative; it can be affirming or deforming. Where we are plagued by the chaos of our own bodies, we pray for a new, different expression by our 'neighbor' in relation to God's call. It may also require that we minister to our 'neighbor' (body) so that it comes to the fullest (self) expression of goodness to us and the overall community.[29] Even so, we ultimately pray and hope for Christ's second

---

28. Some of these ideas concerning increasingly larger, more complex systems were first inspired by reading Joseph Bracken's *Society and Spirit: A Trinitarian Cosmology*. Although I do not support many ideas in his process thinking, he does have some ideas worth pondering. Since I have read Bracken, I could cite many other texts; it is difficult to find many current texts explaining theories of science that do not speak in terms of systems.

29. Two clarifications need to be made. First, for those afflicted in their embodiment by misbehaving chromosomes or cells, their becoming in the world will be shaped by the responses of their bodies to God's call. It is not as though they are *guilty* for the unnurturing behavior of others. It is not as though they can change the responses of

coming, the resurrection of the dead, and the life of the world to come. We pray for the refashioning of the world at Christ's return—the passing away of one manner of existing to participate in another.

Much, if not most, of the chaos experienced by humans is due to their personal injurious relationship with God's self-gifting or the choices of fellow humans.[30] We are affected by chaotic choices made by others even prior to our conception or our birth.[31] We are affected by or constituted by that which precedes our beginning. We are not just affected by contemporaneous influences. We come to be in a world already experimenting with certain expressions of both goodness and chaos.

One illustration: it is fitting that the telling of Israel's story does not start with God's calling of Abram. There is the *history of the whole* which preceded that call. That history informed the context and things already in motion at Israel's beginning. Israel was an inheritor of generations of

---

others and the repercussions. People who are marked by chaos in their bodies are responsible for growing into the fullness of God's self-gifting for them according to what is appropriate for them in their circumstances. They can still choose to express love, beauty, and goodness in the manner(s) they are able. Second, many in the world are oppressed and discreated by their neighbors. They are enslaved in systems of chaos. They are not *guilty* for being marked by the chaos in the environment in which they become. They are responsible, however, to self-express God's call to act in love for the o/Other, doing all they can to be a neighbor to their enemies, praying for them, and nurturing them into the fullness of God's self-gifted goodness for them. They should continue to act in ways that affirm their subjectivity and not just play the part of a de-faced object assigned to them by the system and actions of others. They can keep choosing; they can keep (self) expressing God's self-gifted goodness: they can turn the other cheek, walk the extra mile, and the like. Whatever the cost of their choosing to act righteously, they can entrust themselves to the one who has power over death and the grave; they can be assured of God's ultimate faithfulness to them in the resurrection of the dead. These two examples highlight how notions of individual guilt and individual salvation break down in a relational/communal matrix. Because of the negative actions of others, we cannot help but have our responses affected by that. In the same way, our experience of God's salvific work of new creation is dependent on it being worked out within and among the community.

30. Milgrom says that in the Priestly tradition in the Old Testament they rewrote the beliefs and practices of their neighbors. Where their neighbors tried to fight off the demonic from their sacred spaces, Israel replaced the demonic with inert contamination wrought from human misdeeds. Israel's cultic practices are about avoiding and removing the impurities resulting from human activity that threaten the sacred and bring death. There is no demonic, only human misdeeds (*Leviticus*, 9, 10, 13, 32). See chapter 3n82.

31. An easy example is the possibly chaotic circumstances of our conception, whether it occurred by force, through intercourse by an unwed couple, etc. During gestation, an unborn child can be affected drastically and permanently by the choices of substances the mother puts in her body.

growth into goodness and chaos. Israel also inherited God's prior relationship to and Noahite covenant with creation.

In the case of human conception, children, whose becoming God makes possible, are shaped by the relationships of others to the goodness of God's eccentric calling; unfortunately they are shaped as much by the chaos-riddled relationships into which they are born as the righteousness therein. As Gerald O'Collins says, we pass on to them a "heritage of evil" or an "enduring legacy of evil" as we enculturate them into our chaotic ways of behaving and relating to others.[32] Even though they are not born using the knowledge of good and evil (especially if they do not developmentally have it—Deut 1:39),[33] from infancy they experience the ways of those around them who gorge on the fruit of that tree. They play from youth among fountains of chaos. In our enculturation, the intimate, perpetual relationship with God that is necessary for expressing ourselves in bountifully good and beautiful ways gets fractured.

---

32. O'Collins, *Jesus Our Redeemer*, 62, 63. This heritage of evil does not have to be as obvious as an abusive home. Any chaos in our worldview, our manner of operating in the world, or the like can be passed along. For example, one criticism of capitalism is that it splits up families and communities as people must go to where there is employment for them. By enculturating children into such a system, we may unwittingly be preparing them to participate in the dissolution of the most basic human community: the family. We also ingrain in them a distrusting and isolating spirit of competition with others over a purported scarcity of resources, instead of a habit of thought that is self-emptying for and openly embracing of our fellow community members to whom we are, by God's creative activity, to be neighbor.

33. See, e.g., "If any of you put a stumbling block before one of these little ones *who believe in me*, it would be better for you if a great millstone were hung around your neck and you were thrown into the sea" (Mark 9:42, emphasis added; cf. Matt 18:6; Luke 17:2). In reference to Rahner's position, O'Collins states, "Particular, full individuals in 'a direct relationship' with God from the outset, children exhibit, Rahner wrote, not only a basic orientation to God but also a trust, an open readiness to be controlled by another, and 'the courage to allow fresh horizons' which privilege their response to divine grace" (O'Collins, *Jesus Our Redeemer*, 76). Through God's creative operations by the Spirit and Word, humans are created ready-made to grow into participation in the goodness God makes possible in the cosmic community. Unfortunately, we transition from being trusting children to adults who think we know better (cf. ibid., 77). Zachary Hayes follows a similar line of thinking: "Though no individual is personally culpable except when he or she personally sins, each is born into an environment that is oriented in the wrong direction. It is a world that is insensitive to God and resists him. Thus, even the child, while having no personal culpability, is in the full sense of the word a member of a community which, through the culpable actions of its members, has constituted itself historically in opposition to God" (*What Are They Saying about Creation?* 91).

Participating in these fractured contexts makes each person both guilty and responsible for the part he/she plays.[34]

In keeping with developments in Western thinking, original sin in this paradigm would not be articulated as a static state or a fallen nature in which all humans since the first are created. Instead, it has a history, an ebb and flow. Its history is the history of chaotic expressions in the cosmic community and their contribution to subsequent becoming. Original sin is a matter of ontology insofar as coming to be in a chaotic manner embodies that expression, it undermines community. However, original sin is neither static nor deterministic; in the moment-by-moment creative activity of God there is the possibility of something different, new, good, or the like. Recapitulation via righteous expression is an ever available possibility, even in this lifetime. In becoming in tune with the inseparable creative operations of God, humans can write chaos out of the unloving, destructive ways we have become related. In responding in concert with God, chaotic activity seems foreign, nonsensical; it is outside one's vocabulary of ways to function in relation to others. People can in this life mature into a truly human manner of (self) expressing divine goodness in relation to others and begin to be freed from enslavement to chaos as they await the salvation to be revealed at Christ's second coming (cf. Rom 8:18–25; 1 Cor 15:1–2). God calls us to this holiness of life, this perfection in love. God has joined himself throughin creation to that end.

The number of goodness-denying expressions among humans is essentially limitless. There are, nevertheless, certain themes among the

---

34. I am thankful for an in-class presentation by one of my colleagues at Marquette University, Michael Groen, on some of the recent findings of neuroscience (delivered in November 2007). There are certain emotional, physiological responses that are hardwired into us at birth. However, our social interactions imprint on our brains what bodily reactions (somatic markers) to have when certain situations present themselves. These bodily reactions are unconscious. Our surroundings—our enculturation—truly become embedded in our bodies, our brains. Based on those imprintings, our bodies will present us with unconsciously selected data under certain circumstances. Thus, our "rational" decision making is based on a small selected portion of data given to us by our body. Nevertheless, our upbringing is not determinative. Even though our bodies have been programmed by our upbringing to react in certain ways, we can consciously choose against what our bodies present to us. There is also evidence that the brain is more plastic than once believed. Our brains can be retaught over time to have different somatic markers to certain stimuli. In this case Christian community becomes that much more important in helping us grow into the salvation and creative calling made possible by God.

variations. For example, chaos appears in the hyperactive schedules we keep, in our lack of sleep and rest,[35] in the quantity and quality of our food intake, in the substances to which we expose our bodies, in our choice of work, in our motivation for and manner of our work, in our self-centeredness, in our self-denial/deprecation,[36] in our institutional structures, in our societal structures, in our cultural norms, in our patterns of thinking, in our treatment of others, in our manner of speaking, in discreative activities of prejudice, hatred, murder, and warfare. The list of themes with any possible variation is itself extremely long. Our ingenuity for discreative acts is as limitless as our ingenuity for expressions of goodness, both made possible by the gifting of God's transjective Spirit and transcarnate Word. Instead of discovering with God endless expression of good, humans have invented a vocabulary for acting, thinking, and expressing themselves that transgresses against God, precisely because of the nature of God's self-gifting throughin creation.

Many pious Christians would bristle at some items that have been listed, but there is nothing we do that is not an act in relation to the very divine activity by which the act is possible. Our acts are also in relation to all in the cosmic community who nurture us in our becoming and who we are to nurture in theirs. Every act is righteous to the degree it rings true with God's good, loving nature. If our lack of sleep, exercise, or healthy eating harms us (including the very matter called by God to nurture our unfolding) it is unrighteous. If it takes someone else's daily bread or unnecessarily overtaxes the land, it is unrighteous. If our choices of house and car sizes (or the building materials used)—as well as our consumption of other products—harms the earth or limits our ability to gift of ourselves with our time and money to the needs of others, it is clearly antithetical to the flow of the possibility and call of God and in need of repentance. Many Christians seeking to be holy have been far too narrow in examining areas in need of repentance because their definition of unrighteousness has been limited and/or their enculturation

---

35. Although the Israelites did honor the Sabbath through most all of their history, there is no record that they ever honored sabbatical years, or the year of Jubilee. Centuries later we hardly even go as far as to take a sabbath. The effects on humans, our ways of living, and on the planet are not fully knowable.

36. See Diane Leclerc's *Singleness of Heart*. Leclerc defines original sin in terms of idolatry, either of self (pride) or others (self-denial). Pride by itself is an insufficient definition of humanity's problem. Many humans, especially many women and abuse victims, have no sense of self, let alone an inflated, prideful sense of self.

into systems marked by chaos have helped them perpetuate discreative acts thoughtlessly. There is nothing that exists that has not been called according to God's eccentric goodness. It is against God's self-gifting that all acts must be measured.

Whether we are deliberate in our chaotic acts or even conscious of them is not at issue. What is at issue are instances when the love of God and 'neighbor'—which includes the treatment of our own body and the world—is mis-expressed—or worse, we de-face the other. Any chaotic act is a deformation of our relationship with God and others with whom we are created to commune. Out of love for the o/Other, the act must be repented of and new ground for the imaginative expression of good in the relationship sought out.[37]

Intent

The issue of intentionality has been mentioned several times in regard to chaotic responses. It needs to be addressed directly. During the Enlightenment, where natural human reason was becoming the standard for societal arrangements (including politics, economics, legal systems, etc.) and morality itself (instead of a religious framework or a system thought to be inherent in the cosmos), it became the assumption that evil deeds (or crimes) require malicious intent.[38] The focus was on a facet of the human subject.[39] Without malicious intent in doing the act, the person's action could not be considered criminal.[40]

Susan Neiman writes of this transition as well as the utter confounding of this way of thinking in the aftermath of World War II. When the

---

37. Both Williams, "The Forgiveness of Sins," and Volf, "Forgiveness, Reconciliation, and Justice," are excellent essays that unfold this idea.

38. This shift can be seen in some of the theology done at this time on hamartiology. For example, in the theology of John Wesley (eighteenth century), sin properly so called required a *willful* transgression against a known law of God. All other transgressions committed *unknowingly* and/or *unintentionally* were sin improperly so called.

39. Kant, e.g., taught that intent was the one thing over which we as humans have control. Therefore we should act with right intent regardless of what we think may or may not be the effects of an action; those consequences are largely out of our control (Neiman, *Evil in Modern Thought*, 74).

40. Susan Neiman summarizes: "Before [the eighteenth-century earthquake in] Lisbon, evils were divided into matters of nature, metaphysics, or morality. After Lisbon, the word *evil* was restricted to what was once called moral evil . . . Modern evil is the product of will. Restricting evil actions to those accompanied by evil intention rids the

concentration camps were discovered and investigated in order to bring the people responsible to trial, it was found that the people who carried out both the day to day operations at the camps and the broader infrastructure that made the camps possible had no calculations of genocide or malicious intent toward their victims.[41] Most all of the participants had motives that were utterly banal: for example, motives of personal promotions within the Nazi ranks or a desire not to have their own personal lives disrupted.[42] The totalitarian regime created a system that allowed people to do horrific deeds guilt-free, with little to no reflection on the immorality of their actions. The key ingredient for establishing criminality was absent in this new, banal type of evil. The basic philosophy of morality and law was left silent.

The concentration camps exposed a type of evil that previous accounts of evil could give no account; it was a banal evil done by people participating in a system designed for doing horrific evil thoughtlessly.[43] "In contemporary evil, individuals' intentions rarely correspond to the magnitude of evil individuals are able to cause."[44] This is the great problem with making malicious intent the benchmark in the areas of morality and criminality.

In the framework proposed, chaos is chaos. Whether coming to be (responding to God's call) is chaotic for either banal or murderous

---

world of a number of evils in ways that made sense. Less clear were the concepts of willing and intention themselves" (*Evil in Modern Thought*, 268; cf. 271ff.).

41. Neiman, *Evil in Modern Thought*, 270–71.

42. Ibid., 273.

43. It is easy to pick on World War II Germany, but many Westerners with banal motivations work in industries, do certain leisure activities, and consume goods that not only harm themselves or damage creation but keep other humans in horrifically poor living conditions. Their acts are discreative of the other and yet they are done according to a system that allows them (even encourages them) to do them thoughtlessly again and again and again. E.g., even in the face of global climate change, the first thing it is hoped that Americans will do in a slumping economy is to consume more. This characteristic of Western thought should terrify us; "Precisely the belief that evil actions require evil intentions allowed totalitarian regimes to convince people to override moral objections that might otherwise have functioned" (Neiman, *Evil in Modern Thought*, 275). We cannot unthinkingly go on following culture and convention just because our intention-alarms are not sounding. As Neiman, Rawls, and other Kantian philosophers urge, we should operate in the world in ways that we would rationally design given the chance, not according to the irrationality and injustice that far too abundantly pervade conventions.

44. Neiman, *Evil in Modern Thought*, 273.

intentions, it is still mal-creative or discreative of self and others; as Neiman states: "What counts is not what your road is paved with, but whether it leads to hell."[45] Chaos is chaos; it is a hell of-our-own-making on earth. It is in need of repentance, repair, and new response. It demonstrates ongoing imperfection in love. In short, the notion of chaos in this framework attempts to account for all types of evil. The resultant chaotic circumstance is in need of the same salvific activity of God no matter the nature of the intention.

The entire purpose of questioning intentionality is not to erase responsibility, but to understand it in a new, even deeper way. If anything, it should lead God's people to cry even more earnestly "Have mercy on me, a sinner!" and "Come, Lord Jesus!"—rather than, "Thank you, God, I am not like those people." It also keeps at the forefront our solidarity with the community and how far *we* have left to go toward universally expressing God's goodness.

Recapitulation and Glorification

Within this framework of creative activity and growth from infancy, there is always the possibility of good expression. This good coming-to-be is a positive adjustment within a system marked by chaos; it recapitulates to some degree chaos-marked relationships.

Irenaeus's notion of recapitulation has already been appealed to since it was utilized by Catherine Keller in the cycles of her feedback loops—beginning and beginning again. These loops mean for Keller that there is not the linear progression of creation begun *ex nihilo*. Keller opts for an Irenaean "helical, recapitulatory sense of history."[46] In the recapitulatory loops, the new creation of all things is forever hoped for and possible. Irenaeus himself affirmed that in recapitulation/new creation the substance or thing itself would not be annihilated, it was its fashion of existence that would pass away and be renewed and strengthened.[47] Unfortunately *humans have become old in corruptions*. The making new

---

45. Ibid., 275.

46. Keller, *Face of the Deep*, 56.

47. Steenberg, *Irenaeus on Creation*, 55; cf. *Haer.* 5.31.1. Irenaeus makes it clear that sin and the misuse of freedom are not the problem. Human flesh has the characteristics of being corruptible and finite—weak and passible. These qualities of our immature flesh can be problematic and will naturally come to a mortal end, though not embodiment itself (Steenberg, ibid,123).

of things will make them ready for incorruptibility so that they will not again become old.[48]

Recapitulation is for the sake of establishing goodness-expressing, life-nurturing community through the Call and Possibility of God. The fulfillment of the life-nurturing community in God's love is the end of creation and salvation (new creation). Inherent in creation is the telos of growing into maturity in its expressions of good for the o/Other across all creation. Because creation and salvation have the same end and are part of the same overall economy, there is only slight distinction between them. Salvation is brought about by the creative healing of that which inhibits good expression—that which is mal-creative or deformed. Creation makes possible and nurtures good expression into maturity. Thus, our salvation is the entering into and enjoyment of that toward which we are called by God in creation; it is that which we can and do taste in part in the present because of recapitulatory moments.

Christian hope is ultimately in God's final work of new creation, the making new of all things—the resurrection of the dead and the life of the world to come. The eradication of chaos from creation and creation's perfection into maturity is what we so deeply crave; it is the fulfillment of God's creative and salvific activity. The new creation to be revealed at Christ's second coming also has the quality of incorruptibility, to which we look forward.[49]

The nascent chaos that influences new distortions of every degree, even discreative acts unto the very death (nihilation) of self and other, must be healed. All creation must be freed from these chains of chaos to express unencumbered true and full beauty and goodness. Creation's imagination for self-expressing (divine) goodness will no longer be clouded by a malformed frame of reference, destructive habits, or the

---

48. It is significant that Irenaeus stresses both materiality and divine immediacy in both creation and redemption; he loved the Genesis 2 narrative of God forming Adam out of the dust and breathing into his nostrils. Out of that narrative of dust and breath he stresses that the *image* of God is both body and soul (Steenberg, *Irenaeus on Creation*, 119). Redemption must include a refashioning of what is going on in our bodies. In addition, however, it also means that there can be no reduction of what it means to be creation to the purely material. The "life-giving essence" of one's being is just as crucial as material fashioning. In terms of the framework being proposed here, the eccentric call of God with/as the very possibility of the other is constitutive just as is the shape that the self-expression of the other takes.

49. To say that our glorified bodies will not be corruptible does not mean that there will not be continued discovery and development in expressing the good.

kinesis of incumbent chaos. It will reach fullness of expression. What that day means for humanity in Dabney's view: "That end is not the imposition of divine will upon recalcitrant matter nor the rising of contingent being to the contemplation of its necessary first cause. The end of all things is the cosmic Sabbath, that day in which the human creature as creation's steward will stand before God in worship and thanksgiving and praise and will thereby reflect God's image in the world, being and saying and doing what God is and says and does in God's creation."[50] God will see a family resemblance in creation as his o/Other-driven Spirit and Word's love is expressed therein. Creation will answer the first question posed by the Father in Scripture, "where are you?" with a jubilant childlike cry, "Here I am!"[51]

To that end, God has already been at work. Most powerfully and definitively, God has been reconciling and recapitulating the world in and through Christ. In Christ, the work of the Spirit showed that the Spirit will always be the Possibility of God that any brokenness can be *"taken up anew and made whole."*[52] When Christ returns, the remaining chaos and brokenness will cease. He will be the Omega. All things will 'pass away' (Rev 21:1) to receive full newness of life. The raging nations will be at peace (Ps 46:9; 76:3); their instruments of war will be turned into instruments to tend the earth (Isa 2:4). The animal kingdom will be at peace (Isa 11:6–9). Instead of being subdued, that which lies fractured in chaos will be healed and join in doxology in that day (e.g., Ps 98:6–8; Isa 2:2; Phil 2:9–11). Chaos will be no more, not because it is an *it* (an entity) that will be vanquished, but because that which is marked by a grating dissonance of expression will be made new in the fullness of divine goodness. Creation will be at peace because it will be transformed; that is the hope and promise of our coming salvation, of which we have a tasting in the present.

Another note on soteriology would be helpful to make in regard to recapitulation and creation's destiny. The image of the garden's trees has been used throughout the Christian tradition for theological purposes. In his book on soteriology, Gerald O'Collins makes reference to a poem by John Donne that states: "We think that Paradise and Calvary, Christ's

---

50. Dabney, "The Nature of the Spirit," 110.
51. Ibid.
52. Dabney, "Naming the Spirit," 58 (italics original).

Cross and Adam's tree, stood in one place."[53] In a footnote O'Collins explains that there is an old legend that Christ's cross was actually fashioned out of the tree of the knowledge of good and evil. Thus, Christ paid for Adam's taking of that fruit on the very tree itself.

Donne's words are exactly right, but the legend behind them is wrong. Christ's and Adam's trees stand together. However, given the significance of the two trees in the Garden, Christ's cross is not from the tree of the knowledge of good and evil. Christ's cross *is* the tree of life. When Christ is lifted up on that tree, he becomes the very fruit of the tree of life that humanity was and is to eat—the divine self-giver, Love poured out for the other. When Christ offers himself up, the flaming sword is removed from the path to the tree. Once again, humanity is invited to "Take and eat . . ." Christ is the "the way, and the truth, and the life" (John 14:6).[54]

Christ, who was poured out for others, is the fruit we eat from the tree of life in submitting to the Holy Spirit as daughters and sons of the Father. The goodness of God's self-gifting character—revealed in the Trinity's operations in the birth, life, death, and resurrection of Christ—is that which we are told to eat, that to which we are to be conformed. The very Word who was made flesh and dwelt among us, revealing God to us, is the very same self-giving Word, who with the Spirit, makes creation possible. That character is the pulse of creation. It is our possibility in relation to which we become.

This is consistent with the theological anthropology outlined above. Humanity's imaging of God in the world was not supposed to be due to a static nature intrinsic to it. Humanity was to image God through dynamic relationship to the Triune God by the inseparable operations of God throughin. Humans were supposed to perpetually come to the tree, taking in and learning from the humanity of God.[55] His "self-giving be-

---

53. Quoted in O'Collins, *Jesus Our Redeemer*, 40.

54. Cf. also John's use of the analogy of healing for Christ's death on the cross (John 3:14–15). I must thank Gerald O'Collins for providing the information that inspired this idea that Christ himself is the fruit of the tree of life, even though he did not say it himself. The implications for Christology, a theology of the Eucharist, Christian anthropology, and ecclesiology are exciting. For example, see Revelation 22:2, where the tree of life is said to have twelve kinds of fruit and its leaves are for the healing of the nations. Those who respond to the call to image God in the world become linked with the very self-gifting activity (mission) of God in the world.

55. Humans must "pray without ceasing" (1 Thess 5:17). Christ invites them: "Take my yoke upon you, and learn from me; for I am gentle and humble in heart, and you

havior alone is the norm for human activity."[56] Following him is wisdom; "Trust in the Lord with all your heart, and do not rely on your own insight. In all your ways acknowledge him, and he will make straight your paths. Do not be wise in your own eyes; fear the Lord, and turn away from evil. It will be a healing for your flesh and a refreshment for your body" (Prov 3:5–8).

Last, eternity is not about coming to a predetermined destination which will not be arrived at until checking off all points on God's agenda. There is no goal among true friends. The point is not the destination. The point is not to say that one thing such that nothing more needs to be said. The point of relationship is the joy of the relationship, the shared expressions of love and companionship.

God delights in nurturing the other into the good. In the nurturing of the other, there is delight for both God and creation in the journey together, through the unfolding of each day and the creativity of discovering new ways to manifest goodness, truth, and beauty in the relationship. There will be the utmost joy for God and creation when all creation is rescued from its chaos and communes fully with both God and neighbor. Even at that point, the journey together will only have just begun.

This is in line with the thinking of Irenaeus. He did not define the eschaton as the ending of the current economy by starting a new one, "but the fulfillment, restoration and renewal of that which God originally began in creating 'the heavens and the earth' (Gen 1.1)."[57] At that

---

will find rest for your souls" (Matt 11:29). Irenaeus believed that Christ reveals God to us as we in turn image God in our humanity; "[If] Christ's humanity is not something that sullies or conceals his divinity, but rather makes that divinity available to human perception, then the same is true of the humanity we share with Christ . . . in our humanity we can be, and, indeed, are called to be, revealers of divinity, bearers of divine glory, the means by which God is glorified (AH IV.20.7)" (Minns, *Irenaeus*, 41). The phrase "humanity of God"—used in the text above—is taken from the later writings of Karl Barth, who believed that God's humanity and humanity's togetherness with God was miraculously established in Christ (Barth, *The Humanity of God*, 47).

56. Marshall, "The Fullness of Incarnation," 192. "The presumed 'perfection' of Adam prior to the fall is not the goal of human existence; Christ is" (ibid., 200). The church will be judged based on its faithfulness to the call of the Father by the Spirit in embodying God's humanity, the nature of God displayed in Christ. Judgment does not take place in Christ. It takes place on the basis of Christ. God in Christ is wooing humanity from unbelief into a repaired relationship with God. Those who believe and live in obedience will hear the Father say, "I recognize you; we have a striking family resemblance. Well done!"

57. Steenberg, *Irenaeus on Creation*, 55; see ibid., 84.

time there is a rest that both God and creation will enjoy.[58] Both will be at home with each other. In focusing on the restoration of the earthly paradise the point is not about the heavenly state being a reward; rather, the restoration is more for the purpose of preparation for future growth and glory.[59] The journey of creation with God will continue.

The Ethic and Telos of Creation

An important corollary to the brief mention of glorification in the previous section is to make explicit the telos of creation in the framework, which is manifest in its founding ethic. The *ethic* of God's creative activity is definitive of the relationships among all those in the community that is envisioned by the Priestly source. The ethic of creation's genesis is its telos.

The God who is our possibility is himself oriented eccentrically to act lovingly for the other, nurturing the other into the fullness of self-expressing (divine) goodness. God does not master or coerce, but self-gifts that creation might grow up such that its own voice is transparent to the o/Other orientation of the Possibility and Call creatively operating throughin. Divine creation is teleological. To know the character of God is to know the character for which creation is destined. In the possibility of our beginning is our end. God is calling us forward to participate in him.[60]

In our genesis is our identity and ethic for life as contributors to the cosmic community. The Possibility by which we respond—that which we

---

58. Ibid., 53. Steenberg writes further: "For Irenaeus, God's rest comes only in the perfect completion of his cosmogonic work. When God's nature as creator had been actualized fully in the formation of the cosmos, he was able to rest. So humankind shall find rest only in the perfection of its own nature, for the character of 'Sabbath' is a reality both for God and humankind" (Steenberg, *Irenaeus on Creation*, 100). Human perfection is about joining God's Sabbath. Interestingly, Irenaeus never uses Genesis 2:1–3 "in the context of a distinctly protological discussion. In his reading these verses are chiefly eschatological, and stand as among the most important ancient testimony to the incarnational confession of a chiliastic kingdom" (ibid., 98). The end is defined relative to the beginning for Irenaeus, but never the opposite. Genesis 1 has historicity, but of more import is reading it as a "prophecy of what is to come" (ibid., quoting Irenaeus, 99); "The true Sabbath is not the seventh day of creation, but the kingdom which that seventh day indicates" (ibid., 100).

59. Ibid., 58.

60. There is a growing conversation about the futurity of God. It is claimed that this is in keeping with ideas of God in the Bible—in other words, "the idea of a God who

should most naturally image—is not characterized by exploiting creation (other), self-deprecation, isolation, or by endless growth in knowledge, wealth, and power. The Spirit is the Possibility of God for the other, operating transjectively relative to creation. Our possibility, our eccentric orientation to express good toward the o/Other, is our end. Building up the cosmic community (those in it) is our purpose in existing; it is in our call to be. It is how we express moment by moment to God and neighbor, not just "here *I* am," but "here *I* am *for you*."[61]

To reiterate an earlier point, the goal is not to be part of a ceaseless incremental progression with all humanity and creation wherein we will wake up one day to find we have arrived at perfection. Rather, we seek in this moment that our becoming be a self-expression of divinely-enabled/self-gifted goodness to the o/Other. The aim is the maturation of things/persons/systems in the time in which they exist, the maximal expression of good therein.

This again is in keeping with the spirit of Irenaeus's theology. He does not focus much on the *how* of creation. That was a topic that he believed was speculative and a source for many of the erroneous notions against which he fought.[62] Instead of speculating on *how*, he focused on

---

comes to meet the world out of the realm of the future" (Haught, "Chaos, Complexity, and Theology," 189). This arguably biblical notion fits well with the direction scientific reflections are heading; "it is the promising quality of this divine futurity that leaves the present open to the unpredictable surprise and novelty that the sciences of chaos and complexity are now bringing to our attention" (189–90). Dan Boone, president of Trevecca Nazarene University, in his teaching uses for God an analogy of parents teaching a child how to walk. Parents do not stand behind the child pushing her in the back telling her to go forth. Rather, they stand in front of the child, in the child's field of vision, and beckon the child to come (see, e.g., Exod 13:21–22). Thus, God is the one who in creative expression forever precedes us; he both invites and makes possible our response.

61. Chris Vena, in his dissertation at Marquette University, makes a similar point. One of his main arguments is that care for creation should not be discussed as a matter of stewardship, but within the realm of love of God and neighbor. He was the first to articulate this point for me. My suggestions are compatible with his. In my view, creation is not to be objectified and utilized to the highest utility, but should be seen as an other with whom we are in a co-nurturing relationship.

62. In Irenaeus's words, "we shall not err if we affirm the same thing concerning the substance of matter—namely, that God produced it—for we have learned from the scriptures that God holds the supremacy over all things. But whence or in what manner he produced it, scripture has nowhere declared, nor is it for us to conjecture, forming from our own opinions endless speculations concerning God. Such knowledge should be left to God" (2.14.4; quoted in Steenberg, *Irenaeus on Creation*, 46). The *how* only has value as it relates to the redemption wrought through the incarnation (ibid.).

why God creates. The answer is God's goodness.[63] "God's motivation for creation is his own inherent goodness . . . his nature leads to creation in which his goodness can be expressed."[64] In his description of Irenaeus's position, Steenberg does not use the language of eccentricity; however, he does say that there is an "externalizing character of his nature which only finds fulfillment in sharing its love with another."[65]

It is significant that Irenaeus affirmed the character of God's goodness as such "to 'bring into being an entity other than himself,' to give being to that which has none, that it may ultimately find being in himself."[66] As a result, "God's creative movements are purposeful, intentional, propelled forward by the goodness of a nature that cannot but reach out of itself in creative activity and render perfect the beings it creates—a perfection 'made visible' in the incarnate Christ."[67]

In contrast to Irenaeus's focus on the second person, the language of *possibility* used in this framework was first developed by Dabney in regard to the Spirit. This pushes us to look in different places in Scripture for the ethic of creation. As has already been argued in relation to creation, the Spirit's work in Christ and initial connection to the rearing of the world from obscurity seems to be the broader paradigm in which to interpret the Spirit's ministry within and through those on whom he rests. Going further, within early post-Pentecost communities, the nature of the Spirit's work is seen in the erasing of hierarchical or alienating distinctions in favor of the familial status of brother and sister. The Spirit as Possibility for the o/Other establishes the relational conditions for something good: namely, human equality in fellowship, in mutual submission[68] and loving service. Therefore, the consequent operations

---

63. Cf. Cottrell, *What the Bible Says about God the Creator*, 124.

64. Steenberg, *Irenaeus on Creation*, 33, 34. In another place Steenberg writes, "God will create in order to bring this goodness to another" (*Irenaeus on Creation*, 22; cf. ibid., 84).

65. Ibid., 35.

66. Ibid., 38.

67. Ibid. Irenaeus linked God's externalizing character primarily with the Second Person. He did not start with the Spirit as Genesis 1 and Dabney do. Nevertheless, the roles of the Father, Son, and Spirit from protology to eschatology are the same in Irenaeus's work. There is one overarching economy defined relative to God's goodness in which the persons consistently fulfill their respective parts; see Steenberg, *Irenaeus on Creation*, 72.

68. Submission is an idea that is so easily perverted. Submission is only godly if it is mutual. Otherwise, it is subjugation of one to another; it objectifies or de-faces one party.

of those who dynamically cooperate with the Spirit of Sonship are to participate in God's self-giving dominion of building up the other for participation in the cosmic community, into fellowship in love.

An Advantage of the Proposed Framework and Definition of "Chaos"

One of the goals of this project was not only to articulate a grammar of creation in which to define "chaos," but to develop a grammar that is coherent within a contemporary Western context. There were several reasons for wanting to achieve this goal. First, was to provide a framework with components that are not wholly unfamiliar for people outside Christianity, who may lack familiarity with the worldviews in which orthodox positions on significant Christian doctrines were first articulated. Second, for those inside Christianity, less translation is required between this framework and the wider worldview in which they function in society and their professional work.[69] Specifically, the proposed framework honors the cultural shifts that came of age during the Enlightenment concerning views of human nature and the nature of evil in the world. Thus, it seeks to be a theology that is ready-made for living in the world as the community of faith.

Meeting this goal required some adaptations in the way certain Christian affirmations were articulated. In classic Greek thinking, the

---

It takes mutuality—that both parties respond in kind. In a small-group setting I recall studying Christ's command to "sell all you have and give it to the poor." We were talking about the barriers in the community that inhibit such a move; it requires vulnerability, trust, and dependence on others that when you have need others will help supply from their abundance. When I pushed that our fears and excuses should not stop us from living according to the in-breaking Kingdom, one of the people replied in jest, "You go first." Living in faithfulness to God's call does require a community for life-abundant thriving for all. When we live in fear about scarcity, and hoard resources, we neither trust God for our "daily bread" nor see the miracle that there is enough for everyone (e.g., Matt 14:14–21; 15:32–38). Christ never promised, however, that in this life there would not be pain for living in obedience; we will be quite vulnerable to those who respond improperly to their Creator. Nevertheless, the call to obedience is no less legitimate and authoritative.

69. As Zachary Hayes hopes in the creation of such a contemporary articulation of creation, "it speaks in language that is understandable in terms of modern world-experience, it does not require that the believer, who is modern in his or her daily experience, must become mediaeval or even pre-mediaeval in the world of faith" (*What Are They Saying about Creation?*, 49–50).

nature of humans never changed. Christians claimed, as they sought to articulate their beliefs in that intellectual milieu, that human nature changed once in the fall and has persisted in that broken, sinful state since then.[70] During the Enlightenment that particular formulation of Christianity's belief that all are affected by sin was challenged. It was a time period in which what counts as metaphysics was changing. The first question of philosophy was no longer being. Questions of epistemology gained precedence over metaphysics. The old first question of being was thus being asked and answered in very different ways. The topic of metaphysics was being re-construed in a context where the human subject was becoming the measure of all things. Matters of history, culture, and relationships became viewed as constitutive of a person/thing.[71] Thus, during the Enlightenment, thinkers such as Jean Jacque Rousseau began saying that humans are inherently good. It is simply their enculturation that develops in them virtues and/or vices. Further, those cultures have a history of development. Unfortunately, through the development of social interactions, what humans have become has developed mostly for the worse; one dysfunction has been compounded upon another.

In the thoughts of Rousseau (and Hegel later on) evil arose in history and would be resolved in history.[72] Thus, in the present framework, claims concerning the compounding and complicating of chaos over time, as well as claims concerning recapitulation even in the present, resonate with the broader intellectual culture in the West, which sees evil (chaos) as an issue of developments in history—not an issue of our given/created nature (being).[73] Much of society's aims, in all fields, have

---

70. Neiman, *Evil in Modern Thought*, 44.

71. I am thankful to Dr. Philip Rossi for challenging me after I had made statements that "metaphysics" was no longer an issue; rather, the classic notion of metaphysics was being morphed into new realms or categories in giving an account of what is constitutive of a thing. The history of a thing and its relationships to other things began to define what it is.

72. Neiman, *Evil in Modern Thought*, 44, 94.

73. We are enculturated—we become—in chaotic circumstances. This does not mean that the problem of original sin is inherent to human nature: that we are born with it. There is no inherent breakdown in human capacities or morality due to the manner in which God calls us to respond or our 'neighbors' to respond in love toward us. Our capacities are susceptible to corruption when they operate within and according to the fractured context. E.g., doing what is laudable, good, or right in a consumeristic, capitalistic society may have no reflection of the (divine) goodness to which God calls us; context can dull and deceive our ingenuity for responding to God's call. No matter of our intention to respond well, participating in these fractured contexts makes each

been to resolve the evils or problems that have arisen: in education, politics, economics, agriculture, environment, community development, family dynamics, etc. The hope is to resolve the problems, to recapitulate that which is manifesting chaos (by whatever standard of measure is being used).

It took a shift in worldview from static notions of being for humans to intentionally seek to change their world. As Adorno wrote: "[o]nly when that which is can be changed is that which is not everything."[74] In an intellectual context where societal arrangements were given naturalistic, historical explanations (instead of explanations about the God-given order of reality) those arrangements could be critiqued and changed. In that same landscape, where evil lies at the surface and can be described in historical, relational terms, humans can be thought of as not just being guilty for being evil, but being responsible for their participation in evil and able to participate in solutions.[75]

In Susan Neiman's Kantian framework she focuses on the need for reason to work to be at home in the world where it currently feels homeless; reason should be applied to systems in which people's thoughtless, mundane participation enmeshes them in perpetuating immeasurable evil. In the framework being proposed, reason is a means. It is God, working by the transjective Spirit and transcarnate Word, who is working to make the cosmic community homey for us all. God is working to mature the *tohu wabohu* earth into a nurturing, abundantly full community. It is God who initiates salvation for creation marked by chaos. It is divine goodness/love that is working to be at home in the world.[76]

---

person both guilty and responsible for the part he/she plays.

74. Quoted in Neiman, *Evil in Modern Thought*, 308.

75. In her treatment of Rousseau, Neiman mentions that Augustine made humans guilty for evil (because of their inherited damaged nature), but Rousseau made humans responsible (because of the part they play in evil in history); see Neiman, *Evil in Modern Thought*, 43.

76. "He was in the world, and the world came into being through him; yet the world did not know him. He came to what was his own, and his own people did not accept him. But to all who received him, who believed in his name, he gave power to become children of God, who were born, not of blood or of the will of the flesh or of the will of man, but of God" (John 1:10–13).

One Caution Concerning the Framework

One of the concerns Catherine Keller has with many of the theological positions available is the manner in which they have been used as justifications for one group's power and for the demonization of the (m) other.[77] Living in the proposed paradigm should inspire anything but grabs for power or the demonizing of oneself or others on account of the chaos embodied therein. God's call is neither to war nor to self-preserving defensive posturing. God's call is to love of God and neighbor. The call is to an open-armed, vulnerable embrace of others. That call includes embracing one's enemies and laboring on their behalf that they might come to the fullest (self) expression of (divine) goodness. That labor is both salvific and creative; it is toward freeing others of the chains of chaos and toward coming to fullness in God's self-gift.[78] If there are obstacles in loving others and drawing near to them, most likely immaturity and/or chaos are present; until Christ's return we can be certain it is as much one's own as it is others.' As we can be neighbor to all in the cosmic community—partnering with them in helping us all flourish in goodness/love/beauty—we will see the Kingdom expressed.

The litmus test of what constitutes chaos is not one group's ideals over another's. The test is conformity to God's self-revelation of love in Christ; the test is the degree to which individuals and groups are able to love one another, even unto death.[79] As with Christ, perfect love requires

---

77. See Beal's *Religion and Its Monsters*. He claims that monsters "are paradoxical personifications of otherness within sameness. That is, they are threatening figures of anomaly within the well-established and accepted order of things" (4). There is a tendency for us to build a comfortable, homey place in which we feel restful and secure. So long as unsettling things stay outside our realm of sameness, we are content. If one gets in our space, it threatens our "sense of 'at-homeness,' not from the outside but from *within* the house" (ibid., 4–5). Having the monster (otherness) in one's house (sameness) is deeply disconcerting (ibid., 5). A monster can be many things: "that which invades one's sense of personal, social or cosmic order and security" (ibid., 5). It is anything that cannot be integrated into one's prior hominess; cf. Stuart Chandler's similar suggestion concerning the category of 'chaos' ("When the World Falls Apart," 467–91).

78. Such work is living according to the image of Revelation 22:2, in which the tree of life has twelve kinds of fruit; to be ambassadors of and/or to participate in such work is to image God in the world.

79. "I give you a new commandment, that you love one another. Just as I have loved you, you also should love one another. By this everyone will know that you are my disciples, if you have love for one another" (John 13:34–35; cf. 15:12–14, 17).

we die at the hands of others before we ourselves act in mal-creative, nihilating ways toward them.

Where love is deficient, repentance, healing, and further maturation is needed. We need everyone, all within the cosmic community, to work together in building one another up into the fullness of God's self-gifting. We all need, together, to work out our collective salvation with fear and trembling. It may require submitting mutually to one another that we all might know better our immaturity or blind spots. However, this framework does not justify putting one group in a place of power over others and/or demonizing any part of creation. God's mission is not the annihilation of any of the others he creates, but that they would come to fullness in him and be freed of any instantiations of chaos that would hinder that growth.

Summary

By expanding Lyle Dabney's pneumatology and his notion of *trans*ject into a discussion that focuses equally on the second person, a framework was proposed in the last chapter that sought to move beyond some of the tensions within the tradition related to the doctrine of creation. God exists and operates relative to creation neither as a foreign causative force nor within it in an embodied way such that God/Spirit becomes the subject of natural science. The transjective Spirit and transcarnate Word operate throughin creation as the very possibility for the self-expression of the other with God's call. This makes the creative event a combined act of God with the very other coming into being.

By defining God's creative activity and relationship to creation in this way, it precluded any notions of chaos as a precreation condition or entity. In continuity with the movement of Genesis 1 and the theology of Irenaeus, it was suggested that creation moves from infancy to maturity—the not-yet of barrenness to the fullness of life. Creation does not move from "chaos" to "order." "Chaos" was not defined in opposition to order; it was defined as improper expression, compared against the possibility of divine goodness self-gifted to creation throughin God's eccentric call. The expression was defined as chaotic regardless of whether it was intended maliciously or not. In either case the discordant becoming could have disastrous discreative consequences in need of repair. In either case it is also equally in need of a new, *right*eous relationship to the o/Other.

8

Conclusion

A Context in Motion

ONE PRESUPPOSITION OF THIS BOOK HAS BEEN THAT THEOLOGIANS have been adjusting to changes in the broader Western worldview throughout the centuries. As was tracked in chapter 2, at certain points there have been decisive changes in that worldview that demanded of theologians that they find new ways of articulating the faith.[1] However, since Galileo, theologians for the most part have been less willing to continue to adapt their theological language with the developments in the intellectual and scientific context. Particularly between theology and science "Effective dialogue became impossible, and theology continued its work in the familiar categories of the late Middle Ages while science went on its own way independently of any theological concern."[2] As science ever more was understanding the universe to be in flux and historical consciousness was coming of age, there has grown a divide between the language of the church and its surroundings.[3] Now "the worldview mediated to both believer and unbeliever alike by our modern culture

---

1. As Zachary Hayes states: "As world view changes, the particular shape of the theology of creation changes as well. A comparison between Aquinas, Irenaeus, and the Old Testament would demonstrate this with dramatic clarity" (*What Are They Saying about Creation?*, 33–34)
2. Ibid., 9.
3. Cf. ibid., 11, 15.

is radically different from that which provided some key structural elements for our familiar theological vision and language."[4]

Many proposals, including the present one, have sought to close the gap between articulations of theology and the present worldview. Interestingly, there is in this endeavor much that the biblical traditions have to offer as a dialogue partner. By paying attention to the erosion within biblical studies of certain long-standing assertions of comparative ANE studies, as well as paying attention to the types of interpretive work being done in Genesis 1 outside of those "chaos" laden frameworks, this project attempted to show how suitable the voice of Genesis 1 is for theology in this age.

Where in the biblical view as a whole "creation is related to the gradually emerging future-consciousness of the Old Testament people"—the hope of salvation founded in creation that moves to "new creation"—today, more and more, theology of creation is also linked with theology of history.[5] God's creative activity has a history to it, as it did for the New Testament authors as they spoke of new creation in Christ. Presently *being* is no longer the focus of the definition of creation in the manner it had been for centuries. God's creative activity in the world has both purpose and history;[6] "What comes forth from the creative action of God is not a finished reality but an unfinished world which is being led by God to the end which he has in mind for it."[7] Thus, a view that resonated through Scripture until Irenaeus has found new life in the current context, after many intervening centuries.

---

4. Ibid., 10. Hayes concludes that from these trends in the past few centuries that "By and large, it would be true to say that the reaction of modern theology has been considerably less courageous than was that of Aquinas in the thirteenth century" (ibid., 11).

5. Ibid., 25.

6. In Hayes's view "the purpose or goal of created existence is the realization of loving, transforming union of the creature with the Creator such as has been realized in the incarnation and glorification of Christ. God creates for this purpose because he is, in himself, a mystery of self-communicative love" (*What Are They Saying about Creation?*, 36–37). The implications of this are that "meaning and purpose are not peripheral qualities of finite existence but are deeply rooted in the fact of existence as such" (ibid., 37). Hayes's view is quite compatible with Irenaeus's and what has been proposed in chapter 6.

7. Ibid., 88.

Pointing Forward: Areas for Extending This Work

There are issues that a project such as this raises that can be pursued in subsequent projects. In this case, dialogues concerning 1) the implicit metaphysics of this project, 2) the possibilities for the area of soteriology, and 3) the possibilities for discussions about Christian holiness stand out as significant and timely among the possibilities. It is hoped that these areas for future work will be taken up and addressed.

Metaphysics

As was mentioned in the introductory chapter, there are many issues of metaphysics that naturally surround any discussion of God's creative activity and the relationship between God and creation. It is important to investigate the implications of any proposal. The aim of this project was not to outline current conversations in metaphysics and show how the grammar of creation that is proposed herein relates to the various positions. The goal was also not to directly enter those conversations by proposing a way through any debates within contemporary metaphysics. In looking at the history of development within Western thinking about the world and the corresponding adjustments in the church's theology concerning creation, the goal was to suggest a way of articulating creation theology where we currently stand and to propose a specific way to understand and use the term "chaos" for theological purposes. There is work that needs to be done in going forward of outlining the metaphysical implications of this framework and evaluating them.

In addition to searching out any metaphysical implications of the proposed theology of creation, these implications need to be compared and contrasted with those in other frameworks. So much of the church's tradition of creation theology consists of a journey through centuries of variations on Classical metaphysics, whether those variations were predominantly Platonic or Aristotelian. Even centuries beyond the cataclysmic shifts in relation to these philosophical frameworks within the West, there are some theologians who continue to champion the merits of positions forged by certain theological giants in response to issues within those contexts. There is no arguing against the service to the church of these greats of the tradition and their insightfulness in the ways they carefully shaped the theological imaginations of generations within their context, emphasizing certain affirmations of the Christian faith and guarding against patterns of thinking in those contexts that would undermine the spirit of the faith. It is right that these theologians and their work are applauded. Nevertheless, Western thinking has changed in multiple ways, multiple times since those once-dominant Platonic and Aristotelian paradigms in which they worked were displaced.

Developments in philosophy and science in the seventeenth century onward in many ways were a direct assault on previous ways of thinking. Thus, there is some important work that needs to be done in explicitly stating how the metaphysics of the proposed framework differs from the classical contexts up through the Middle Ages, perhaps even through the Modern era as well.

For example, the language developed by Lyle Dabney about the Spirit being the Possibility of God for the o/Other was an intentional attempt to speak about God in the present context, in place of classical notions in which God and God's creative activity is conceptualized in terms of Being and primary causation. In Aquinas's position, for instance, as explained by David Burrell, God as primary cause not only causes things to be, but causes each "to be the cause that it is (*ST* 1.105.5)."[8] This type of causation is unique to God because "only God's activity can enter into the actions of creatures in such a way as to make them actions."[9] However, when it comes to matters of subjectivity and freedom, God's relationship to creation is one of *exteriority* as Aristotle's Unmoved Mover resided in the outermost sphere of the cosmos; that is, in Aquinas's words, while "the very meaning of voluntary activity denotes an internal principle within the subject, this...does not have to be the utterly first principle, moving yet unmoved by all else. The proximate principle is internal, but the ultimately first moving principle is external, as indeed it is for natural movement, this being the cause setting nature in motion" (*ST* 1—2.9.4.1).[10]

As Burrell continues his presentation it becomes all the more clear how much Aquinas spoke according to his era where motion was

---

8. Burrell, *Freedom and Creation in Three Traditions*, 68–69.

9. Ibid., 69. This is a good example of primary causation, wherein God is the underlying foundation or cause for cause and effect (secondary causation) in the creaturely realm.

10. Quoted by Burrell, ibid., 91. In addition to this issue of causation, also distinct from Aquinas, the proposed position does not see all initiation by humans (creation) as a failure to act the good, to freely participate "in the very being of God" (ibid., 100), or "'re-

thought to be external to objects, an accident. This changed significantly in Western thinking after Spinoza, regardless of Newton's best efforts. In his pneumatology, Dabney's language of "possibility" and "transject" seeks to get theology through some of these internal/external problems[11] and the dissolved category of primary causation in broader Western thinking;[12] it starts with God's activity as possibility instead of God as the Real, the first cause.[13]

Beyond making contrasts, however, further work can be done showing how the distinctly Christian concerns of Thomas Aquinas's

---

fusing' to enter into the process initiated by actively willing 'the good.' In the Thomistic view, we can be 'like unto God,' but only in a self-destructive manner" (ibid., 91). In the present framework, humans do not passively float on God's river of goodness (see ibid., 123, 125), they are called to act; even so, they do not act as parrots of God's call, but in response to it. One type of initiatory activity that has been labeled as chaos in this book; it is eating from the wrong tree and is destructive of both self and others. Nevertheless, righteous expression does not exclude input from the creature; such self-expression is anything but a failure to act the good, a lack. Both becoming in right relation and becoming in disharmony are activities of God's other. On the other side, the position of Duns Scotus has not been proposed in this project, that God has "endowed creatures with a capacity to originate activity" as autonomous entities (Burrell, 94). Creation does not have that type of autonomy from the transjective Spirit and transcarnate Word, nor does creation possess them. Burrell believes that Scotus is guilty of constructing a zero-sum game where either God or humans act. However, Aquinas was just as guilty of this problem when all activity and motion (due to primary causation) was on God's side of the balance sheet. By changing the language from cause to possibility, creaturely response and activity can still be dependent on God, but there is not the zero-sum balance sheet with all motion, activity, existence, agency, etc., being ultimately traceable *back* to God, in terms of primary causation; this is how grace is introduced in Aquinas: "no created nature can 'proceed to its act unless it be moved by God' (ST 1—2.109.1)" (ibid., 148; cf. ibid., 153 where he says that even *human* response in redemption comes from *God*); grace elevates fallen nature above its hindrances (ibid.,149; cf. ibid., 113 as a possible response to this zero-sum accusation). Where God is said to relate to creation in terms of causation, qualifications must be inserted in order to answer issues of theodicy; e.g., the omnipotent God is able to cause things to be different but has chosen to operate in creation according to some other manner that honors the otherness of creation. God's omnipotent nature is placed in tension with a decision of God according to God's loving nature. Where God is the possibility for the other, the issue of evil does not fall upon God in that way.

11. See, e.g., Burrell, *Freedom and Creation in Three Traditions*, 127. Cf. Dabney and his discussion of this ongoing dilemma in the Christian tradition concerning pneumatology: "Starting with the Spirit," 3–27; Dabney, "Naming the Spirit," 28–40; and Dabney, "The Nature of the Spirit," 511–12, 516–18.

12. There is a need to examine the relation between 1) Dabney's theology, 2) the framework proposed herein, and 3) Burrell's claims about the merits of seeing being as act (cf. Burrell, *Freedom and Creation in Three Traditions*, 100–101, 126–27).

13. See Dabney, "The Nature of the Spirit," 102.

metaphysic and theology of creation—as outlined by contemporary scholars such as David Burrell and his one-time student Rahim Acar[14]—are, in this book, placed in new language appropriate for notions within the broader present context. There has been a concerted effort to keep the proposed framework within the spirit of the tradition. For example, God's creative activity is affirmed as a free choice by God.[15] Creation happens instantaneously; there is not a formation of a subject that is then animated or brought into reality. God's triune operations, which are the very possibility of the response of an other, are instantaneous with the response.

The coloring of panentheistic talk with the emphasis on "in" is also rejected in keeping with the tradition by the prefix *trans* in *trans*ject and *trans*carnate. God is not embodied in creation even though there is no speaking of creation apart from God's perpetual operation throughin it. There is furthermore a shared sense in which God has a unique activity in creating because only God is the Possibility and Call by which there is the responding other. There is no grammar of primary and secondary causation in the proposed framework; this is in part because the manner of being (influenced by what would be secondary causes for Aquinas) is taken less to be an accident to things than constitutive of them in the contemporary setting; relations through time are given more ontic weight.[16] Lastly, in the paradigm of Aquinas, there is more concern for the reality of sinful action than the quality of a person's intention; regardless of intention we are responsible.[17] Aquinas's concern that we were created "to act intelligently rather than heedlessly" has been affirmed here.[18]

It is appropriate not only to look backward and make comparisons, it is also appropriate to look at the present proposal relative to other contemporary positions. For example, there are some who are beginning to see God not as primary cause, with the existence of the world and secondary causation being the effect. Rather, they are looking at God in terms of futurity, God standing *before*, beckoning creation to God's-self. For creation, having its destiny in God is not a matter of *return* back to its

14. Acar, *Talking about God and Talking about Creation*.

15. See, e.g., Burrell, *Freedom and Creation in Three Traditions*, 45.

16. Compare Burrell, ibid., 96f, with Hayes, *What Are They Saying about Creation?*, 92.

17. Burrell, *Freedom and Creation in Three Traditions*, 125.

18. Ibid. Cf. Susan Neiman, *Evil in Modern Thought*; her position is Kantian, but it still relates well to this situation.

source; it is a matter of coming forward into a fulfillment made possible in God's creative activity.[19] As has been suggested, God calls and makes possible the other's response. God does not push it into being; creation is not actualizing possibilities God makes available to it. The result at the eschaton will be the righteous expression(s) of creation, having matured into the full self-expression of God's self-gift of divine goodness.[20] Evaluating the relationships between these positions is work that is yet to be done.

Last, the merits of the creation theology in this book for the present context need to be evaluated. The proposed framework was developed as an attempt to articulate a Christian theology of creation for the present context, a theology that has a very specific notion of chaos in it. It was developed not only in an attempt to be sensitive to the intellectual context (specifically within the physical sciences), but also to provide a theology of creation that is tenable enough to the contemporary imagination such that it could help provide a framework for making sense of the world we encounter and for shaping the way we communicate those experiences. This is to suggest a role for theology that it has not had in quite some time; it does not simply work with a context *given* to it that is based on non-Christian presuppositions.[21] Theology should help provide the narrative, in dialogue with other academic disciplines, which shapes our experience of the world but also is adequate (for a time) for hanging our experiences of the world upon. This framework, with its notion of chaos, was developed to that end. Now the work of evaluating its suitability for that end in our contemporary Western context needs to be carried out.[22]

Soteriology

Works on soteriology and atonement theories have been abundant in recent years. There has been a flurry of activity in both Old and New

---

19. See, e.g., Hayes, *What Are They Saying about Creation?*, 96.

20. Hayes has a similar vision of the eschaton: "It will be that final state of existence with God in which the creative power of God's self-giving love will totally suffuse all creaturely relations, transforming all into the final perfection of love and mutuality; and 'God will be all in all' (1 Cor. 15:28)" (*What are they Saying about Creation?*, 98).

21. See, e.g., the work of D. Stephen Long that challenges the foundational presuppositions of the given context of capitalism as an example of a theology that does this (*Divine Economy: Theology and the Market*).

22. This should at least be qualified in that there is no single Western context. Each

Testament theology on these issues, as well as within and between various theological traditions. As with the turbulence in creation theology, much of this trend is fueled by the growth of historical consciousness developed during and out of the Enlightenment. Many atonement theories have been linked with the social contexts in which they arose. The concurrent social relationships, notions of justice and/or law, theological anthropology, etc. all shaped the way the biblical texts and their terms were read.

It was not until the critical methodologies developed since the seventeenth century by thinkers such as Spinoza were employed that there was careful attention paid to the differences in the way terms have been used across time and by different authors. This has put into question the degree and manner to which several dominant theological positions on atonement from various eras can be said to rest on the witness of Scripture.

The debates to preserve, revise, or replace these long-standing theories (e.g., vicarious satisfaction, penal substitution, Christus victor) are far from over. Nevertheless, as with the dilemma of creation theology in the current cultural milieu, it is assumed here that new contexts demand fresh articulations of the faith—as Aquinas did at the transition from a Platonic to an Aristotelian worldview. If the proposed creation theology, with its accompanying notion of chaos, is indeed fitting for the present context, then the task of articulating God's salvific response to chaos in the framework needs to be addressed. Some trajectories were mentioned in chapter 7, but a great deal more needs to be done. Fitting articulations of God's response to chaos within the proposed framework need to be found.

According to what has been proposed, each creation's destiny has always been maturation into perfect self-expression in relation to God's triune creative activity—that is, the pervasive self-expression of God's love/goodness among the cosmic community by God's self-gifting throughin. Nevertheless, the scarring, miring, and enslaving character of chaos on creation's subsequent expressions is an evolving condition in ongoing becoming from which creation needs salvation.

It has already been suggested that the o/Other oriented love made flesh in God's humanity, even unto and in his death, is the fruit of the tree

---

academic field or culture in itself is diverse. However, there may be ways in which this proposal is well suited for the broader trends in thinking since the Enlightenment.

of life from which God intended humanity to eat since the beginning.[23] Humans are called to a unique vocation in their living in the dynamic of God's o/Other oriented love that God self-gifts; humans are to image their creator in the community. Even though God self-gifts himself to all creation in his creative operations, humans have a special role in giving themselves to others in the cosmic community. It is an activity unique and appropriate to them. Nurturing the whole community into self-expression of goodness according to both their gifting and the extent of their abilities is humanity's occupation through which they pour themselves out as they eat from the tree of life. It should also not be underestimated the significance of God engaging humans in literal conversation, and humans being able to construe worlds with their speech.

In seeking to articulate God's salvific work there are several things to which we must attend. First, just as Scripture and the early tradition of the church affirm, God's salvific work must be understood to include all creation, not just humanity. It was out of this concern that certain positions were taken in developing this framework. Second, any account of God's salvific activity should be understood to culminate in Christ, not just begin with Christ. Thus a narrative of God's salvific enterprise is inadequate by New Testament precedents if it does not include God's prior and continuing relationship with the descendants of Abraham, God's covenant people. Both the Law and the Prophets affirm that through Abraham and his descendents all the families on earth will be blessed.

A third issue that needs to be addressed in relation to this proposed framework is perhaps the most important. In the preceding chapters the grammar of "transcarnation" and "throughin" was used. That the Word became *in*carnate marks a radically different relationship of God with creation and activity therein. The creative and soteriological implications in regard to the proposed framework will need to be explored. The brief treatment of God's salvific work offered to this point did not address this difference of incarnation. It was suggested that in the self-expression made possible by the call of God that reverberates in the one who hung on the tree that there is recapitulation from chaos. This is a

---

23. God's incarnation and *life* in Christ must be included in God's salvific activity. This was a common theme in some early church theologians (e.g., Irenaeus), but, in the face of penal substitution theories, has become superfluous, a nearly nonsensical component in soteriology. According to Andrew P. Klager, the early fathers avoided notions of penal substitution precisely because it "systemically undermines the centrality of the incarnation" ("Retaining and Reclaiming the Divine," 445).

transformation beyond a simple moral influence; this is a shift in relationships that has true ontic import. There is a freeing from many of chaos's chains; there is new, fertile life that grows on the other side of sin's scars. There is the possibility for many relationships, to the extent that it is up to the convert, to be re-birthed in justice—to be justified. The initial righteous-coming-to-be upon God's call in Christ is to begin in a creative moment to become what God forever self-gifts to creation. It is to take a new road at that bifurcation point; it is to turn/repent.

A fourth point that needs to be explored is the possibility that in Christ the Triune God acts in a decisive way that goes even beyond the dynamic of creation, of making possible the expression of an other; such an action can be described as nothing short of God's rescue and adoption of the other. The issue of whether God acts on behalf of the other without their consent and the manner in which God does so must be faced. For example, in Exodus the Israelites yearned for and called out to God for deliverance from slavery. Nevertheless, it was not entirely known to the Israelites all that their deliverance would entail. That for which they were asking unknowingly entailed far more than a change in geography and governance. It also required a change in their thinking and habits. God often acted in response to their prayer in spite of their protests and wandering astray.

All creation continues to groan for deliverance from chaos. Only God knows all that the answer to that prayer entails. For example, the book of Acts is full of instances when God went beyond the disciples' expectations and they had to react in order to keep in line with God's in-breaking kingdom. It at least appears God does not always act in ways that were fully anticipated and thus invited. In Christ, God tore through all parts of creation—through the heavens to earth and through the earth to below the earth (Mark 1:10; 15:38).[24] God annexed the entirety

---

24. When Christ exhaled his final breath, the temple curtain was torn from top to bottom. Dominic Rudman has found first-century descriptions of the curtain in which the four colors of thread used to weave it were understood to represent the four elements of creation. The tearing of the curtain is symbolic of the tearing through of creation itself (Rudman, "The Crucifixion as Chaoskampf:" 107). I believe this aspect of the curtain tearing that Rudman suggests has symbolism in Mark's Gospel beyond the rending of creation. Earlier in the narrative there is a 'tearing' of the heavens when the Spirit descends on Jesus at his baptism (1:10). Now there is a 'tearing' of creation at the death of Jesus (15:38). These two places are the only use of the verb *skidzō* in Mark. Just as the Word has a two-tiered kenosis in becoming incarnate and then dying in the flesh (cf. Phil 2:5–8), the narrative imagery indicates that the Spirit has a two-tiered kenosis by

of creation for his kingdom, even death itself. No aspect of creation is exempt from God's enlivening work of rescue and restoration.

The end of God's cleansing of all creation from the destructive cancer of chaos is no different than the end of God's creative operation. All creation is being freed to participate in the holy vocation of love of the o/Other. By each member being transformed into right/just relationship within the community, creation is freed to grow into maturity in its life-supporting/nurturing destiny, into the Glory of God. There is much about that activity, nevertheless, that remains to be explored.

In the debates concerning the contextual limitations of various atonement theories and the similarities and differences of those theories from the thought-worlds of the biblical texts, there have been several different proposals put forward on how the tradition should proceed from here. Many of the new proposals advocate for a non-violent view of the atonement. How the proposed framework might be useful in developing non-violent atonement theories needs to be examined. These theories outright reject the way violence can be seen to be condoned by God within some of the more traditional theories.[25] The reasons for rejecting notions of divine violence in the atonement are: first, its questionability on biblical grounds, second, the rejection of violence in early Christian witness, and, third, the unattractiveness of such a teaching in our present context.

There have been many suggestions based on Scripture for why the cross should not be viewed as an act of violence by God or willed by God.[26] For instance, that the Son spoke of being forsaken unto his violent

---

tearing through the heavens at Jesus's baptism and then in tearing through creation into Sheol at Jesus's death. The movement of the Word and Spirit is through the three parts of the cosmos: above the earth, on the earth, and below the earth. Often the tearing of the curtain is seen as the opening of a direct path between God and humanity, a tearing down of the barrier; Rudman does not exclude this. However, what is being communicated in the language and images of the narrative is that the *who* behind the curtain (God's presence) also is plunging through creation into uncreation, into Sheol. This experience of and/or descent into death itself is arguably one of the key reasons God's incarnation within human flesh is necessary for creation's ultimate salvation. How else could the Living God have personally entered into such complete nullification for the sake of sanctifying death, apart from becoming what God was not via the incarnation?

25. Cf., e.g., Anthony Bartlett's critique of violence in the Christian tradition in *Cross Purposes: The Violent Grammar of Christian Atonement*.

26. Cf. Jersak, "Nonviolent Identification and the Victory of Christ." Jersak believes that Jesus's death could not have been an act of violence by God against the Son as a substitute for humanity because it would undermine Jesus's teachings (ibid., 34).

death on the cross does not logically entail that God either carried out the violence or willed that it should have happened. Not intervening on behalf of the Son such that he was not spared from death—a result of the cruelty of humanity—arguably shows a pacifistic character to God. The teaching of Jesus to turn the other cheek, to love one's enemies, and to pray for one's persecutors is demonstrated to be the mode of God's operation in Christ.

Second, God's instructions to the Hebrew Priests about animal sacrifice were that it was supposed to be done with as little pain and trauma inflicted on the animal as possible. God did not demand that the priest torture the animal in proportion to the sinner's transgressions. Thus, the magnitude of Christ's sufferings in his sacrifice shows nothing of the magnitude of our debt or punishment that God exacted on Christ in our place; it has no relation to the sacrificial significance of his death. The magnitude of Christ's sufferings only shows the layers of twistedness in humanity's discord with God's creative operations.

As a last example, it has been suggested that God had to see that "justice" was fulfilled or God himself would be guilty of being unjust, that God is bound by his own code of justice. God cannot simply forgive a debt (e.g., Matt 18:23–35) or pardon a transgression (e.g., John 8:1:11) without such an act being a failure to maintain his justice. This logic concerning justice reveals certain notions of *justice* and *law* in the contexts of Anselm and the Reformers more than it does the biblical narrative.[27] It appears, however, that God is ready and able to forgive

27. Anselm's *Cur Deus Homo* is often criticized by supporters of nonviolent atonement theories. However, the summarization of the work that they criticize rarely bears resemblance to the actual position of Anselm. It should be noted that Anselm did not point to God the Father as the one who was willing or performing violence against the Son. The Father would be unjust to do such a thing to an innocent person whose life was not owed to him. The Father simply willed that the Son should always live in obedience to the Father. If living in that way led to the Son's death at the hands of sinful humans, then only indirectly can it be said that the Father willed that the Son should die. Anselm's position on this particular point is not irreconcilable with nonviolent atonement theories; the Father cannot be said to be condoning the violence, only the Son's obedience. It is only Anselm's medieval notion of a debt of honor that could be satisfied by the surplus merits of Christ's unnecessary death that should be questioned. So that the Father was not left holding a surplus that was not rightfully his to take and so the scales of justice could be balanced, the merits of Christ's death, which were more than sufficient, were awarded toward all the debts of all humanity. Even for Irenaeus, long before Anselm, the reason for Christ being killed was that by his *obedience*, by hanging on the tree, he was *undoing* (i.e., recapitulating) the *disobedience* of Adam by taking from the tree (cf. Klager, "Retaining and Reclaiming the Divine," 465–66).

without payment or punishment (i.e., retributive justice). The Ninevites, the prodigal son, the woman caught in adultery, and others in the Bible were all beneficiaries of this divine quality; it was typically the human onlookers who wanted retributive justice. It should not be assumed that John the Baptist's baptism of repentance *for the forgiveness of sins* (Luke 3:3) or Jesus's words of forgiveness in the Gospels were contingent upon Christ's subsequent satisfaction of "justice." God does not require death as a prerequisite to forgiveness or for reconciliation. Other reasons for Christ's death need to be explored.

Several contemporary theologians appeal to the early church's witness to non-violence in rejecting certain traditional atonement theories. The testimony of the Gospel, demonstrated in the faithfulness of the martyrs even unto death, shows the character of nonviolence among early Christ followers. There is also an explicit rejection of violence in some early theologians; Irenaeus is popularly referenced. Irenaeus wrote that God in Christ "did righteously turn against that apostasy, and redeem from it his own property, *not by violent means,* as the [apostasy] had obtained dominion over us at the beginning, when it insatiably snatched away what was not its own, but by means of persuasion, as became a God of counsel, *who does not use violent means to obtain what He desires; so that neither should justice be infringed upon,* nor the ancient handiwork of God go to destruction."[28] The point of not only Christ's death, but also his life, for Irenaeus, was to eliminate death and vivify humanity, to "ensure humanity entrance into the divine."[29] There is much in the tradition that should give theologians pause for claiming that God or God's "justice" demanded Christ's death or that God was satisfied by such a horror. There is room in the tradition to say that Christ was falsely accused, convicted, and murdered because he chose to live attuned to the Father even in the face of chaos in the world. The ways in which Christ's death (and subsequent resurrection) was used by God to save and recapitulate all creation is a different issue than the cause of the death.[30] The manner

---

28. *Haer.* 5.1.1; quoted in Jersak, "Nonviolent Identification and the Victory of Christ," 34; italics Jersak's.

29. Klager, "Retaining and Reclaiming the Divine," 452; cf. ibid., 468.

30. One advantage of viewing Christ's death nonviolently is that it helps to hold the resurrection together with what God worked in and through Christ's death. The whole loop of death and resurrection becomes the atonement. Atonement is not centrally about payment or punishment satisfied in Christ's death. The Good News is about the abundance of life offered in the new creation worked in and through Christ's death and resurrection.

in which the proposed framework can be integrated with a non-violent atonement theory needs to be examined.

Examining the Usefulness of the Proposed Framework for Articulating a Doctrine of Christian Holiness and/or Entire Sanctification

Within the Wesleyan-holiness theological tradition their doctrine of Christian holiness and/or entire sanctification is of great import. In recent decades, there have been discussions in certain circles of this tradition whether to continue to emphasize a crisis moment in a believer's faith journey in which they are instantaneously and enduringly transformed in holiness—i.e., perfected in love. Some have advocated diminishing the stress on a single drastic event in favor of stressing progressive transformation and growth in holiness throughout one's life, with significant moments along the way.

Neither of these options is fully precluded in the framework provided. However, there is ample room to explore what a fully articulated doctrine of Christian holiness (a more general notion) would look like within this framework. It is hoped that this framework not only provides an attractive grammar for understanding and articulating what holy living means within a community, but that it can also provide a basis for talking about both the what and how of entire sanctification—the how being crisis moments (bifurcation points) and the continued growth to which we all look forward.

In regard to holiness, since we are shaped to a great degree by our community, we look forward to continued growth in response to the eccentric mission of God therein, which will bring the community-dynamic toward greater expression of God's goodness. We look forward to our participation in the community's perfection of relationships. As the church, we also look forward to participating in God's sanctifying work beyond our microcosm, into the world. These types of theological explorations will hopefully continue out of this work.

Summary and Conclusions

In the second chapter, a sketch was offered of some ways in which creation theology has changed in the tradition through different contexts.

Today, within the ongoing conversations concerning creation theology in the midst of the erosion of past foundations and in the uncertainty about what to do with the current context, one of the ways theologians have tried to talk about creation is by incorporating the language of "chaos" with various accompanying notions. Some have tried to use the term as it is used in science, while others have embraced suggestions that, as in the literature of Israel's neighbors, chaos is part of the biblical narrative.

These sources from which theologians have drawn have been examined and critiqued. On the side of science, the manner in which reality has been labeled as chaos based on the epistemological limitations of humans was questioned. Also, the implications of the way in which science linguistically construes the world, at times equating entropy with chaos, was questioned. The aim was to suggest that there is probably a better way in which "chaos" can be used in science and thus in the science-theology dialogue. Similarly, the way in which "chaos" has been used in biblical studies, particularly in relation to Genesis 1 was examined. Serious questions have been raised here and by others concerning both the appropriateness of the ways in which the term is used and the implications of some of the notions that are grouped under it. It was suggested that there are more appropriate ways to read the Genesis text without those commonly used notions of "chaos." In that suggestion, the pattern of creation was viewed to be from immaturity to maturity (or, death to life) instead of from chaos/disorder to order. Also, God's activity in creating was seen to be more collaborative with creation than creation being by divine fiat.

In the fifth chapter Catherine Keller's use of "chaos" to depict *creativity* within process thought was questioned. She provides a sophisticated attempt to overcome the duality of process thought by bringing "God," "chaos"/*tehom*, and "Spirit" together as a trinity. Even though the way she uses the term "chaos" is rejected, she does provide some helpful ideas that were brought into the framework proposed in this project. Her ideas of feedback loops, recapitulation, and discreative acts all influenced the suggestions made in chapters 6 and 7.

Finally it was suggested that Lyle Dabney's pneumatology in which the Spirit operates as *trans*ject to creation be expanded to the second person; thus the Word is *trans*carnate to creation. In the use of this one prefix, God's immanence and transcendence is suggested. The goal is to bypass not only the traditional problem of interiority/

exteriority of God relative to creation, but also to provide a grammar that moves beyond the zero-sum problem of who is operative, God or creation, in various circumstances.

Since the ways in which "chaos" has been used in theology had been put in question earlier in this project, it was then suggested that its place is in the self-expression of creation for which God is the possibility. Chaos is a coming to be of creation, organic and inorganic, in disharmony with the Spirit and Word—the Possibility and Call of God—and thus others in the cosmic community as well. Chaos does not pre-exist creation, stand at the opposite polarity from creation, or exist as its own entity in creation. Rather, where creation comes to be in discord to God and others, it instantiates chaos in the would-be community; creation comes to be in a way that is not related to others in the cosmic community in goodness, beauty, and love. There is always room for maturation and further discovery in expressing God's self-gift; immaturity is not the problem. The problem is the introduction of chaos into creation and its distorting effects on subsequent expressions of creation. Chaos, as it has been defined here, is that from which creation needs rescue and recapitulation.

Bibliography

Acar, Rahim. *Talking about God and Talking about Creation: Avicenna's and Thomas Aquinas' Positions.* Islamic Philosophy, Theology and Science: Texts and Studies 58. Leiden: Brill, 2005.

Albright, William Foxwell, and Theodore J. Lewis. *Archaeology and the Religion of Israel.* The Old Testament Library. Louisville: Westminster John Knox, 2006.

Alster, Bendt. "Tiamat." In *Dictionary of Deities and Demons in the Bible*, edited by Karel van der Toorn et al., 1634–39. Leiden: Brill, 1995.

Anderson, Bernhard W. *Creation in the Old Testament.* Issues in Religion and Theology 6. Philadelphia: Fortress, 1984.

———. *Creation versus Chaos: The Reinterpretation of Mythical Symbolism in the Bible.* New York: Association Press, 1967.

———. "Introduction: Mythopoeic and Theological Dimensions of Biblical Creation Faith." In *Creation in the Old Testament*, 1–24. Philadelphia: Fortress, 1984.

———. "The Persistence of Chaos in God's Creation: Order and Chaos Belong Together in God's Creation, but Potential Chaos of Another Kind was Introduced When God Created Human Beings Endowed with Freedom." *Bible Review* 12 (1996) 19, 44.

Angel, Andrew R. *Chaos and the Son of Man: The Hebrew Chaoskampf Tradition in the Period 515 BCE to 200 CE.* Library of Second Temple Studies 60. London: T. & T. Clark, 2006.

Angell, Norman. *From Chaos to Control.* New York: The Century Co., 1932.

Aulen, Gustaf E. H. "Chaos and Cosmos: The Drama of the Atonement." *Interpretation* 4 (1950) 156–67.

Baker, Sharon. "The Repetition of Reconciliation: Satisfying Justice, Mercy, and Forgiveness." In *Stricken by God? Nonviolent Identification and the Victory of Christ*, edited by Brad Jersak and Michael Hardin, 220–41. Grand Rapids: Eerdmans, 2007.

Bangert, Byron C. "Why Owls Matter, Mosquitoes Bite, and Existence Remains a Mystery: A Case for *Creatio Ex Chaos.*" *Quarterly Review* 15 (1996) 415–25.

Barth, Karl. "The Humanity of God." In *The Humanity of God.* Translated by John Newton Thomas. Richmond: John Knox, 1960.

Bartlett, Anthony W. *Cross Purposes: The Violent Grammar of Christian Atonement.* Harrisburg, PA: Trinity, 2001.

Batto, Bernard F. *Slaying the Dragon: Mythmaking in the Biblical Tradition.* Louisville: Westminster John Knox, 1992.

Bavinck, Herman. *In the Beginning: Foundations of Creation Theology.* Edited by John Bolt. Translated by John Vriend. Grand Rapids: Baker, 1999.
Beal, Timothy K. *Religion and Its Monsters.* New York: Routledge, 2002.
Bechtel, Lyn. "Genesis 2.4b—3.24: A Myth about Human Maturation." *Journal for the Study of the Old Testament* 67 (1995) 3–26.
———. "Rethinking the Interpretation of Genesis 2:4b—3:24." In *A Feminist Companion to Genesis*, edited by Athalya Brenner, 77–117. The Feminist Companion to the Bible 2. Sheffield: Sheffield Academic, 1993.
Benz, Arnold O., et al. *The Future of the Universe: Chance, Chaos, God?* New York: Continuum, 2000.
Bird, Phyllis A. "'Male and Female He Created Them': Genesis 1:27b in the Context of the Priestly Account of Creation." In *I Studied Inscriptions from before the Flood: Ancient Near Eastern, Literary, and Linguistic Approaches to Genesis 1–11*, edited by Richard S. Hess and David T. Tsumura, 329–61. Sources for Biblical and Theological Study 4. Winona Lake, IN: Eisenbrauns, 1994.
Bonhoeffer, Dietrich. *Creation and Fall: A Theological Interpretation of Genesis 1–3.* London: SCM, 1959.
Bonting, Sjoerd L. "Chaos and Creation: A Reply to R. William Carroll." *Sewanee Theological Review* 47 (2004) 447–49.
———. "Chaos Theology: A New Creation Theology and its Applications." *Journal of Faith and Science Exchange* 4 (2000) 143–59.
———. *Chaos Theology: A Revised Creation Theology.* Saint Paul University Research Series. Ottawa: Novalis, 2002.
———. *Creation and Double Chaos: Science and Theology in Discussion.* Minneapolis: Fortress, 2005.
———. "God's Action in the World: Influencing of Chaos Events?" *Sewanee Theological Review* 47 (2004) 372–401.
———. "Of Burning Bushes and Barren Fig Trees." *Sewanee Theological Review* 47 (2004) 436–38.
———. "The Problem of Evil." *Sewanee Theological Review* 47 (2004) 402–12.
Bouteneff, Peter C. *Beginnings: Ancient Christian Readings of the Biblical Creation Narratives.* Grand Rapids: Baker Academic, 2008.
Bracken, Joseph A. *Society and Spirit: A Trinitarian Cosmology.* Selinsgrove: Susquehanna University Press, 1991.
Brague, Rémi. *The Wisdom of the World: The Human Experience of the Universe in Western Thought.* Chicago: University of Chicago Press, 2003.
Brandon, S. G. F. *Creation Legends of the Ancient Near East.* London: Hodder & Stoughton, 1963.
Brierley, Michael W. "Naming a Quiet Revolution: The Panentheistic Turn in Modern Theology." In *In Whom We Live and Move and Have Our Being: Panentheistic Reflections on God's Presence in a Scientific World*, edited by Philip Clayton and Arthur Peacocke, 1–15. Grand Rapids: Eerdmans, 2004.
Brightman, Edgar Sheffield. "Chaos and Cosmos: A Meditation for Our Times." *Religion in Life* 9 (1940) 16–30.
———. *Chaos and Cosmos: A Meditation for our Times.* Nashville: Abingdon, 1939.
Brodie, Thomas L. *Genesis as Dialogue: A Literary, Historical & Theological Commentary.* Oxford: Oxford University Press, 2001.

Brown, William P. "Divine Act and the Art of Persuasion in Genesis 1." In *History and Interpretation: Essays in Honour of John H. Hayes*, edited by M. Patrick Graham et al., 19–32. Journal for the Study of the Old Testament Supplement Series 173. Sheffield: JSOT Press, 1993.

———. *The Ethos of the Cosmos: The Genesis of Moral Imagination in the Bible*. Grand Rapids: Eerdmans, 1999.

———. *Structure, Role, and Ideology in the Hebrew and Greek Texts of Genesis 1:1—2:3*. Society of Biblical Literature Dissertation Series 132. Atlanta: Scholars, 1993.

Brueggemann, Walter. "Kingship and Chaos: A Study in Tenth Century Theology." *Catholic Biblical Quarterly* 33 (1971) 317–32. Reprinted in *David and His Theologian: Literary, Social, and Theological Investigations of the Early Monarchy*, edited by K. C. Hanson, 82–100. Eugene, OR: Cascade Books, 2011.

———. "Weariness, Exile and Chaos: A Motif in Royal Theology." *Catholic Biblical Quarterly* 34 (1972) 19–38.

Bruteau, Beatrice. *God's Ecstasy: The Creation of a Self-Creating World*. New York: Crossroad, 1997.

Buckley, Michael J. *At the Origins of Modern Atheism*. New Haven: Yale University Press, 1987.

Burrell, David B. "Distinguishing God from the World." In *Language, Meaning, and God: Essays in Honor of Herbert McCabe*, edited by Brian Davies, 75–91. 1987. Eugene, OR: Wipf & Stock, 2010.

———. *Freedom and Creation in Three Traditions*. Notre Dame: University of Notre Dame Press, 1993.

Carroll, R. William. "A Word in Defense of Creatio Ex Nihilo: A Response to Sjoerd Bonting." *Sewanee Theological Review* 47 (2004) 439–46.

Cassuto, Umberto. *A Commentary on the Book of Genesis*. Vol. 1, *From Adam to Noah*. Publications of the Perry Foundation for Biblical Research in the Hebrew University of Jerusalem. 1st English ed. Jerusalem: Magnes, Hebrew University, 1961.

Chandler, Stuart. "When the World Falls Apart: Methodology for Employing Chaos and Emptiness as Theological Constructs." *Harvard Theological Review* 85 (1992) 467–91.

Childs, Brevard S. "Enemy from the North and the Chaos Tradition." *Journal of Biblical Literature* 78 (1959) 187–98.

———. *Myth and Reality in the Old Testament*. 2nd ed. Studies in Biblical Theology 27. London: SCM, 1962.

Clayton, Philip, and Arthur Peacocke, editors. *In Whom We Live and Move and Have Our Being: Panentheistic Reflections on God's Presence in a Scientific World*. Grand Rapids: Eerdmans, 2004.

Clifford, Richard J. *Creation Accounts in the Ancient Near East and the Bible*. The Catholic Biblical Quarterly Monograph Series 26. Washington, DC: Catholic Biblical Association, 1994.

Clifford, Richard J., and John Joseph Collins, editors. *Creation in the Biblical Traditions*. Catholic Biblical Quarterly Monograph Series 24. Washington, DC: Catholic Biblical Association of America, 1992.

Clines, David J. A. "Themes in *Genesis 1–11*." In *I Studied Inscriptions from before the Flood: Ancient Middle Eastern, Literary, and Linguistic Approaches to Genesis*

1–11, edited by Richard S. Hess and David T. Tsumura, 285–309. Sources for Biblical and Theological Study 4. Winona Lake, IN: Eisenbrauns, 1994.

Cohen, Jack, and Ian Stewart. *The Collapse of Chaos: Discovering Simplicity in a Complex World.* New York: Penguin, 1995.

Cohen, Robert S. "Cosmic Order and Human Disorder." In *Cosmology, History, and Theology*, edited by Wolfgang Yourgrau and Allen D. Beck, 335–45. New York: Plenum, 1977.

Colling, Richard G. *Random Designer: Created from Chaos to Connect with the Creator.* Bourbonnais, IL: Browning, 2004.

Copan, Paul, and William Lane Craig. *Creation out of Nothing: A Biblical, Philosophical, and Scientific Exploration.* Leicester, UK: Apollos, 2004.

Cotter, David W. *Genesis.* Berit Olam Studies in Hebrew Narrative & Poetry. Collegeville, MN: Liturgical, 2003.

Cottrell, Jack. *What the Bible Says about God the Creator.* What the Bible Says Series. Joplin, MO: College Press, 1983.

Craigie, Peter C. "Ugarit and the Bible: Progress and Regress in 50 Years of Literary Study." In *Ugarit in Retrospect: Fifty Years of Ugarit and Ugaritic*, edited by G. D. Young, 99–111. Winona Lake, IN: Eisenbrauns, 1981.

Cross, Frank Moore. *Canaanite Myth and Hebrew Epic; Essays in the History of the Religion of Israel.* Cambridge: Harvard University Press, 1973.

Cupitt, Don. *Creation out of Nothing.* London; Philadelphia: SCM, 1990.

Dabney, D. Lyle. "The Justification of the Spirit: Soteriological Reflections on the Resurrection." In *Starting with the Spirit*, edited by Gordon Preece and Stephen Pickard, 59–82. Task of Theology Today 2. Hindmarsh: Australian Theological Forum, 2001.

———. "'Justified by the Spirit': Soteriological Reflections on the Resurrection." *International Journal of Systematic Theology* 3 (2001) 46–68.

———. "Naming the Spirit: Towards a Pneumatology of the Cross." In *Starting with the Spirit*, edited by Gordon Preece and Stephen Pickard, 28–58. Task of Theology Today. Hindmarsh: Australian Theological Forum, 2001.

———. "The Nature of the Spirit: Creation as a Premonition of God." In *Starting with the Spirit*, edited by Gordon Preece and Stephen Pickard 83–110. Task of Theology Today 2. Hindmarsh: Australian Theological Forum, 2001.

———. "The Nature of the Spirit: Creation as a Premonition of God." In *Work of the Spirit: Pneumatology and Pentacostalism*, edited by Michael Welker, 71–86. Grand Rapids: Eerdmans, 2006.

———. "*Pneumatologia Crucis*: Reclaiming *Theologia Crucis* for a Theology of the Spirit Today." *Scottish Journal of Theology* 53 (2000) 511–24.

———. "Starting with the Spirit: Why the Last Should Now Be First." In *Starting with the Spirit*, edited by Gordon Preece and Stephen Pickard. Task of Theology Today 2. Hindmarsh: Australian Theological Forum, 2001.

Davies, Paul C. W. "Introduction: Toward an Emergentist Worldview." In *From Complexity to Life: On the Emergence of Life and Meaning*, edited by Niels Henrik Gregersen, 3–16. Oxford: Oxford University Press, 2003.

Davis, John Jefferson. "Theological Reflections on Chaos Theory." *Perspectives on Science and Christian Faith* 49 (1997) 75–84.

Day, John. *God's Conflict with the Dragon and the Sea: Echoes of a Canaanite Myth in the Old Testament*. University of Cambridge Oriental Publications. Cambridge: Cambridge University Press, 1985.

———. *Yahweh and the Gods and Goddesses of Canaan*. Journal for the Study of the Old Testament Supplement Series 265. Sheffield: Sheffield Academic, 2000.

Deroche, Michael P. "Isaiah XLV 7 and the Creation of Chaos." *Vetus Testamentum* 42 (1992) 11–21.

———. "The *Rûah 'Ĕlōhîm* in Gen 1:2c: Creation Or Chaos?" In *Ascribe to the Lord: Biblical and Other Essays in Memory of Peter C. Craigie*, edited by Lyle Eslinger and Glen Taylor, 303–18. JSOT Supplements 67. Sheffield: JSOT Press, 1988.

Dobson, Geoffrey P. *A Chaos of Delight: Science, Religion and Myth and the Shaping of Western Thought*. London: Equinox, 2005.

Douglass, Scot. *Theology of the Gap: Cappadocian Language Theory and the Trinitarian Controversy*. American University Studies Series 7. Theology and Religion 235. New York: Lang, 2005.

Drees, Willem B. *Creation: From Nothing until Now*. London: Routledge, 2002.

Eslinger, Lyle. "Freedom or Knowledge? Perspective and Purpose in the Exodus Narrative (Exodus 1:15)." In *The Pentateuch*, edited by John W. Rogerson, 186–202. Biblical Seminar 39. Sheffield: Sheffield Academic, 1996.

Fergusson, David. *The Cosmos and the Creator: An Introduction to the Theology of Creation*. Cunningham Lectures. London: SPCK, 1998.

Frankfort, H., and H. A. Frankfort. "The Emancipation of Thought from Myth." In *The Intellectual Adventure of Ancient Man: An Essay on Speculative Thought in the Ancient Near East*, 363–87. Chicago: University of Chicago Press, 1977.

———. "Myth and Reality." In *The Intellectual Adventure of Ancient Man: An Essay on Speculative Thought in the Ancient Near East*, 3–27. Chicago: University of Chicago Press, 1977.

Fretheim, Terence. "The Book of Genesis." In *The New Interpreter's Bible*, edited by Leander E. Keck et al., 1:319–674. Nashville: Abingdon, 1994.

Frymer-Kensky, Tikva Simone. "Creation Myths Breed Violence: The Chaoskampf Myth of Creation Sets Up a Cosmic Cycle of Violence: Can It Ever Bring Peace?" *BR* 14 (1998) 17, 47.

Galambush, Julie. "*Ādām* from *Ādāmâ*, *'Iššâ* from *'Îš*: Derivation and Subordination in Genesis 2.4b—3.24." In *History and Interpretation: Essays in Honour of John H. Hayes*, edited by M. Patrick Graham et al., 33–46. JSOT Supplements 173. Sheffield: Sheffieled Academic, 1993.

Geertz, Armin W. "A Chaos of Delight: Science, Religion and Myth and the Shaping of Western Thought." *Numen* 54 (2007) 502–7.

Gilkey, Langdon. *Maker of Heaven and Earth: The Christian Doctrine of Creation in the Light of Modern Knowledge*. Lanham, MD: University Press of America, 1985, 1959.

Girardot, N. J. "Chaos." In *The Encyclopedia of Religion*, edited by Mircea Eliade et al., 3:213–18. New York: Macmillan, 1987.

Gorman, Michael J. *Cruciformity: Paul's Narrative Spirituality of the Cross*. Grand Rapids: Eerdmans, 2001.

Gowan, Donald E. *Theology in Exodus: Biblical Theology in the Form of a Commentary*. Louisville: Westminster John Knox, 1994.

Greene-McCreight, Kathryn. *Ad Litteram: How Augustine, Calvin, and Barth Read the "Plain Sense" of Genesis 1–3*. Issues in Systematic Theology 5. New York: Lang, 1999.

Gregersen, Niels Henrik. "From Anthropic Design to Self-Organized Complexity." In *From Complexity to Life: On the Emergence of Life and Meaning*, 206–34. Oxford: Oxford University Press, 2003.

———. "Three Varieties of Panentheism." In *In Whom We Live and Move and Have Our Being: Panentheistic Reflections on God's Presence in a Scientific World*, edited by Philip Clayton and Arthur Peacocke, 19–35. Grand Rapids: Eerdmans, 2004.

Gregersen, Niels Henrik, and Ulf Görman, editors. *Design and Disorder: Perspectives from Science and Theology*. Issues in Science and Theology. London: T. & T. Clark, 2002.

Gunkel, Herman. "The Influence of Babylonian Mythology upon the Biblical Creation Story (1895)." In *Creation in the Old Testament*, edited by Bernhard W. Anderson. Issues in Religion and Theology 6. Philadelphia: Fortress, 1984.

Gunkel, Hermann, with Heinrich Zimmern. *Creation and Chaos in the Primeval Era and the Eschaton: A Religio-Historical Study of Genesis 1 and Revelation 12*. Translated by K. William Whitney Jr. Grand Rapids: Eerdmans, 2006.

Gunton, Colin E. *Christ and Creation*. Carlisle, UK: Paternoster, 1993.

———, editor. *The Doctrine of Creation: Essays in Dogmatics, History and Philosophy*. Edinburgh: T. & T. Clark, 1997.

———. "The End of Causality? The Reformers and their Predecessors." In *The Doctrine of Creation: Essays in Dogmatics, History and Philosophy*, 63–82. Edinburgh: T. & T. Clark, 1997.

Hahn, Andrew Mayer. "*Tohu Va-Vohu*: Matter, Nothingness and Non-being in Jewish Creation Theology." PhD diss., Jewish Theological Seminary of America, 2002.

Hamilton, Victor P. *The Book of Genesis: Chapters 1–17*. New International Commentary on the Old Testament. Grand Rapids: Eerdmans, 1990.

Harlow, Daniel C. "After Adam: Reading Genesis in an Age of Evolutionary Science." *Perspectives on Science and Christian Faith* 62 (2010) 179–95.

Harrison, Peter. "Original Sin and the Problem of Knowledge in Early Modern Europe." *Journal of the History of Ideas* 63 (2002) 239–59.

Haught, John F. "Chaos, Complexity, and Theology." In *Teilhard in the 21st Century: The Emerging Spirit of Earth*, edited by Arthur Fabel and Donald St. John, 181–94. Maryknoll, NY: Orbis, 2003.

Hauser, Alan J. "Genesis 2–3: The Theme of Intimacy and Alienation." In *I Studied Inscriptions from before the Flood: Ancient Near Eastern, Literary, and Linguistic Approaches to Genesis 1–11*, edited by Richard S. Hess and David T. Tsumura, 383–98. Sources for Biblical and Theological Study 4. Winona Lake, IN: Eisenbrauns, 1994.

Hayes, Zachary. *What Are They Saying about Creation?* New York: Paulist, 1980.

Heermance, Edgar L. *Chaos and Cosmos*. New York: Dutton, 1922.

Hefner, Philip J. "God and Chaos: The Demiurge versus the *Ungrund*." *Zygon* 19 (1984) 469–85.

Heidel, Alexander. *The Babylonian Genesis: The Story of Creation*. Phoenix Books. Chicago: University of Chicago Press, 1963.

Hess, Richard S. "One Hundred Fifty Years of Comparative Studies on *Genesis 1–11*: An Overview." In *I Studied Inscriptions from before the Flood: Ancient Near*

Eastern, Literary, and Linguistic Approaches to Genesis 1–11, edited by Richard S. Hess and David T. Tsumura, 3–26. Sources for Biblical and Theological Study 4. Winona Lake, IN: Eisenbrauns, 1994.

Hess, Richard S., and David Toshio Tsumura, editors. *I Studied Inscriptions from before the Flood: Ancient Near Eastern, Literary, and Linguistic Approaches to Genesis 1–11*. Sources for Biblical and Theological Study 4. Winona Lake, IN: Eisenbrauns, 1994.

Huchingson, James E. *Pandemonium Tremendum: Chaos and Mystery in the Life of God*. Cleveland: Pilgrim, 2001.

Inch, Morris A. *Chaos Paradigm: A Theological Exploration*. Lanham, MD.: University Press of America, 1998.

Israel, Jonathan Irvine. *Enlightenment Contested: Philosophy, Modernity, and the Emancipation of Man, 1670–1752*. Oxford: Oxford University Press, 2006.

Jacobsen, Thorkild. "The Battle between Marduk and Tiamat." In *Essays in Memory of E. A. Speiser*, edited by William W. Hallo, 104–8. New Haven: American Oriental Society, 1968.

———. "Mesopotamia: The Cosmos as a State." In *The Intellectual Adventure of Ancient Man: An Essay on Speculative Thought in the Ancient Near East*, 125–84. Chicago: University of Chicago Press, 1977.

Jenson, Robert W. "Aspects of a Doctrine of Creation." In *The Doctrine of Creation: Essays in Dogmatics, History and Philosophy*, edited by Colin E. Gunton, 17–28. Edinburgh: T. & T. Clark, 1997.

Jersak, Brad. "Nonviolent Identification and the Victory of Christ." In *Stricken by God? Nonviolent Identification and the Victory of Christ*, edited by Brad Jersak and Michael Hardin. Grand Rapids: Eerdmans, 2007.

Jersak, Brad, and Michael Hardin, editors. *Stricken by God? Nonviolent Identification and the Victory of Christ*. Grand Rapids: Eerdmans, 2007.

Kaiser, Christopher B. *Creation and the History of Science*. The History of Christian Theology 3. London: Pickering, 1991.

———. *Creational Theology and the History of Physical Science: The Creationist Tradition from Basil to Bohr*. Studies in the History of Christian Thought 78. Leiden: Brill, 1997.

Kauffman, Stuart. "The Emergence of Autonomous Agents." In *From Complexity to Life: On the Emergence of Life and Meaning*, edited by Niels Henrik Gregersen, 47–71. Oxford: Oxford University Press, 2003.

Keller, Catherine. *Apocalypse Now and Then: A Feminist Guide to the End of the World*. Boston: Beacon, 1996.

———. *Face of the Deep: A Theology of Becoming*. London: Routledge, 2003.

———. *God and Power: Counter-Apocalyptic Journeys*. Minneapolis: Fortress, 2005.

Kelsey, David H. "The Doctrine of Creation from Nothing." In *Evolution and Creation*, edited by Erman McMullin, 176–96. University of Notre Dame Studies in the Philosophy of Religion 4. Notre Dame, IN: University of Notre Dame Press, 1985.

Kitchen, Kenneth A. *The Ancient Orient and Old Testament*. Downers Grove, IL: InterVarsity, 1966.

Klager, Andrew P. "Retaining and Reclaiming the Divine: Identification and the Recapitulation of Peace in St. Irenaeus of Lyons' Atonement Narrative." In *Stricken by God? Nonviolent Identification and the Victory of Christ*, edited by Brad Jersak and Michael Hardin 442–80. Grand Rapids: Eerdmans, 2007.

Knight, Douglas A. "Cosmogony and Order in the Hebrew Tradition." In *Cosmogony and Ethical Order*, edited by Robin W. Lovin and Frank E. Reynolds, 133–57. Chicago: University of Chicago Press, 1985.

Küng, Hans. *The Beginning of All Things: Science and Religion*. Grand Rapids: Eerdmans, 2007.

Lambert, Wilfred G. "A New Look at the Babylonian Background of Genesis." In *"I Studied Inscriptions from before the Flood": Ancient Near Eastern, Literary, and Linguistic Approaches to Genesis 1–11*, edited by Richard S. Hess and David T. Tsumura. Sources for Biblical and Theological Study 4. Winona Lake, IN: Eisenbrauns, 1994.

Lambert, W. G. et al. *Atra-Ḫasīs: The Babylonian Story of the Flood*. Oxford: Clarendon, 1969.

Leclerc, Diane. *Singleness of Heart: Gender, Sin, and Holiness in Historical Perspective*. Pietist and Wesleyan Studies 13. Lanham, MD: Scarecrow, 2001.

Levenson, Jon Douglas. *Creation and the Persistence of Evil: The Jewish Drama of Divine Omnipotence*. San Francisco: Harper & Row, 1988.

———. *Sinai and Zion: An Entry into the Jewish Bible*. San Francisco: Harper & Row, 1987.

Levering, Matthew. "Jon D. Levenson on the God of Israel." In *Scripture and Metaphysics: Aquinas and the Renewal of Trinitarian Theology*, 77–82. Challenges to Contemporary Theology. Malden, MA: Blackwell, 2004.

Levine, Baruch A. *In the Presence of the Lord: A Study of Cult and Some Cultic Terms in Ancient Israel*. Studies in Judaism in Late Antiquity 5. Leiden: Brill, 1974.

Lodahl, Michael. *All Things Necessary to Our Salvation: The Hermeneutical and Theological Implications of the Article on the Holy Scriptures in the Manual of the Church of the Nazarene*. Monograph Series 4. San Diego: Point Loma Press, 2004.

———. *The Story of God: A Narrative Theology*. 2nd ed. Kansas City, MO: Beacon Hill, 2008.

Long, D. Stephen. *Divine Economy: Theology and the Market*. Radical Orthodoxy. London: Routledge, 2000.

Löning, Karl, and Erich Zenger. *To Begin with, God Created . . . : Biblical Theologies of Creation*. Translated by Omar Kaste. Collegeville, MN: Liturgical, 2000.

Luyster, Robert. "Wind and Water: Cosmogonic Symbolism in the Old Testament." *Zeitschrift für die alttestamentliche Wissenschaft* 93 (1981) 1–10.

Maddox, Randy L. *Responsible Grace: John Wesley's Practical Theology*. Nashville: Kingswood, 1994.

Marshall, Molly T. "The Fullness of Incarnation: God's New Humanity in the Body of Christ." *Review & Expositor* 93 (1996) 187–201.

May, Gerhard. *Creatio Ex Nihilo: The Doctrine of "Creation Out of Nothing" in Early Christian Thought*. Translated by A. S. Worrall. Edinburgh: T. & T. Clark, 1994.

McCarthy, Dennis J. "'Creation' Motifs in Ancient Hebrew Poetry (1967)." In *Creation in the Old Testament*, edited by Bernhard W. Anderson. Issues in Religion and Theology 6. Philadelphia: Fortress, 1984.

McDonagh, Enda. *Between Chaos and New Creation: Doing Theology at the Fringe*. Dublin: Gill & Macmillan, 1986.

Mettinger, Tryggve N. D. "Fighting the Powers of Chaos and Hell: Towards the Biblical Portrait of God." *Studia Theologica* 39 (1985) 21–38.

Middleton, J. Richard. "A New Heaven and a New Earth: The Case for a Holistic Reading of the Biblical Story of Redemption." *Journal for Christian Theological Research* 11 (2006) 73–97. Online: http://www2.luthersem.edu/ctrf/JCTR/Vol11/Middleton_vol11.pdf/.

Milgrom, Jacob. *Cult and Conscience: The Asham and the Priestly Doctrine of Repentance*. Studies in Judaism in Late Antiquity 18. Leiden: Brill, 1976.

———. *Leviticus 1–16: A New Translation with Introduction and Commentary*. Anchor Bible 3. New York: Doubleday, 1991.

———. *Leviticus: A Book of Ritual and Ethics*. Continental Commentaries. Minneapolis: Fortress, 2004.

———. *Studies in Cultic Theology and Terminology*. Studies in Judaism in Late Antiquity 36. Leiden: Brill, 1983.

Mills, Donald H. *The Hero and the Sea: Patterns of Chaos in Ancient Myth*. Wauconda, IL: Bolchazy-Carducci, 2003.

Minns, Denis. *Irenaeus*. Washington, DC: Georgetown University Press, 1994.

Moltmann, Jürgen. *God in Creation: A New Theology of Creation and the Spirit of God*. The Gifford Lectures, 1984–1985. Minneapolis: Fortress, 1993.

Morales, José. *Creation Theology*. Dublin: Four Courts, 2001.

Murray, Robert. *The Cosmic Covenant: Biblical Themes of Justice, Peace and the Integrity of Creation*. Heythrop Monographs 7. London: Sheed & Ward, 1992.

Neiman, Phyllis G. "The Myth of Chaos: Implications for Jewish Religion." DHL diss., Jewish Theological Seminary of America, 2002.

Neiman, Susan. *Evil in Modern Thought: An Alternative History of Philosophy*. Princeton: Princeton University Press, 2002.

Niditch, Susan. *Chaos to Cosmos: Studies in Biblical Patterns of Creation*. Scholars Press Studies in the Humanities 6. Chico, CA: Scholars, 1985.

Norris, Richard A. *God and World in Early Christian Theology*. New York: Seabury, 1965.

O'Collins, Gerald. *Jesus Our Redeemer: A Christian Approach to Salvation*. Oxford: Oxford University Press, 2007.

Otten, Willemien. "Nature and Scripture: Demise of a Medieval Analogy." *Harvard Theological Review* 88 (1995) 257–84.

———. "Reading Creation: Early Medieval Views of Genesis and Plato's Timaeus." In *The Creation of Heaven and Earth: Re-Interpretations of Genesis I in the Context of Judaism, Ancient Philosophy, Christianity, and Modern Physics*, edited by George H. van Kooten, 225–43. Themes in Biblical Narrative 8. Leiden: Brill, 2005.

Otzen, Benedikt. "The Use of Myth in Genesis." In *Myths in the Old Testament*, edited by Benedikt Otzen et al., 22–61. London: SCM, 1980,

Ouro, Roberto. "The Earth of Genesis 1:2: Abiotic or Chaotic?" *Andrews University Seminary Studies* 36 (1998) 259–76.

Page, Ruth. *God and the Web of Creation*. London: SCM, 1996.

Pannenberg, Wolfhart. *Systematic Theology*. Vol. 3. Translated by Geoffrey W. Bromiley. Grand Rapids: Eerdmans, 1998.

Peacocke, A. R. *Creation and the World of Science: The Re-Shaping of Belief*. Oxford: Oxford University Press, 2004.

Peat, F. David. *From Certainty to Uncertainty: The Story of Science and Ideas in the Twentieth Century*. Washington, DC: Joseph Henry, 2002.

Pederson, Ann. "James Huchingson's Constructive Theology." *Zygon* 37 (2002) 421–31.

Pelikan, Jaroslav. *What Has Athens to Do with Jerusalem? Timaeus and Genesis in Counterpoint*. Jerome Lectures 21. Ann Arbor: University of Michigan Press, 1997.

Pennington, Jonathan T., and Sean M. McDonough, editors. *Cosmology and New Testament Theology*. T. & T. Clark Library of Biblical Studies. Library of New Testament Studies 355. London; New York: T. & T. Clark, 2008.

Pickard, Stephen K., and Gordon Preece, editors. *Starting with the Spirit*. Task of Theology Today 2. Hindmarsh, South Australia: Australian Theological Forum, 2001.

Polkinghorne, John C. *Quarks, Chaos and Christianity*. Rev. ed. New York: Crossroad, 2005.

———. *The Work of Love: Creation as Kenosis*. Grand Rapids: Eerdmans, 2001.

Powell, Samuel M. *Participating in God: Creation and Trinity*. Theology and the Sciences. Minneapolis: Fortress, 2003.

Prigogine, Ilya, and Isabelle Stengers. *Order Out of Chaos: Man's New Dialogue with Nature*. New York: Bantam, 1984.

Reynolds, Frank E., and Theodore M. Ludwig. "Introduction—A Methodology Appropriate for the History of Religions." In *Transitions and Transformations in the History of Religions: Essays in Honor of Joseph M. Kitagawa*, edited by Frank E. Reynolds and Theodore M. Ludwig, 11–21. Studies in the History of Religions, Supplements to Numen 39. Leiden: Brill, 1980.

Rousseau, Jean-Jacques. *On Philosophy, Morality, and Religion*. Edited by Christopher Kelly. Hanover, NH: Dartmouth College Press, 2007.

Rudman, Dominic. "The Crucifixion as Chaoskampf: A New Reading of the Passion Narrative in the Synoptic Gospels." *Biblica* 84 (2003) 102:7.

Russell, Robert John. "Entropy and Evil." *Zygon* 19 (1984) 449:68.

Russell, Robert John et al. *Chaos and Complexity: Scientific Perspectives on Divine Action*. Vatican Observatory, 1995.

———. *Chaos and Complexity: Scientific Perspectives on Divine Action*. 2nd ed. Vatican City: Vatican Observatory, 1997.

———. *Quantum Mechanics: Scientific Perspectives on Divine Action*. Vatican City: Vatican Observatory, 2001.

Sacks, Robert D. *A Commentary on the Book of Genesis*. Ancient Near Eastern Texts and Studies 6. Lewiston, NY: Mellen, 1990.

Saggs, H. W. F. *The Encounter with the Divine in Mesopotamia and Israel*. Jordan Lectures in Comparative Religion 12. London: Athlone, distributed by Humanities Press, 1978.

Samuelson, Norbert M. *Judaism and the Doctrine of Creation*. Cambridge: Cambridge University Press, 1994.

Sarna, Nahum M. *Exodus: The Traditional Hebrew Text with the New JPS Translation*. Philadelphia: Jewish Publication Society, 1991.

———. *Genesis: The Traditional Hebrew Text with the New JPS Translation*. Philadelphia: Jewish Publication Society, 1989.

Sasson, Jack M. "On Relating 'Religious' Texts to the Old Testament." *Maarav* 3 (1982) 217–25.

Seo, John. "Creation and Conflict in the Beginning: A Study of the Ancient Near Eastern Background, Historical Context, and Theological Role of the 'God's Battle with Chaos' Model of Creation in Isaiah 40–55." PhD diss., Drew University, 2002.

Sharpe, Kevin J., and Jonathan Walgate. "The Emergent Order." *Zygon* 38 (2003) 411–33.

Shults, F. LeRon. "A Theology of Chaos: An Experiment in Postmodern Theological Science." *Scottish Journal of Theology* 45 (1992) 223–35.

Sjöberg, Åke W. "Eve and the Chameleon." In *In the Shelter of Elyon: Essays on Ancient Palestinian Life and Literature in Honor of G. W. Ahström*, edited by W. Boyd Barrick and John R. Spencer, 217–25. Journal for the Study of the Old Testament Supplement Series 31. Sheffield: JSOT Press, 1984.

Smedes, T. A. *Chaos, Complexity, and God: Divine Action and Scientism*. Studies in Philosophical Theology 26. Leuven: Peeters, 2004.

Smith, Mark S. *The Ugaritic Baal Cycle: Introduction with Text, Translation and Commentary of KTU 1.1—1.2*. Supplements to Vetus Testamentum 55. Leiden: Brill, 1994.

Sölle, Dorothee, with Shirley Cloyes. *To Work and to Love: A Theology of Creation*. Philadelphia: Fortress, 1984.

Sorabji, Richard. *Time, Creation, and the Continuum: Theories in Antiquity and the Early Middle Ages*. Ithaca, NY: Cornell University Press, 1983.

Speiser, E. A. *Genesis*. Anchor Bible 1. Garden City, NY: Doubleday, 1964.

Sponheim, Paul R. *The Pulse of Creation: God and the Transformation of the World*. Minneapolis: Fortress, 1999.

Spronk, Klaas. "Rahab." In *Dictionary of Deities and Demons in the Bible*, edited by Karel van der Toorn et al., 1292–95. Leiden: Brill, 1995.

Sproul, Barbara C. *Primal Myths: Creating the World*. San Francisco: Harper & Row, 1979.

Stadelmann, Luis I. J. *The Hebrew Conception of the World: A Philological and Literary Study*. Analecta Biblica 39. Rome: Pontifical Biblical Institute Press, 1970.

Steenberg, M. C. *Irenaeus on Creation: The Cosmic Christ and the Saga of Redemption*. Supplements to Vigiliae Christianae 91. Leiden: Brill, 2008.

Stordalen, Terje. *Echoes of Eden: Genesis 2–3 and Symbolism of the Eden Garden in Biblical Hebrew Literature*. Contributions to Biblical Exegesis and Theology 25. Leuven: Peeters, 2000.

Tanner, Kathryn. *God and Creation in Christian Theology: Tyranny Or Empowerment?* Oxford: Blackwell, 1988.

Taylor, Charles. *Philosophy and the Human Sciences*. Philosophical Papers 2. Cambridge: Cambridge University Press, 1985.

Thunberg, Lars. "The Cosmological and Anthropological Significance of Christ's Redeeming Work." In *The Gospel and Human Destiny*, edited by Vilmos Vayta, 64–89. The Gospel Encounters History Series. Minneapolis: Augsburg, 1971.

Thweatt-Bates, Jennifer J. "Chaos and the Problem of Evil." *Stone-Campbell Journal* 6 (2003) 53–70.

Torrance, Alan. "*Creatio ex Nihilo* and the Spatio-Temporal Dimensions, with special Reference to Jürgen Moltmann and D. C. Williams." In *The Doctrine of Creation: Essays in Dogmatics, History and Philosophy*, edited by Colin E. Gunton, 83–103. Edinburgh: T. & T. Clark, 1997.

Torrance, Thomas F. *Divine and Contingent Order: Nihil constat de contingentia nisi ex revelatione*. Oxford: Oxford University Press, 1981.

———. "Fundamental Issues in Theology and Science." In *Science and Religion*, edited Jan Fennema and Iain Paul, 35–46. Dordrecht: Kluwer Academic, 1990.

———. *The Ground and Grammar of Theology*. The Richard Lectures for 1978–79, University of Virginia. Charlottesville: University Press of Virginia, 1980.
Tracy, Thomas F. "Particular Providence and the God of the Gaps." In *Chaos and Complexity: Scientific Perspectives on Divine Action*, edited by Robert John Russell et al., 289–324. Vatican City: Vatican Observatory, 1997.
Tsumura, David Toshio. *Creation and Destruction: A Reappraisal of the Chaoskampf Theory in the Old Testament*. Winona Lake, IN: Eisenbrauns, 2005.
———. *The Earth and the Waters in Genesis 1 and 2: A Linguistic Investigation*. Journal for the Study of the Old Testament Supplement Series 83. Sheffield: JSOT Press, 1989.
———. "The Earth in Genesis 1." In *I Studied Inscriptions from before the Flood: Ancient Near Eastern, Literary, and Linguistic Approaches to Genesis 1–11*, edited by Richard S. Hess and David T. Tsumura, 310–28. Sources for Biblical and Theological Study 4. Winona Lake, IN: Eisenbrauns, 1994.
———. "Water." In *New Dictionary of Biblical Theology*, edited by T. Desmond Alexander and Brian S. Rosner, 840–41. Downers Grove, IL: InterVarsity, 2000.
Uehlinger, Christoph. "Leviathan." In *Dictionary of Deities and Demons in the Bible (DDD)*, edited by Karel van der Toorn et al., 956–64. Leiden: Brill, 1995.
Volf, Miroslav. "Forgiveness, Reconciliation, and Justice." In *Stricken by God? Nonviolent Identification and the Victory of Christ*, edited by Brad Jersak and Michael Hardin. Grand Rapids: Eerdmans, 2007.
Wakeman, Mary K. *God's Battle with the Monster: A Study in Biblical Imagery*. Leiden: Brill, 1973.
Walsh, Jerome T. "Genesis 2:4b—3:24: A Synchronic Approach." In *I Studied Inscriptions from before the Flood: Ancient Near Eastern, Literary, and Linguistic Approaches to Genesis 1–11*, edited by Richard S. Hess and David T. Tsumura, 362–82. Sources for Biblical and Theological Study 4. Winona Lake, IN: Eisenbrauns, 1994.
Watson, Rebecca S. *Chaos Uncreated: A Reassessment of the Theme of "Chaos" in the Hebrew Bible*. Beihefte zur Zeitschrift für die alttestamentliche Wissenschaft 341. Berlin: de Gruyter, 2005.
———. "The Theme of Chaos in the Psalter: A Reassessment." PhD diss., University of Oxford, 2002.
Welker, Michael. "What Is Creation? Rereading Genesis 1 and 2." *Theology Today* 48 (1991) 63–71.
———. *The Work of the Spirit: Pneumatology and Pentecostalism*. Grand Rapids: Eerdmans, 2006.
Wenham, Gordon J. *Genesis 1–15*. Word Biblical Commentary 1. Waco: Word, 1987.
———. "Sanctuary Symbolism in the Garden of Eden Story." In *I Studied Inscriptions from before the Flood: Ancient Near Eastern, Literary, and Linguistic Approaches to Genesis 1–11*, edited by Richard S. Hess and David T. Tsumura, 399–404. Sources for Biblical and Theological Study 4. Winona Lake, IN Eisenbrauns, 1994.
Wenk, Matthias. *Community-Forming Power: The Socio-Ethical Role of the Spirit in Luke-Acts*. Journal of Pentecostal Theology Supplement Series 19. Sheffield: Sheffield Academic, 2000.
Westermann, Claus. *Genesis 1–11: A Commentary*. Translated by John J. Scullion. Continental Commentaries. Minneapolis: Augsburg, 1984.
Wicken, Jeffrey S. "The Cosmic Breath: Reflections on the Thermodynamics of Creation." *Zygon* 19 (1984) 487–506.

Williams, Rowan. "The Forgiveness of Sins: Hosea 11:1–9; Matthew 18:23–35." In *Stricken by God? Nonviolent Identification and the Victory of Christ*, edited by Brad Jersak and Michael Hardin, 214–19. Grand Rapids: Eerdmans, 2007.

Wilson, John A. "Egypt: The Nature of the Universe." In *The Intellectual Adventure of Ancient Man: An Essay on Speculative Thought in the Ancient Near East*, 31–61. Chicago: University of Chicago Press, 1977.

Wolff, Hans Walter. *Anthropology of the Old Testament*. Philadelphia: Fortress, 1974.

Wyatt, Nick. *The Mythic Mind: Essays on Cosmology and Religion in Ugaritic and Old Testament Literature*. BibleWorld. London: Equinox, 2005.

Yeago, David S. "The New Testament and the Nicene Dogma: A Contribution to the Recovery of Theological Exegesis." In *The Theological Interpretation of Scripture: Classic and Contemporary Readings*, edited by Stephen E. Fowl, 87–100. Blackwell Readings in Modern Theology. Malden, MA: Blackwell, 1997.

www.ingramcontent.com/pod-product-compliance
Lightning Source LLC
Chambersburg PA
CBHW071242230426
43668CB00011B/1557